MW00965756

booksonline

Getting Started with Web Dynpro ABAP™

Dominik Ofenloch and Roland Schwaiger

Getting Started with Web Dynpro ABAP™

Bonn • Boston

Galileo Press is named after the Italian physicist, mathematician and philosopher Galileo Galilei (1564–1642). He is known as one of the founders of modern science and an advocate of our contemporary, heliocentric worldview. His words *Eppur se muove* (And yet it moves) have become legendary. The Galileo Press logo depicts Jupiter orbited by the four Galilean moons, which were discovered by Galileo in 1610.

Editor Stefan Proksch
English Edition Editor Kelly Grace Harris
Translation Lemoine International, Inc., Salt Lake City, UT
Copyeditor Jutta VanStean
Cover Design Jill Winitzer
Photo Credit Getty Images/Garry Gay
Layout Design Vera Brauner
Production Editor Kelly O'Callaghan
Assistant Production Editor Graham Geary
Typesetting Publishers' Design and Production Services, Inc.
Printed and bound in Canada

ISBN 978-1-59229-311-7

1st Edition 2010
1st German edition published 2009 by Galileo Press, Bonn, Germany

Library of Congress Cataloging-in-Publication Data
Ofenloch, Dominik.
[Einstieg in Web Dynpro ABAP. English]
Getting started with Web Dynpro ABAP / Dominik Ofenloch, Roland Schwaiger.
p. cm.
Includes bibliographical references and index.
ISBN-13: 978-1-59229-311-7 (alk. paper)
ISBN-10: 1-59229-311-5 (alk. paper)
1. Web sites — Design. 2. User interfaces (Computer systems) 3. Web Dynpro. 4. ABAP/4 (Computer program language) I. Schwaiger, Roland. II. Title.
TK5105.888.O38713 2009
006.7 — dc22 2009037255

Contents at a Glance

Contents

Preface

We know from experience with training courses, projects, and our day-to-day work that considerable demand exists for a simple, well-founded treatment of the topic of Web Dynpro ABAP. Experienced ABAP developers find Web Dynpro technology easy to learn and appreciate its simplicity. However, for developers to be able to effectively implement the full scope of this technology, they need a good understanding of the various aspects of Web Dynpro. Providing this understanding is the goal of this book. It will introduce you to Web Dynpro technology one step at a time, using several practical examples that you will be able to apply to your own projects.

This book covers everything from architecture to the main UI elements and standard components to the questions that Web Dynpro beginners typically have and that arise in practical work. It covers the most important basic functions and special features of Web Dynpro ABAP and the relevant development environment. The book's structure lets you learn about the basic concepts first, which you will then apply using practical exercises. The exercises consist of step-by-step instructions (indicated by the pen icon) accompanied by screenshots and sample code. Each chapter concludes with a summary so you will get a chance to revisit what you have learned.

Target groups

This book aims to give developers who already have some ABAP knowledge an easy introduction to component-based UI development and a solid basis for developing complex applications on the basis of Web Dynpro ABAP. After reading this book, you will understand the architecture of the Web Dynpro framework, be familiar with the relevant development tools, and be able to independently create business-critical Web Dynpro applications.

Structure of the book

This book is divided into nine chapters. The first three cover the basics of Web Dynpro technology. The next five give you insight into advanced Web Dynpro concepts, with a particular focus on the practical application of the exercises. The ninth and final chapter describes how to extend Web Dynpro UIs.

The following is a detailed overview of the contents of each chapter:

- **Chapter 1**, Introduction, covers the basic aspects of modern user interface technologies and describes how SAP user interfaces are developed. The Model View Controller architecture pattern, which was first introduced decades ago, is still an important factor in this context. After describing the basics, this chapter looks at the historical development of SAP UI technologies, which have progressed rapidly in recent years.
- **Chapter 2**, Web Dynpro Architecture, covers — on a less technical level — the architecture of Web Dynpro applications. This chapter describes the basic components of Web Dynpro user interfaces: components, applications, views, controllers, and context. Short, simple exercises are used to gradually guide you to a point at which you can program Web Dynpro applications.
- **Chapter 3**, Developing Web Dynpro Applications, teaches you how to implement the knowledge you gained in Chapters 1 and 2 by developing a Web Dynpro application. You will also obtain a deeper understanding of the following: programming contexts, view layouts, and containers; using important UI elements, tables, input help, and messages; and internationalization. In this chapter, it is our intent to give you a good understanding of the procedure used to develop Web Dynpro applications and, at the same time, provide you with a wide range of examples and techniques that will make it easier for you to use Web Dynpro in practice.
- **Chapter 4**, Dynamic Web Dynpro Applications, discusses applications that differ from the applications discussed up until now. These were based on requirements and information fully known during the development period. However, it can happen that information becomes available only during the development period — information that influences the structure of the controller contexts, the view layouts, and the assignment of actions to view elements. Dynamic programming provides the tools that are required to make changes during development.

- **Chapter 5**, Web Dynpro Standard Components, discusses multi-component architectures and standard components. By dividing a complex UI architecture across several Web Dynpro components, you can structure your UIs semantically. Multi-component architectures also simplify team-based development work considerably, thanks in part to a number of standard components provided by SAP. This chapter covers the most important standard components.
- **Chapter 6**, Input Helps and Semantic Helps, describes the input helps in a Web Dynpro application, which support the user in a number of ways. For example, they enhance usability, speed up the pace of work, reduce input errors on the part of the user, and reduce the workload of hotline staff. Web Dynpro offers a wide range of options for the implementation of input helps. These options can be divided into two main sub-categories: selection options and input helps. This chapter contains an extensive, example-based treatment of the technical aspects to help you understand this topic in greater depth, and it also describes the various technical alternatives for providing the user with various kinds of content-based help, from short help texts to detailed documentation.
- **Chapter 7**, Configuration, Customizing, and Personalization, addresses the fact that, in practice, it is sometimes necessary to adapt existing Web Dynpro applications — whether they are standard SAP applications or custom applications — to individual requirements. This chapter covers the available options in all three areas, ranging from the requirements of customizing functionality on an enterprise-wide level to industry-specific requirements to user-specific changes to the interface or the navigation. These requirements are fulfilled using configuration, Customizing, and personalization.
- **Chapter 8**, Practical Tips and Hints, shows you how to optimize the performance of your Web Dynpro applications. This chapter also introduces the new Web Dynpro debugger, the Web Dynpro change log, and hotkeys for a range of actions. It also explains how to use context menus.
- **Chapter 9**, Web Dynpro in the Enhancement Framework, will be very helpful if you want to adapt a Web Dynpro application that exists in a different namespace. The Enhancement Framework enables you to

quickly and easily adapt third-party Web Dynpro architectures to your own requirements. For example, exit methods are used to adapt Web Dynpro controllers.

System requirements

This book was written for SAP NetWeaver 7.01 with Support Package 3. However, if you do not have access to this system, do not panic. Aside from some newer technologies such as hotkeys and delta rendering, the topics covered in this book are also valid for older versions of Web Dynpro, especially the basic concepts that are the subject of Chapters 1 to 4.

SAP provides an *ABAP trial version* (previously known as a *sneak preview*) that allows you to test ABAP technology. This trial version is available for both Windows and Linux, although the two versions are different. It is very easy to use the trial version. Proceed as follows:

1. Open the Download area of the SAP Developer Network (*https://www.sdn.sap.com/irj/scn/nw-downloads*).
2. Open the trial version of your choice (if you are using Linux, note that Web Dynpro ABAP is available in version 2004s only).
3. Start the download process and follow the installation instructions.

Acknowledgments

Bringing a book like this to fruition requires many months of hard toil. Many pages of this book were completed in the evening and night hours after a full day's work. Others were written over more cold autumn and winter weekends than we care to remember. The reliable and ever-available support of our editor, Stefan Proksch, was a great help from day one of the writing process. We would also like to thank the Web Dynpro development team for their hard work.

I, Dominik Ofenloch, would particularly like to thank my proofreaders, Stefanie Mayer and Thomas Rösch, for their commitment and their positive feedback. They were my valued advisers in the writing process and a great support at all times. My thanks also go to Karin Voss in ALV Basis development for her editing work. Finally, I want to thank my partner, Elisa Castenholz, for her patience and unfailing ability to motivate me to keep writing. Without her support, I would never have had the courage to commit myself to such a time-consuming project.

There is not enough space for me, Roland Schwaiger, to thank everyone who deserves thanks. Let me thus extend a collective thank you to everyone who is close to me for their professional and personal support in every aspect of my life. However, there are a few people whom I cannot fail to thank by name. Heartfelt thanks go to my parents, Margot and Wolfgang Schwaiger, who guided me and my brothers, Wolfgang, Martin, and Christian, through the stormy seas of life. In their daily efforts, they demonstrated to us one of the most important principles of life, and continue to do so to this day: to value production over consumption. Lastly, I must mention my dear wife Ursula, who is a constant source of support and strength to me and our precious children, Elisa, Marie, and Nico. Without them, I would not have been able to contribute to this book. Thank you for everything and for being the wonderful people you are!

Dominik Ofenloch and **Roland Schwaiger**

Web Dynpro technology has become established in the SAP world as the standard for new user interfaces and this chapter explains the basic principles behind the development of Web Dynpro user interfaces. It also describes how SAP user interfaces evolved over the years, right up to the development of Web Dynpro.

1 Introduction

Web-based user interfaces have undergone rapid technological advancement in recent years. Roughly ten years ago, at the beginning of the Internet boom, web pages consisted largely of static content and there were only a small number of scripts available that enabled knowledgeable and experienced Internet users to program the first dynamic web functions such as guest books.

Today's websites have very little in common with those of ten years ago. Today, easy-to-use content management systems such as Joomla have become Internet standards and asynchronous JavaScript and XML (AJAX) technology has heralded the next generation of dynamic web pages.

SAP and web-based applications

In the past, it was difficult to predict the implications of all of these developments. Today's market, especially regarding SAP, requires web-based applications that can be opened directly in any web browser without complicated installation or maintenance. To fulfill this requirement, SAP initially adapted the former dynpro user interfaces (UIs) (see Section 1.2.2, Dynpros) so that they could be displayed in web browsers using Internet Transaction Server (ITS). However, this was only an interim solution because the two technologies were too different and several compromises had to be made. SAP then developed business server pages (BSP), a technology that was specifically tailored to the Internet; however, this technology was also not mature enough to establish itself as the successor to the original dynpros.

With the introduction of Web Dynpro in 2005, SAP was finally able to offer a comprehensive and easy-to-program technology that fulfilled the description of a worthy successor to dynpro in the application area.

Topics Discussed

This chapter discusses the following topics:

- Developing web technologies
- Significance and structure of the Model View Controller (MVC) architecture pattern
- Evolution of UI technologies in the SAP world, including the console, dynpro, ITS, BSP, and Web Dynpro

1.1 Model View Controller

Before we take a detailed look at SAP UIs and Web Dynpro technology, it is important that you understand the basics of modern UI design, including Web Dynpro. Today, architecture patterns play an increasingly central role in UI design, describing the basic structure of applications. In the SAP environment, for example, the three-tier architecture is the best-known of these patterns. It describes how the data layer (the database), the application layer (the application server), and the presentation layer (the client) are separated.

Origins of MVC

The *Model View Controller (MVC) architecture pattern* has become an indispensable part of UI design. The MVC is a pattern for separating the user interface (the view) from the program control element (the controller) and the underlying data model. MVC has its origins in 1979, when the Norwegian software developer Trygve Reenskaug first implemented it in a programming language called Smalltalk. Figure 1.1 illustrates the basic access principle of the MVC pattern.

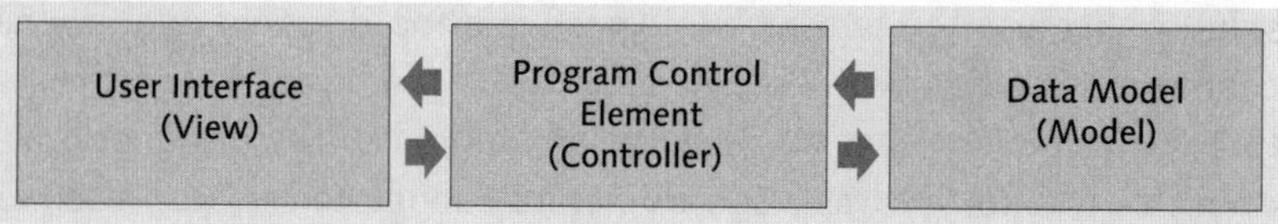

Figure 1.1 Simplified Representation of the MVC Architecture Pattern

MVC modularization

Applications that are modularized in accordance with the MVC pattern have clearer code, which makes it easier for programmers to reuse individual components. The UIs of such applications can therefore be changed – and their usability improved – without the need to change the program control or the data model. Also, any number of applications and any kind of application can access the same UI. MVC modularization also enables the programmers involved in a development project to specialize. For example, a programmer who specializes in UI development does not require any knowledge of the data model; he only needs to know about the program control interfaces.

Section 1.1.1 (Model), Section 1.1.2 (View), and Section 1.1.3 (Controller) describe the classes of the MVC architecture pattern and where they fit in to the three-tier architecture. Section 1.1.4, MVC Interaction Example, describes how the MVC layers interact with each other.

1.1.1 Model

In the MVC architecture pattern, the *model* represents the persistent data layer. For this purpose, it provides both the view layer and the controller layer with interfaces for data retrieval and data processing while remaining invisible to both the controller and the view.

Where the model fits into the MVC pattern

Normally, the application logic, the business logic, or both are located in the model. An application can be based on one model, or several models, which are dynamically selected by the controller at runtime. For example, Figure 1.2 shows an example in which every view has its own model. The controller uses either model X or model Y, depending on whether view A or view B is being displayed.

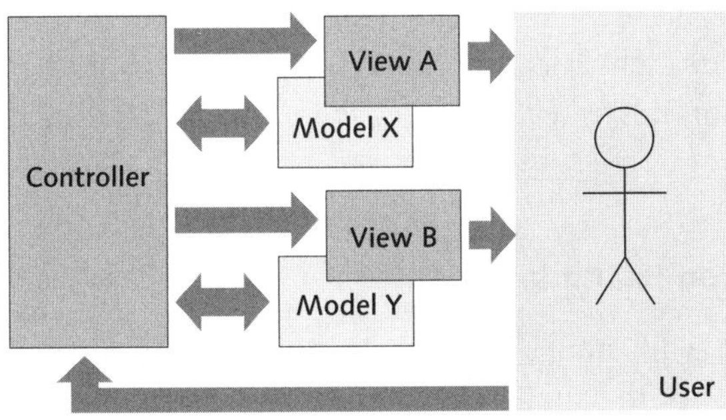

Figure 1.2 Example of the Structure of an MVC Scheme

The model is unaware of both the calling view and the calling controller. The entire process of communication with the two other layers is handled by the methods and interfaces provided by the model. The model accesses the actual (raw) data using a backend service, which is usually a database.

1.1.2 View

A *view* is used to represent data in a UI. Every view is designed to display specific data or screen content. For example, one view might display the login area of an application, while another might show a table of overdue orders. Therefore, an application consists of several differently structured views.

Examples of views

Views contain various UI elements such as buttons, input fields, and tables but no data or control logic. Therefore, you would not be able to navigate from the first view to the second view using only a login view and a "welcome" view, for example – you would also need a controller. The controller processes the data the user enters into the login view, as well as the actions that follow such as a click on the login button.

1.1.3 Controller

The *controller* is primarily responsible for program control and view management. It processes all input and reacts appropriately to this input by sending messages to the model or deciding which view should be displayed. However, as you now know, the controller does not contain any application logic or business logic; this logic is contained only in the model.

As with the model layer and the view layer, an application may contain one or several controllers, which can be interchanged as required at runtime. The next section describes this process in greater detail and provides an example.

1.1.4 MVC Interaction Example

The diagram in Figure 1.3 illustrates the sample application described in Section 1.1.2, View. After the application is started, the user sees the login view, which becomes the welcome view after the user enters his data and clicks on the login button. The processes that are triggered by these actions are hidden from the user.

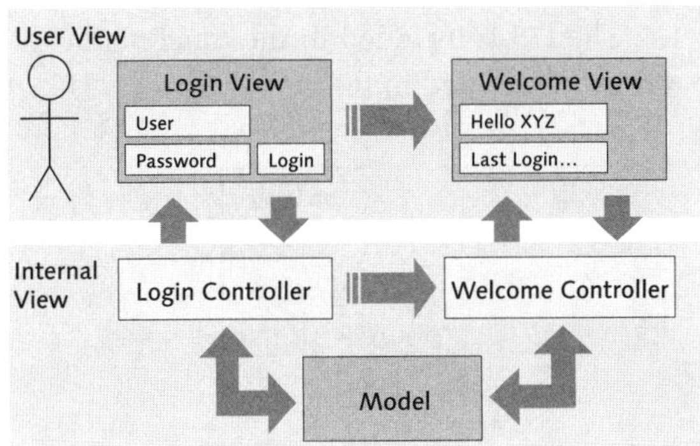

Figure 1.3 Login with Two Views and Controllers

Process cycle

Internally, the application is started and the login controller is loaded. The login controller then creates the login view and sends it back to the client for display. The user enters his data and clicks on the login button. This action is sent back to the login controller. The login controller creates the model and compares the input data with the user database. If the login is successful, the welcome controller is created and opened. This process cycle is then repeated in a similar manner, and the user is passed on from controller to controller within the application.

This is just an example of the possible interactions within the MVC architecture pattern. A central controller or a distributed model are other options, and several other combinations are also possible.

1.2 Evolution of SAP User Interfaces

As you know from the first paragraphs of this chapter, the MVC architecture pattern was not always a standard in the UI area. Instead, the first SAP UIs were based on console technology; consoles were the standard for UIs for a relatively long time.

SAP UIs are based on technology that is always changing, and changing quickly. For example, in recent years, two innovations developed in parallel: BSP and Web Dynpro. The latter has been available since 2005 for both Java and ABAP applications.

The following sections give you a comprehensive overview of the evolution of UI technologies developed by SAP over the years, as illustrated on a timeline in Figure 1.4. The ITS is included in the timeline for the sake of completeness, but it is not covered in this book.

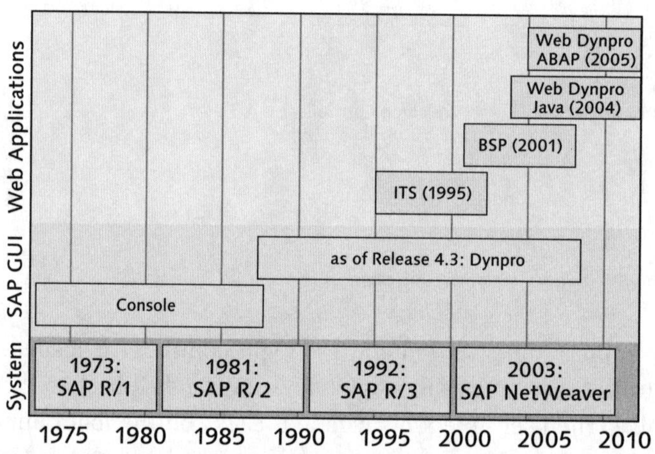

Figure 1.4 Evolution of SAP User Interfaces

1.2.1 Console

Until the late 1980s, SAP programs were based on *console technology*. The main feature of consoles was a direct terminal connection to mainframe servers. Because their application logic is implemented in servers rather than in the client, consoles are known as "zero clients."

Properties of consoles

Both SAP R/1 and SAP R/2 were fully written in Assembler and based on consoles. Consoles were controlled via the keyboard only; thus, users had to learn several key combinations and transaction codes. Modern developments such as the mouse and menus were still unknown.

Only after more advanced versions of SAP R/2 came onto the market at the end of the 1980s were consoles rendered obsolete by dynpro technology. The main features of dynpros were greater ease of use and a client-side presentation layer.

Due to the strict client-server architecture and very limited uses, SAP consoles do not offer any advantages and are rarely used in today's environments.

1.2.2 Dynpros

As mentioned earlier, dynpros were introduced as the successor to console technology at the end of the 1980s, with SAP R/2 (release 4.3). The term "dynpro" is short for "dynamic program." Dynpros are displayed in the SAP GUI and they are still the most important UI technology in the SAP world today. Therefore, although most new SAP applications are developed exclusively in Web Dynpro, the Web Dynpro ABAP development tools – collectively known as the ABAP Workbench – are based entirely on dynpro technology. Unlike many modern UI technologies, dynpros do not use the object-oriented approach to software programming. Instead, they consist of two subcomponents:

- **Screen definition**
  The screen definition describes the structure and layout of screen elements in the dynpro. A wide range of screen definitions is available, including text fields, input and output fields, checkboxes, radio buttons, subscreens, and table controls for table display. In most cases, programmers program the screen definition using the *Screen Painter*. However, in a few special applications, the screen definition is dynamically generated at program runtime.
- **Flow logic**
  The dynpro flow logic describes the two process blocks *process before output (PBO)* and *process after input (PAI)*. These blocks are run sequentially in the dynpro either before or after a user action (see Figure 1.5):
  - The PBO block is run at initialization and before each dynpro is updated. The relevant modules for loading and formatting the data to be displayed are opened in this block. For example, the descriptive text for an input field is loaded in the PBO block. The results are then transferred to the user's client using identically-named global variables, where they are displayed on the screen by the presentation application – the SAP GUI – in the form of a dynpro.

- The PAI block is started after each user action in the dynpro. A user action could be a change to a date or a mouse click. The PAI block then loads the relevant modules for processing the input.

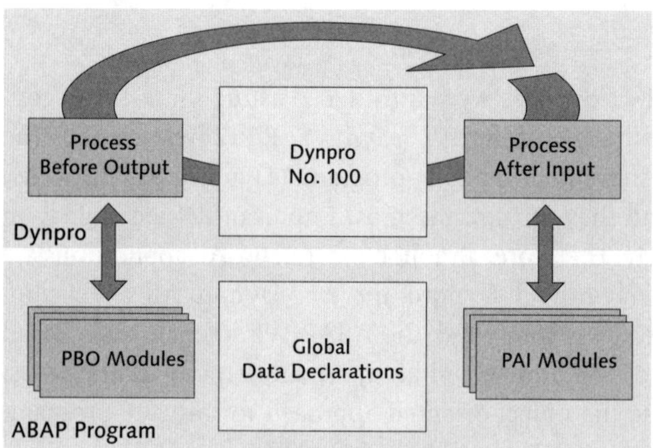

Figure 1.5 Flow Logic of Dynpro Number 100

The two main elements of the interaction process between dynpros are the *calling logic* and the *data transport*. Dynpros within a program have a unique identification number and it has become established practice at SAP to use number 100 for the welcome dynpro in applications. The ABAP statement `CALL SCREEN 100` starts the PBO flow logic and loads the dynpro, and the statement `SET SCREEN <dynno>` can be used to navigate between dynpros. You can thus create any sequence of dynpros, like in the example shown in Figure 1.6.

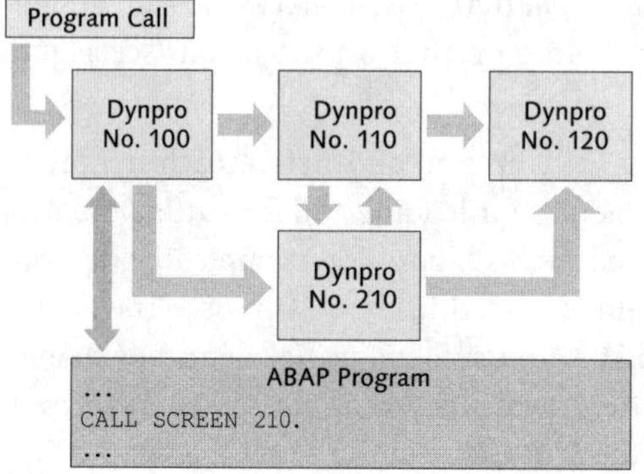

Figure 1.6 Interaction Between Dynpros

The data transport between dynpros uses global variables that can be used by all the dynpros in a program.

Assessment of Web Dynpro technology

Dynpro has become an established and mature technology. It is still the fastest SAP UI and offers the best ease of use. However, its structures are very inflexible compared to modern programming techniques. For example, unlike modern programming environments, dynpro does not allow for event-based control. One exception to this is the SAP List Viewer (also known as the ABAP List Viewer [ALV]), which includes event-based control and is used to display complex tables in dynpros. However, despite some disadvantages, the most advanced dynpros are still the main SAP technology used for facilitating interaction between the user and the SAP system.

1.2.3 Business Server Pages

Until 2001, the *SAP ITS* – which was first released in 1995 – was the only Internet connection solution available in SAP R/3. The ITS was an external system with only limited functionality and was not integrated into the SAP system. BSP technology was developed to overcome these disadvantages.

BSP, released with SAP Web Application Server (Web AS) 6.10 in July 2001, was the first Internet connection solution to be fully integrated into the SAP system landscape. BSPs allowed SAP programmers to generate HTML pages for web-based applications directly in the application server. Generally speaking, BSPs are similar to *Java Server Pages (JSPs)* from Sun Microsystems.

Example of a Simple Dynamic BSP Application

Listing 1.1 shows the code for a very simple BSP application and gives you an initial idea of how BSPs are structured:

```
<%@page language="abap"%>
<HTML>
  <HEAD>
    <TITLE>Hello World Application</TITLE>
  </HEAD>
  <BODY>
```

```
    <% DO 5 TIMES. %>
      <FONT size=<%=sy-index %>>Hello World!<br></FONT>
    <% ENDDO. %>
  </BODY>
</HTML>
```

Listing 1.1 Server-Side Scripting with BSP

In this HTML code, ABAP statements are enclosed in `<%...%>` tags. `@page language="abap"` in the first line sets the server-side scripting language to ABAP (JavaScript could also be used). The code contained in the `DO n TIMES` statement is executed n times; the loop counter system variable `sy-index` increments by 1 at each execution.

At runtime, the server interprets this BSP page, generates the relevant HTML code, and sends this code to the calling browser. In the browser, the sentence "Hello World!" appears five times in succession, with increasing text size (see Figure 1.7).

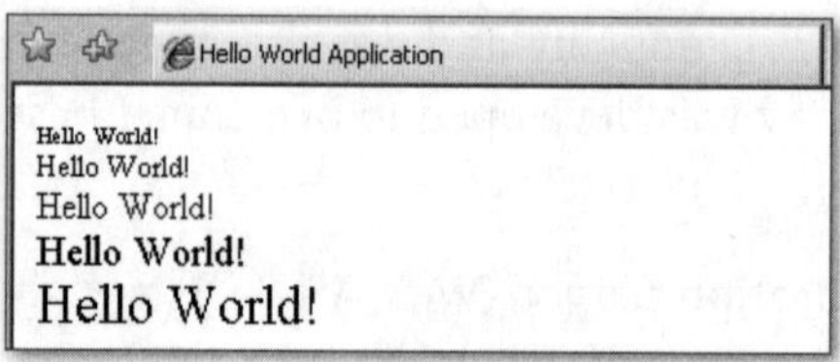

Figure 1.7 "Hello World" with BSP

BSPs and the MVC Pattern

Layer separation, as defined in the MVC architecture pattern, has been supported in BSPs only since Web AS 6.20. This layer separation is achieved by deriving model and controller classes from abstract superclasses. These superclasses are called `CL_BSP_MODEL` and `CL_BSP_CONTROLLER2`:

- The controller is derived from `CL_BSP_CONTROLLER2`. The inheritance concept enables any number of main controllers and sub-controllers to be created with ease. The controller can use the interface class to create any number of views at runtime and to control both their interaction and the data flow between the layers. To do this, it can also access the methods of the model.

- The model is derived from the `CL_BSP_MODEL` class; thus, it already contains several important basic classes for database communication. It accesses the Data Dictionary, among other things, and converts input on the basis of the relevant data type.

Note

As of Web AS 6.20, BSPs contain two controller classes to ensure downward compatibility: `CL_BSP_CONTROLLER2` and `CL_BSP_CONTROLLER`. The former is a fully modernized version of the latter.

However, BSP MVC applications can still be combined with the classic UI programming model in any way, without layer separation. Figure 1.8 illustrates the difference between the two UI programming models.

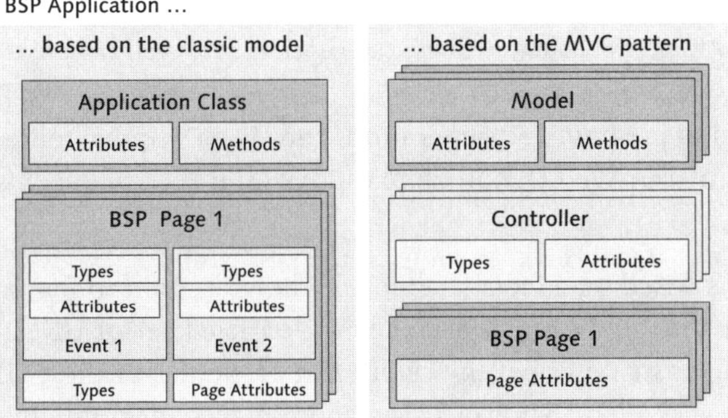

Figure 1.8 Classic UI Design vs. MVC-Based Design

Structure of BSP views

The view of a BSP application consists of HTML files that contain ABAP code and that are stored on the server. Access can be gained to the library of HTML modules for the BSP extension HTMLB from within these BSP pages. HTMLB is a collection of common screen elements such as input fields and tables. The existence of page attributes with the same names makes it possible for data to be transferred between the view and the controller.

Assessment of BSP technology

With the release of BSPs, SAP brought to market the first technology to be optimized exclusively for web browsers; ITS, the previous internet connection technology, could only emulate dynpros in web browsers.

However, because BSP programming is done at a very basic level, it requires a lot of time and advanced HTML knowledge as compared to modern Web Dynpro technology.

1.2.4 Web Dynpro

Within the framework of the SAP NetWeaver strategy, Web Dynpro is the official UI technology for SAP applications. It can be programmed in both Java and ABAP. Web Dynpro has been available on the SAP Java platform since the first release of SAP NetWeaver in 2004; the ABAP version was released at the end of 2005.

Naming Convention

The Web Dynpro version that is based on ABAP is often abbreviated to WD4A or WDA (Web Dynpro for ABAP). Because this book deals exclusively with Web Dynpro ABAP, we will continue to use the general term, Web Dynpro.

Benefits of Web Dynpro over BSP

All that is needed to use both BSP applications and Web Dynpro applications is a web browser. Web Dynpro applications offer several benefits over BSPs:

- Web Dynpro is based on a metadata model. The Web Dynpro framework provides the application developer with a fixed set of UI elements. The metadata describes the layout and properties of these UI elements for every Web Dynpro UI. The entire process of communication between the application and the Web Dynpro framework takes place in ABAP only, and at fixed points. With Web Dynpro, application developers do not need any knowledge of HTML or JavaScript to develop web-based UIs. Also, thanks to the strict separation of application logic and display technology, developers can create UIs without any technical knowledge of the underlying display technology. This also makes it possible for developers to adapt complex applications to new display technology by simply changing the client-specific Web Dynpro implementation.
- The Web Dynpro component model makes it easy for Web Dynpro UIs to be reused – Web Dynpro components are used to structure UIs. Chapter 2, Web Dynpro Architecture, discusses these components in detail. Thanks to the component model, Web Dynpro is considerably

more powerful than BSP technology and SAP already provides developers with a range of reusable Web Dynpro standard components.

- Like the SAP GUI-based dynpros, Web Dynpro provides an automatic connection to the input helps of Data Dictionary objects.
- The rigorous encapsulation of the Web Dynpro framework and the application logic means that Web Dynpro offers a high level of investment protection. The encapsulation of the UI technology ensures that it will be easy to adapt Web Dynpro applications to future display technologies, such as smart clients.

A look ahead

You now have an initial impression of the benefits of Web Dynpro and you will see them in the exercises and chapters to come.

1.3 Summary

In this chapter, we gave you a brief overview of the development of UIs, with particular regard to SAP technologies.

The underlying architecture of Web Dynpro applications is explained in detail in Chapter 2, Web Dynpro Architecture.

Since its first release in 2005, the Web Dynpro framework has evolved substantially. The current release, for example, contains a considerably extended set of UI elements, while existing elements have been optimized. However, there is one thing that has not changed – the architecture of the Web Dynpro framework. Based on intuitive examples, this chapter provides a detailed description of this architecture.

2 Web Dynpro Architecture

Web Dynpro programming model

Now that you have some insight into the history and development of user interfaces from reading Chapter 1, Introduction, this chapter describes the basic architecture of applications in Web Dynpro ABAP. In contrast to BSP, Web Dynpro applications are not based on the imperative but on the declarative programming model. Consequently, user interfaces and their relationships are not programmed (as in the imperative model); rather, they are constructed in a graphical editor. The editor saves the information obtained through the user interface declaratively as metadata. In principle, this metadata allows you to generate source code in any programming language; however, currently only ABAP and Java for Web Dynpro are supported.

Firmly defined exit points within the source code allow developers to implement their own source code at certain points in the application. Subsequently, the compiler translates all of the information into an executable application. Figure 2.1 shows the Web Dynpro programming model.

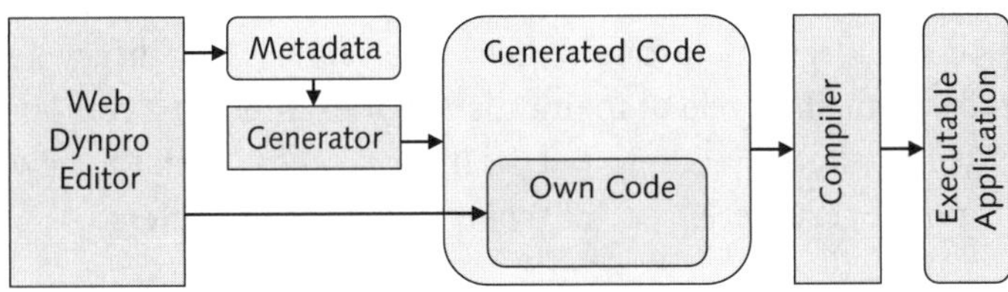

Figure 2.1 Web Dynpro Programming Model

Web Dynpro clients

The use of the declarative model greatly facilitates using Web Dynpro on separate clients. As a result, you need to implement only one interface for the respective client technology in the SAP NetWeaver Application Server to obtain Web Dynpro support. The current Web Dynpro ABAP release only supports HTML. As of release 7.01, Lightspeed-Rendering will be included and thus represent a Web Dynpro AJAX client.

Both Web Dynpro Java and Web Dynpro ABAP are based on the same architecture. The following sections provide a detailed description of this architecture using Web Dynpro ABAP as a reference for the examples.

Topics Discussed

The following topics are discussed in this chapter:

- The design and structure of Web Dynpro components, windows, views, and applications
- Views, UI elements, and their properties
- Navigating between different views using windows and plugs
- Different types of controllers and their interaction
- Hook methods
- Assistance classes
- Context programming: data binding, mapping, and supply functions

2.1 Components and Applications

Components represent the central Web Dynpro building blocks. They combine logically related Web Dynpro objects and processes into groups. Components primarily include controllers, windows, views, and Web Dynpro applications, which will all be described in this chapter. Simply speaking, from the point of view of the MVC architecture pattern, components consist of a set of views and controllers.

Reusing components

Components are reusable, which means that they can be used by other components and addressed through their interfaces. Their lifecycle depends heavily on the lifecycle of their callers. For example, if a component is generated by another component, its lifecycle ends when the new component is no longer referenced, or when it is manually deleted.

Web Dynpro applications

You should make sure not to mistake components in Web Dynpro for Web Dynpro applications. Web Dynpro applications represent entry points in components. Put simply, a Web Dynpro application consists merely of a server address that can be called from your web browser and is linked internally with the view of the respective component that should be called. Therefore, a Web Dynpro application has nothing in common with the usual meaning of the term application.

You cannot execute a component without an application. However, its interfaces enable other components to integrate a component into applications. Consequently, a Web Dynpro component can have zero, one, or any number of Web Dynpro applications.

2.1.1 Example: Library

The library example shown in Figure 2.2 displays the interaction between components and applications. A librarian can use a web browser to launch the Web Dynpro application `Administration`, which is loaded for display by the `Search` view of the `Administration` component. Whenever necessary, the component interface then enables `Administration` to access data and views of the `Books` component; for instance, to display the books borrowed by a specific customer. The `Books` component, on the other hand, cannot be accessed directly because it does not contain an application as an entry point. However, the views and data provided by `Books` can be accessed by any number of other components.

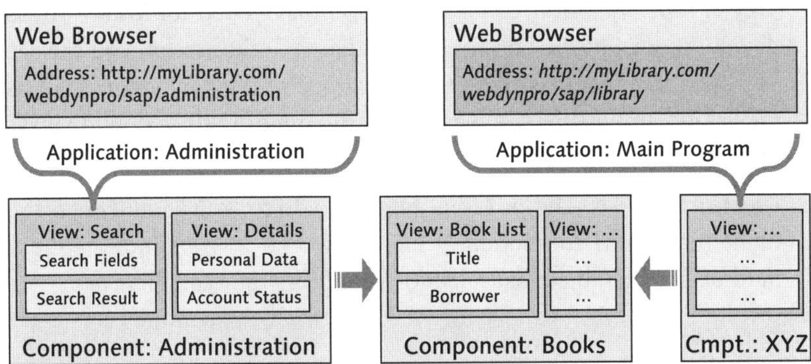

Figure 2.2 Web Dynpro Applications (Simplified Display)

Your own first Web Dynpro application

Now that you have acquired basic knowledge about Web Dynpro components and applications, the following sections will introduce you to the Web Dynpro development environment, and you will create your first "Hello World" component. In this context, you will get to know the Web Dynpro programming model step by step, both in theory and in its practical use.

Initially, your component will contain only one application and one view with the text "Hello World." Later in this chapter, the component will be gradually extended by input fields, buttons, and a second view to display the data that has been entered. This exercise does not involve the graphical design of the views or details for the individual objects of the framework. These details will be described in great detail in later chapters so that at this stage, you can fully concentrate on creating your component.

2.1.2 Web Dynpro Explorer

[✎] The Web Dynpro development environment – the Web Dynpro Explorer – is fully integrated in the ABAP Workbench (Transaction SE80).

Starting the Web Dynpro development environment

1. Start the ABAP Workbench. You will find the WEB DYNPRO EXPLORER under the WEB DYNPRO COMP./INTF entry in the object list selection of the Repository Browser.

   Figure 2.3 displays a screenshot of the Web Dynpro Explorer containing the Web Dynpro component you will create in this chapter. The Web Dynpro Explorer contains all the tools needed for Web Dynpro developments. In the bottom left-hand area of the screen, you can see an object tree that lists all objects contained in the component such as views and applications. The right-hand pane of the window displays the respective object details.

Creating the component

2. Create a new Web Dynpro component. To do so, you should enter the name of the new component – `ZWDC_02_HELLO_WORLD` – into the input field below the object list selection and press the `Enter` key.

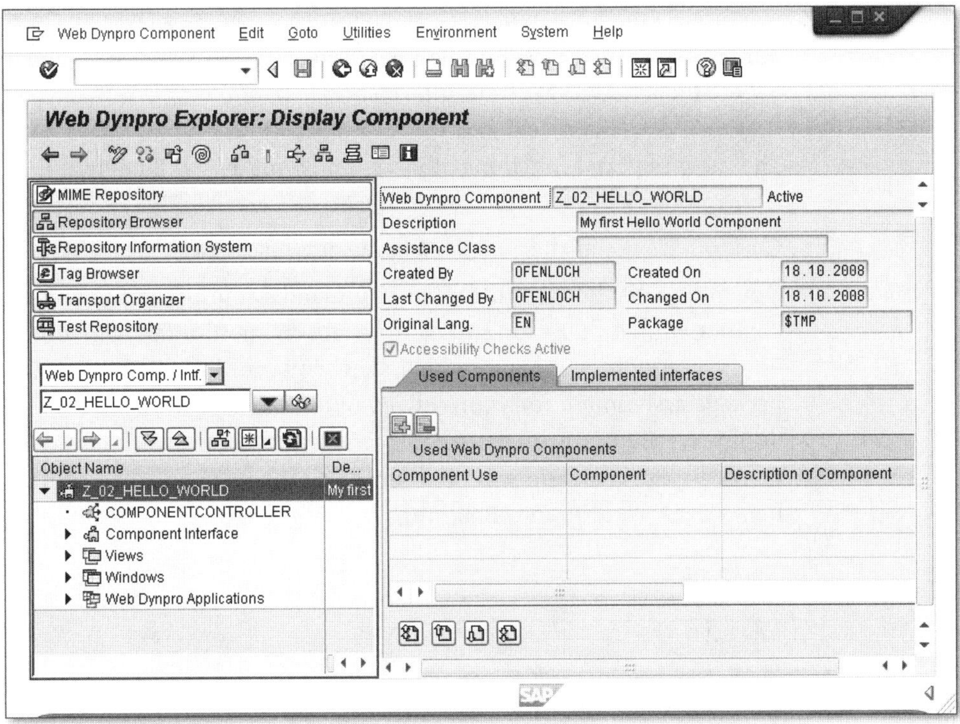

Figure 2.3 Web Dynpro Explorer – First Component

3. A dialog box appears, asking you whether you want to create the new component that does not yet exist. Confirm this query with YES.
4. A second dialog box displays, in which you can enter details for the new Web Dynpro component. Enter a description for the new component, as shown in Figure 2.4.

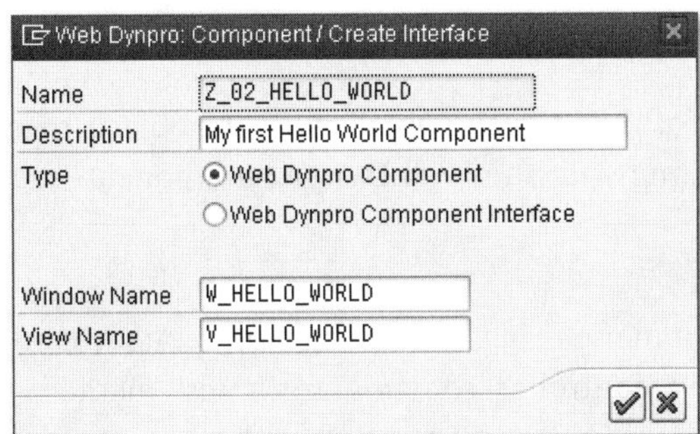

Figure 2.4 Creating the First Web Dynpro Component

5. Next, select the WEB DYNPRO COMPONENT type; the WEB DYNPRO COMPONENT INTERFACE type will be discussed in geater detail in Chapter 5, Section 5.1.3, Component Interfaces. Then, enter `W_HELLO_WORLD` in the WINDOW NAME field and `V_HELLO_WORLD` in the VIEW NAME field. The meanings and functions of views and windows will be described later in this chapter.
6. Click on the green checkmark to confirm your entries.
7. Depending on the system configuration and namespace of your new component, you may have to confirm the creation of the component in a subsequent step. In the final step, you will be asked about the package assignment for your new component (see Figure 2.5). If you do not want to transport the component, you should click on LOCAL OBJECT. After this, you will be returned to the newly created component in the Web Dynpro Explorer.

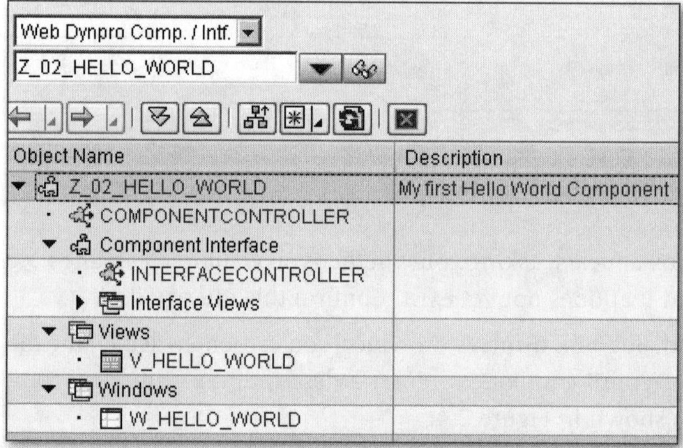

Figure 2.5 Package Assignment for the New Web Dynpro Component

Structure of a Web Dynpro component

8. The object list on the left of your screen now displays the objects that are created by default, along with the Web Dynpro component (see Figure 2.6):
   - **Component controller**
     Every Web Dynpro component has exactly one component controller. The component controller contains attributes, methods, events, and a context. Section 2.4, Context, describes the context

in greater detail. Within the component, the component controller is available to all objects and is therefore of essential importance.

- **Views**
  Views contain the visible part of Web Dynpro components. Consequently, they consist primarily of UI elements. Additionally, the view controller allows for responding to user actions.
- **Windows**
  A Web Dynpro component has at least one window. Windows integrate views and enable you to navigate between them. We will discuss windows in greater detail later in this chapter.
- **Component interface**
  Each Web Dynpro component contains one instance of the component interface that enables the design of cross-component Web Dynpro architectures.

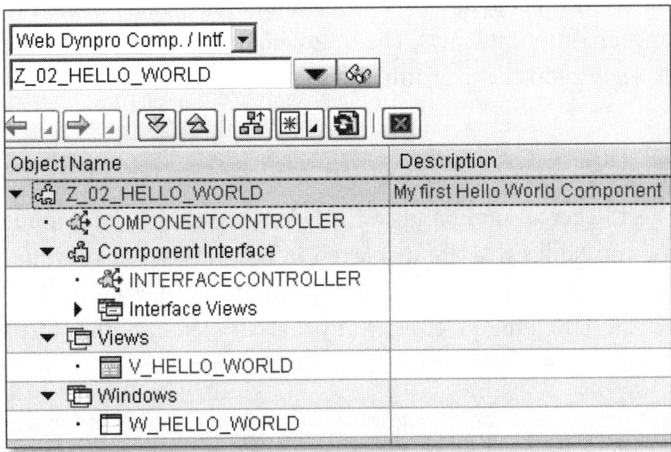

Figure 2.6 Object List of the New Web Dynpro Component

9. At this stage, you should play around and click through the component to familiarize yourself with the Web Dynpro Explorer and the different objects. For example, by double-clicking on the component name, you can view or edit the components used or integrated by your component. That being said, you will not need these options in this chapter because you are working with a new and rather simple component.

You have now created your first Web Dynpro component. Theoretically, you could activate it at this point; however, there are still two things missing for you to be able to use the component:

- First, the Hello World text is missing in the view. The following section provides a detailed description on how to use views.
- Second, you need an application as an entry point into the Web Dynpro component. The application will be integrated into the component after the view has been completed.

2.2 View

This section provides a detailed description of the view and the Web Dynpro elements related to it. For this purpose, we will take a closer look at views, windows, and plugs. As mentioned earlier, windows are on a higher hierarchy level than views, and contain plugs that enable the navigation between different views. The following section describes how you can create views and the user interface.

2.2.1 Views

Structure of a view

A view contains the actual input and control elements such as text input fields, buttons, and tables that are displayed in the browser at runtime. In Web Dynpro, all of these elements are referred to as *UI elements*. It is possible that some UI elements consist of other UI elements that form the structure of a hierarchical tree of UI elements.

The UI element `Group`, shown in Figure 2.7 (located directly under the view root), is an example of such a hierarchical tree because it contains labels and input fields for describing and displaying data. Within the web browser, the UI elements contained in a `Group` are surrounded by a colored frame. UI elements that contain other UI elements are also referred to as *container elements*.

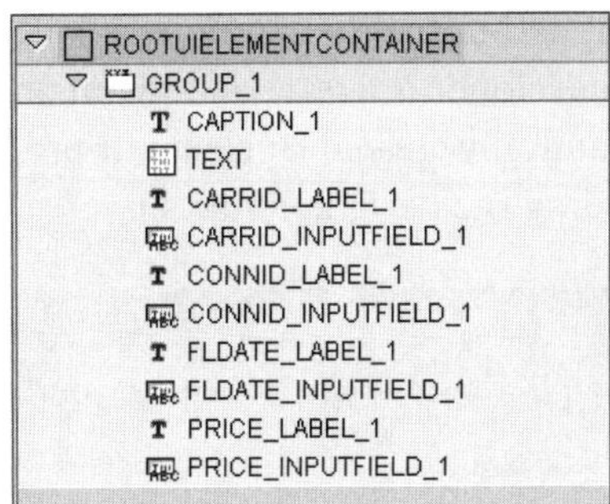

Figure 2.7 Example of a UI Group at Design Time

Container Elements in Practice

In addition to the `Group` element, you will frequently use the UI elements `TransparentContainer` and `ViewContainer` in your daily work:

- Similar to the `Group` element, transparent containers allow for an easy arrangement of UI elements within a view. However, in contrast to the `Group` element, transparent containers do not display in the user interface.
- View containers enable you to integrate views in defined portions of other views. This allows you to compile your UIs flexibly from multiple views. It also enables the simultaneous display of multiple views. Using view containers requires knowledge of developing Web Dynpro windows, which is described in Section 2.2.2, Windows and Plugs.

Layouts in Web Dynpro

In this hierarchical structure, the position of the UI elements is not fixed in the UI. For example, percentage specifications such as "Width: 100%" can easily cause elements to shift into a different position. In contrast to traditional dynpros, the arrangement of UI elements is flexible and changes according to the amount of space available in the web browser window. Developers who want to customize the layout can choose from four different layout types, some of which are commonly used in the Java world: `FlowLayout`, `RowLayout`, `GridLayout`, and `MatrixLayout`. These layout types are described in much detail in Chapter 3, Developing Web Dynpro Applications.

There are two different ways to create UI elements in views:

- Declaratively, using the View Editor at design time
- Dynamically, within coding of the view

If necessary, you can also combine both methods with each other in one view. Although it is much easier for a developer to create and maintain UI elements using the View Editor, dynamically created UI elements provide a higher degree of flexibility regarding the design of views.

> **Note**
>
> Don't worry! Most of the time – and also in this book – you will create your views declaratively using the View Editor.

Actions

As is required by the MVC architecture, views do not contain any application logic (provided they are properly programmed). However, some UI elements such as buttons can respond to user actions and trigger what are called *actions*. When an action is triggered, the respective view controller executes an *event handler method* that is assigned to the action. This method could then initiate the navigation to a subsequent view, for instance.

Creating the First View

[✎] You will now create a second view for the Hello World component. This view will be used at a later stage to display the entries in the first view.

Creating the first view

1. Right-click on the component and select CREATE • VIEW from the context menu (see Figure 2.8).

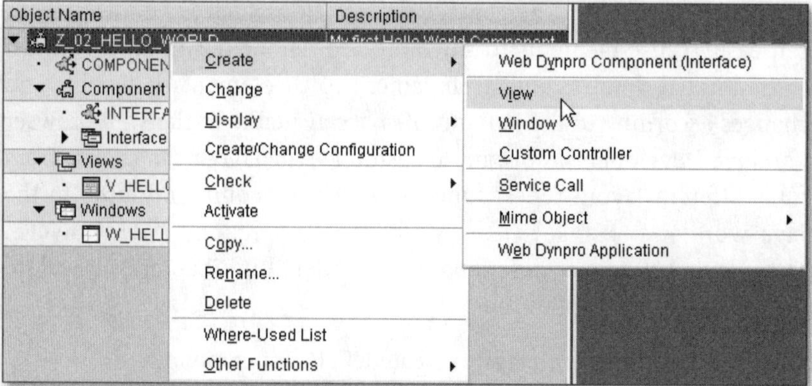

Figure 2.8 Creating a New Web Dynpro View

2. Enter the name of the view in the dialog box that appears. Enter V_RESULT, as shown in Figure 2.9, and provide a description. Confirm your entries by clicking on the green checkmark in the bottom right-hand corner.

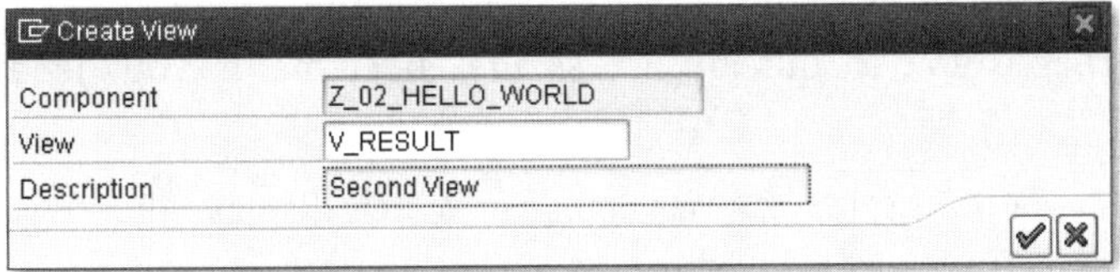

Figure 2.9 Entering View Information

3. After that, the system takes you to the editor of the new view. At this stage, the newly created view does not yet display in the object list of the component. To include it in the list, click on the SAVE button in the ABAP Workbench toolbar. Navigate back to the first view.

Structure of the view editor

By default, the LAYOUT tab of the view editor is selected when you display Web Dynpro views (see Figure 2.10). This tab allows you to design your views at design time using a WYSIWYG editor.

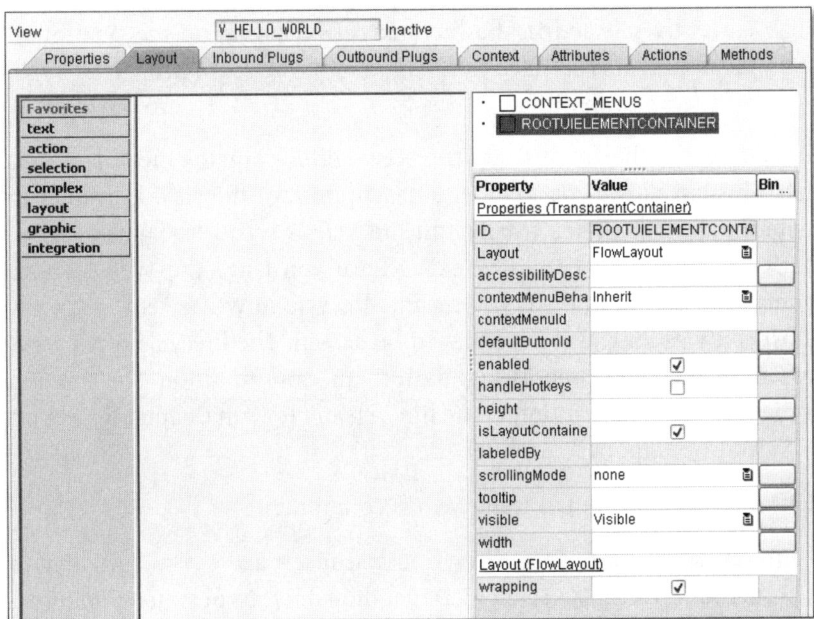

Figure 2.10 Layout Tab of the View Editor

The layout editor is divided into three main areas:

Layout tab

- The area on the left contains a *toolbar* with a library of all available Web Dynpro UI elements. These elements are categorized by multiple tabs according to their usage or degree of complexity. You can drag and drop individual elements from the tabs to the FAVORITES tab. Favorites enable you to quickly access the UI elements you need most.
- The central area represents the *view designer,* which displays the view at design time. You can drag and drop the UI elements from the toolbar into the designer, where you can change their position and arrange them according to your requirements.
- The area on the right consists of two subareas:
  - The upper subarea displays a hierarchy of the statically defined UI elements of the view. The starting point of a view is always the UI element ROOTUIELEMENTCONTAINER, which is predefined by Web Dynpro in each view. Right-clicking your mouse enables you to insert, edit, or delete UI elements in the hierarchy via a context menu.
  - The lower subarea displays the *properties* of the UI element that is currently selected in the hierarchy. Depending on the type of UI element that is selected in the hierarchy, the set of properties available to you can differ.

Properties tab

In addition to the LAYOUT tab, the view editor contains the PROPERTIES tab. This tab allows you to enter a description for the view as well as to determine its lifecycle. The default lifecycle is set to FRAMEWORK CONTROLLED. In this case, a view exists until you leave the Web Dynpro component. In contrast, if you set the lifecycle to WHEN VISIBLE, a view exists only as long as it is displayed on screen. The lifecycle of views is essential regarding memory and performance optimization. You can find a more detailed description of the lifecycle of views in Chapter 5, Section 5.1, Multi-Component Architectures.

Adding new UI elements

Let us now complete the Hello World component:

1. To do so, return to the LAYOUT tab and insert a TextView UI element into the V_HELLO_WORLD view. Depending on your personal preferenc-

es, you can integrate the element into your UI in two different ways, as shown in Figure 2.11:

- Drag the TextView UI element from the TEXT tab on the view editor toolbar into the view editor. When you do so, Web Dynpro automatically assigns a unique ID to the new element.
- Right-click on the ROOTUIELEMENTCONTAINER element in the element hierarchy and select INSERT ELEMENT. Enter TV_HELLO_WORLD as the element name in the dialog box that opens and select TextView as the element type.

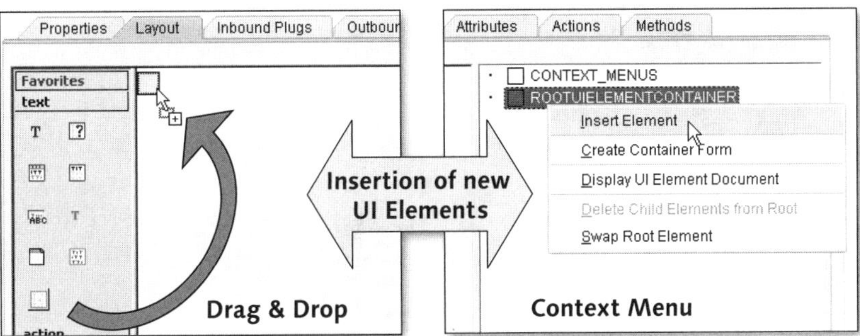

Figure 2.11 Adding New UI Elements

Performance Hint

In your daily work, you will generally insert only one container element such as Group under the root of a view – the ROOTUIELEMENTCONTAINER. Because – from a technical point of view – the view root is also a container, it makes sense to use Group directly as the root of the view. This way you can avoid using a redundant container element.

To do so, right-click on the ROOTUIELEMENTCONTAINER element and select SWAP ROOT ELEMENT. Select your preferred alternative root element type from the dialog box that opens. The SWAP ROOT ELEMENT function is only available for selection if the view does not contain any elements.

By replacing the root element with a more specific element you can reduce the number of nesting levels of the user interface. This affects both the amount of data transferred to the client and the time required for rendering the frontend.

Properties of UI elements

2. Let us now take a look at the properties of UI elements. To do so, select the new `TextView` element from the element hierarchy in the top right-hand area of your screen. As you can see in Figure 2.12, the properties area of UI elements is divided into two sections: one for the actual element properties (and their events, if available for the respective type) and one for the layout data of the element. Chapter 3, Developing Web Dynpro Applications, provides a detailed overview of the layout types available in Web Dynpro.

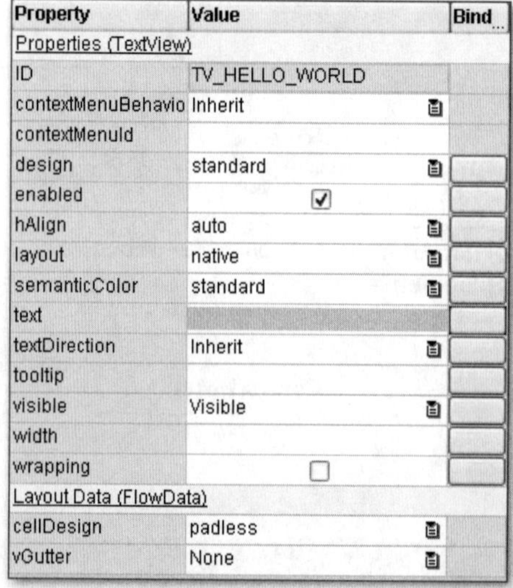

Property
Value
Bind...
Properties (TextView)
ID
TV_HELLO_WORLD
contextMenuBehavio
Inherit
contextMenuId
design
standard
enabled
hAlign
auto
layout
native
semanticColor
standard
text
textDirection
Inherit
tooltip
visible
Visible
width
wrapping
Layout Data (FlowData)
cellDesign
padless
vGutter
None

Figure 2.12 Properties of the TV_HELLO_WORLD Text View

Depending on the UI element you use, the sets of available UI element properties may differ substantially. However, there are a few default properties that are available for almost all UI elements. These include, first and foremost, the ENABLED property for enabling and disabling UI elements, and the VISIBLE property, which allows you to control the visibility of UI elements.

The most important properties of the `TextView` element are TEXT, TOOLTIP, and DESIGN. Because the TEXT property for the `TextView` UI element is a mandatory field that has not yet been filled out, the respective input field is highlighted in red. The DESIGN property enables you to customize the appearance of the text according to your requirements. To do so, you can choose from a set of predefined designs stored in a central stylesheet.

3. You should now design the `TextView` element as per your personal preferences. When doing so, you should try out the different design options. For example, if you want to enlarge the size of the text, you can use HEADER1. Additionally, you should attach the Hello World text to the element and select an appealing design.

Design options

Creating a Web Dynpro Application

What you still need at this point is a Web Dynpro application to be able to test your development.

Creating Web Dynpro applications

1. Similar to creating views, you can create a Web Dynpro application by right-clicking on the component root. Then, select CREATE • WEB DYNPRO APPLICATION from the context menu (see Figure 2.13).

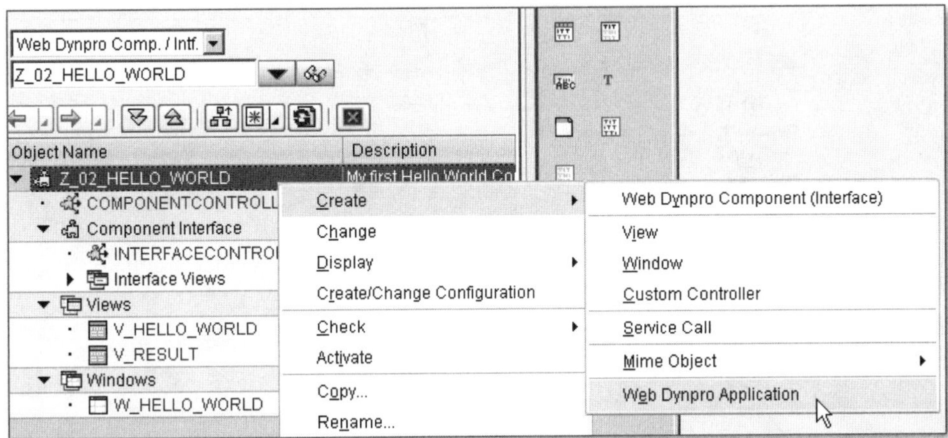

Figure 2.13 Creating Web Dynpro Applications

2. The dialog box that appears specifies the component name as the name of the application. This name will later become part of the URL. As shown in Figure 2.14, you should now enter `z_hello_world` as the name of the application and a description for the development. Then, confirm your entries.

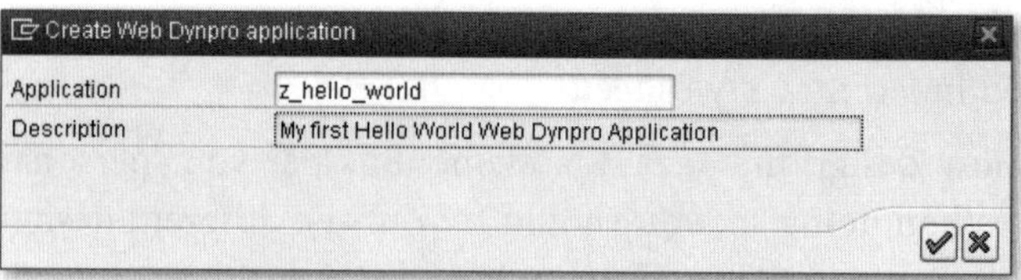

Figure 2.14 Entering the Web Dynpro Application Name

3. The system then displays a tab on which you can specify the properties of the application (see Figure 2.15). The properties have been filled automatically with default values from the component: the COMPONENT field contains the name of the current component; the INTERFACE VIEW contains the name of the only window available at this stage; and the PLUG NAME field has been assigned the only plug that is currently available from the component (see Section 2.2.2, Windows and Plugs).

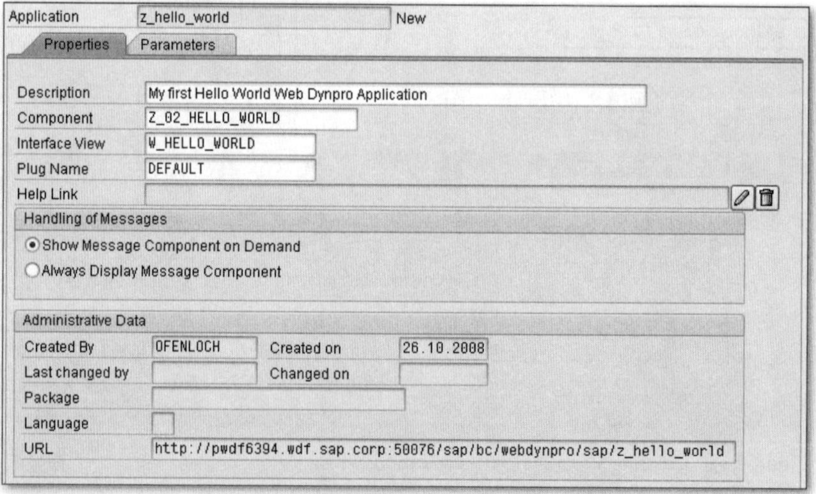

Figure 2.15 Properties of the New Web Dynpro Application

Parameters in applications

4. The PARAMETERS tab allows you to define import parameters. When starting the application, users can append these parameters to the URL and evaluate them as import parameters in the window. You can also set static parameter values on the PARAMETERS tab. The third option you have is to combine the two methods. In this case, the

static parameters remain valid as long as they are not overwritten by the URL parameters.

5. Save the application and activate the component. To do so, select the ACTIVATE item from the context menu.

Activating the component

6. After the activation, you have completed the development of your first Web Dynpro component. Congratulations!

Testing the first Web Dynpro application

You should now test the component. To do so, right-click on the application and select the TEST item from the context menu. Alternatively, you can also copy the URL from the application's properties. As shown in Figure 2.16, your own Web Dynpro application opens in a browser window.

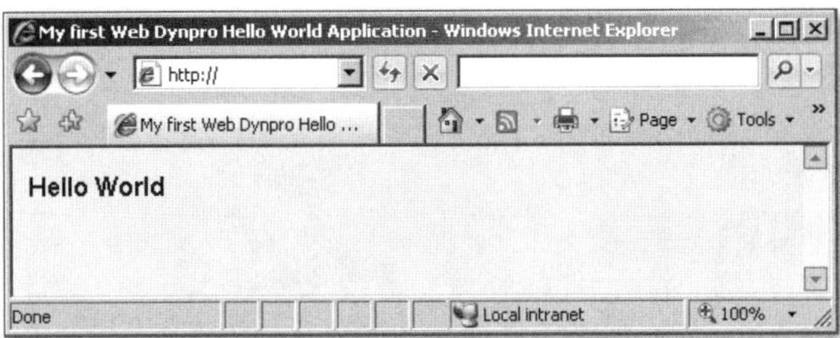

Figure 2.16 Hello World in Web Dynpro

You now know how to create views and how to position UI elements in views. Moreover, creating Web Dynpro applications should no longer be a problem for you. However, so far the component only uses the V_HELLO_WORLD view. The second view – V_RESULT – is still empty and unused. Therefore, the following section describes how you can navigate between different views of the sample component using two buttons.

2.2.2 Windows and Plugs

Windows in the Web Dynpro framework

Now that you have a sound basic understanding of views, the following sections describe the concept of *windows* and *plugs* used in the Web Dynpro framework. Although the MVC architecture pattern contains only views, Web Dynpro provides an additional feature – the window. Web Dynpro windows group all views to be displayed into a relevant context and enable navigation between individual views.

A web browser can only display a view if the view is embedded in a window. Each window uses one or more logically related views. You can only display one window, including one embedded view, at a time; however, it is possible to display additional views by creating view hierarchies. To create view hierarchies, you must use ViewContainer UI elements that are embedded in their respective parent views. Chapter 3 provides more details about this topic.

Example of using windows

Figure 2.17 shows the embedding of views in windows on the basis of the W_HELLO_WORLD window of the component. This window was created together with the ZWDC_02_HELLO_WORLD component and the V_HELLO_WORLD view (see Figure 2.4). At that stage, the V_HELLO_WORLD view was automatically integrated into the window. Therefore, you were able to test the view without any additional preparatory work or additional knowledge about the window by simply creating the application.

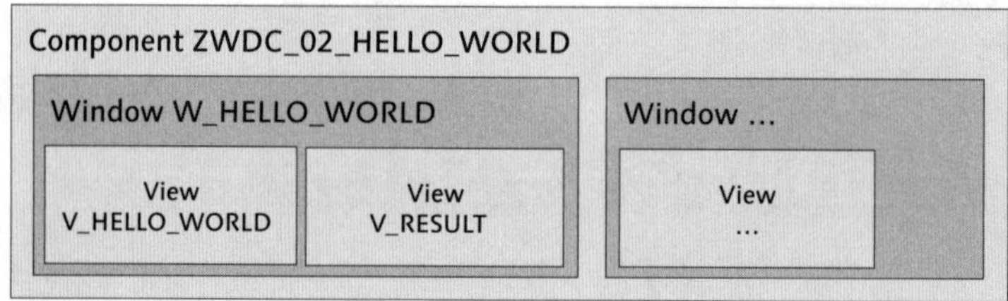

Figure 2.17 Example of Embedding Views in Windows

As shown in Figure 2.17, the V_RESULT view, which was also created at that time, has not been embedded in the window yet. This scenario is described in the following section. Note that the component could contain many other windows in addition to the W_HELLO_WORLD window.

Navigating between views

Aside from the basic structure of views and windows, you should also know how to enable navigation between individual views within a window. To navigate and interact with each other, views require entry and exit points which are referred to as *inbound* and *outbound plugs* in Web Dynpro. The link between an inbound plug and an outbound plug is called a *navigation link*. The creation of navigation links in a window enables you to navigate between the individual views of that window.

You can define outbound and inbound plugs both in views and in windows. The plugs you define in views can only be used to navigate within the respective Web Dynpro component. On the other hand, the plugs you define in windows provide additional navigation options (via three plug types each). These are discussed in greater detail in the following sections.

Example of a navigation

Figure 2.18 illustrates the concept of plugs. The figure is based on a component to which you are later (in the practical section) going to add two buttons, both used for navigating between the views. For this purpose, the views V_HELLO_WORLD and V_RESULT will be extended by one button each, as well as by a related outbound and inbound plug. The W_HELLO_WORLD window contains the views V_HELLO_WORLD and V_RESULT.

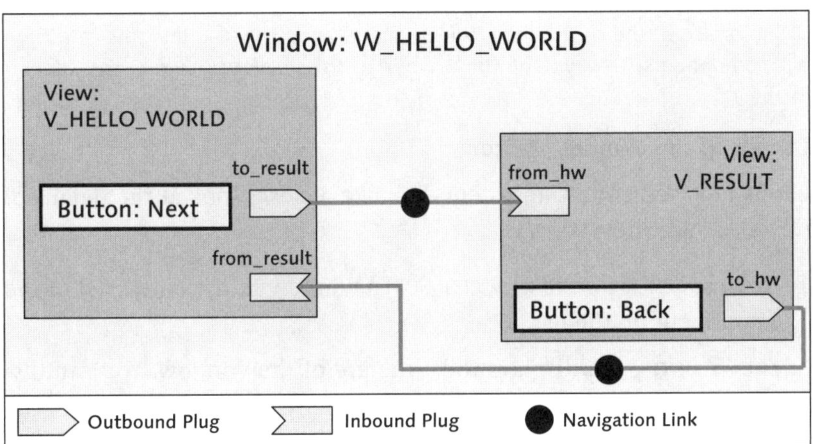

Figure 2.18 Navigating Between Views

After you have launched the application, the V_HELLO_WORLD view displays by default. Within the W_HELLO_WORLD window, the to_result outbound plug was linked with the from_hw inbound plug (from Hello World). When you click on the NEXT button, the to_result outbound plug is triggered for navigation to the V_RESULT view. Users can return to the initial view by clicking on the BACK button in the V_RESULT view. Of course, the related to_hw and from_result plugs must first be linked with each other in the window for this to happen.

Should I define an Outbound Plug in the View or in the Window?

You can define outbound and inbound plugs both in views and in windows. Depending on the intended use of the plug, you should follow the definition recommendations below:

- **View**
  You should define an outbound plug in the view if you want to call the target view only from within the source view. An example of this is the navigation from a simple to a complex search screen and back. This type of plug is referred to as a *local plug*.
- **Window**
  You should define a plug in the window if you want to call the target view from different locations. It usually makes sense to define an outbound plug in the window if you want to carry out complex navigation operations such as the navigation to a complex view that contains many subviews. Additionally, you can include plugs that are defined within a window into the interface of the component, which enables you to reuse the plug in other components. This type of plug is referred to as a *global plug*.

Details of the Window Editor

[✎] Let us now return to the system and take a closer look at the details of the window editor:

1. To do so, click on the W_HELLO_WORLD window in the object list of the component on the left.

Window tab

2. The WINDOW tab displays the structure of the window. You can display the views embedded in the window by expanding the W_HELLO_WORLD node. As shown in Figure 2.19, the window should use only the V_HELLO_WORLD view at this stage.

   In addition to the views, you can also see all plugs that have been defined in the views and windows. You will use the drag-and-drop method later on to link the outbound plugs with the inbound plugs. The yellow background color of the view within the hierarchy, as well as the checkmark next to the DEFAULT property of the view, indicate that the V_HELLO_WORLD displays by default when you open the window.

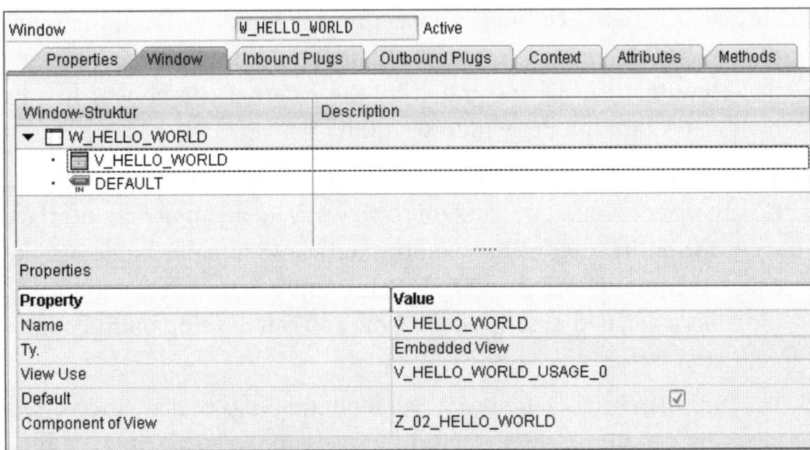

Figure 2.19 W_HELLO_WORLD Window prior to Restructuring

3. The PROPERTIES tab displays the administrative data of the window (see Figure 2.20). Here, you can also enter a description for the window. Properties tab

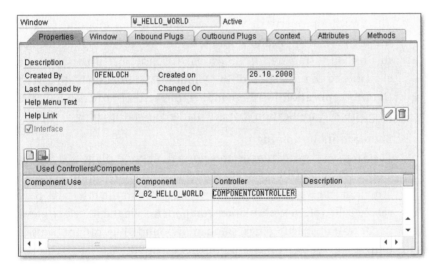

Figure 2.20 Properties of a Window

If you check the INTERFACE flag, you can use the window for entering the component via applications. In addition to this, setting this checkmark allows you to reuse the window of the component from within other components. For this purpose, the Web Dynpro framework creates what is called an interface view for the window. From the point of view of the external component, the window appears to be a normal view that can be integrated by the external component like its own views through the window editor.

4. You can display interface views in the object list of the component via COMPONENT INTERFACE • INTERFACE VIEWS. When you use an interface view, the entire logic of the window and views remains hidden to the external component. Chapter 5, Web Dynpro Standard Components, provides a detailed description of how you can develop multi-component architectures.

Inbound Plugs tab

5. The INBOUND PLUGS tab displays all inbound plugs of the window in a table. By default, the Web Dynpro framework creates a STARTUP type inbound plug called `default` with each window (see Figure 2.21). A method is created for each inbound plug in the window controller. The following three different types of inbound plugs are available to windows:

   - **Startup plug**
     The STARTUP property declares the option for an inbound plug to use the plug in applications and thus, to instance components. For this reason, using startup plugs makes sense only if they are also available to the interface of the window. When you create a Web Dynpro application for the window, the system provides only the plugs for the application that are marked as startup plugs.
   - **Standard inbound plug**
     The STANDARD property declares normal inbound plugs that do not have any specific properties and enable simple navigation between individual views. If these plugs are integrated in the interface, they can be called from within other components via the interface view. In contrast to startup plugs, standard inbound plugs cannot be used to instance Web Dynpro components via applications.
   - **Resume plug**
     Resume plugs are described in greater detail in the following sections. Furthermore, when we take a look at outbound plugs, suspend plugs will also be discussed.

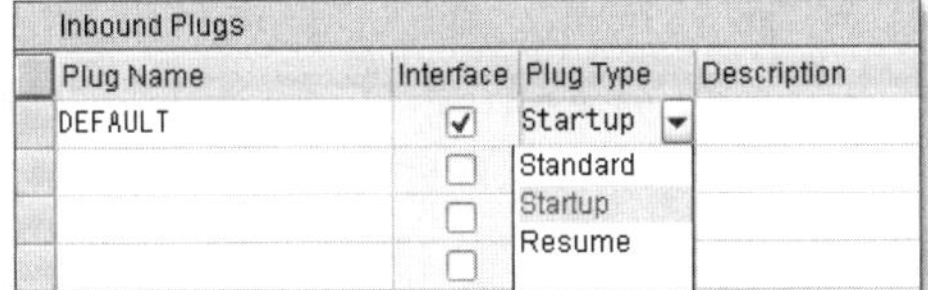

Figure 2.21 Inbound Plugs in the Window

Outbound Plugs tab

6. The OUTBOUND PLUGS tab allows you to define the outbound plugs of the window (see Figure 2.22).

Outbound Plugs

Plug Name	Interface	Plug Type	Description
	☐	Standard ▾	
	☐	Standard	
	☐	Exit	
	☐	Suspend	

Figure 2.22 Outbound Plugs in the Window

By checking the INTERFACE flag, you can transfer an outbound plug into the interface view of the window. You can define any number of transfer parameters for each outbound plug. To do so, you must select the respective outbound plug by double-clicking on it and entering the parameters in the lower table.

Web Dynpro distinguishes between three different types of outbound plugs:

- **Standard outbound plugs**
  Standard outbound plugs are the most frequently used type of outbound plug in windows. This type of plug represents the counterpart of the standard inbound plug, which triggers the navigation between views.

- **Exit plugs**
  Exit plugs are the counterpart of startup plugs, which are used to start the application instance; however, exit plugs are less frequently used. They enable you to explicitly terminate a Web Dynpro application. Note that unlike other plugs, exit plugs do not require a navigation link to accomplish this.

  In addition to using exit plugs without any parameters, you can define the two optional parameters `url` (type: `STRING`) and `close_` `window` (type: `WDY_BOOLEAN`) for an exit plug. Then, if you fill the `close_window` parameter with `X` when triggering an exit plug, Web Dynpro tries to close the browser window. Alternatively, you can specify an alternative target address via the `url` parameter.

- **Suspend and resume plugs**
  Suspend plugs allow you to navigate to another independent Web Dynpro application without closing the running application. Calling a suspend plug is similar to calling an exit plug insofar as both plugs enable you to leave a running Web Dynpro ABAP application. However, in contrast to exit plugs, suspend plugs enable you to return to the original application after you have closed the second application. Whenever an exit plug is triggered in the secondary Web Dynpro application, this application terminates and the resume plug of the primary application is called.

7. The remaining three tabs, CONTEXT, ATTRIBUTES, and METHODS are part of the window controller and will be described in detail in Section 2.3, Controllers.

More Details about Windows and Views

In Web Dynpro, you can display only one window with one view at a time. However, there are some exceptions to this rule:

- **Views with view containers**
  The `ViewContainer` UI element and window enable you to integrate any number of views into another view that serves as a frame. When doing so, you can position the view containers in any way you like between the UI elements within the frame view. Using these container elements also enables you to create view hierarchies.
- **Windows within popups**
  Another way to display two windows at the same time is to use popup windows. For example, if, within a view, you click on a link that opens a popup, this popup displays another window at a new level. Note, however, that you cannot access the lower level as long as the popup is open. Chapter 8, Practical Tips and Hints, provides a detailed description of how to create popups.

- **Integrating windows from within other components**
  The third option to include multiple windows in a view consists of reusing windows from within external components through the view interface. This option enables you to divide your UI architecture into components. For example, it is advisable to develop a separate component for frequently used UIs, such as address master data. This component could then be reused by any number of other components. However, for performance reasons, you should not make extensive use of this method and avoid creating a separate view for each new component. Chapter 5, Web Dynpro Standard Components, provides a detailed description of reusing components.

Windows and Plugs

You should now try to apply your new knowledge of windows and plugs in the system. The goal of this exercise is to create a navigation between the two views, V_HELLO_WORLD and V_RESULT. For this purpose, you will insert a button as well as an inbound plug and an outbound plug to each view. After this, you will establish a link in the window between the plugs you created in the views. [✎]

1. Go to the LAYOUT tab of the V_HELLO_WORLD view. Switch to change mode.
2. Insert a new button into the view. To do so, drag the Button UI element from the toolbar group ACTION into the view editor and drop it after the existing TextView element. Adding buttons

   Alternatively, you can create the new element via the context menu in the element hierarchy. To do so, right-click on the ROOTUIELEMENTCONTAINER element and select INSERT ELEMENT. Then, enter BTN_NEXT as the element name and select the Button element type, as shown in Figure 2.23.

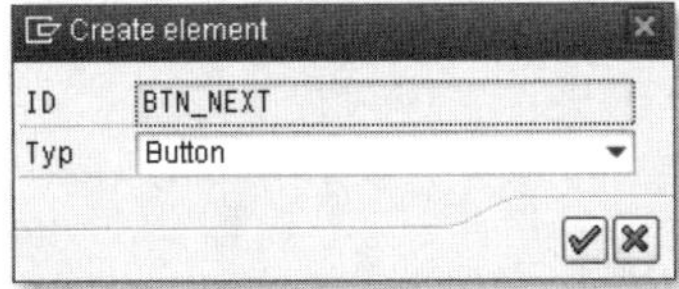

Figure 2.23 Creating the Navigation Button

3. Select the new element in the element hierarchy. Set the DESIGN to next. This adds an arrow pointing to the right to the button. Then, enter Next as the label into the TEXT property field. This label will then be displayed in the button within the view editor.

Actions of UI elements

4. At this stage, the creation of the button is completed. However, the button has no function yet. If you activated the view in its current state and started the z_hello_world application, the system would display the button but you would not be able to use it because you still need a button event handler for the onAction event. Therefore, you must now click on the CREATE button in the BINDING column to define a new action for the onAction event (see Figure 2.24).

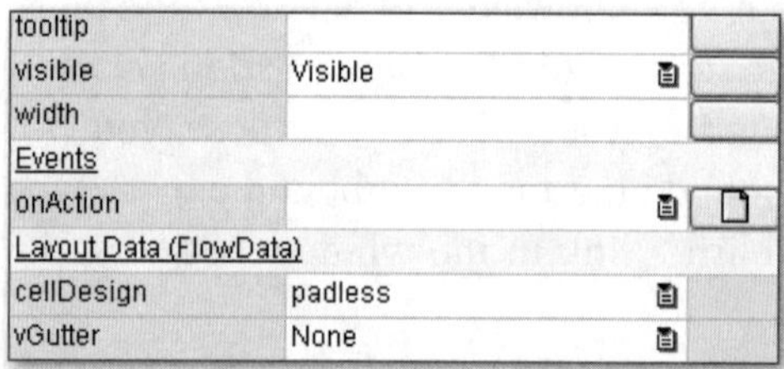

Figure 2.24 Create New Action Button

Creating actions

5. The dialog shown in Figure 2.25 opens in a popup; this dialog enables you to create new actions. Enter the name of the new action into the ACTION field; in this example, the name is NAVIGATE_TO_RESULT. Then, enter a short description for your action.

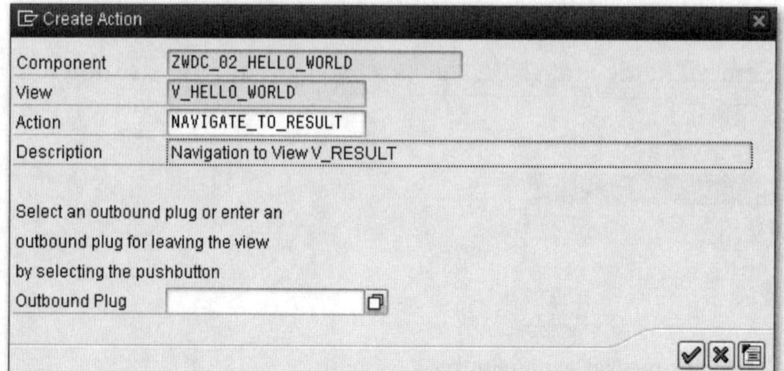

Figure 2.25 Creating an Action for Navigating Between Views

Next, finish the creation of the action. However, at this stage you should take the time to create the outbound plug that lets you navigate to the `V_RESULT` view. To do so, enter `to_result` into the OUTBOUND PLUG field and confirm your entry by clicking on the green checkmark.

6. Because you are creating the `to_result` outbound plug directly with the action and not through the OUTBOUND PLUGS tab, the system asks you again whether you want to create a new outbound plug. Confirm the prompt with YES.
7. You have now created both the action and the outbound plug. Double-check this by selecting the OUTBOUND PLUGS tab. Also, you should now take a brief look at the view controller by selecting the ACTIONS tab. Double-clicking on the action takes you to the `onactionnavigate_to_result( )` method, which has been automatically generated into the `NAVIGATE_TO_RESULT` action. In this method, the `to_result` outbound plug is called via the `wd_this->fire_to_result_plg( )` statement.

Convention

Outbound plugs are called via the `wd_this->fire_<plug name>_plg( )` method call. In this method call, the `wd_this` attribute represents a self-reference to the current view (comparable to the `me` self-reference in classes). If transfer parameters were defined for an outbound plug, they can be transferred as in normal method calls.

Caution: The outbound plug itself – and thus, the controller of the view – do not contain any information about the destination of the triggered navigation. The connection to the selected inbound plug of a subsequent view must be established via a navigation link in the layout of the window.

[✎] Using the outbound plug you defined, the view has now been prepared for navigating to the subsequent view. However, before you can eventually turn to the `V_RESULT` view, you must first define an inbound plug for navigating into the opposite direction; that is, toward the view.

Creating inbound plugs

1. To do so, go to the INBOUND PLUGS tab. Enter `from_result` in the PLUG NAME column, as shown in Figure 2.26. Then, add a description. The EVENT HANDLER column displays the name of the event handler method defined for the inbound plug; we will describe this method in greater detail in a moment.

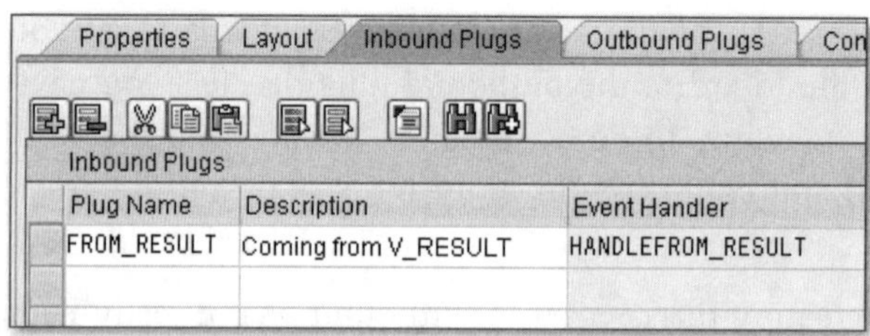

Figure 2.26 Defining an Inbound Plug,

Editing the V_RESULT view

2. Go to the V_RESULT view, which still has not been assigned a value. There, you must perform several steps similar to those you performed for the V_HELLO_WORLD view.
3. Insert a new button called BTN_BACK in the view. Enter "Back" as the label for this button (TEXT property). Select previous for the DESIGN. This will add an arrow pointing to the left on the left-hand side of the button.
4. Next, click on the CREATE button next to the onAction event to define a new action called NAVIGATE_TO_HW for the BTN_BACK button. Enter the same values as for the NEXT button in the respective fields. Use to_hw as the name of the outbound plug. Confirm the creation of the new button in the final step.
5. Then, complete editing the V_RESULT view by adding the from_hw inbound plug. Save the view and activate the inactive objects.

[✎] You should now turn your attention to the W_HELLO_WORLD window. In this window, you must still define a navigation link to connect the V_HELLO_WORLD view with the V_RESULT view and another one in the opposite direction.

Editing the W_HELLO_WORLD window

1. Switch to change mode and select the WINDOW tab. Expand the W_HELLO_WORLD node and its sub-nodes to obtain an overview of the current structure of the window.
2. As you can see in the window structure (see Figure 2.27), at this stage, the window contains only the V_HELLO_WORLD view and the new plugs you defined within the view display underneath it.

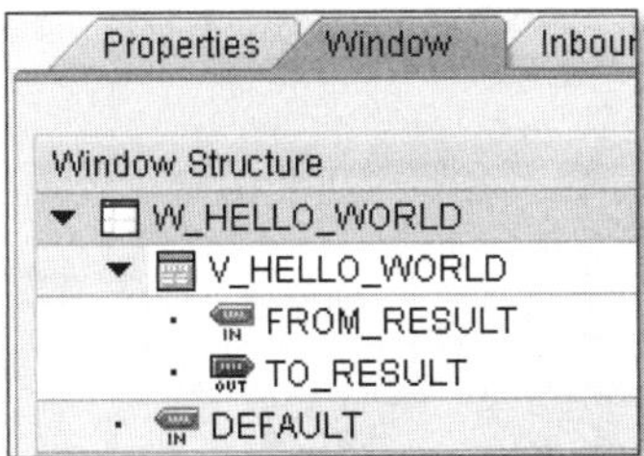

Figure 2.27 Window Structure after Defining the Plugs

Embedding views

3. Insert the V_RESULT view into the window structure. To do so, right-click on the W_HELLO_WORLD node element and select EMBED VIEW (see Figure 2.28).

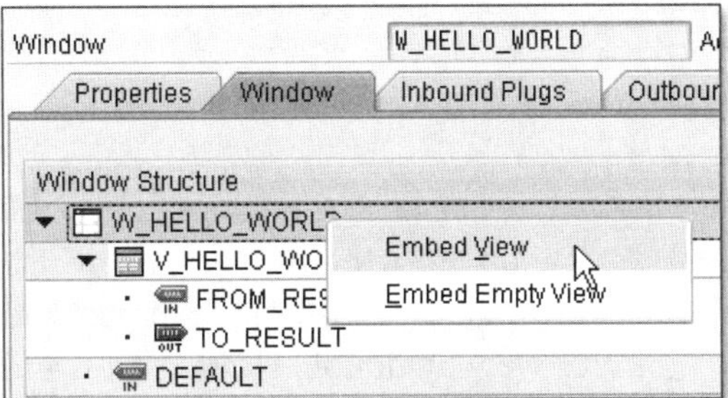

Figure 2.28 Adding a New View to the Window Structure

Embedding Views via Drag-and-Drop

An even faster way to embed views in windows is to use drag-and-drop instead of the context menu. To do so, select the view to be embedded from the object list and drag-and-drop it to the required position in the window.

4. A popup window opens in which you can select the view to be embedded in the window (see the top right-hand area in Figure 2.29). In addition to the COMPONENT and WINDOW fields, which already contain default values, the popup window provides three other fields for selecting the view to be embedded as well as its origin (see Chapter 5, Web Dynpro Standard Components).

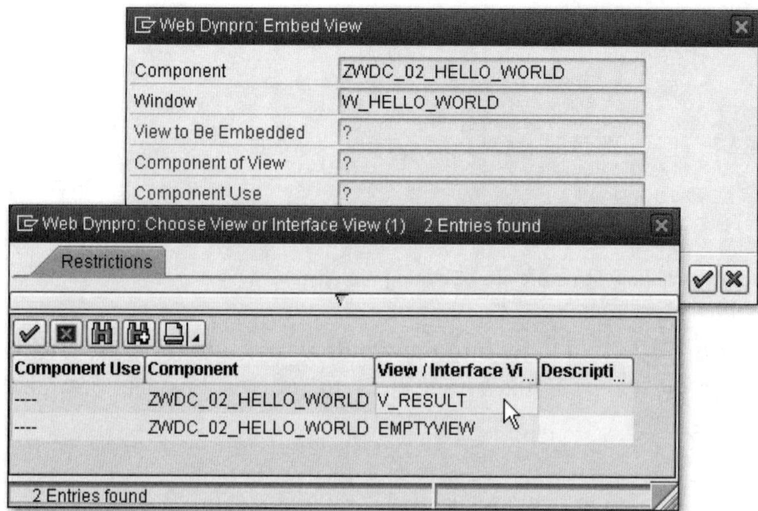

Figure 2.29 Embedding Views in Windows

Position the cursor in the VIEW TO BE EMBEDDED field and open the associated input help (F4). A new popup window opens in which you can select one of the available views, as shown in the foreground of Figure 2.29. Select the `V_RESULT` view by double-clicking on it and close the selection dialog by clicking on the green checkmark.

Empty Views

During the last practical exercise, you may have noticed that each Web Dynpro component automatically contains what is called an EMPTY VIEW. Empty views represent a specific type of view that is automatically provided by the Web Dynpro framework in each window.

These are used as placeholders for empty windows and empty view containers. If you do not embed a view in a window, the Web Dynpro framework integrates the empty view implicitly into that window. Empty views play an essential role primarily in the area of performance optimization, which is why they are discussed in greater detail in Chapter 8, Practical Tips and Hints.

Creating navigation links

5. In the final step, you need to connect the two views with each other using a navigation link. You can do so either via drag-and-drop or by right-clicking on the outbound plug and using the respective context menu.

If you want to use the drag-and-drop method, click on the `to_result` outbound plug and hold the mouse button, as shown in Figure 2.30. Then, move the mouse cursor to the `from_hw` inbound plug of the `V_RESULT` view and release the mouse button. A new window opens, displaying detailed information about the new navigation link. Click on the green checkmark to confirm the information.

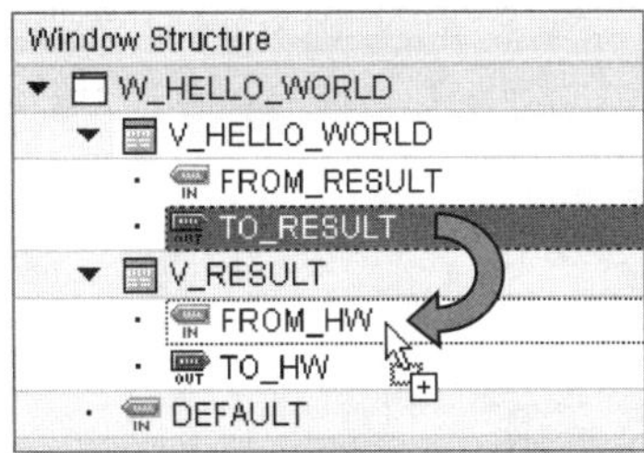

Figure 2.30 Creating Navigation Links via Drag-and-Drop

6. Next, you should create the navigation link from the `V_RESULT` view to the `V_HELLO_WORLD` view. To do so, repeat the last step, starting from the `to_hw` outbound plug.

   This time, however, you should try to create the navigation link via the context menu. To do so, right-click on the `to_hw` outbound plug and select Create Navigation Link. As was the case when you created the first navigation link, the window for defining navigation links opens (see Figure 2.31).

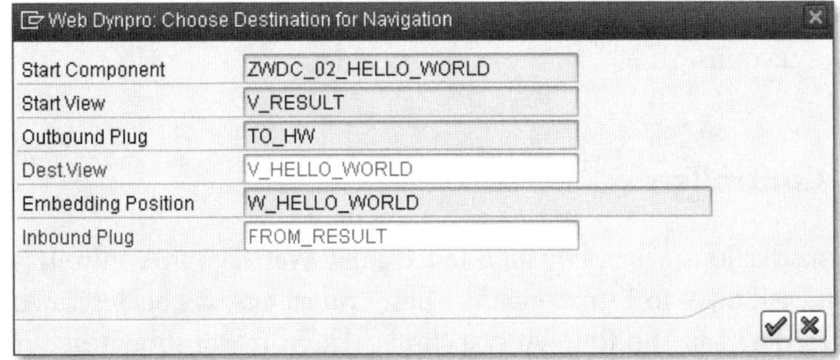

Figure 2.31 Defining Navigation Links

Open the input help for the DEST. VIEW field and select the V_HELLO_WORLD view as the destination. The INBOUND PLUG field was automatically assigned the from_hw inbound plug. Then, click on the green checkmark to confirm the entries.

Testing the application You have almost made it. Activate the component and start the z_hello_world application. It should now open in a new window, as shown in Figure 2.32. The NEXT and BACK buttons enable you to navigate between the two views.

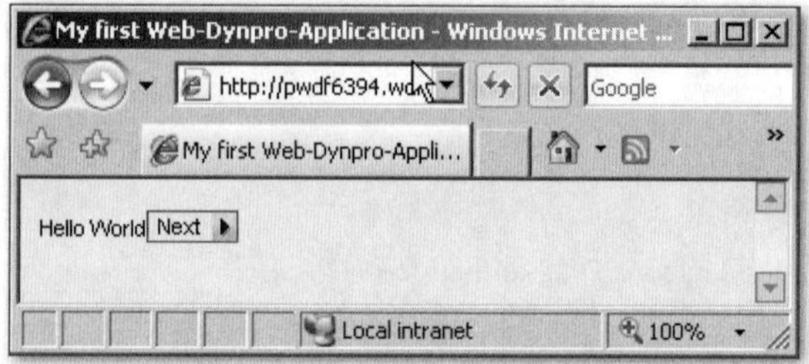

Figure 2.32 Testing your First Navigation Application

Summary and outlook At this point, you have completed editing the W_HELLO_WORLD window. You have learned how to create views and UI elements and how to link views with each other via windows and plugs. This enables you to create small Web Dynpro components.

However, you will soon reach a point at which you want to display data from the system in the UI or enter data into the system through the UI. To do so, you need controllers and contexts, which are described in the following sections.

2.3 Controllers

In previous sections, we briefly mentioned a few Web Dynpro controllers and even used them to a small extent. These controllers will be described in greater detail in the following sections. Then, to consolidate your newly acquired knowledge, you will perform a few short exercises.

Types of controllers The Web Dynpro framework distinguishes between five different types of controllers:

- **Component controllers**
  Component controllers represent the global point of access within each Web Dynpro component. They contain constructor and destructor methods that are executed during the creation or deletion of a component. Component controllers are particularly useful for cross-component communication and model binding. Additionally, they can be used together with contexts – which will be described later in this chapter – to act as a global data exchange interface between the windows and views of a component.
- **View controllers**
  View controllers are only visible within their respective view, and each view has its own controller. The main task of view controllers consists of responding to actions triggered by the user, checking user entries for accuracy regarding firmly defined rules within the controller, and controlling the properties of UI elements contained in the view.
- **Window controllers**
  In contrast to view controllers, window controllers are visible within their respective windows as well as in the views contained therein. When you start a Web Dynpro application, the respective window controller is addressed by inbound plugs defined within the window. Each instance of a component can only use one window at a time. To enable views to access a window controller, the respective window must be explicitly made known to the views.
- **Interface controllers**
  A component interface controller publishes methods and actions of the component controller in the component interface. Therefore, the methods of this controller must always be defined via the component controller because the interface controller is actually an interface rather than a controller in the narrow sense of the word. The respective method becomes visible across different components if you set the INTERFACE flag in the component controller.
- **Custom controllers**
  You can develop any number of custom controllers. They provide the same features as component controllers and are thus, specifically useful for exchanging data across views and windows, as well as for binding models.

Table 2.1 provides an overview of the different controller types.

Controller	Actions	Events	Plugs	Visibility
Component		x		Component-wide
View	x		x	Local view
Window			x	Component-wide (Local window)
Interface		x	x	External
Custom		x		Component-wide

Table 2.1 Controller Features

Controller attributes

As is the case with ABAP classes, you can create separate attributes and methods for each controller. You should create attributes to store all non-UI-relevant application data such as object references. (Note that for UI-relevant data, you must use contexts; see Section 2.4, Contexts).

Figure 2.33 shows the ATTRIBUTES tab of a component controller. This tab contains a table that lists all attributes defined in the controller. To make attributes visible to the remaining controllers within the component, you must set the checkmark in the PUBLIC column.

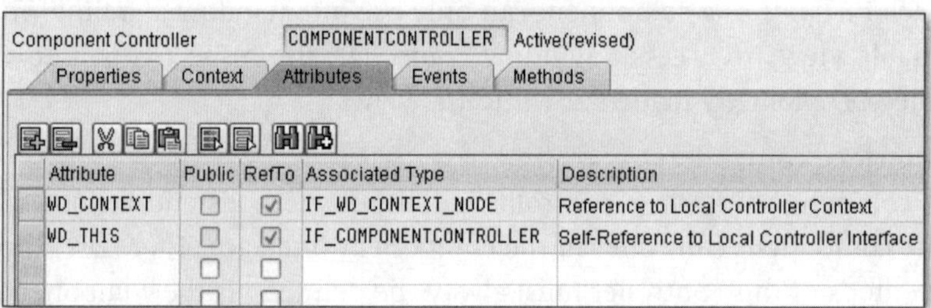

Figure 2.33 Attributes in the Component Controller

Standard attributes

By default, each controller contains the attributes `wd_this` and `wd_context`. The `wd_this` attribute represents a self-reference to the respective controller. This self-reference allows you to access the controller's methods and attributes. The statement `wd_this->fire_to_result_plg( )` is an example of this. The `wd_context` attribute is a reference to the respective context and will be described in greater detail in Section 2.4, Contexts. Moreover, view controllers and window controllers contain the `wd_comp_controller` attribute by default. This attribute enables you to directly access the methods and attributes of the component controller from a view or window, provided they have been defined as PUBLIC.

Controller methods

Figure 2.34 shows the METHODS tab of the component controller. Depending on the controller type, Web Dynpro provides a range of standard methods that enable developers to interfere with the program flow at a particular point in time. Because these methods can only be called by the runtime at a fixed point in time, they are also referred to as *hook methods*. The most important hook methods and their flow sequence are described in Section 2.3.1, Hook Methods' Flow Sequence.

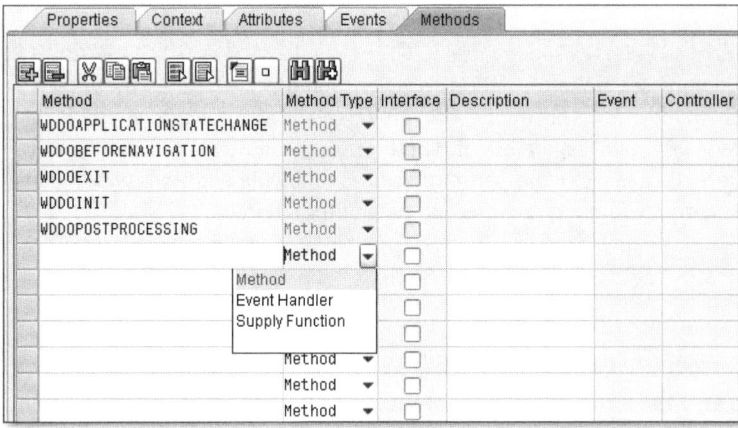

Figure 2.34 Method Types in the Web Dynpro Framework

Method types

Regarding the controller methods, Web Dynpro distinguishes between three different types of methods (see Figure 2.34):

- **Methods**
  These are methods in the traditional object-oriented sense. You can create them by entering the method name in the METHOD column of the METHODS tab. To navigate from the method list to the body of the method, double-click on the method name. In addition to entering the coding within the method body, you can also define any number of transfer parameters here.

- **Event handlers**
  Within the component and custom controllers, you can define events for the purpose of cross-controller and cross-component navigation. After an event has been triggered, the runtime automatically calls the associated event handler in all controllers registered for the event.

  You can register the respective method for available events by selecting the EVENT HANDLER type. You can even execute events across different components by including them in the component interface. Section 2.3.3, Actions and Events, covers the topic of events.

- **Supply functions**
  Supply functions are used to automatically fill context nodes upon request. They are described in greater detail in connection with contexts in Section 2.4.4, Supply Functions.

Web Dynpro-Specific Characteristics of Controller Methods

Web Dynpro component methods or event handlers are called by the Web Dynpro framework. The framework provides all Web Dynpro method parameters with data, regardless of whether the parameters are actually used. Therefore, it does not make sense to use the following additions within controller methods to query the method parameter interface:

- `IS REQUESTED`
- `IS SUPPLIED`

Outlook on the exercises to follow

The exercises that will follow in this section will introduce you to controllers and the context in the system. For this purpose, you will extend the exercise you started in earlier sections of this chapter. At the end of the exercise, you will be able to enter an unlimited number of ice cream flavors through an input field in the `V_HELLO_WORLD` view and a `Dropdown` UI element in the `V_RESULT` view will allow you to scroll through the list of flavors you entered. Furthermore, a REMOVE button will let you remove individual flavors from the list.

In the first step, you will create a new method called `add_icecream( )` in the component controller of the `ZWDC_02_HELLO_WORLD` component. You will need this method later to save the ice cream flavors in the context. Proceed as follows:

1. Select the METHODS tab of the component controller.
2. Enter `add_icecream` in a free cell of the METHOD column and make sure that the associated METHOD type `Method` is selected. Optionally, you can enter a description for the method, as shown in Figure 2.35.

Method	Method Type	Interface	Description
WDDOAPPLICATIONSTATECHANGE	Method	☐	
WDDOBEFORENAVIGATION	Method	☐	
WDDOEXIT	Method	☐	
WDDOINIT	Method	☐	
WDDOPOSTPROCESSING	Method	☐	
ADD_ICECREAM	Method	☐	Adds a new icecream to the context

Figure 2.35 Creating Controller Methods

3. Double-click on the method name to go to the method body. Then, add a new importing parameter called `name` of data type `CHAR_LG_32`, which enables you to enter the ice cream flavor. Provide a corresponding short description and enter a brief commentary into the method, as shown in Figure 2.36.

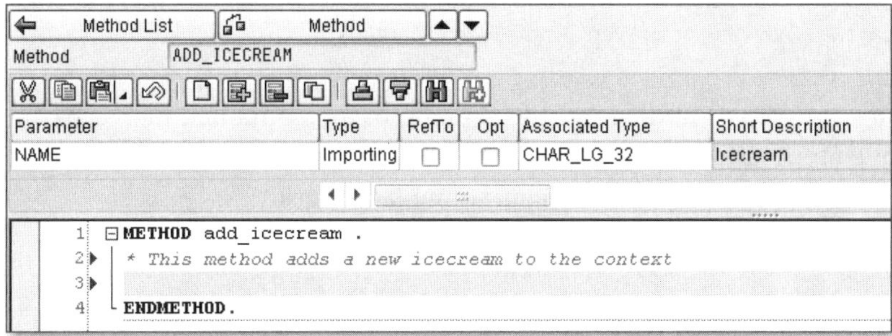

Figure 2.36 Body of Method add_icecream( )

This completes the creation of the new method, `add_icecream( )`, which will be extended in the following sections and be used by the methods of other controllers.

2.3.1 Hook Methods' Flow Sequence

Hook methods

Depending on the type, a controller provides a range of different standard methods that enable you to interfere with the program flow at a particular point in time. These methods are also referred to as *hook methods*. In this context, each type of controller offers a different set of methods to interfere with the component. The sequence of individual method calls is described in what is called the *phase model*. The following paragraphs describe this model as well as the hook methods.

However, before learning about the phase model for hook methods, you should be familiar with all of the hook methods available. Table 2.2 provides a list of all controllers and the hook methods contained in them.

Controller	Available Hook Methods
Component	wddoinit( ), wddoexit( ), wddobeforenavigation( ), wddopostprocessing( ), wddoapplicationstatechange( )
Window	wddoinit( ), wddoexit( ), wddoonopen( ), wddoonclose( )
View	wddoinit( ), wddoexit( ), wddobeforeaction( ), wddoafteraction( ), wddomodifyview( )
Custom	wddoinit( ), wddoexit( )

Table 2.2 Overview of all Web Dynpro Hook Methods

wddoinit( ) and wddoexit( )

The wddoinit( ) and wddoexit( ) methods are contained in every controller type and can be compared to the constructor or destructor of objects in object-oriented programming languages.

- wddoinit( ) is called every time a controller is instanced anew. For example, you can instance auxiliary classes or set initial values of attributes and the context within this method.
- In turn, the wddoexit( ) method allows you to clean up; that is, to delete auxiliary objects and release locks when leaving the controller.

wddoinit( ) and wddoexit( ) are two of the most important standard methods.

Let us now take a look at the phase model for instancing a component (see Figure 2.37). When a component is instanced – for example, ZWDC_02_HELLO_WORLD – via the application, it is first and foremost the wddoinit( ) method of the component controller that enables you to initialize your own attributes and objects. In a subsequent step, the system calls the wddoinit( ) method of the window. In the final step, the views that are visible in the window are instanced.

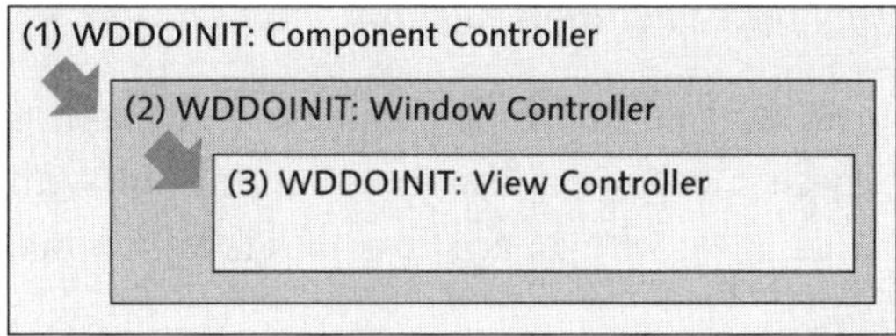

Figure 2.37 Phase Model for Component Instancing

Hook methods of the component controller

In addition to the wddoinit( ) and wddoexit( ) methods, the component controller contains three other hook methods:

- The wddoapplicationstatechange( ) method is run through every time the state of an application changes; that is, at exactly the point at which the application changes from running mode into suspend mode and is then resumed via the resume plug. This method is not discussed further in this book.
- The wddobeforenavigation( ) method is used primarily for validating user entries in more complex applications. If an error occurs during the validation process, the application developer can terminate the navigation within the method.
- Shortly before the rendering phase of the user interface starts, the wddopostprocessing( ) method allows for one last access to the component. You can use this method, for example, to carry out application-specific cleanup tasks.

Hook methods of the window controller

Each window controller contains the two hook methods wddoonopen( ) and wddoonclose( ). These methods are run through only when a window is opened as a dialog window or is closed. Because the opening of a dialog window is not linked to a navigation, no inbound plug is called and no associated event handler method is processed at that time. Therefore, the wddoonopen( ) method can optionally be used to implement initializations of the window.

Hook methods of the view controller

Next to `wddoinit( )` and `wddoexit( )`, the `wddomodifyview( )` method is arguably the most important hook method. This method is called prior to the generation of the view and allows for the dynamic modification of the view at runtime. Accordingly, it is only available in the view controller. Chapter 4, Dynamic Web Dynpro Applications, provides a detailed description of the topic of dynamic view modification.

In addition, the view provides the two methods `wddobeforeaction( )` and `wddoafteraction( )`. These methods allow you to interfere with the flow sequence prior to or after the execution of view actions, respectively.

Phase model of the hook methods

Figure 2.38 shows the flow sequence of the respective component and view controller methods within a phase model. All methods of this model are processed in the sequence shown here with each action in the UI. For example, for the execution of the `wddobeforenavigation( )` method, it is irrelevant whether the preceding action has started a navigation between views. If an error occurs during the event handling process and is displayed to the user via a Web Dynpro notification, the system blocks all navigation steps until the error is removed from the list of messages. However, even this does not affect the flow sequence of hook methods.

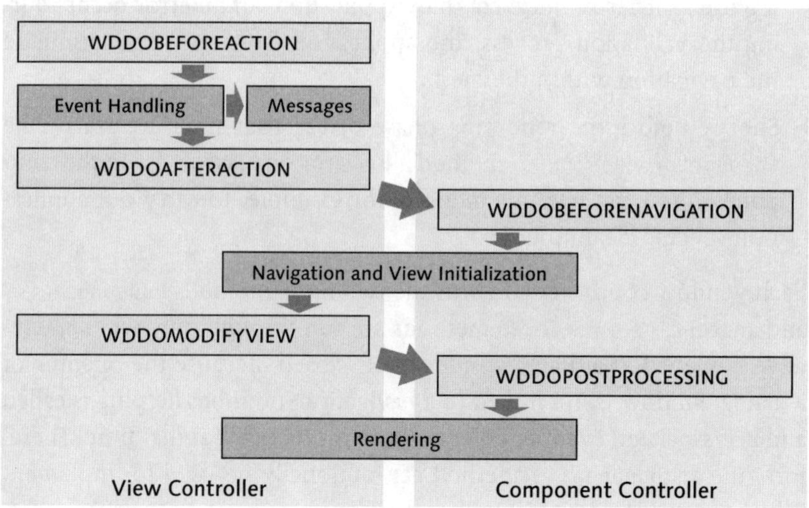

Figure 2.38 Phase Model for a Roundtrip

Output of Messages in Web Dynpro

The Web Dynpro framework provides a tool called Message Manager for the output of system and application messages. When this tool receives a message, it is automatically integrated into the system, either in the upper area of the browser window or in another, specifically defined position within the view. Chapter 3 provides a more detailed description of the Message Manager.

Viewing hook methods in the debugger

Don't worry if the large number and sequence of hook methods has confused you a little. The majority of hook methods are not particularly important for beginners or small applications. Furthermore, the three methods emphasized – `wddoinit( )`, `wddoexit( )`, and `wddomodifyview( )` – let you perform a large portion of the standard tasks in your daily work.

Yet, to better understand the methods, it is advisable to take a look at them in the debugger. To do so, you should set a breakpoint within the hook methods of the `ZWDC_02_HELLO_WORLD` component and restart the application.

2.3.2 Usage and Visibility of Controllers

Up until now, we have looked at each controller separately. Thus, you already know the most important aspects of controller types and their standard methods. The self-reference `wd_this`, which is available in every controller, enables you to access the methods and attributes of the respective controller.

However, we have not yet dealt with another important aspect of controller programming – calling methods across different controllers. For example, it is often useful to store methods within the component or window controller instead of the view controller. This allows you to reuse methods from within other controllers.

Different uses of controllers

For a Web Dynpro controller A to be able to access the methods and attributes of another controller B, controller B must first be made known to controller A. This can be done by entering a controller usage on the PROPERTIES tab of controller A. You can then use `wd_this->get_<ControllerName>_ctr( )` to obtain a reference of interface data type `ig_<ControllerName>` to controller B.

You should practice using controllers with the V_RESULT view and the W_HELLO_WORLD window. The goal of this exercise is to obtain a reference to the window controller in the view controller.

1. In the window controller, create a new method called remove_icecream( ), without parameters. You will later use this method along with a REMOVE button to delete an ice cream flavor from the list or context, respectively.

Creating controller usages

2. Navigate to the PROPERTIES tab of the V_RESULT view. The controller usages already entered in the view display under the general view properties in the USED CONTROLLERS/COMPONENTS table. The usage of the component controller is automatically entered for all views and windows.
3. Click on the CREATE icon directly above the table. A dialog appears in which you can select from the available controller usages (see Figure 2.39). Select the window controller W_HELLO_WORLD.

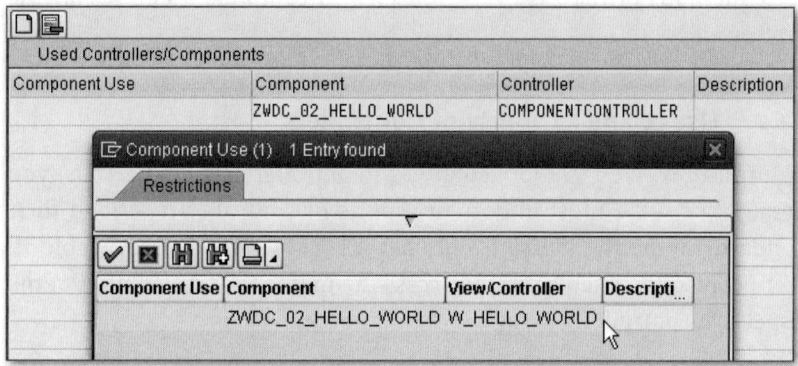

Figure 2.39 Adding Controller Usages

4. Then, go to the METHODS tab and open the wddoinit( ) method. In the following steps, you will enter the coding into this method, which allows you to access the controller.

Web Dynpro Code Wizard

5. Launch the Web Dynpro Code Wizard. This wizard makes your daily work easier because it provides patterns for a number of standard Web Dynpro actions. To launch the wizard, either click on the asso-

ciated TOOLBAR button (see Figure 2.40) or use the [Ctrl] + [F7] key combination.

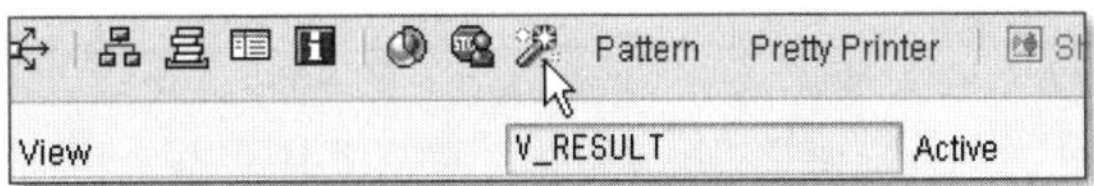

Figure 2.40 Launching the Web Dynpro Code Wizard

6. Select the GENERAL tab in the window that appears. This tab provides possible options to create access to the window controller and its methods:
   - The METHOD CALL IN CURRENT CONTROLLER option allows you to select the `get_w_hello_world_ctr( )` method. In this case, the wizard generates the coding for accessing the interface of the window controller.
   - The METHOD CALL IN USED CONTROLLER option enables you to directly access the methods of the window controller.

   Because you do not yet need the `remove_icecream( )` method of the window controller created in the first step, you should select the first option, as shown in Figure 2.41, and exit the code wizard by clicking on the green checkmark.

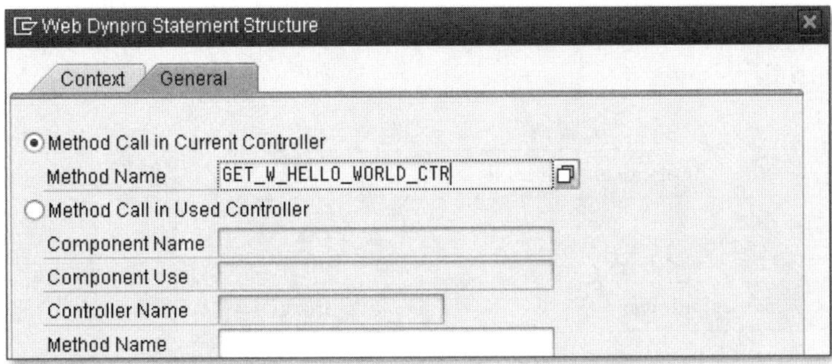

Figure 2.41 Web Dynpro Pattern of the Code Wizard

7. The code wizard has generated the following coding, which provides access to the window controller:

```
DATA lo_w_hello_world TYPE REF TO ig_w_hello_world.
lo_w_hello_world = wd_this->get_w_hello_world_ctr( ).
```

The new lo_w_hello_world attribute is currently only visible within the wddoinit( ) method. To be able to also access the attribute from other methods of the view, you must include it in the attributes list of the view controller.

Adding view attributes

8. To do so, go to the ATTRIBUTES tab and enter a new attribute called go_w_hello_world with data type ig_w_hello_world. Then, modify the wddoinit( ) method in such a way that you delete the data declaration and replace the lo_w_hello_world string in the second line with wd_this->go_hello_world. This enables you to access the window controller in all view methods via the wd_this->go_hello_world attribute.

At this point you have successfully completed the exercise.

The component controller represents a special case regarding controller usages. Because this controller is among the most frequently used, all views and windows already contain a controller usage for the component controller. You can use this controller usage directly and without any further initializations via the wd_comp_controller reference.

Visibility of controller usages

However, you cannot link all controllers with each other using controller usages. The diagram in Figure 2.42 shows the controller usages that are allowed. For example, you cannot have external access to a view controller, whereas a view controller can access any other controller. The bolded arrows in the figure represent the automatically created component controller usages.

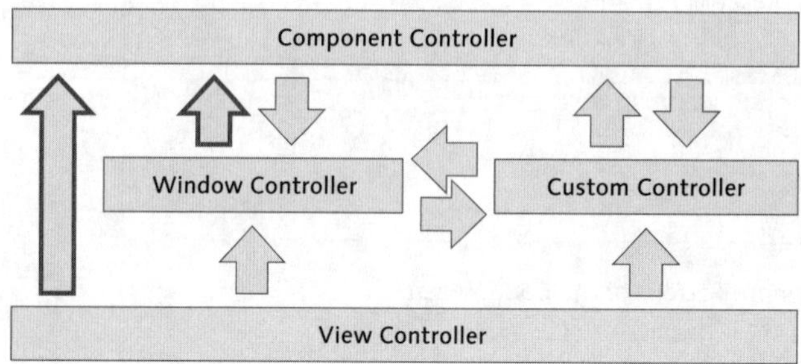

Figure 2.42 Visibility of Controllers

2.3.3 Actions and Events

As described in Section 2.3.2, Usage and Visibility of Controllers, you cannot define any controller usages for accessing view controllers. Thus, all views are completely separated from the perspective of the remaining controller types. For example, it is not possible to call a view method from within a component controller. However, Web Dynpro provides some alternatives to this scenario – *events*.

Events

You can define events to enable cross-controller interactions between components and custom controllers. These events can then be triggered (fired) in the respective controller using the predefined fire_<event name>_evt( ) method. After an event has been triggered, the runtime automatically calls the associated event handler in another controller. For this purpose, a usage of the triggering controller must have been entered and an event handler defined in the other controller.

You can register any number of other controllers for an event. For example, it is possible to catch an event triggered by the component controller both within a view and within a window. As is the case with methods, events can transfer both mandatory and optional parameters.

[✎]

You should now create a new event called SET_PROPERTIES in the component controller. You will use this event later for the property handling of the REMOVE button in the V_RESULT view. Proceed as follows:

Defining events

1. Go to the EVENTS tab of the component controller. Enter the new SET_PROPERTIES event into the events table, as shown in Figure 2.43. Set the INTERFACE flag to integrate the event in the interface controller and thereby make it visible within the entire component.

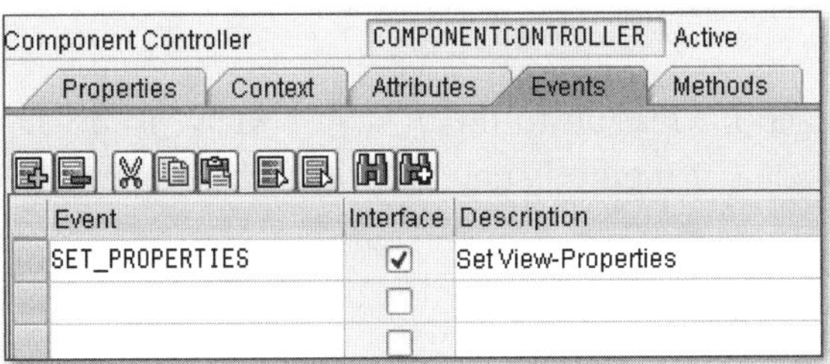

Figure 2.43 Defining Events

You have now defined the event; it can be triggered at any time in the component controller via the `fire_set_properties_evt( )` method. However, what you still need is an event handler that reacts to the event.

Defining event handlers

2. Therefore, you must now define an event handler in the `V_RESULT` view. To do so, go to the METHODS tab of the view and create a new EVENT HANDLER type method called `on_set_properties( )`. This method will be implemented at a later stage.
3. Register the new method for the component controller event `SET_PROPERTIES`. To do so, click into the EVENT column of the event handler method and open the associated input help (see Figure 2.44). By registering the event, you ensure that the event handler method will be automatically triggered after the event has been fired in the component controller.

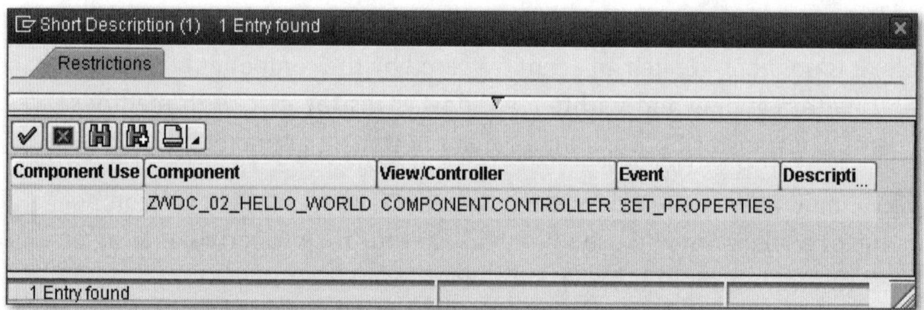

Figure 2.44 Registration for the SET_PROPERTIES Event

Registering for events

4. After opening the input help, select the `SET_PROPERTIES` event by double-clicking on it. This action will automatically close the popup window, and the `on_set_properties( )` method is registered for the `SET_PROPERTIES` event.
5. Call the event with each navigation to the `V_RESULT` view. To do so, access the `handlefrom_hw( )` method and enter the following line:

   ```
   wd_comp_controller->fire_set_properties_evt( ).
   ```

   This ensures that the button properties in the `V_RESULT` view will already be set accurately during the instancing process.

Review of the exercise

This concludes the exercises for the time being. In the last two exercises, you created methods and events and defined controller usages. In doing so, you have laid the foundation for the handling of actions and contexts, which will be part of the following sections and exercises.

Events and Inbound Plugs

For each inbound plug, an EVENT HANDLER type method is automatically created in the respective controller of the plug. This method is automatically called during a navigation process, using the inbound plug for initializing a view or window controller. You can use this method, for example, to load data to be output or to prepare the output. You would use this, for example, to show or hide view elements.

The naming convention for event handler methods of the inbound plug is `handle<inbound plug name>`.

Actions

Several UI elements can trigger actions. Actions are specific events that are triggered by certain user operations in an application's interface. The associated event handler methods then control the subsequent flow of the application. Does this ring a bell? We already briefly touched on the topic of actions back in Section 2.2.2, Windows and Plugs, when creating buttons and plugs. In that section, you created the `NAVIGATE_TO_RESULT` and `NAVIGATE_TO_HW` actions, as well as the outbound plugs `to_result` and `to_hw`, from within the UI element `Button`.

Creating actions

You can create actions either from within the respective UI element or via the ACTIONS tab of the view controller (see Figure 2.45). For each action, an event handler method is automatically created based on the naming convention `onaction<action name>`. For example, the `NAVIGATE_TO_RESULT` action has the event handler method `onactionnavigate_to_result( )`.

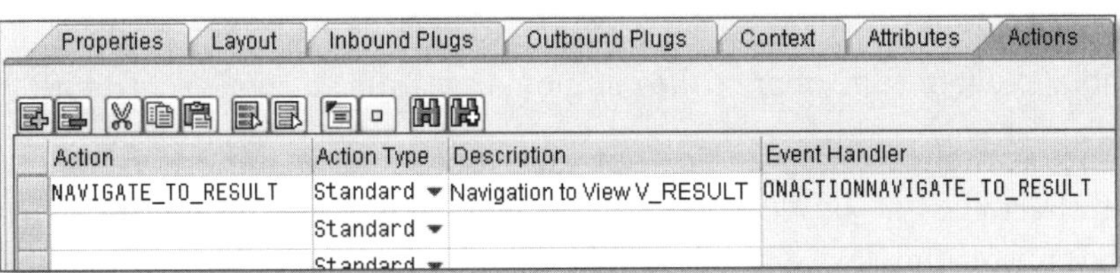

Figure 2.45 Actions Tab in the V_HELLO_WORLD View

As is the case with other event handlers, you can also add your own programming code to the event handler methods of actions. Double-clicking on the action takes you to the body of the respective event handler method.

Web Dynpro distinguishes between two types of actions:

- **Standard actions**
  Standard actions are triggered only if all available data required for executing the action is accurate. For example, if you enter a letter into a date field, then none of the actions linked with the date field will be triggered.
- **Validation-independent actions**
  Validation-independent actions are executed irrespective of the result of the data validation.

Tip

It is advisable to always create new actions directly from within the respective UI element. Some UI elements even provide the option to automatically enter additional UI element parameters into the parameters list of the corresponding event handler method. The `InputField` UI element, which will be described in Chapter 3, is an example of this. It provides an event called `onEnter`. If you create the associated action directly via the UI element, the system automatically transfers two additional parameters into the method of the action. This way, you not only obtain a context element, but also the name of the associated UI element.

2.3.4 Assistance Class

For each Web Dynpro component, you can create a uniquely assigned assistance class, which will be instanced automatically along with its associated component. The instance of the assistance class is then made available to every controller of the component via the `wd_assist` attribute.

The assistance class should (but does not have to) inherit from the abstract class `CL_WD_COMPONENT_ASSISTANCE`. This way, it inherits methods for reading text symbols within the inheriting class. The constructor of the assistance class cannot have any parameters.

Use cases

Using assistance classes is advisable in the following cases:

- **Model binding**
  You can use an assistance class as an interface between the Web Dynpro component and the model.
- **Text symbols**
  Because assistance classes allow you to store text symbols, you can use them as a storage location for your texts (see Chapter 3, Developing Web Dynpro Applications).
- **Performance**
  In general, we recommend that you use classes to store any coding that is not directly related to a controller or the UI. From a performance perspective, method calls of assistance classes perform much better than method calls of Web Dynpro controllers.

Defining assistance classes

If you decide on using an assistance class, you can enter it in the ASSISTANCE CLASS field in the header area of the component (see Figure 2.46).

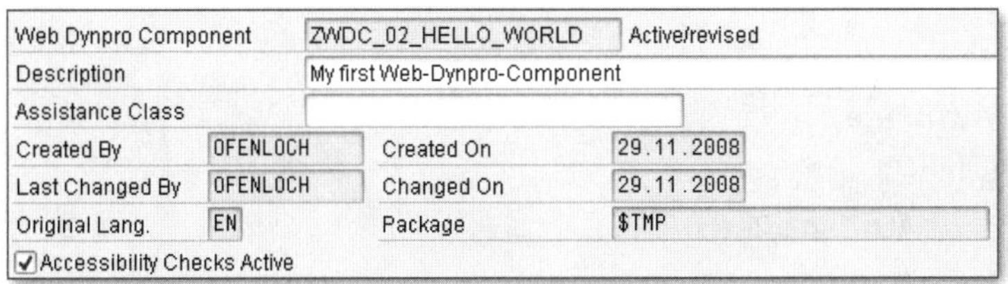

Figure 2.46 Entering Assistance Classes

2.4 Context

At this point, you have learned about almost all of the basic features needed for developing Web Dynpro UIs. For example, you can create views and windows, link them with each other using navigation links, and work with controllers and their methods.

The only thing you still need to learn to round off this chapter on the Web Dynpro architecture is the concept of the context. The context represents the interface for data between the UI and the system. The following sections describe the basic principle and importance of the context for Web Dynpro, both in theory and in your daily work.

Context and controllers

The context is the central building block for storing data and for exchanging UI-relevant data between the browser, views, controllers, and components. Each Web Dynpro controller has exactly one context. The visibility of each context depends on its controller. For example, the context of the component controller is visible across the entire component, whereas a view context is only visible within the view. Concerning the visibility of a context, the same rules apply as for the respective controller.

2.4.1 Structure of a Context

Context at design time

A context is a hierarchical tree structure that consists of *nodes* and *attributes*. A node can have any number of children. These children exist either as other nodes or as attributes that contain the data stored in the context. Because attributes cannot have any children, you can compare them to the leaves of a tree. Likewise, nodes represent a branch within the tree structure. Figure 2.47 shows a sample context structure at design time.

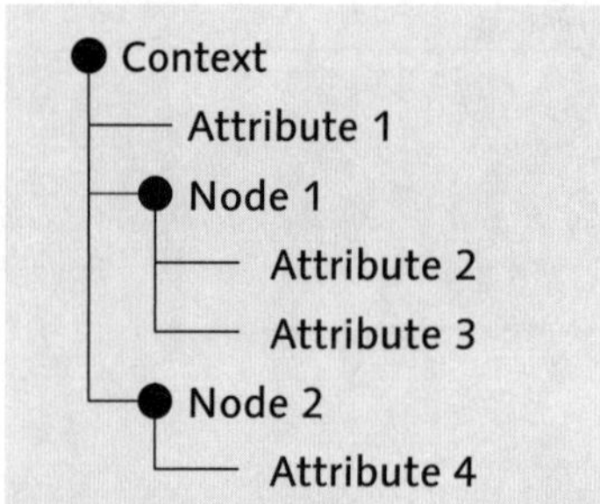

Figure 2.47 Sample Context at Design Time

Comparable to tables

You can also regard contexts as an object-oriented version of internal tables. In a context, tables are represented by nodes. Tables are based on row structures, which in turn consist of fields. The table rows are represented by elements in the context. The element contains the structure of the row. The fields of the structure are referred to as attributes in the element. In addition to the structure, elements also contain references to subnodes that may exist. You can use methods to navigate through the hierarchy of nodes and elements.

Each node has a number of properties that can be set in the editor; the most important of these is the cardinality. It specifies how many elements of a node you can create at runtime. You can choose among the following cardinalities:

Cardinality

- `0..1`
  You can create either zero or one version of the node.
- `1..1`
  Exactly one version of the node exists.
- `1..n`
  Any number can be available; but at least one must exist.
- `0..n`
  Any number can be available and even zero is possible.

You can use the `0..n` cardinality, for instance, to display tables. However, if you want to display only a single input field instead of an entire table, you should use the `1..1` cardinality.

Context at runtime

At runtime, the framework generates object instances from the context nodes defined at design time. During this process, each node is mapped as an object of reference type `IF_WD_CONTEXT_NODE`. The attributes defined in the context node are grouped in another object, which is referred to as the context element. This object is based on the `IF_WD_CONTEXT_ELEMENT` type. Depending on the cardinality and number of nodes within a context node, the same number of context elements may exist.

For example, if you set cardinality `1..1` for a context node, this node will always have exactly one child instance in the form of a context element. If, in turn, you set cardinality `0..n`, the corresponding context node can have either none or any number of child elements (and object instances).

The diagram shown in Figure 2.48 provides a simple example of this scenario: Node 1, which exists as a node object at runtime, contains a total of three child elements. The objects contain a value of Attributes 2 and 3 each. You can now use several different access methods of the node and element – which will be further described in the following sections and chapters – to modify the data stored in the nodes and elements, as per your requirements.

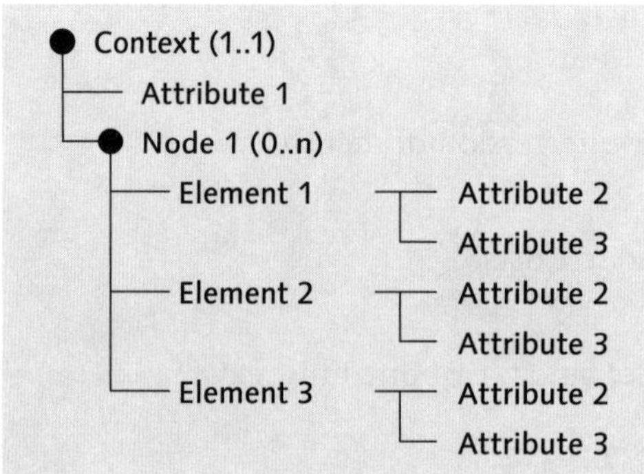

Figure 2.48 Sample Context at Runtime

Context editor

At this point, we will end the theoretical discussion and take a look at the CONTEXT tab of the `V_HELLO_WORLD` view (see Figure 2.49). The context editor is divided into three areas:

- **Context at design time**
  The upper left-hand area of the editor displays the structure of the context at design time. Here, the nodes and attributes of the context are displayed in a tree structure. Each context has a root node called `CONTEXT`. You can access this root node at runtime via the `wd_context` attribute.
- **Properties of the selected context object**
  The lower area of the context editor displays the properties of the node or attribute you select in the upper left. One of the properties that are displayed here is the cardinality, for example.
- **Controller usages**
  The upper right-hand area displays buttons for all controller usages that have been entered previously in the controller. By clicking on these buttons, you can view the respective external controller context. Figure 2.49 shows the context of the component controller. Section 2.4.3, Mapping, describes how you can use contexts across different controllers.

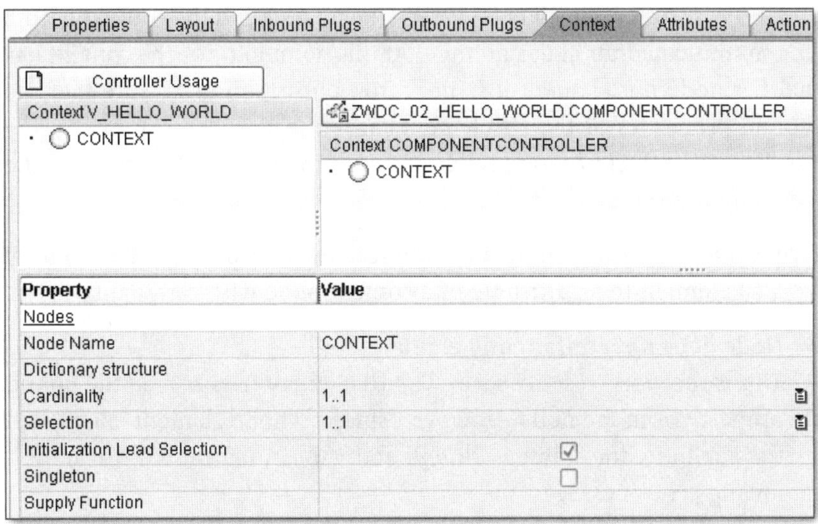

Figure 2.49 Context Editor

2.4.2 Data Binding

Context and UI elements at design time

You can bind properties of UI elements to context attributes via a few clicks of the mouse in the view editor. This process is referred to as *data binding* or *binding*. By binding a UI element, you can build a direct relationship between the UI element and the selected context attribute.

Depending on the type of UI element, the properties available to you for binding can vary substantially. Take the `InputField` UI element, for example, which is required in the following exercise. This UI element contains the properties `value` and `visible`, among others. If you bind the `value` property to an attribute, you can create a relationship between the UI and the context. Then, if you change the text in the input field of the browser, this change will be immediately reflected in the respective context element/attribute. The context also enables you to manipulate the UI element in the browser. For example, if you bind the `visible` property to a context attribute of the `WDY_BOOLEAN` type, you can control the visibility of the input field by setting the attribute value either to "`X`" or " " (blank).

Data binding of UI elements at runtime

The process of binding data between UI elements and the context occurs in the context editor at design time. At this point in time, the context has neither node nor element instances. You must then make sure that the bound properties of the UI element can be read in the context during runtime. Incorrect programming can result in errors and even cause the program to terminate.

We will now go through the possible scenarios for binding the property of a UI element to an attribute of a context node with cardinality `0..n`:

- **Node does not contain any element**
  This is the worst case scenario. The UI element tries to read the bound property from the node. However, since no node element exists with the attribute, the framework will abort the application with the following error message:

  Cannot resolve context binding of property <property name>: Node <node name> does not contain any elements.

- **Node contains exactly one element**
  The UI element can read and display the property without any problem from the node or element in the context. Note, however, that the automatic initialization of the lead selection is a prerequisite for this, which will be described in the following sections.

- **Node contains several elements**
  The UI element can read and display the property without any problem from the node or element in the context. However, because the node contains several elements, the question is this: From which of the existing elements should the bound property be read? The lead selection, which is described in the following sections, gives us the answer.

Selection

When looking at Figure 2.49, you may have noticed that you can maintain the property SELECTION for each context node. Here, you can choose from the same options that are available for the cardinality. The node property SELECTION indicates how many elements of a context node can be selected at runtime. Therefore, this property is primarily important for displaying tables:

- For example, if you select SELECTION `0..1` for a node, at runtime, you can select a maximum of one row in a table.

- If you select `1..n`, at least one table row is always selected. You can then select any number of additional table rows using the `Ctrl` and `Shift` keys. A method provided by the context node returns the selected elements.

Lead Selection

Within each node, a single element can contain the *lead selection*. The lead selection represents a selected element that plays a specific role in the interaction with UI elements. For example, the lead selection determines from which of the existing context elements the UI element properties bound to node attributes will be read. In other words: Which of the available node elements should be displayed in the UI? Figure 2.50 illustrates the importance of the lead selection for the data binding of UI elements.

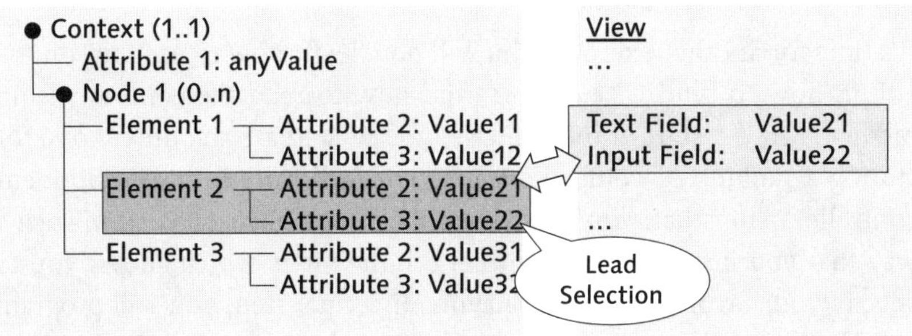

Figure 2.50 Data Transport between Context and View

Setting the lead selection

You can set the lead selection in several different ways, for example by using methods in the context or via specific UI elements. The `DropDownByIndex` UI element represents a useful example in this respect: If you select an item from a dropdown list that is based on a context node, the lead selection is automatically set for the selected element. In tables, it is always the first selected row for which the LEAD SELECTION flag is set. All subsequent selected elements are only assigned the SELECTION flag. You can recognize the lead selection in tables by its stronger background color as compared to the other selected rows.

Automatic Initialization of the Lead Selection

Imagine the following scenario: You want to bind the content of an input field to an attribute from a context node with cardinality `1..1`. This means that the node always contains exactly one context element. However, the input field always requires a set lead selection to resolve the binding to the node. If the lead selection is not set, Web Dynpro aborts the application.

You have the following two options: You can set the lead selection manually for the only existing element, or you can check the checkmark for the INITIALIZATION LEAD SELECTION property in the node properties. This property determines whether the lead selection should be set automatically when needed, in case it has not yet been set.

Note that the automatic initialization of the lead selection does not depend on the selected cardinality. If a node contains more than one element, the first element of the node is set as the lead selection.

Context Editor and Context

[✎] It's time for another exercise! You will now learn how to use the context editor, how to bind UI elements, and how to read the context within methods. At the start of the exercise, you will create a context node for storing a ranking of your favorite ice cream flavors in the component controller. After that, you will design the `V_HELLO_WORLD` view in such a way that you insert a new input field in the view, which allows you to specify your favorite ice cream flavors. In a final step, you will program a method that allows you to read and then delete the values in the input field. Follow these steps:

Creating a node

1. Go to the CONTEXT tab of the component controller. Right-click on the CONTEXT root and select CREATE • NODE, as shown in Figure 2.51.

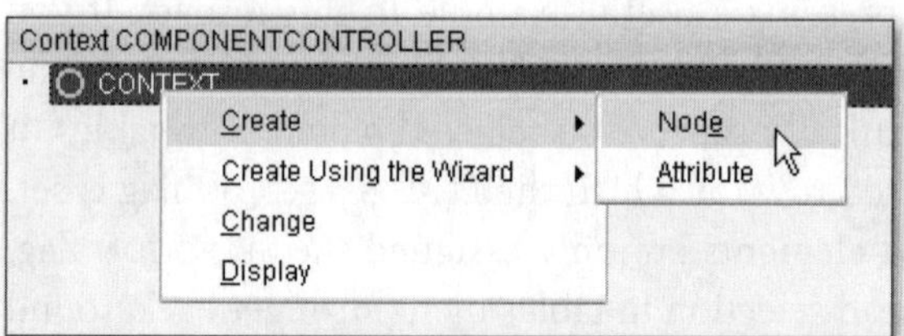

Figure 2.51 Creating a New Context Node

2. Enter ICECREAM as the node name, and select cardinality 0..n. Make sure that all properties are set as shown in Figure 2.52. Then, click on the green checkmark on the left (the one without a label) to create the node.

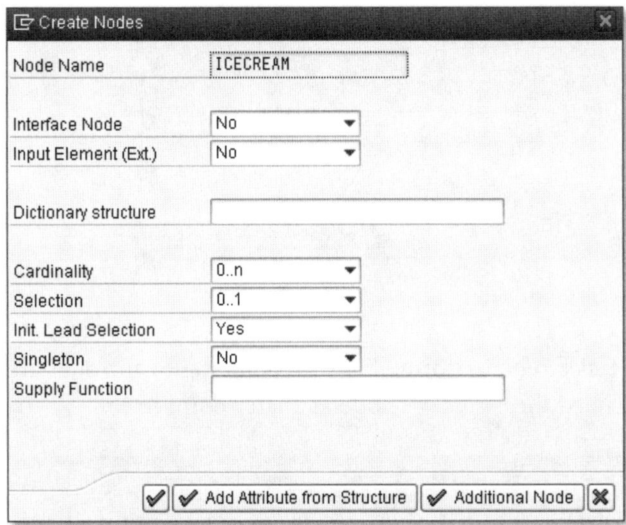

Figure 2.52 Properties of the New Node

3. This takes you back to the context editor. So far, the new node is still empty. To add attributes to the node, right-click on the node and select CREATE • ATTRIBUTE.

Adding attributes

4. The dialog shown in Figure 2.53 appears; it lets you define the properties of the new attribute.

   Create two new attributes with the following properties:

   - ATTRIBUTE NAME: RANKING, TYPE I
   - ATTRIBUTE NAME: NAME, TYPE CHAR_LG_32

   The RANKING attribute will be used to store the rankings of the respective ice cream flavors (NAME attribute).

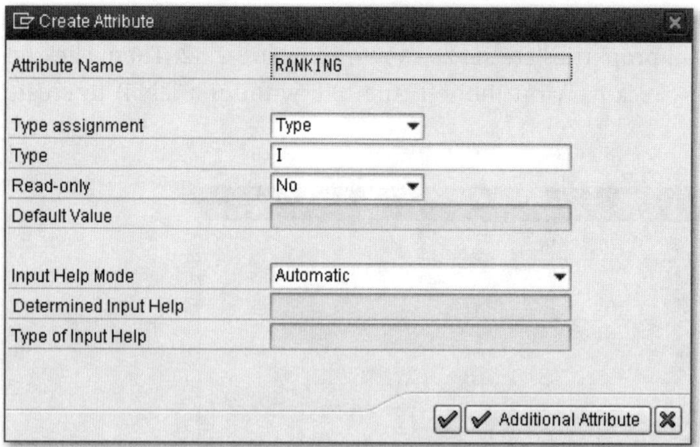

Figure 2.53 Creating New Attributes

At this point, the tasks to be performed in the component controller are finished. You will need the `ICECREAM` node at a later point in time.

Using Contexts Accurately

You can store any data type such as structures, tables, and objects, within a context. However, you should not use a context as an alternative storage for controller attributes; use it only for UI-relevant data.

[✎] In the next step, you should create a new attribute that allows you to enter ice cream flavors in the context of the `V_HELLO_WORLD` view.

Creating an attribute

1. Go to the CONTEXT tab of the `V_HELLO_WORLD` view.
2. Create a new `VALUE` attribute with data type `CHAR_LG_32`, directly under the CONTEXT root.
3. Then, select the LAYOUT tab. Delete the `TextView` element `TV_HELLO_WORLD`. You will not need this element for the rest of this exercise.

[✎] In the following steps, you will create an element label (`Label`) and an input field for the `VALUE` attribute in the view editor. You must manually create and maintain these two UI elements, as well as their properties, in the view editor.

Web Dynpro Code Wizard

At this point, we would like to again point out the options provided by the Web Dynpro Code Wizard (see Figure 2.40). This wizard enables you to generate forms and tables in the view editor. To do so, you must select a context node after launching the wizard. You can then choose those attributes from the node for which you want to generate UI elements.

Creating an input field

1. Insert a new UI element called `IF_ICECREAM` of the `InputField` type into the `V_HELLO_WORLD` view. Position this element before the NEXT button.
2. Bind the UI element `IF_ICECREAM` to the context attribute `VALUE`. To do so, click on the BINDING button of the VALUE property (see Figure 2.54). Then, select the `VALUE` attribute by double-clicking on it in the window that opens. The input field is now bound to the attribute.

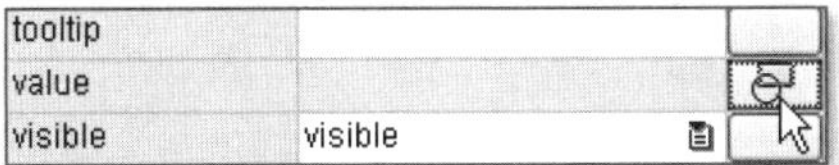

Figure 2.54 Data Binding to the Context

Creating a label

3. Create a label for the input field. To do so, you should insert a new UI element called `LB_ICECREAM` of the `Label` type before the input field.
4. Bind the label to the `IF_ICECREAM` input field. To do so, select `IF_ICECREAM` from the dropdown list of the LABELFOR property, as shown in Figure 2.55.

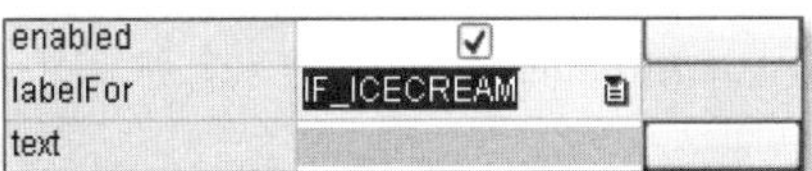

Figure 2.55 Defining the Label Reference

Adding text for the label

5. Due to the binding between the label and the input field, the label property TEXT will be read automatically from the data element of the bound context attribute. Consequently, you typically do not need to maintain any extra text in the label. However, in our example, we used a generic data element. Therefore, you should now enter the string "my ice cream favorites" under TEXT in the label properties.

[✎] You have now created an input field with a label and bound it to an attribute of the context. In the next step, you will ensure that the VALUE attribute will be read and the value of the component controller method add_icecream( ) will be transferred every time you press the Enter key. The IF_ICECREAM input field should then be emptied again to allow for entering another ice cream flavor.

Creating the ADD_ICECREAM action

1. To do so, create the new ADD_ICECREAM action for the onEnter event in the properties of the IF_ICECREAM input field.

ADD_ICECREAM action

2. Go to the method body of the new action. The easiest way to do this is to double-click on the action name in the UI element.
3. Enter the code shown in Listing 2.1 into the method. This code reads the ice cream flavor entered by the user and transfers it to the add_icecream( ) method in the component controller.

```
DATA: lv_icecream TYPE char_lg_32.
* Read VALUE attribute from input field/context
CALL METHOD wd_context->get_attribute
  EXPORTING
    name  = 'VALUE'
  IMPORTING
    value = lv_icecream.
* Rank ice cream in list of favorite ice cream flavors
wd_comp_controller->add_icecream( name = lv_icecream ).
* Delete value VALUE input field/attribute
CALL METHOD wd_context->set_attribute
  EXPORTING
    name  = 'VALUE'
    value = ''.
```

Listing 2.1 Reading and Emptying the VALUE Attribute

Testing the application

Activate the component and test the application. It should look like the one shown in Figure 2.56. You can now enter any ice cream flavor in the input field. The Enter key enables you to transfer the ice cream flavor entered to the currently empty add_icecream( ) method in the component controller. The content of the input field is then deleted so that the next ice cream flavor can be entered.

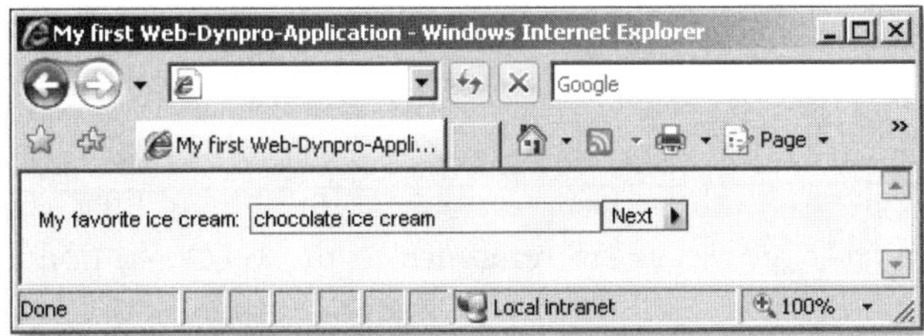

Figure 2.56 Testing the Application

Because the add_icecream( ) method in the component controller is still empty, the ice cream flavors you enter will not yet be stored in the context of the component controller. In the following steps, the flavors should be stored in the ICECREAM context node in the sequence of their entry.

1. Go to the METHODS tab of the component controller and open the add_icecream( ) method.
2. Launch the Web Dynpro Code Wizard. The wizard enables you to generate the code for reading node elements, as well as for editing and adding new elements with a few clicks of the mouse.

Appending Code Wizard elements

3. After launching the wizard, go to the CONTEXT tab and then select the APPEND option and then the ICECREAM context node. To do so, click on the node selection icon (see the mouse pointer in Figure 2.57) and select the node by double-clicking on it in the window that appears. Click on the green checkmark to terminate the Web Dynpro Code Wizard.

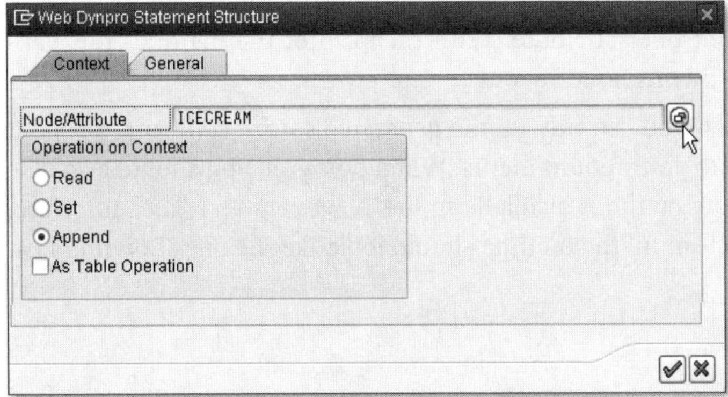

Figure 2.57 Code Wizard – Appending New Elements

Analyzing the generated code

4. At this stage, the Code Wizard has generated the code for appending a new row structure and has inserted it in the method. You should now take a closer look at this code.

   After the data declaration, the `get_child_node( )` method of the `CONTEXT` node fills the `lo_nd_icecream` reference to the `ICECREAM` node. Then, the call of the `bind_structure( )` method appends the `ls_icecream` structure at the end of the node. The `set_initial_elements = abap_false` parameter prevents an overwriting of existing node elements and appends the structure as a new table row.

Local Types for Data Declarations within the Context

The Web Dynpro framework creates two local data types in the controller – one for a row structure and one for a table structure – for each statically defined context node. You can use these data types in the respective controllers when entering definitions via the `DATA` statement.

- Row structure: `wd_this->element_<name_of_node>`
- Table structure: `wd_this->elements_<name_of_node>`

In addition, the framework creates a constant for each node based on the `wdctx_<name_of_node>` scheme.

5. Before you can bind the `ls_icecream` structure to the node, you must fill it with the ice cream flavor and ranking. For this purpose, you must fill the `NAME` field of the structure with the import parameter `name`.

6. In the last step, you need to store the ranking of the ice cream flavor in a global variant called `gv_ranking_counter` of data type `I` as a component controller attribute. With each call of the method, this variable must be increased by one.

Tidying up the code

7. If you want, you can tidy up the generated source code and format it according to your requirements. When doing so, you should also take a look at the methods available in the `IF_WD_CONTEXT_NODE` interface. After the cleanup, the method should look like the one shown in Listing 2.2.

```
* This method adds a new ice cream flavor to the context
DATA: lo_nd_icecream TYPE REF TO if_wd_context_node,
      ls_icecream    TYPE wd_this->element_icecream.
lo_nd_icecream = wd_context->get_child_node(
  name = wd_this->wdctx_icecream ).
```

```
* Fill ICECREAM row structure
ADD 1 to wd_this->gv_ranking_counter.
ls_icecream-ranking = wd_this->gv_ranking_counter.
ls_icecream-name    = name.
* Append row structure to node
lo_nd_icecream->bind_structure(
  new_item             = ls_icecream
  set_initial_elements = abap_false ).
```

Listing 2.2 add_icecream( ) Method (Component Controller)

2.4.3 Mapping

What is mapping?

So far, we have treated individual contexts separately. However, Web Dynpro also allows you to share nodes and attributes across different contexts. This process is referred to as *mapping*.

The process of mapping allows you to copy the structure of the original and to create a reference from the mapped context to the original. At runtime, the data is not copied, only referenced. Consequently, the data exists only once in the original context. If a controller changes mapped data, these changes will have an immediate effect on all other controllers that reference the same data.

Why use mapping?

Why should you use mapping? Mapping allows you to share a context across several controllers. For example, if you have two views that frequently require similar data, it makes sense to store the common data in a controller context that can be accessed by both views. Usually, this is the component controller. However, you can also use the window controller or a custom controller for this purpose.

Mapping examples

Regarding the ZWDC_02_HELLO_WORLD component, it is advisable to map the component controller node ICECREAM to the V_RESULT view and the W_HELLO_WORLD window. For example, mapping the node to the V_RESULT view allows for the display of data that originates from the component controller. The window requires access to the node to provide data to the remove_icecream( ) method. (You may wonder why the method is stored separately in the window controller and not in the component controller like add_icecream( ). This is because the exercises in this chapter are structured in such a way that they cover the largest possible number of aspects of the Web Dynpro architecture.)

To familiarize yourself with the mapping functionality, you should use it right away. For this purpose, in the next exercise, you will define a mapping from the component controller to the window and view controllers. Then, you will add a `Dropdown` UI element through the view controller, which will enable you to scroll through the previously entered list of ice cream flavors.

Mapping by drag-and-drop

1. Select the CONTEXT tab of the window. Drag the `ICECREAM` node from the window area on the right and drop it in the local window context (see Figure 2.58).

   This way, you have created a mapping between the component and the window controller. The arrow pointing to the right in the node indicates that the node has been mapped.

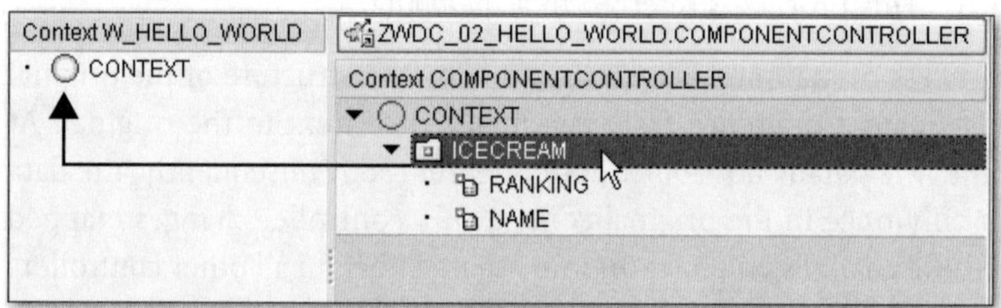

Figure 2.58 Mapping between Component Controller and Window Controller

Deleting elements

2. Complete the `remove_icecream( )` method in the window controller. The method should be called from within the `V_RESULT` view using a new button, and it deletes the element containing the lead selection from the context node. You can then set the lead selection in the view via a `DropDownByIndex` UI element.

   To delete the element that contains the lead selection, you can use the `get_lead_selection( )` and `remove_element( )` methods of the node. To do so, you must first retrieve the selected element via the first of the two methods and then delete it by transferring to the `remove_element( )` method. Listing 2.3 contains the complete method.

```
DATA: lo_nd_icecream TYPE REF TO if_wd_context_node,
      lo_el_icecream TYPE REF TO if_wd_context_element.
lo_nd_icecream =
      wd_context->get_child_node( wd_this-
>wdctx_      icecream ).
```

```
lo_el_icecream = lo_nd_icecream->get_lead_selection( ).
lo_nd_icecream->remove_element( lo_el_icecream ).
wd_comp_controller->fire_set_properties_evt( ).
```

Listing 2.3 remove_icecream() Method

3. Go to the CONTEXT tab of the V_RESULT view. As was the case with the window, you should now map the ICECREAM node to the view.

V_RESULT view

Updating Mapped Nodes

Imagine the following scenario: You have created a node in the component controller and integrated this node into the context of a view using a mapping. Shortly thereafter, you notice that you forgot an important attribute when creating the original node. What can you do now?

Add the missing attribute to the original node of the component controller. Then, right-click on the mapped context node. Select the UPDATE MAPPING item from the context menu. This way, you can ensure that all attributes of the original node are transferred again to the mapped node. After you have updated the mapping, the node in the view is up-to-date again.

Adding a dropdown list

4. Change to the layout view. Insert a DropDownByIndex element called DDBI_RANKING after the BACK button. This UI element enables you to display an attribute of a context node in a dropdown list. During runtime, you can set the lead selection by selecting an item from the dropdown element.
5. Bind the TEXTS property to the RANKING attribute of the ICECREAM node. This causes the element to display the ranking of individual ice cream flavors, but not the flavors themselves (NAME attribute). In addition, you can select the individual rankings via the element.
6. Create a new action called APPLY_CONTEXT_CHANGE for the onSelect event in the dropdown element. Leave this action empty.

   When you select this action from the dropdown list to call it, the web browser sends a roundtrip to the application server. The application server, in turn, processes the result and at the same time updates the view. If you had not implement this method, you would have needed an APPLY button for updating the view.

Creating an empty action

7. Insert a TextView element called TV_NAME directly behind the dropdown element. Bind its TEXT property to the ICECREAM node attribute

NAME. Similar to the Dropdown element, this UI element will always display the value of the node attribute NAME of the respective lead selection at runtime.

8. Finally, you should insert a button called BTN_REMOVE behind the Text element. This button should call the remove_icecream( ) method in the window controller. Add the label "Remove" to the button. Then, generate a new action called REMOVE from within the button and enter the following line in the event handler method of the action:

```
wd_this->go_w_hello_world->remove_icecream( ).
```

Testing the application

This step completes the exercise. Perform a syntax check and activate the component. Then, test the application. Enter several of your favorite ice cream flavors on the first page and use the NEXT button to view the result. The dropdown list now allows you to browse through the ranking of ice cream flavors (see Figure 2.59). After you have selected a rank in the dropdown list, the text field containing the flavor is automatically updated. This is due to the lead selection. Whenever you select an element in the dropdown list, the lead selection is set anew and all UI elements bound to the node are updated on the basis of the new lead selection. The REMOVE button enables you to delete a selected element from the list or node.

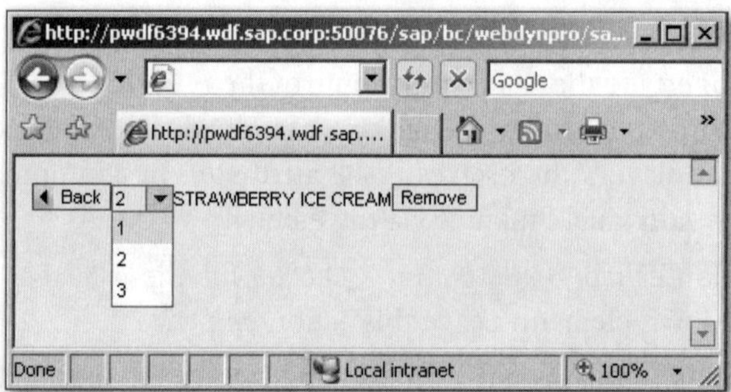

Figure 2.59 Testing the Application – Selecting Ice Cream Flavors

Program termination

Watch out when deleting elements! If you delete the last element from the ICECREAM node or if you navigate directly to the second view without entering an ice cream flavor, the system will abort the process and display the following error message:

The following error text was processed in the system NSP: Adapter error in INPUT_FIELD "ROOTUIELEMENTCONTAINER_T1" of view "ZWDC_GOS_USER.V_MAIN": Context binding of property VALUE cannot be resolved: Node V_MAIN.1.TEST does not contain any elements.

This error message occurs whenever the property of a UI element has been bound to a context attribute at design time and the path to the attribute element cannot be resolved at runtime (empty node). Several options are available to resolve this error:

Filling nodes automatically with data

- You can make sure that the node is always filled with at least one element. To do so, you can either set the cardinality of the node to `1..n` or use supply functions to automatically fill the node with data. The following section describes supply functions in greater detail.

Controlling the visibility of UI elements

- As a preemptive measure, you can also use the ENABLED property of the REMOVE button as well as the VISIBLE property of the text field to prevent the program from terminating. This is described in Section 2.4.5, Controlling the Visibility of UI Elements via the Context.

2.4.4 Supply Functions

Supply functions enable you to automatically initialize context nodes with data. You can create a separate supply function for each node. These supply functions are called by the framework every time the data of their respective nodes is accessed at runtime, provided the nodes do not contain any data yet or have been invalidated in a previous step.

Supply functions in the ICECREAM node

Regarding the exercise in this chapter, you could use a supply function every time the user skips entering ice cream flavors in the first view and navigates directly to the second view, `V_RESULT`. At that point, the `ICECREAM` node is empty. However, because the TEXT property of the text field is bound to the node and requires an element for binding, the supply function is called by the framework to fill the node.

[✎]

You will now create a supply function:

1. Go to the CONTEXT tab of the component controller.
2. Click on the `ICECREAM` node and enter the value `SUPPLY_ICECREAM` in the SUPPLY FUNCTION field (see Figure 2.60).

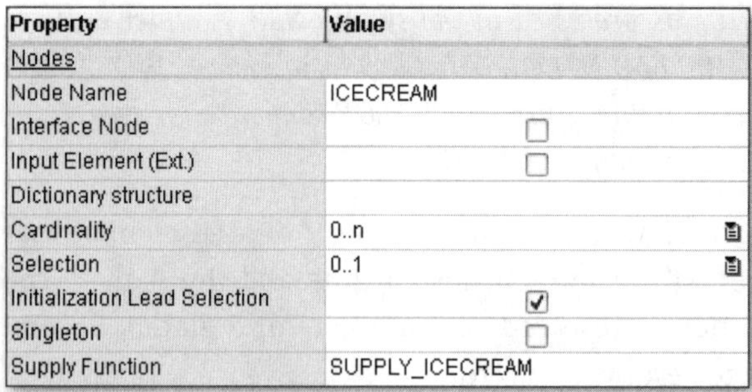

Property	Value
Nodes	
Node Name	ICECREAM
Interface Node	☐
Input Element (Ext.)	☐
Dictionary structure	
Cardinality	0..n
Selection	0..1
Initialization Lead Selection	☑
Singleton	☐
Supply Function	SUPPLY_ICECREAM

Figure 2.60 Creating a Supply Function for the ICECREAM Node

3. Double-click on the function to display the source code of the supply function method. You can find the necessary coding for binding a table at the end of the commentary block of the method. Remove the commentary characters and fill the table with one or two rows. Your method should then look like the one shown in Listing 2.4.

```
* Data declaration
DATA: lt_icecream TYPE wd_this->elements_icecream,
      ls_icecream LIKE LINE OF lt_icecream.
* Create a table with two standard ice cream flavors
ADD 1 to wd_this->gv_ranking_counter.
ls_icecream-ranking = wd_this->gv_ranking_counter.
ls_icecream-name    = 'Vanilla ice cream'.
APPEND ls_icecream TO lt_icecream.
ADD 1 to wd_this->gv_ranking_counter.
ls_icecream-ranking = wd_this->gv_ranking_counter.
ls_icecream-name    = 'Chocolate ice cream'.
APPEND ls_icecream TO lt_icecream.
* Transfer the table to ICECREAM node
node->bind_table(
  new_items            = lt_icecream
  set_initial_elements = abap_true ).
```

Listing 2.4 Supply Function SUPPLY_ICECREAM

Testing the supply function

Activate the component and test the application. When you navigate to the `V_RESULT` view without entering an ice cream flavor, the supply function interferes and fills the `ICECREAM` node with data. The supply function is not called until the rendering takes place.

2.4.5 Controlling the Visibility of UI Elements via the Context

Something is still missing: If you use the REMOVE button to remove the last element from the ICECREAM node, the application aborts due to the missing binding between the text field and the node. In this case, even the supply function cannot provide any help because it is only called for initial nodes and not after the deletion of the last node element of a node that has already been initialized.

[✎] Fortunately, you can solve this problem easily. Because the text field has no more data to display after the last element has been deleted, it can be integrated by the view and set to invisible. In addition, the REMOVE button can be disabled after the deletion of the last element. The UI elements TV_NAME and BTN_REMOVE provide the ENABLED and VISIBLE properties for this purpose. In the following, final exercise of this chapter, you will bind these elements to the context:

1. Go to the V_RESULT view. Open the context editor and create a new attribute called VISIBLE_AND_ENABLED of the WDY_BOOLEAN type.
2. Bind the VISIBLE property of UI element TV_NAME to the VISIBLE_AND_ENABLED attribute. Then, bind the ENABLED property of element BTN_REMOVE to the same attribute.

   Binding the visible and enabled properties
3. Complete the previously created event handler method on_set_properties( ). This method is called every time ICECREAM is changed.
4. As soon as the node contains at least one element, the value of the VISIBLE_AND_ENABLED attribute must be set to true. To verify this, you can use the get_element_count( ) method of the node. You should first try to program the method without looking at Listing 2.5.

```
DATA: lo_nd_icecream TYPE REF TO if_wd_context_node,
      lv_bool        TYPE wdy_boolean.
lo_nd_icecream =
  wd_context->get_child_node( wd_this->wdctx_icecream ).
IF lo_nd_icecream->get_element_count( ) > 0.
  lv_bool = abap_true.
ENDIF.
wd_context->set_attribute(
  EXPORTING
    name  = 'VISIBLE_AND_ENABLED'
    value = lv_bool ).
```

Listing 2.5 Event Handler Method on_set_properties( )

Testing the component

After activating the component, you can test the entire application. If you delete all ice cream flavors from the list, the TV_NAME text field gets hidden, and the REMOVE button is grayed out (see Figure 2.61). The BACK button enables you to return to the input field and re-enter the ice cream flavors.

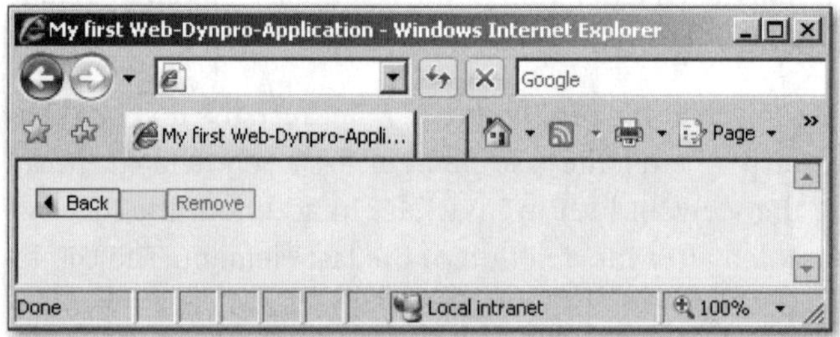

Figure 2.61 Testing the V_RESULT View

At this point, there is still room for further improvement of the application. For example, the ranking of ice cream flavors by deleting and inserting elements can easily become messy; also, it would be conceivable not to set the NEXT button to active mode until at least one flavor has been entered. However, these optimization tasks exceed the scope of this book and are not discussed here.

2.5 Summary

In this chapter, you have been introduced to the basic Web Dynpro architecture as well as to the fundamental techniques of programming Web Dynpro user interfaces. At this point, you know almost everything you need to know to develop complex UIs in Web Dynpro.

Chapter 3, Developing Web Dynpro Applications, will further enhance this knowledge and introduce you to a large number of new UI elements. Moreover, the next chapter will further strengthen your knowledge of context programming and describe how you can arrange UI elements using the layouts provided by Web Dynpro.

Web Dynpro applications represent the view to one or more Web Dynpro components for a user. In this chapter, you will learn how Web Dynpro applications are developed and how you can put their different features to use.

3 Developing Web Dynpro Applications

Web Dynpro — deepening and broadening your knowledge

In this chapter, you will use the knowledge you have gained so far to develop a Web Dynpro application. You will also get deeper insight into programming the context into view layouts and containers, using important UI elements, tables, input help, and messages, as well as internationalizing texts, which is known as internationalization or I18N.

Example of a Web Dynpro application

The different topics discussed in this chapter will be integrated step by step into a Web Dynpro application we will create to show you how the theory is applied in practice. In this chapter, we will pursue four goals, as follows:

- Presenting and conveying detailed information about the elements of Web Dynpro development
- Explaining the procedure for developing a Web Dynpro application and using the presented techniques in practical examples
- Providing a complete – from the perspective of an operational Web Dynpro application – and integrated set of examples that you can reuse as templates for your development projects
- Presenting additional topics such as Run Time Type Identification (RTTI) or service calls that will make your life easier

The application we will develop in this chapter has been named *class browser*. In this application, users can enter search criteria for an ABAP class. If the ABAP class is found, the description and methods for the ABAP class are displayed, both in a tree and in a table.

Web Dynpro toolbox

As you can already guess, you will need numerous techniques from the Web Dynpro toolbox to implement this Web Dynpro application; thus, we have structured the sections in this chapter accordingly. We will begin with programming the context. You will create a Web Dynpro component, define a context structure, and then use the tools for designing and programming the view. You will also use layouts, containers, and a number of view elements for designing the view layout.

Topics Discussed

We will discuss the following topics in this chapter:

- Context programming
- Layouts and containers
- Using important view elements
- Messages and internationalization

3.1 Context Programming

As you have already learned, each controller has a *context* in which used data is hierarchically stored. *Context nodes* and *context attributes* are the basic elements used for context structuring. In this section, we will discuss in more detail how to create, change, and delete data in the context.

[✎] In this chapter, you will create the ZWDC_03_CLASS_BROWSER Web Dynpro component as a warm-up exercise and review of what you have already learned. The component, which you will create as a LOCAL OBJECT, will be built incrementally throughout the chapter. Call the view you create V_MAIN_LAYOUT and the window W_MAIN. Aside from the Web Dynpro component, you will also create a Web Dynpro application called ZWDC_03_CLASS_BROWSER_APP. (If you have any difficulties with this task, you can find the information you need in Section 2.1, Components and Applications.)

Building a context structure

To program the context, you must either build context structures or define context nodes using *ABAP Dictionary structure types*.

ABAP Dictionary Structure Types

Structure variables are provided in ABAP to combine several scalar variables (simple data types such as date, time, and whole number values) in one unit. If you need the structure variable setup (type) several times, you can create a *structure type* in the ABAP Dictionary (Transaction SE11), which you can then use for typing structure variables. There are three kinds of structure types in the ABAP Dictionary; which one you use depends on the planned area of application for the structure type:

- **ABAP Dictionary structure**
  You create ABAP Dictionary structures primarily for typing variables and interface parameters.
- **Transparent table**
  A transparent table is a database table you define in the ABAP Dictionary and then create in the database. You can use it like an ABAP Dictionary structure for typing purposes.
- **ABAP Dictionary view**
  This is a virtual table that does not contain any data; instead, it is an application-oriented view of one or more ABAP Dictionary table(s).

The structure type elements are known as *fields* or *components*.

Building a context structure with a structure type

Recall the context nodes and attributes you created individually in Section 2.4, Context. First, you created the context node and then, you individually created every context attribute required for the context node. As an alternative to this method, you can proceed as follows:

1. Define a structure type in the ABAP Dictionary with the required structure components.
2. Create a context node in the required controller. For the typing, use the structure type you previously created.

Let us look at an example of the described procedure. The user should be offered a selection screen to search for ABAP classes and must enter the name of the ABAP class he wants to find. If the ABAP class is found, its description is displayed in the selection screen. To be able to implement this requirement, you must (if you follow the described procedure) first create an ABAP Dictionary structure for the selection criteria in the ABAP Dictionary:

Creating a structure type

1. Switch to the initial screen of the ABAP Dictionary using Transaction SE11.
2. As described, several kinds of structure types are available. Because you will only use the structure type for typing the node and variables, choose the structure as the structure type. Select the DATA TYPE radio button in the ABAP Dictionary Initial Screen.
3. Enter the structure name `ZST_03_WD_CLASS_SEL_CRIT` in the input field for the DATA TYPE radio button. The name begins with the letter `Z` and is therefore in the customer namespace.
4. Click on the CREATE button and set the STRUCTURE radio button in the selection dialog box that appears. Click on the green checkmark to confirm your entry.
5. In the maintenance screen for the structure, assign a short description such as "Class Selection Criteria" for the ABAP Dictionary structure.

Now, create the components for the structure. The name and description of an ABAP class are required as components:

- **Name**
  - COMPONENT: `NAME_CLASS`
  - COMPONENT TYPE: `SEOCLSNAME`
- **Description**
  - COMPONENT: `DESCR_CLASS`
  - COMPONENT TYPE: `SEODESCR`

Determining a data element

1. To determine the component types, we will analyze the initial screen of the Object Navigator (Transaction SE24) in this example. The input field for the name of an ABAP interface or ABAP class is available there. The semantic help for the input field appears when you place the cursor in the OBJECT TYPE input field and press the [F1] key. If you now click on the TECHNICAL INFORMATION button, the technical information for the input field appears. In the DATA ELEMENT display field of the FIELD DATA group, you will find the name of the data element (`SEOCLSNAME`) that was used for typing the input field.

Enhancement category

2. You still have to define how the `ZST_03_WD_CLASS_SEL_CRIT` structure can be enhanced in the future. To do this, use the EXTRAS • ENHANCEMENT CATEGORY... menu path. In the next selection dialog box that

appears, set the CAN BE ENHANCED (DEEP) radio button and confirm your entry using the CHECKMARK button.

3. Select the structure by pressing the ACTIVATE (Ctrl + F3 key combination) button. The result of your previous work is displayed in Figure 3.1.

Activating

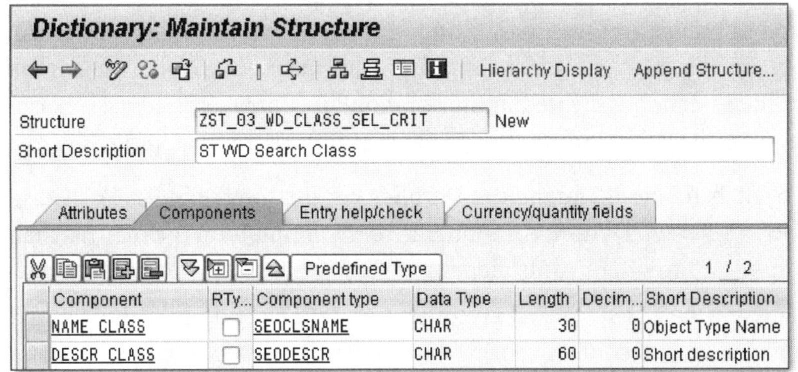

Figure 3.1 ZST_03_WD_CLASS_SEL_CRIT Structure in ABAP Dictionary

You have now created the complete ZST_03_WD_CLASS_SEL_CRIT ABAP Dictionary structure and can use it in defining the context structure. Beforehand, however, you have to perform another exercise to consolidate your knowledge. Create an ABAP Dictionary structure that will be used for typing the context node for ABAP class methods. Call the ABAP Dictionary structure ZST_03_WD_CLASS_METHOD. Table 3.1 contains the required components and their types. Do not forget to set the enhancement category and to activate the structure.

Component	Component Type
NAME	SEOCPDNAME
KIND_ICON	ICONNAME
IS_CLASS	WDY_BOOLEAN
IS_INTERFACE	WDY_BOOLEAN
IS_REDEFINED	WDY_BOOLEAN

Table 3.1 Components and Component Types for the ZST_03_WD_CLASS_METHOD ABAP Dictionary Structure

Defining a context structure

Everything is now ready to define the context structure in the ZWDC_03_CLASS_BROWSER Web Dynpro component. As already mentioned, you need a context node that can transfer the data from the selection screen and a node that can include the methods found for an ABAP class.

Context node for the selection

We will begin with the context node for the selection criteria. The data from the selection view should also be available for the component controller because accesses to the context that are implemented later are all executed by the component controller. This means that the context node for the selection is created in the component controller; later, access can be made available for other controllers using context mapping.

1. Switch to the component controller context of the ZWDC_03_CLASS_BROWSER Web Dynpro component. You will find it on the CONTEXT tab in the component controller.

Creating nodes

2. Create the CLASS_SEL_CRIT context node: Selecting first the context menu on the context root node and then the CREATE • NODES menu option opens the maintenance dialog box for the context node (see Figure 3.2).
3. Enter the context node name CLASS_SEL_CRIT in the NODE NAME input field (❶).

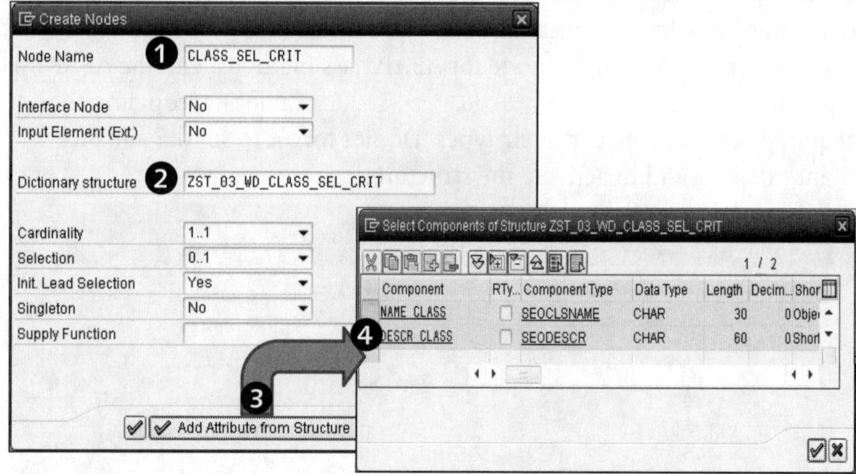

Figure 3.2 Creating the CLASS_SEL_CRIT Context Node Using an ABAP Dictionary Structure

4. The next step is a new feature. In the DICTIONARY STRUCTURE input field, enter the name of the ABAP Dictionary structure you created for the selection criteria: `ZST_03_WD_CLASS_SEL_CRIT` (❷). By doing so, you define the structure type from which you want context attributes to be determined for the context node.
5. Click on ADD ATTRIBUTE FROM STRUCTURE to select the attributes you need (❸). A selection dialog box appears for the components of the specified structure.

   Adding attributes
6. Select all components to change them to attributes (❹).
7. Finally, click on the button with the green checkmark to confirm your selection.

You have now created a context node with context attributes. This method of creating context nodes is used frequently in practice because context nodes created using the structure type offer advantages over context attributes created individually such as environment-sensitive input help. The result of your efforts is illustrated in Figure 3.3.

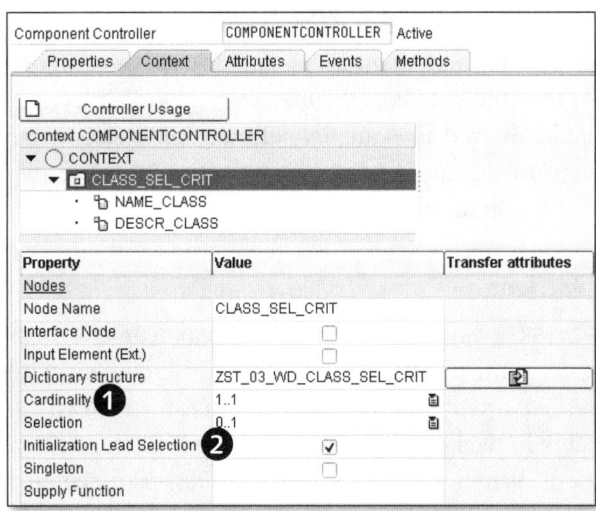

Figure 3.3 CLASS_SEL_CRIT Context Node with Context Attributes

Properties

When you look at some of the properties of the `CLASS_SEL_CRIT` context node, you will discover that exactly one context element is created from this context node. This element is defined by the CARDINALITY 1..1 (❶). In addition, the Web Dynpro framework performs the INITIALIZATION LEAD SELECTION, because this property is selected (❷).

These two settings ensure that a context element is available for transferring the input data from the selection view still to be created.

[✎] Now, create the METHODS context node in the component controller context. For this, use all of the components from the ZST_03_WD_CLASS_METHOD ABAP Dictionary structure, as described for the ZST_03_WD_CLASS_SEL_CRIT ABAP Dictionary structure. Set the CARDINALITY of the context node to the 0..n value because no methods may be found for the ABAP class; thus, the 0 lower limit. However, you may also have a situation where several methods are found; thus, the n upper limit.

You have now created the prerequisites to get started with the discussion of context programming. In the following sections, you will see how you can create and manipulate data in the context.

3.1.1 Changing Attribute Values of an Element

Setting default values

To be able to explain how to implement access to context, we assigned the following task for the application: If the user starts the Web Dynpro application, he should be offered a default value for an ABAP class name in the selection screen; for example, CL_GUI_ALV_GRID. There are two options you can use here: default values or programming.

Default Value of an Attribute

Assign the CL_GUI_ALV_GRID value to the DEFAULT VALUE context property for the NAME_CLASS context attribute. You should be familiar with this procedure from ABAP programming whereby you can assign an initial value to the variable to declare a variable using the VALUE addition for the DATA statement. When you assign initial values in the context properties of the NAME_CLASS context attribute, the result (❶) should appear as shown in Figure 3.4.

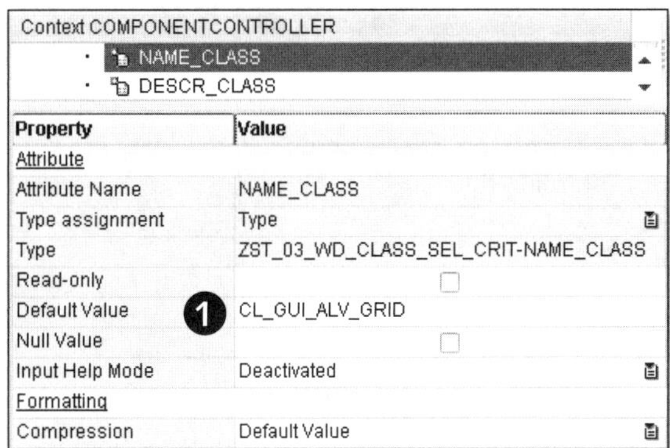

Figure 3.4 Setting the Default Value of a Context Attribute

Programming

The programming involves assigning the CL_GUI_ALV_GRID value to the NAME_CLASS context attribute using context programming. We will take a closer look at the basic procedure for this option.

Navigating in the context hierarchy

To be able to access the NAME_CLASS context attribute, you have to navigate through the context hierarchy. Navigation begins with the CONTEXT root node. From there, you navigate to the CLASS_SEL_CRIT subnode that contains the NAME_CLASS attribute. You then access the content of the context attribute using the element for the context node (see Section 2.4, Context). Because the CARDINALITY property of the CLASS_SEL_CRIT context node was set to 1..1, the element is available for the context node. If you have access to the element, you can set the value for the NAME_CLASS context attribute.

get_child_node( )

We will use the IF_WD_CONTEXT_NODE ABAP interface for working with context nodes; for example, for creating, reading, changing, and deleting node elements. Table 3.2 contains the most important methods from this interface, which we will discuss and use in this section.

Method	Description
get_child_node( )	Determines the subnode reference
get_element( )	Determines the element from the node collection

Table 3.2 Selected Methods of the IF_WD_CONTEXT_NODE ABAP Interface

Method	Description
get_element_count( )	The number of elements in the node collection
get_static_attributes_table( )	All attributes of all elements in the form of an internal table
create_element( )	Creates an element
bind_element( )	Adds a node collection element
bind_structure( )	Creates and adds an element in the node collection from the structure
bind_table( )	Creates and adds, per entry, an element in the node collection from an internal table
remove_element( )	Removes an element from the node collection

Table 3.2 Selected Methods of the IF_WD_CONTEXT_NODE ABAP Interface (Cont.)

Under the controller attributes for each controller, you will find the wd_context attribute that is typed with this ABAP interface. The get_child_node( ) ABAP interface method from this particular ABAP interface is used to determine the reference to a child node. This means that this ABAP interface method enables you to navigate in the context hierarchy.

child_node An analysis of the interface for the method, which you can see in Figure 3.5, shows that the child_node returning parameter is an IF_WD_CONTEXT_NODE type. (If you are not familiar with analyzing the interface of a method, you can find additional information about this in the Analyzing a Method Interface box.)

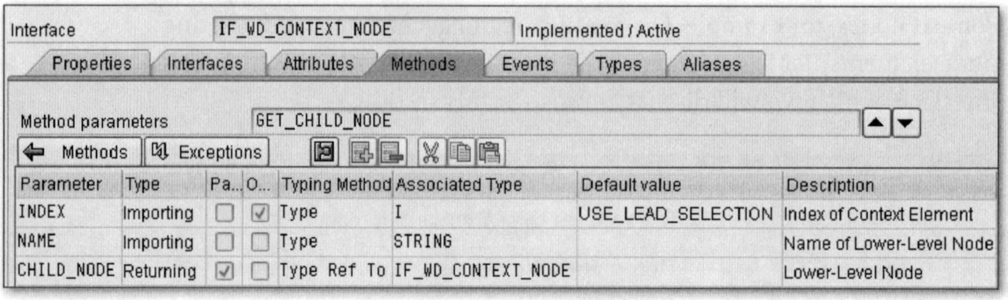

Interface IF_WD_CONTEXT_NODE Implemented / Active

Properties | Interfaces | Attributes | Methods | Events | Types | Aliases

Method parameters GET_CHILD_NODE

Methods | Exceptions

Parameter	Type	Pa...	O...	Typing Method	Associated Type	Default value	Description
INDEX	Importing	☐	☑	Type	I	USE_LEAD_SELECTION	Index of Context Element
NAME	Importing	☐	☐	Type	STRING		Name of Lower-Level Node
CHILD_NODE	Returning	☑	☐	Type Ref To	IF_WD_CONTEXT_NODE		Lower-Level Node

Figure 3.5 get_child_node( ) Method Interface

You will also find the optional `index` importing parameter for determining the element index in the higher-level node to which the node instance belongs. If you do not use the `index` importing parameter, the lead selection of the higher-level node is used for determining the element.

index

Analyzing a Method Interface

The methods for ABAP classes or ABAP interfaces have parameters known as *formal parameters* that can transfer data from the caller or return it to the caller (*actual parameters*). The parameters as a whole are referred to as the *interface* or *signature* of a method. The parameters are divided into groups (*types*) depending on their intended purpose:

- **Importing parameters**
  You can use these parameters to transfer data to the method.
- **Exporting parameters**
  You can use these parameters to return data to the caller.
- **Changing parameters**
  These parameters provide a combination of importing and exporting parameters.
- **Returning parameters**
  The returning parameter is a value that can be returned to the caller. When you use this parameter type, you can define a *functional method* that can be called directly in expressions.

To be able to establish the parameters a method provides and type the data transferred to the parameters, switch to the Class Builder (Transaction SE24), then to an ABAP class or interface, and then to the METHODS tab. Place the cursor on the required method and click on the PARAMETERS button. You will now get a list of formal parameters, including parameter types.

The `IF_WD_CONTEXT_ELEMENT` ABAP interface enables you to read, change and set the attribute data of an element. Table 3.3 shows the most important methods from this interface, which we will be discussing and using in this section.

set_attribute( )

Method	Description
`set_attribute( )`	Changes the value of an attribute in an element
`set_static_attributes( )`	Changes the value of attributes using a structure

Table 3.3 Selected Methods of the IF_WD_CONTEXT_ELEMENT ABAP Interface

Method	Description
get_attribute( )	Reads an attribute from the element
get_static_attributes( )	Reads all attributes from the element

Table 3.3 Selected Methods of the IF_WD_CONTEXT_ELEMENT ABAP Interface (Cont.)

The `set_attribute( )` method is provided in this ABAP interface to be able to change the value of an individual context attribute. The name of the context attribute (`name` parameter) and the new value (`value` parameter) must be transferred to the method for this purpose (see Figure 3.6).

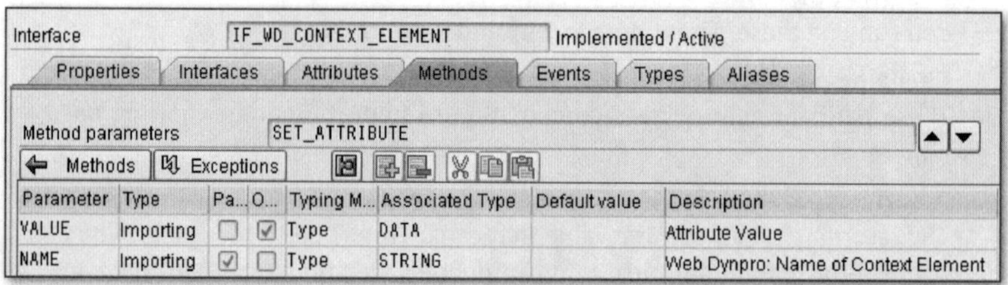

Figure 3.6 set_attribute( ) Method Interface

To use an example of the methods mentioned, you will develop a method to set the value of the `NAME_CLASS` context attribute from the `CLASS_SEL_CRIT` context node. Proceed as follows:

setctx_class_sel_crit( )

1. Switch to the component controller and then select the METHODS tab.
2. Create the `setctx_class_sel_crit( )` method with the `is_value` importing parameter of the `ZST_03_WD_CLASS_SEL_CRIT` type (see Figure 3.7).

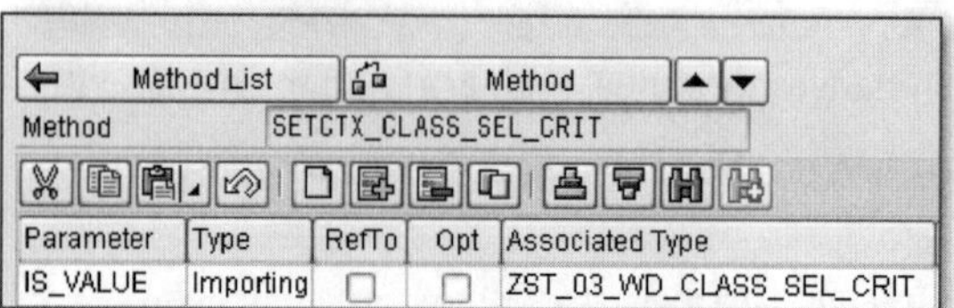

Figure 3.7 setctx_class_sel_crit( ) Method Interface

3. In this method, you will implement setting the `NAME_CLASS` context attribute. To do this, switch to the `setctx_class_sel_crit( )` method.

Web Dynpro Code Wizard

4. Open the Web Dynpro Code Wizard and select the CONTEXT tab. Choose the `NAME_CLASS` context attribute in the CLASS_SEL_CRIT context node in the NODE/ATTRIBUTE field and select the SET option in the OPERATION ON CONTEXT group.
5. Click on the button with the green checkmark to confirm your entry. Your result should correspond to Listing 3.1 (except variant 2).

```
METHOD setctx_class_sel_crit .
* Node reference
DATA: lo_nd_class_sel_crit TYPE REF TO
        if_wd_context_node,
* Element reference
      lo_el_class_sel_crit TYPE REF TO
        if_wd_context_element.
* From <CONTEXT> to <CLASS_SEL_CRIT> with lead selection
lo_nd_class_sel_crit = wd_context->get_child_node(
  name = wd_this->wdctx_class_sel_crit ).
* Element via lead selection
lo_el_class_sel_crit =
  lo_nd_class_sel_crit->get_element( ).
* No lead selection handling
IF lo_el_class_sel_crit IS INITIAL.
  EXIT.
ENDIF.
** Variant 1 - single **
* Set attribute
lo_el_class_sel_crit->set_attribute(
  name =  `NAME_CLASS`
  value = is_value-name_class ).
** Variant 2 - structure **
*lo_el_class_sel_crit->set_static_attributes(
*  static_attributes = is_value ).
ENDMETHOD.
```

Listing 3.1 Determining the Element Reference of the CLASS_SEL_CRIT Node

Description

What have you achieved so far? You have determined the reference to the `CLASS_SEL_CRIT` subnode and in this case, used the `get_child_node( )`

method. You have also read the element reference for this context node using the `get_element( )` method. If an element is not set as the lead selection, the method is exited using `EXIT`. The attribute value for the `NAME_CLASS` attribute is changed using the `set_attribute( )` method from the `IF_WD_CONTEXT_ELEMENT` ABAP interface.

set_static_attributes( )

If you have a large number of attributes, setting them individually can be very time-consuming and can lengthen the source code considerably. The `set_static_attributes( )` method is available in the `IF_WD_CONTEXT_ELEMENT` ABAP interface to enable you to transfer changes to the element reference using a single call. You can transfer a structure with the attribute values to this method using the `static_attributes` formula parameter. This call was inserted into the variant 2 source code section in Listing 3.1.

Call

To ensure that the attributes are initialized before the selection screen is displayed for the first time, you must call the `setctx_class_sel_crit( )` method in the `wddoinit( )` method of the component controller.

[✎]

1. To implement the call, switch to the `wddoinit( )` method and start the Web Dynpro Code Wizard (see Figure 3.8).

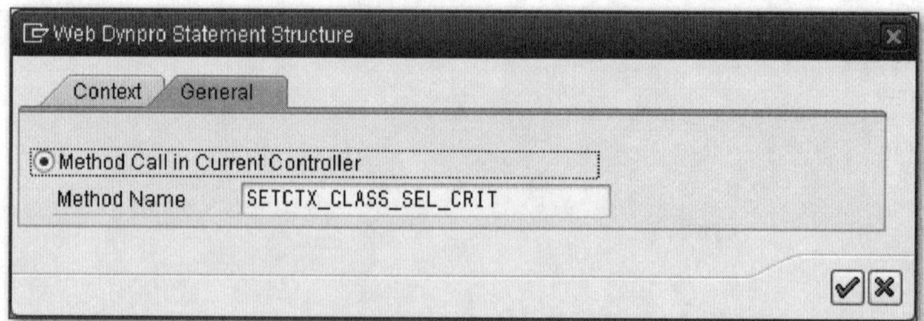

Figure 3.8 Statement Structure for Calling a Method

Web Dynpro statement structure

2. Select the General tab and choose the Method Call in Current Controller option. Enter the name of the `setctx_class_sel_crit( )` method or call it using the input help. Click on the button with the green checkmark to confirm your entry and to generate the source text.
3. In the `wddoinit( )` method, you still have to assign current values to a structure of type `ZST_03_WD_CLASS_SEL_CRIT` and transfer the

structure to the setctx_class_sel_crit( ) method. You must perform these steps manually. Listing 3.2 contains the fully implemented wddoinit( )method.

```
METHOD wddoinit .
DATA: ls_class_sel_crit TYPE
wd_this->element_class_sel_crit.
* Set current data
ls_class_sel_crit-name_class = 'CL_GUI_ALV_GRID'.
ls_class_sel_crit_descr__class = 'ALV List Viewer'.
* Initialize selection criteria
wd_this->setctx_class_sel_crit(
  is_value = ls_class_sel_crit ).
ENDMETHOD.
```

Listing 3.2 Calling the Initialization of Selection Criteria

4. Because no views have been created for displaying data (see Chapter 8, Section 8.2, Debugging Web Dynpro Applications), you can test functions using the Web Dynpro debugger.

Web Dynpro debugger

You are now ready to put what you have learned about changing element attribute values into practice. But how can you read the attribute values of an element? We will look at this next.

3.1.2 Reading Attribute Values of One or More Elements

Three methods

The methods for reading attribute values from an element include three in particular, all of which we will discuss in more detail in the following sections:

- get_attribute( )
  This method from the IF_WD_CONTEXT_ELEMENT ABAP interface enables you to determine the value for a specific attribute. If the transferred attribute name is not known, a CX_WD_CONTEXT exception is thrown.
- get_static_attributes( )
  This method from the IF_WD_CONTEXT_ELEMENT ABAP interface returns the values of all attributes for an element in a structure. The structure for transferring the name to the method may differ in terms of the structure for the formula parameter. In the method implementation, the values are transferred using the MOVE-CORRESPONDING ABAP statement.

▶ `get_static_attributes_table( )`
This method from the `IF_WD_CONTEXT_NODE` ABAP interface returns the values of all attributes of all elements in an internal table.

As a result, there should be no further problem with developing a method for reading the context contents. To enhance the `ZWDC_03_CLASS_BROWSER` Web Dynpro component, you need the selection criteria values from the `CLASS_SEL_CRIT` context node. Although the values were initialized in the attributes, the user may have changed them – in fact, you can assume that they have been changed.

get_attribute( ) method

getctx_class_sel_crit( )

To encapsulate reading the context node, create the `getctx_class_sel_crit( )` method in the component controller. This method should return the selection criteria values as a structure. The `getctx_class_sel_crit( )` method interface consists of the `ZST_03_WD_CLASS_SEL_CRIT`-type `rs_value` returning parameter. You can use it later to execute a functional method call.

[✎]

1. Create the `GETCTX_CLASS_SEL_CRIT` method in the component controller.
2. Define the method interface (see Figure 3.9):
    - PARAMETER: `rs_value`
    - TYPE: `Returning`
    - REFTO: `ZST_03_WD_CLASS_SEL_CRIT`

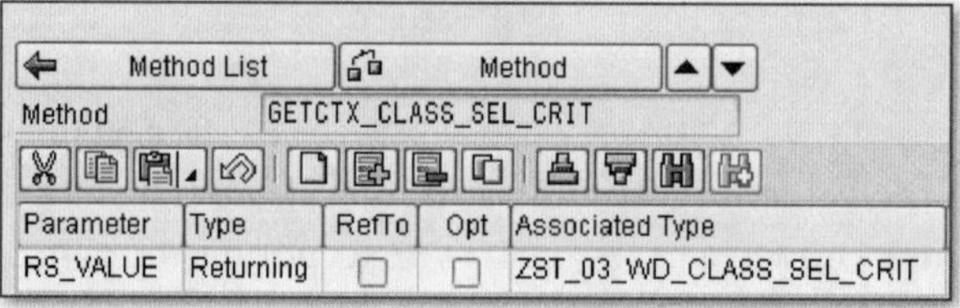

Figure 3.9 getctx_class_sel_crit( ) Method Interface

3. Switch to the method implementation and individually determine the values for the context attributes for each context attribute. To do this, call the Web Dynpro Code Wizard and use the CONTEXT tab. From the context, choose the `NAME_CLASS` attribute in the `CLASS_SEL_CRIT`

node and set the OPERATION ON CONTEXT option to the READ value (see Figure 3.10).

Note the structure of the path for the context attribute. It consists of the node name, a period, and the attribute name. We will need this structure in Chapter 4, Dynamic Web Dynpro Applications.

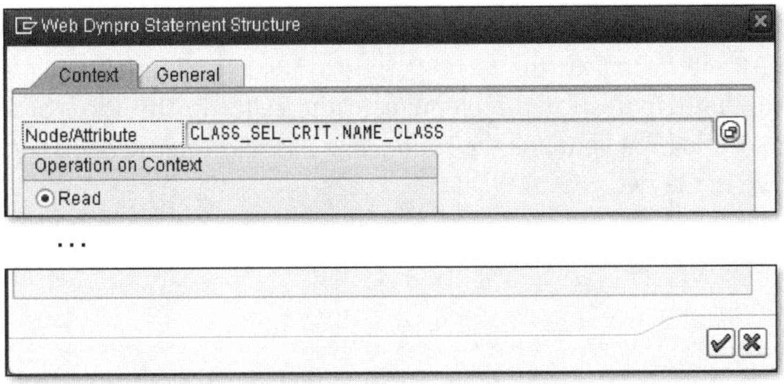

Web Dynpro Statement Structure

Context | General

Node/Attribute: CLASS_SEL_CRIT.NAME_CLASS

Operation on Context

(•) Read

...

Figure 3.10 Reading an Attribute Using the Web Dynpro Code Wizard

4. Click on the button with the green checkmark to confirm your entry and to insert the source text for reading the NAME_CLASS context attribute.
5. To transfer the context attribute value, you still have to transfer the rs_value-name_class structure component to the value exporting parameter of the get_attribute( ) method.

Providing interfaces

This means that the context attribute reading from the lead selection is now fully implemented. As an exercise, you can implement the DESCR_CLASS context attribute reading. Listing 3.3 contains the relevant source code passages for comparison with your solution.

```
** Variant 1: single **
* Read NAME_CLASS attribute from element
lo_el_class_sel_crit->get_attribute(
  EXPORTING
    name =  `NAME_CLASS`
  IMPORTING
    value = rs_value-name_class ).
```

Listing 3.3 Reading Values for the NAME_CLASS and DESCR_CLASS Context Attributes Using the get_attribute( ) Method

You will now probably wonder whether the context attributes cannot be read in a more compact way; for example, by reading all attribute values at once. The good news is, yes, they can. We will describe this in the following section.

get_static_attributes( ) Method

The GET_STATIC_ATTRIBUTES( ) method from the IF_WD_CONTEXT_ELEMENT ABAP interface uses the static_attributes exporting parameter to return all attributes for the element to the caller in the form of a structure. Listing 3.4 contains the source text passage you can use as an alternative to the two get_attribute( ) calls.

```
* Variant 2 - structure *
lo_el_class_sel_crit->get_static_attributes(
  IMPORTING
    static_attributes = rs_value ).
```

Listing 3.4 Using the get_static_attributes( ) Method in the getctx_class_sel_crit( ) Method of the Component Controller

Error message

If you test the method in the debugger, the following error message might be displayed in the browser:

Attribute <attribute name> could not be found.

This message appears if the transferred attribute name cannot be found when you call the get_attribute( ) method. This could occur if the attribute name you transferred has a typo. You also have to use uppercase spelling when transferring the attribute name because, due to performance factors in implementing the get_attribute( ) method, uppercase spelling is not converted.

get_static_attributes_table( ) Method

So far, we have discussed reading individual attribute values and all attribute values of an element. The get_static_attributes_table( ) method from the IF_WD_CONTEXT_NODE interface at last provides us with the functions to read all attribute values for all elements of a context node.

As an example to illustrate this, the METHODS context node should be read completely. The METHODS elements you will create for the reading should return all attributes to the caller in the form of an internal table. The type for this internal table is contained in the component controller interface.

Component controller interface

When you switch to the component controller attributes and double-click on the IF_COMPONENTCONTROLLER reference type of the wd_this attribute, the definition of the component controller interface displayed in Figure 3.11 appears.

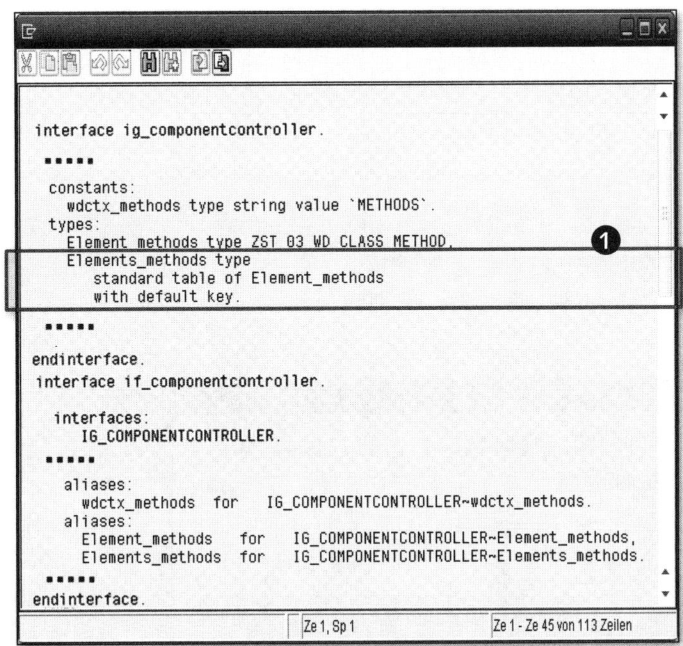

interface ig_componentcontroller.
.....
constants:
wdctx_methods type string value `METHODS`.
types:
Element_methods type ZST_03_WD_CLASS_METHOD.
1
Elements_methods type
standard table of Element_methods
with default key.
.....
endinterface.
interface if_componentcontroller.
interfaces:
IG_COMPONENTCONTROLLER.
.....
aliases:
wdctx_methods for IG_COMPONENTCONTROLLER~wdctx_methods.
aliases:
Element_methods for IG_COMPONENTCONTROLLER~Element_methods,
Elements_methods for IG_COMPONENTCONTROLLER~Elements_methods.
.....
endinterface.
Ze 1, Sp 1
Ze 1 - Ze 45 von 113 Zeilen

Figure 3.11 IG_COMPONENTCONTROLLER Interface

Table types in the component controller interface

The name of the table type for the METHODS context node is elements_methods and is typed as a standard table with the row type element_methods (❶). This, in turn, is standardized with the ZST_03_WD_CLASS_METHOD structure type; in other words, the structure type used for defining the METHODS context node. To be able to address the table type when typing the method interface, you must specify the fully qualified name; that is, `ig_componentcontroller=>elements_methods`. You are now ready to implement the read method.

1. Create the `getctx_methods( )` component controller method.
2. Define the `rt_methods` returning parameter for the method with the `ig_componentcontroller=>elements_methods` type. Figure 3.12 displays the result of typing the interface.

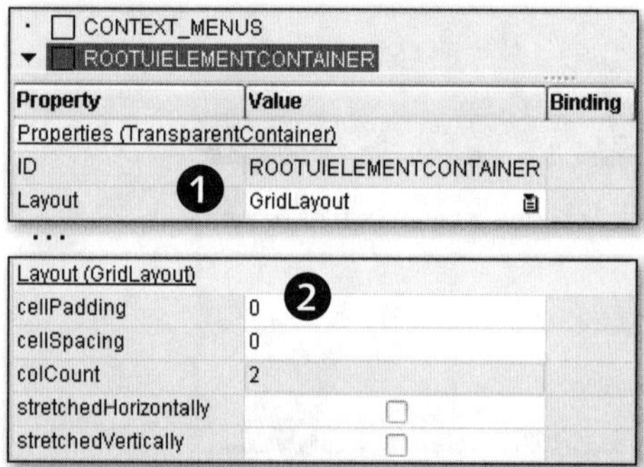

Figure 3.12 Typing the Interface for getctx_methods( )

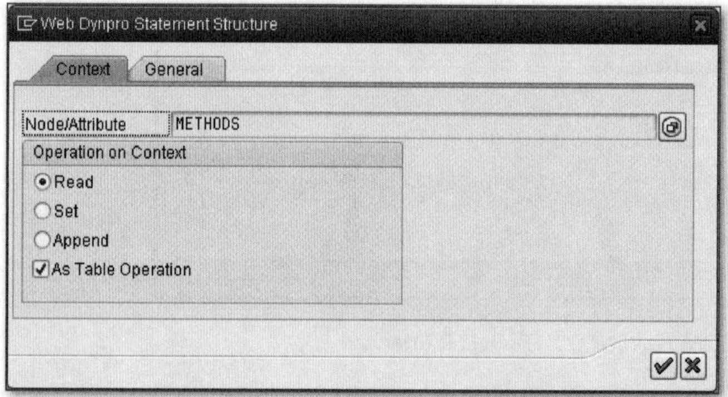

Figure 3.13 Reading the Context with a Table Operation

Web Dynpro Code Wizard and table operations

3. You now need to implement the method again with the support of the Web Dynpro Code Wizard (see Figure 3.13): Open the wizard and choose the `METHODS` context node as the value for the NODE/ATTRIBUTE input field. Select the READ value for the OPERATION ON CONTEXT option and set the checkbox for the AS TABLE OPERATION field.

4. Click on the button with the green checkmark to confirm your entries and to generate the source text (see Listing 3.5).

Generating source text

```
METHOD getctx_methods .
DATA lo_nd_methods TYPE REF TO if_wd_context_node.
* Navigate to <METHODS> node
lo_nd_methods = wd_context->get_child_node(
    name = wd_this->wdctx_methods ).
* Provide element attributes in a table
lo_nd_methods->get_static_attributes_table(
  IMPORTING
    table = rt_methods ).
ENDMETHOD.
```

Listing 3.5 Implementing the getctx_methods( ) Component Controller Method

We have now discussed in detail the options for reading data from the context. But where does the data come from in the context? We have already shown you one way: manually entered by the user. However, you also need to be able to place the data in the context functionally. This will be the topic of the next section.

3.1.3 Creating Context Elements

Creating new context elements

Previously, we only accessed existing elements and only read or changed data from attributes. But how can you create new elements for a node? The `IF_WD_CONTEXT_NODE` interface offers three method alternatives for creating elements:

- `create_element( )`
  This method in combination with `bind_element( )` enables you to create an element, assign it individual values or a structure, and add it to the node collection.
- `bind_structure( )`
  With this method, you can create a new structure-based element compactly in the node collection.
- `bind_table( )`
  This method allows you to use an internal table for creating several elements in the node collection.

All three alternatives enable you to decide whether the new element(s) replace the existing element(s) or are added to the nodes collection. To create a new element for a node, you must first determine the reference to the relevant node. Another look at Section 3.1.1, Changing Attribute Values of an Element, would be useful at this point.

create_element( ) and bind_element( ) Methods

Look at the first option, using the `create_element( )` and `bind_element( )` methods to create a new element and add it to the node collection (see Figure 3.14). First, you must create a new element (❶), and set the element data (❷). Next, you must add the new element to the node collection (❸).

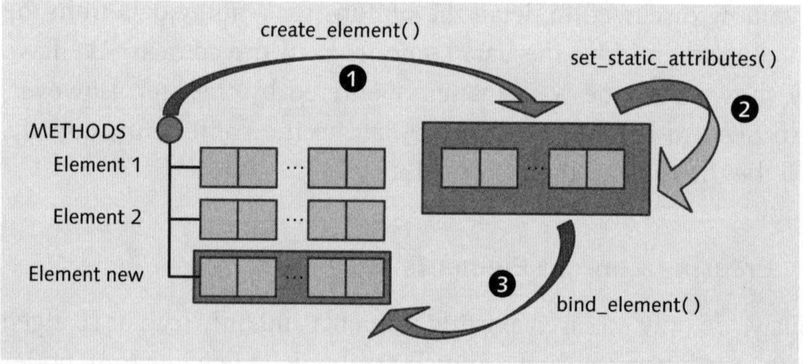

Figure 3.14 Creating a New Element and Adding it to the Node Collection

create_element( )

To create a new element, you must call the `create_element( )` method using the determined node reference. The Web Dynpro Code Wizard does not provide support for this. Instead, use object-oriented statement structures, which you can use as in programming with ABAP objects (see Listing 3.6).

```
** Variant 1 **
* Create element above node
lo_el_method = lo_nd_methods->create_element( ).
* Fill element with structure
lo_el_method->set_static_attributes(
    static_attributes = is_method ).
```

Listing 3.6 Creating the METHODS Node Element and Filling it with the set_static_attributes( ) Method

Setting element values

The `create_element( )` method is called for the node where the new element should be created. As the return value, it returns a reference to an `IF_WD_CONTEXT_ELEMENT` object; in other words, a new element you still have to transfer to be able to set the attribute values. To set the attribute values of the element, you can either use the `set_attribute( )` method, `set_static_attributes( )` method or the `static_attribute_values` parameter of the method.

However, this element is not yet part of the node collection. The next task will be to add the element to the node collection (see Listing 3.7).

```
* Add element to collection
lo_nd_methods->bind_element(
    new_item              = lo_el_method
    set_initial_elements = abap_false ).
```

Listing 3.7 Adding the METHODS Node Element to the Node Collection

bind_element( )

You use the `bind_element( )` method from the `IF_WD_CONTEXT_NODE` interface to add an element. This method contains three parameters:

- `new_item`
  This parameter is used to transfer the element reference.
- `set_initial_elements`
  This parameter is used to determine the insert mode.
  - If you assign the `ABAP_TRUE` value to this parameter, this element replaces all existing elements in the node collection.
  - If you assign the `ABAP_FALSE` value to the parameter, the new element is added to the node collection and the existing elements are retained. Of course, you must look out for the cardinality of the context node.
- `index`
  This parameter is used to indicate an insertion point in the node collection. If an index is not specified, the element is inserted at the end of the node collection.

You have now seen how you can create an element and add it to the node collection. However, the more elongated source code seems a little time-consuming; therefore, we will look at an implementation method that performs the tasks of adding a new element more efficiently.

bind_structure( ) Method

The `bind_structure( )` method from the `IF_WD_CONTEXT_NODE` ABAP interface combines creating a new element with setting attribute values and adding it to the node collection (see Figure 3.15, ❶). In this case, the `bind_structure( )` method provides the same parameters as the `bind_element( )` method.

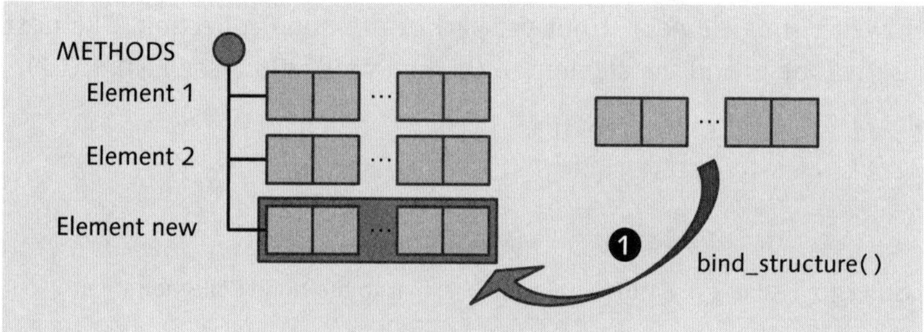

Figure 3.15 Creating a New Element Using bind_structure( )

Listing 3.8 shows that the `bind_structure( )` method is used as an alternative to the previously discussed approach.

```
** Variant 2 **
* Append element to collection
lo_nd_methods->bind_structure(
  new_item = is_methods
  set_initial_elements = abap_false ).
```

Listing 3.8 Creating a New Element Using the bind_structure( ) Method

Description The `bind_structure( )` method creates an individual new element in the node collection. If you now have to create several elements – for example, every row of an internal table should be stored as an element in the context node – you would have to call the `bind_structure( )` method for each element.

bind_table( ) Method

You can, of course, create several elements more compactly using the `bind_table( )` method from the `IF_WD_CONTEXT_NODE` interface (see

Figure 3.16, ❶). First, you will need to fill an internal table with data. Next, you will have to add the internal table data to the node collection as a new element.

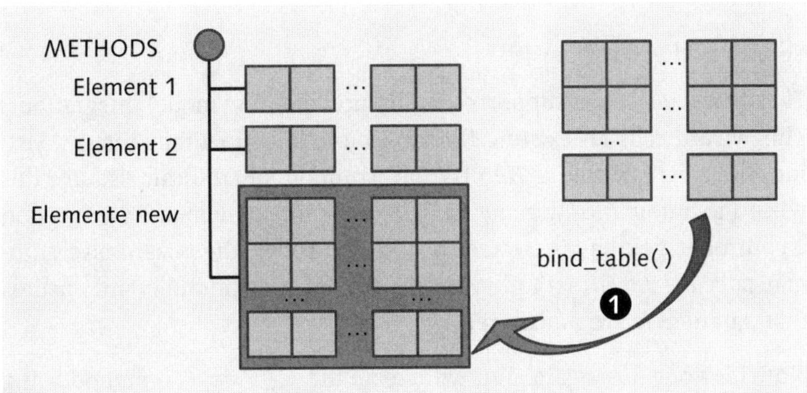

Figure 3.16 Creating Elements Using the bind_table( ) Method

We will develop this example further to illustrate this method. You will use this method to store data for the methods of an ABAP class in the `METHODS` context node. You will create a total of three component controller methods, with different focuses on development:

- `is_class( )`
  This method checks whether the name the user has entered in the selection screen corresponds to the ABAP class name. This method is created using a *service call*.
- `setctx_class_methods( )`
  This method sets the data of the methods for the ABAP class in the `METHODS` context node with the `bind_table( )` method.
- `getmodel_class_description( )`
  This method determines a description object for an ABAP class using *RTTI*, which enables ABAP class descriptions to be determined during runtime. Some of the information included in the description are methods of the ABAP class.

is_class ( ) component controller method)

The first method you will develop is the `is_class( )` component controller method. When implementing this method, which is also an example of *model integration*, you use already existing implementations so that you will have to produce as little of your own source code as possible.

Service Call Wizard

Description

The *service call wizard* supports you in implementing model integrations. This wizard calls an existing function module or methods for an existing ABAP class within a Web Dynpro component. You can also use this wizard to automatically generate all of the context elements you need in a controller you have selected. In this controller, the wizard also automatically creates a method that calls the function module and ensures that parameters are transferred.

[✎] Now it's your turn again. You will create the `is_class( )` method using the service call wizard. Figure 3.17 shows the wizard steps you will go through when creating the service call.

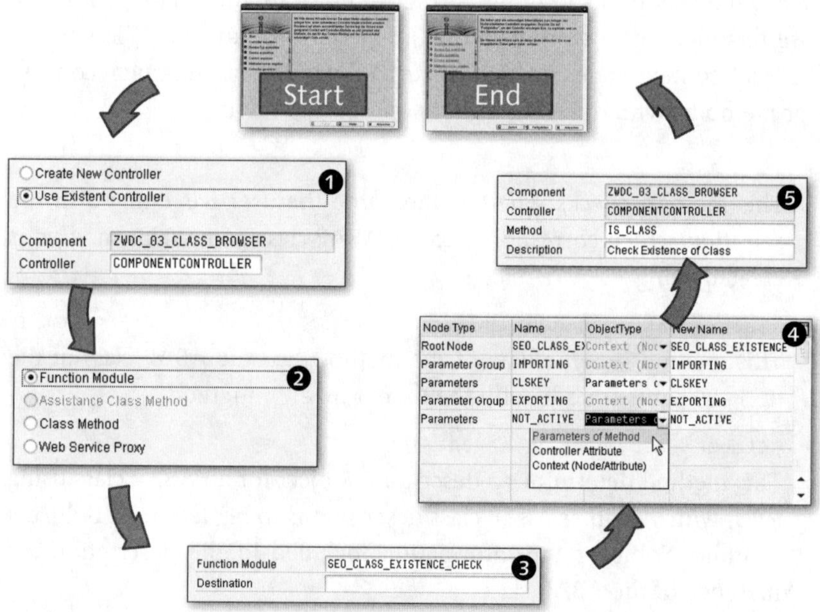

Figure 3.17 Service Call Wizard for Creating the is_class( ) Component Controller Method

1. Start the wizard using the CREATE • SERVICE CALL context menu option of the Web Dynpro component in the object list.
2. When the initial START screen with basic explanations about the wizard displays, click on the CONTINUE button to go to the next screen.
3. In the SELECT CONTROLLER (❶) step, define where the service call is generated. Choose the USE EXISTENT CONTROLLER option and enter the `COMPONENTCONTROLLER` value for CONTROLLER. Click on CONTINUE to go to the next step.
4. The SELECT SERVICE TYPE (❷) step involves defining the reuse component type where the functions are wrapped. The options available are FUNCTION MODULE, CLASS METHOD, and WEB SERVICE PROXY. Choose the FUNCTION MODULE option because the functions you will reuse are implemented in a function module, and click on CONTINUE to move to the next step.

Integrating models using a reuse component

5. In the SELECT SERVICE (❸) step, specify the name of the function module you want to be called in the service. The standard SAP function module for checking whether an ABAP class exists is called `SEO_CLASS_EXISTENCE_CHECK`. Because you do not perform a remote function call (RFC) call for the function module, you are not allowed to maintain the DESTINATION (target system). Click on CONTINUE to go to the next step.
6. In the ADAPT CONTEXT (❹) step, you must define the object type through which you want the interface parameters of the function module to be represented. Three object types are available:

Integrating interfaces

   - PARAMETERS OF METHOD
   - CONTROLLER ATTRIBUTE
   - CONTEXT (NODE/ATTRIBUTE)

   You want to be able to call the `is_class( )` method in such a way that parameters are transferred to the method and results are returned to the caller, again through parameters. To do this, choose the PARAMETERS OF METHOD object type for `clskey` and `not_active` and click on CONTINUE to move to the next step.
7. In the SPECIFY METHOD NAME (❺) step, you assign the name of the component controller method. Enter the name `is_class` in the METHOD input field and click on CONTINUE to go to the last step.

Method name

8. In the last step, GENERATE CONTROLLER, you create the is_class( ) component controller method and SEO_CLASS_EXISTENCE context node. To do this, you must click on the FINISH button.

Manual adjustments

You have now created the is_class( ) component controller method for model integration using the service call wizard. If you use existing reuse components, this wizard can save you a lot of time when creating methods.

To be able to use the method for the example, you still have a few adjustments to make. The changes will mainly affect interface parameters typings, to synchronize them with previously used types. Follow these steps:

1. Delete the SEO_CLASS_EXISTENCE context node. You do not need it because the is_class( ) method communicates through its interface, not through the context.
2. Change the interface for the is_class( ) method.
3. Change the clskey importing parameter type to SEOCLSNAME, which you used in the selection criteria.
4. Change the not_active exporting parameter type to WDY_BOOLEAN.
5. Insert the new ed_exists exporting parameter of the WDY_BOOLEAN type, which lets the caller know whether the ABAP class actually exists.
6. Change the implementation of the is_class( ) method to take into account interface parameter changes. Take a look at Listing 3.9, where the changes to be implemented start with Start manual change and end with End manual change.

```
METHOD is_class .
* declarations for context navigation
* declarations for parameters
* Start manual change
DATA: ls_seoclskey TYPE seoclskey.
* End manual change
* get all involved child nodes
* get input from context
* Start manual change
ls_seoclskey-clsname = clskey.
ed_exists = abap_false.
```

```
* End manual change
* the invocation - errors are always fatal !!!
  CALL FUNCTION 'SEO_CLASS_EXISTENCE_CHECK'
    EXPORTING
      clskey = ls_seoclskey "Manual change
...
* error handling
CASE sy-subrc.
* Start manual change
  WHEN 0. "Class exists!
    ed_exists = abap_true.
* End manual change
    WHEN  1.
```

Listing 3.9 Manual Adjustments in the is_class( ) Method

You have now completed generating and implementing the is_class( ) component controller method. This will be used later to check the data entered by the user. Because of the knowledge you have gained about using the service call wizard, the path is now clear for you to be able to integrate models "cleanly." This means that you separate the display aspects from the model aspects, as required for the model view controller approach (see Section 1.1, Model View Controller).

Additional exercise

As an additional exercise for using the service call wizard, create the new getmodel_class_information( ) service call in the component controller to determine an ABAP class description. Use the SEO_CLASS_READ function module for step (❸) from Figure 3.17. Then, map the provided parameters to PARAMETERS OF METHOD. After you create the getmodel_class_information( ) component controller method, change the class exporting parameter typing to VSEOCLASS and the clskey importing parameter type to SEOCLSNAME. Also delete the redundant SEO_CLASS_READ context node from the component controller context.

Use the is_class( ) component controller method when implementing the method. You will use the getmodel_class_information( ) method in Section 3.3.3, Button, to determine an ABAP class description.

The is_class( ) method you previously implemented checks whether an ABAP class exists. If a class does exist, you should create the method names of the ABAP class as an element in the METHODS context node. This will be the task of the next method you will implement. Here, you will use aspects of RTTI (which you will learn about in more detail in the next section) and the `bind_table( )` method.

1. Create the `setctx_class_methods( )` component controller method and define the `io_classdescr` importing reference parameter of the `CL_ABAP_CLASSDESCR` type (see Figure 3.18).

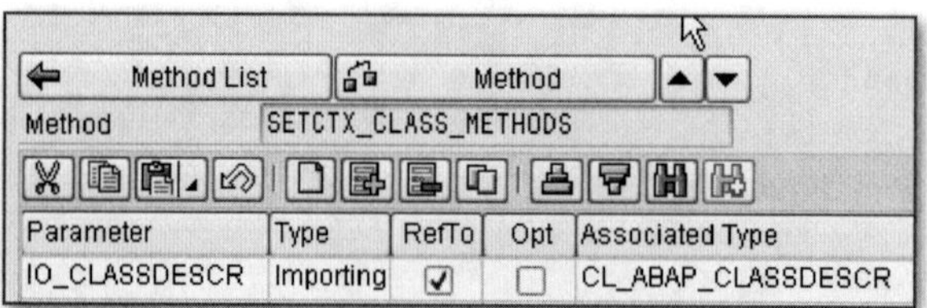

Figure 3.18 setctx_class_methods( ) Method Interface

The `CL_ABAP_CLASSDESCR` ABAP class is part of RTTI and is used as a type for class description objects. The `CL_ABAP_CLASSDESCR` ABAP class has the public `methods` instance attribute, where the method names for the ABAP class are stored in an internal table.

Creating elements

2. Change the method implementation. Read the methods from the `ir_classdescr->methods` internal table row by row and store each method as an element in the `METHODS` context node. How would you implement this requirement? Think about this for a little while before taking a closer look at Listing 3.10.

```
METHOD setctx_class_methods .
* Reference to METHODS node
DATA lo_nd_methods TYPE REF TO if_wd_context_node.
* Internal table to METHODS node
DATA lt_methods TYPE wd_this->elements_methods.
* Structure of a METHODS element
DATA ls_method TYPE wd_this->element_methods.
* A line from model data for methods
FIELD-SYMBOLS: <ls_model_method>
               LIKE LINE OF io_classdescr->methods.
* Determine node reference for METHODS
  lo_nd_methods = wd_context->get_child_node(
    name = wd_this->wdctx_methods ).
* Transform model data into node data
IF io_classdescr IS BOUND.
  LOOP AT io_classdescr->methods ASSIGNING <ls_model_
```

```
method>.
* Transport model data into context structure
    MOVE-CORRESPONDING <ls_model_method> TO ls_method.
* Set icon for method type
    CASE abap_true.
      WHEN ls_method-is_class.
        ls_method-kind_icon = 'ICON_OO_CLASS_METHOD'.
      WHEN ls_method-is_interface.
        ls_method-kind_icon = 'ICON_OO_INTERFACE'.
      WHEN OTHERS.
        ls_method-kind_icon = 'ICON_OO_INST_METHOD'.
    ENDCASE.
* Append to context table
    APPEND ls_method TO lt_methods.
  ENDLOOP.
ENDIF.
* Append table to node
lo_nd_methods->bind_table(
  new_items = lt_methods
  set_initial_elements = abap_true ).
ENDMETHOD.
```

Listing 3.10 Implementing the setctx_class_methods( ) Component Controller Method

Implementation details

The method implementation begins by determining the reference for the METHODS context node. Then, the ir_classdescr->methods internal table is read row by row. The <ls_model_method> field symbol was used to determine references to the entries in the internal table. The MOVE-CORRESPONDING statement moves the model data of the same name to the data structure for the context element. This means a method-local internal table is built that is then transferred to the context node using the bind_table( ) method and then creates all elements there.

> **Note**
>
> Was the task difficult to solve? Experience shows that this is a typical type of task in developing Web Dynpro applications, which is why we presented it to you here. Implementing a method usually begins with reading data from a context. This data is then used as the basis for business logic or display logic. After these logics are processed, the new or changed data is placed back into the context at the end of the method implementation.

Run Time Type Identification

The method you will implement next will introduce you to another key topic of context programming, Run Time Type Identification (RTTI). RTTI provides the mechanisms to determine descriptions of types, including descriptions of ABAP classes, during runtime. This occurs in the form of description objects that are typed with ABAP classes from RTTI. Figure 3.19 shows the inheritance hierarchy of RTTI ABAP classes.

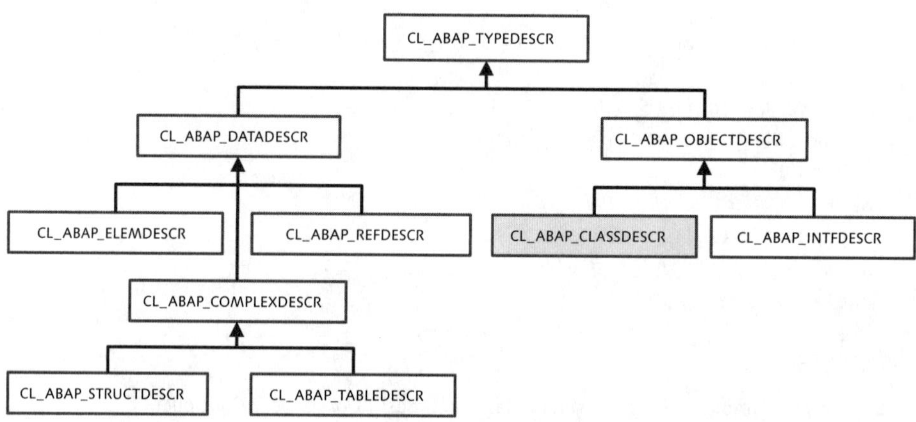

Figure 3.19 Inheritance Hierarchy of RTTI ABAP Classes

CL_ABAP_TYPEDESCR The `CL_ABAP_TYPEDESCR` class is the RTTI root class, and enables descriptions of runtime objects such as ABAP classes to be created during runtime. One of the methods that plays an important role here is `describe_by_name( )`: This method returns the description object to the caller. RTTI is part of *Run Time Type Services (RTTS)*, which also encompasses *Run Time Type Creation (RTTC)*. This, however, is not relevant for our tasks, so we will not discuss it in further detail.

Casting The important thing to know is that the `describe_by_name( )` method always returns a `CL_ABAP_TYPEDESCR`-type object. For the user, this means that a *downcast* must be performed on the corresponding type to be able to access interesting details such as the list of methods for an ABAP class. To do this, a subclass such as the `CL_ABAP_CLASSDESCR` ABAP class highlighted in Figure 3.19 must be used.

We will shortly look more closely at using RTTI within the framework of implementing the getmodel_class_description( ) component controller method. This method determines the description object for an ABAP class based on what the user enters. You must check whether the ABAP class exists and also store the methods from the description object in the context. You will use the two previously implemented is_class( ) and setctx_class_methods( ) methods in the new getmodel_class_description( ) method for this purpose – a great example of reuse.

getmodel_class_description( )

1. Create the getmodel_class_description( ) method in the COMPONENTCONTROLLER. Define two exporting parameters, ed_exists and not_active, for this method, each with the WDY_BOOLEAN type (see Figure 3.20).

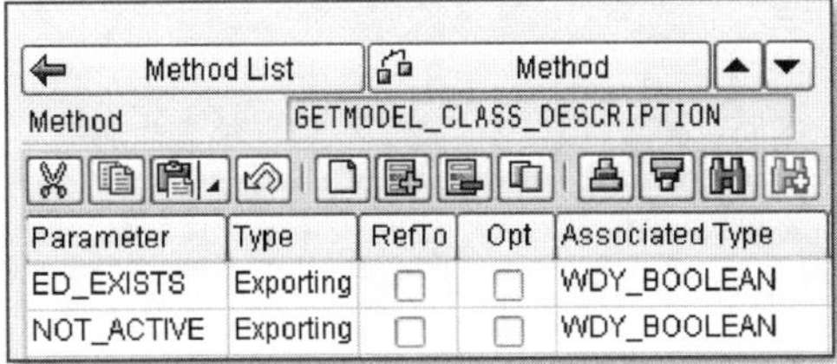

Figure 3.20 getmodel_class_description( ) Method Interface

Implementation

2. Change the method implementation. Try to implement the method step by step. If you need guidance, take a look at Listing 3.11.

```
METHOD getmodel_class_description .
* Exception object
DATA: lo_exception TYPE REF TO cx_root,
* Class description
      lo_classdescr    TYPE REF TO cl_abap_classdescr,
* Type description for class
      lo_typedescr TYPE REF TO cl_abap_typedescr,
* Selection criteria
      lv_rs_value TYPE wd_this->element_class_sel_crit.
* Get class name from context
lv_rs_value = wd_this->getctx_class_sel_crit( ).
* Check if class name is valid
TRY.
  wd_this->is_class(
    EXPORTING
```

```
        clskey = lv_rs_value-name_class
      IMPORTING
        ed_exists = ed_exists
        not_active = not_active ).
  * Determine RTTI description
    CALL METHOD cl_abap_typedescr=>describe_by_name
      EXPORTING
        p_name          = lv_rs_value-name_class
      RECEIVING
        p_descr_ref     = lo_typedescr
      EXCEPTIONS
        type_not_found = 1
        OTHERS          = 2.
  * Class does not exist
    IF sy-subrc <> 0.
      ed_exists = abap_false.
      not_active = abap_true.
    ENDIF.
  * Cast from CL_ABAP_TYPEDESCR to CL_ABAP_CLASSDESCR
    lo_classdescr ?= lo_typedescr.
  CATCH cx_root INTO lo_exception.
  * Class does not exist
    ed_exists = abap_false.
    not_active = abap_true.
  ENDTRY.
  * Store reference in attributes
    wd_this->go_class_description = lo_classdescr.
  * Format data for context
    wd_this->setctx_class_methods(
      io_classdescr = lo_classdescr ).
  ENDMETHOD.
```

Listing 3.11 Implementing the getmodel_class_description( ) Component Controller Method

Description In the first step, the method should read the selection criteria from the context. It does not do this directly, however; instead, it uses the previously implemented `getctx_class_sel_crit( )` method. The `is_class( )` method is then used to see if the search name corresponds to the ABAP class name.

If the search is successful, the static `cl_abap_typedescr=>describe_by_name( )` method is used to determine the class description. After the downcasting has been performed, the description object for the ABAP class is stored in the component controller attributes. You still have to define the public go_class_description attribute of the CL_ABAP_CLASSDESCR type. The setctx_class_methods( ) method is used at the end of this method to put the data in context. This completes the implementations. You can now test them using the Web Dynpro debugger (see Chapter 8, Tips and Tricks from Practical Experience).

We have now explained the options for creating elements in the context. In the next section, we round off the topic of context programming with a discussion of removing context elements.

3.1.4 Removing Context Elements

remove_element( )

The remove_element( ) method for removing elements is available in the IF_WD_CONTEXT_NODE interface (see Figure 3.21).

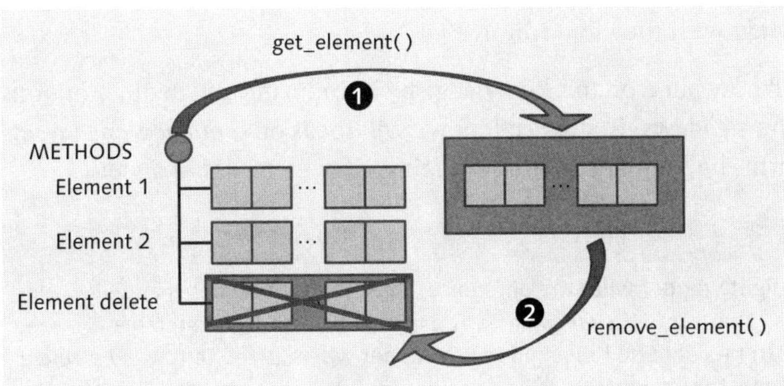

Figure 3.21 Removing an Element Using remove_element( )

You can use the get_element( ) method to determine the element reference to be deleted (❶). The reference to the element to be removed must be transferred to the remove_element( ) method (❷) by the element importing parameter. The has_been_removed parameter is also available as a ABAP_BOOL returning parameter to identify whether the element already existed (ABAP_TRUE) or not (ABAP_FALSE).

This completes our introduction to context programming. In addition to information about removing an element, we introduced RTTI as a key resource in context programming and described examples of how you can use it in practice. The most important method when using RTTI is `cl_abap_typedescr=>describe_by_name( )`.

Service call wizard

The service call wizard is very useful for integrating models. You have seen how existing reuse components are easily reused and can be utilized in the sample application.

The next section will help you understand how to define and program views. Specifically, we will describe layouts and containers, as well as the most important view elements, in detail.

3.2 Layouts and Containers

WYSIWYG editor

In Section 2.2, View, we already discussed the basics of views and windows and you learned that a WYSIWYG editor (*view designer*), with which you already have some experience, is available for designing and creating a view with the view editor.

View elements and UI elements

We will now build on this knowledge by introducing you to other options for defining views. In this section, we will focus on *containers and layouts* that form the foundations for arranging view elements in a view.

The Difference Between View Elements and UI Elements

You might wonder what the difference is between UI elements and view elements. The term *UI element* means an independent user interface element that can be contained in a general container whereas the term *view element* also refers to subelements of composite user interface elements. For example, `TabStrip` is a UI element, but the `Tab` subelement is a view element because it cannot be used independently – it can only be used for structuring a `TabStrip` UI element. We therefore cannot refer to the `Tab` subelement as a UI element.

Containers

Containers and layouts are the tools you can use to define the design for a view in relation to grouping and laying out a UI element. In this context, containers are specialized elements for grouping UI elements. By assigning UI elements hierarchically, you create a parent-child relationship between a container and the assigned UI elements. The most important containers are TransparentContainer with the most well-known representative being ROOTUIELEMENTCONTAINER) and ViewContainerUIElement, which is used for composing views.

Layouts

Layouts are responsible for arranging UI elements in a container. The different layouts available are FlowLayout, RowLayout, MatrixLayout, and GridLayout. The difference in layouts lies mainly in the way elements are arranged, either in *rows* (FlowLayout and RowLayout) or in *columns* (MatrixLayout and GridLayout).

3.2.1 Containers

Hierarchical view structure

The view elements for a view are maintained in a hierarchical view structure. The hierarchy is based on *aggregations* (relationships between objects) such as the parent-child relationship between a UI element container and UI elements, or the relationship between a composite UI element and its subelements (for example: the TabStrip UI element and its Tab subelement).

The higher-level element in this hierarchy is a UI element container that is enhanced for the view or already exists such as ROOTUIELEMENTCONTAINER, for example (see Figure 3.22). ROOTUIELEMENTCONTAINER is a TransparentContainer type (❶) with two children, VC_CLASS_SELECTION and VC_CLASS_METHODS, each of the ViewContainerUIElement type (❷). The preview for the parent-child relationship is shown in the view designer (❸).

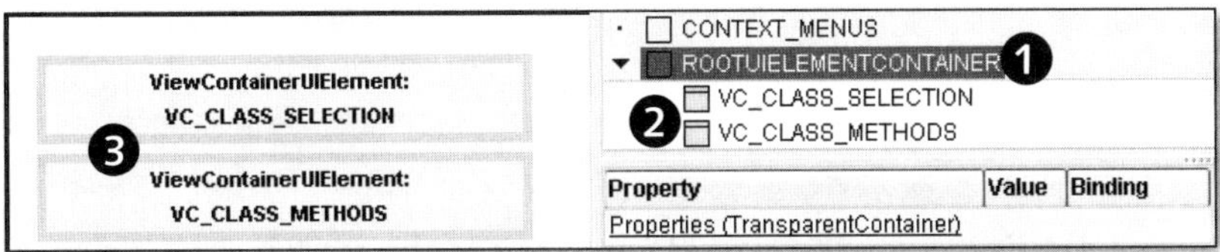

Figure 3.22 ROOTUIELEMENTCONTAINER and ViewContainerUIElement

The parent-child relationship between the UI element container and UI element provides a general mechanism for the hierarchical structure of the view. You can include any number of UI elements and other UI element containers in a UI element container.

There are special UI elements such as the `TabStrip` UI element that can be regarded as containers. However, unlike the UI element container, these elements can only contain special subelements. In the case of the `TabStrip` UI element, this is the `Tab` view element.

Transparent Container

Examples of UI element containers are the `Group`, `TransparentContainer`, and `Tray` UI elements. The most prominent representative of the `TransparentContainer` UI element is `ROOTUIELEMENTCONTAINER`. An important property offered by the `TransparentContainer` UI element is SCROLLINGMODE. This property enables scrollbars to be displayed, which allows the user to scroll to areas that cannot be displayed all at once in the displayable area.

ViewContainer UIElement

Another particularly important UI element for designing the view is the `ViewContainerUIElement` UI element. It is used to display other views, similar to a subscreen area in a classic dynpro, where you can display a subscreen dynpro.

UI element containers are displayed in a rectangular shape or occupy a rectangular area in the view. In the view designer, you may find container elements such as the `TransparentContainer` or `ViewContainerUIElement` UI elements in the UI category layout.

Layout data

You can use the LAYOUT UI element property to define how the lower-level UI elements should be assigned for container UI elements. The following layouts are available for this purpose:

- `FlowLayout`
- `RowLayout`
- `MatrixLayout`
- `GridLayout`

Layout data is assigned to every UI element in the container UI element. This layout data specifies the layout properties of the UI element such as the position in the grid defined by the layout, for example.

Now you know the interrelationships between UI element containers, UI elements, layouts, and layout data. In the following section, we will deepen your knowledge of layouts and specifically discuss how the layout affects the way UI elements are arranged.

3.2.2 Layouts

Layouts

In this section, we will look in detail at the different layouts possible with Web Dynpro ABAP. We will explain the basic layout properties and use examples to illustrate how the layout you choose affects the way UI elements are arranged.

FlowLayout

FlowLayout is the default layout for containers. All UI elements in a container with FlowLayout are displayed in a row. If the area for displaying UI elements is not wide enough, they are displayed in the next row. The wrapping is inserted during runtime.

Layout (FlowLayout)

Figure 3.23 shows the layout properties for ROOTUIELEMENTCONTAINER. The value of the LAYOUT property is set to FlowLayout (❶). The property available for the layout is called WRAPPING (❷). The property instance defines whether the UI elements can be wrapped in the next row. If the value for the property is ABAP_FALSE (depicted by a checkbox not being set), the UI elements will not be wrapped. If the display area is too small, the elements will not be shown in a row, but scrollbars will be added.

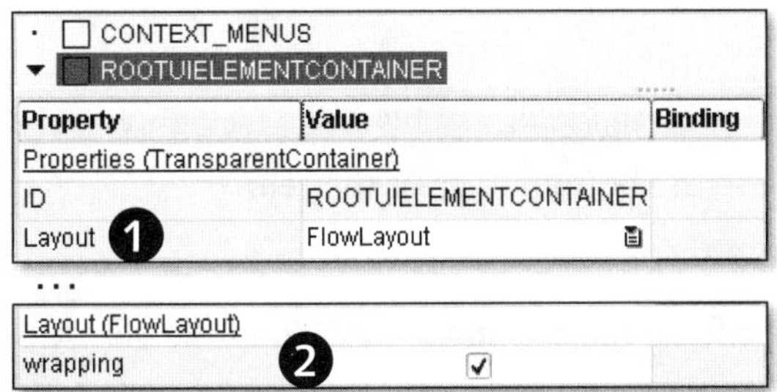

Figure 3.23 FlowLayout with Layout(FlowLayout)

Layout data (FlowData)

Layout data properties for a UI element are set in the properties for the UI element. Figure 3.24 displays the properties for the Label UI element. The layout data properties defined by FlowLayout are CELLDESIGN and VGUTTER (❶). The available properties are based on the layout selected in the higher-level container.

Keeping and arranging spacing

The effects of setting layout data properties may generally be as follows:

- Spacing is kept between the individual UI elements and between the `UI Element` and the grid cell
- The UI elements within the grid are arranged horizontally and vertically
- Setting the width and height of UI elements in the grid cell

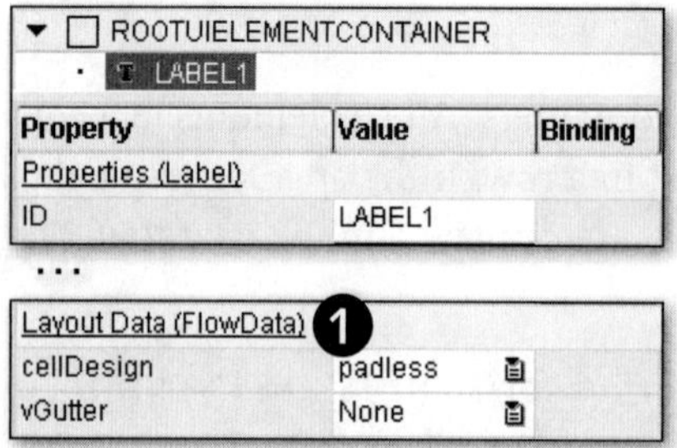

Figure 3.24 Layout Data (FlowData) Properties for a UI Element

cellDesign property

The CELLDESIGN property controls the UI element spacing in a cell to the cell border. Figure 3.25 shows the effects of the `lPad`, `rPad`, `lrPad`, `lrNoPad`, and `padless` instances on the spacing to the cell edge:

- l in a cell stands for the cell content spacing to the left edge of the cell.
- r stands for the spacing to the right edge of the cell.
- b stands for the spacing to the bottom edge of the cell.
- t stands for the spacing to the top edge of the cell.

One of the reasons for specifying the spacing is to prevent the contents of successive cells from getting "joined to one another." We recommend setting the CELLDESIGN property to the `rPad` value.

vGutter property

You can use the VGUTTER property to add more spacing to the left cell edge. You can also determine whether you want a vertical line (*rule*) to be shown for defining the spacing. Figure 3.26 shows the effect of `FlowLayout` and the WRAPPING property instance on the layout of the UI element when the width of the browser window is changed. If the width of the browser window is big enough (❶), all elements are arranged in a row.

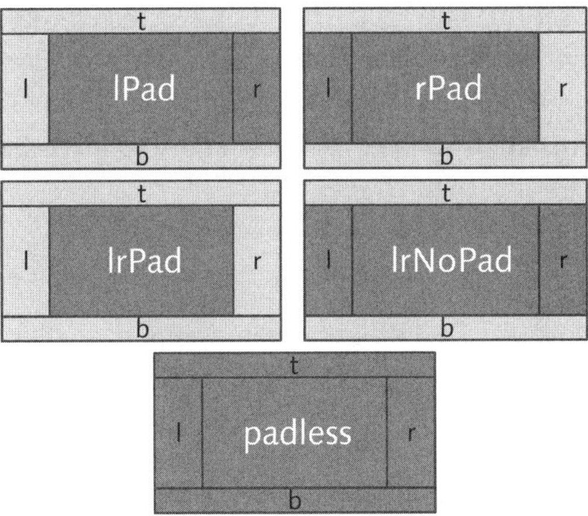

Figure 3.25 cellDesign Property Instances

The value of the WRAPPING property controls the layout of the elements if the user changes the width of the browser window in such a way that there is not enough space available in a row for all UI elements.

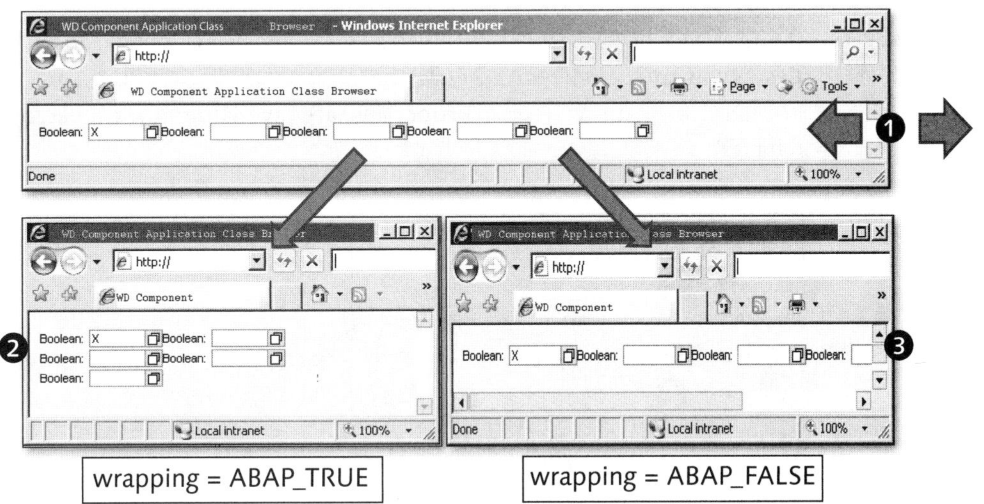

Figure 3.26 Effect of FlowLayout on the Layout of UI Elements

If the WRAPPING property is set to ABAP_TRUE (checkbox is selected) (❷), the elements that do not have enough space in the row are displayed in the next row. If the WRAPPING property is set to ABAP_FALSE (checkbox is not selected) (❸), the elements are displayed in a row and scrollbars are provided to navigate to the undisplayed UI elements.

RowLayout

RowData and RowHeadData

The lower-level UI elements for the RowLayout container inherit the layout data property. This property can have the RowHeadData and RowData values:

- RowHeadData ensures that this element is arranged in a new row in the browser window.
- RowData adds the UI element to the currently valid row.

If the width of the browser window is not sufficient for displaying a UI element, this UI element is moved to the next row. This layout may also be referred to as a *ragged setting* because the UI elements are not aligned in columns, as in the case of MatrixLayout, for example.

Layout data properties

If you assign the RowHeadData value to a UI element for layout data properties, as you can see in Figure 3.27 (❶), the HALIGN, ROWBACKGROUNDDESIGN, ROWDESIGN, and VGUTTER properties are available for the layout data (❷).

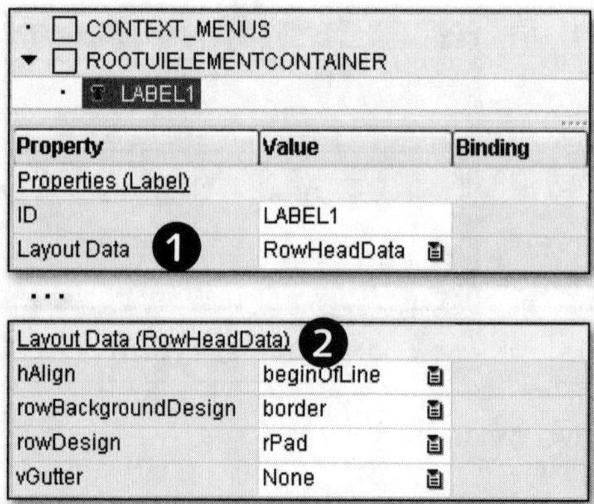

Figure 3.27 Layout Data (RowHeadData) for a UI Element

- HALIGN
  You use the HALIGN property to horizontally arrange UI elements belonging to this row.
- ROWBACKGROUNDDESIGN
  You use ROWBACKGROUNDDESIGN to set the background color for all cells in this row.
- ROWDESIGN
  You use ROWDESIGN to define the spacing of the cell content to the cell border.

Description

Figure 3.28 shows an example of the changed layout for `RowLayout` after the width of the browser window has been changed (❶). Here, the UI elements are arranged in rows: Two UI elements have the layout data property with the `RowHeadData` value and they consequently introduce a new row. Figure 3.28 shows these UI elements with `RowHeadData 1` and `RowHeadData 2`. The value of the ROWBACKGROUNDDESIGN property for the `RowHeadData 1` UI element was set to `border`, which resulted in a background color for the row. The remaining UI elements were set to the `RowData` layout data property. If the width of the browser window is not sufficient, the UI elements are moved to the next row (❷).

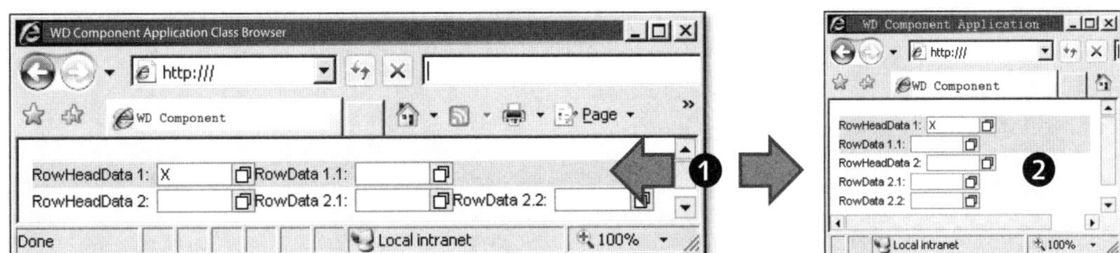

Figure 3.28 Effect of RowLayout on the Layout of UI Elements

MatrixLayout

Layout in tables

`MatrixLayout` arranges the layout of UI elements in tables. The `MatrixLayout` layout can be assigned to a container such as `ROOTUIELEMENTCONTAINER`, as shown in Figure 3.29 (❶), for example. The STRETCHEDHORIZONTALLY and STRETCHEDVERTICALLY properties (❷) are available for `MatrixLayout`.

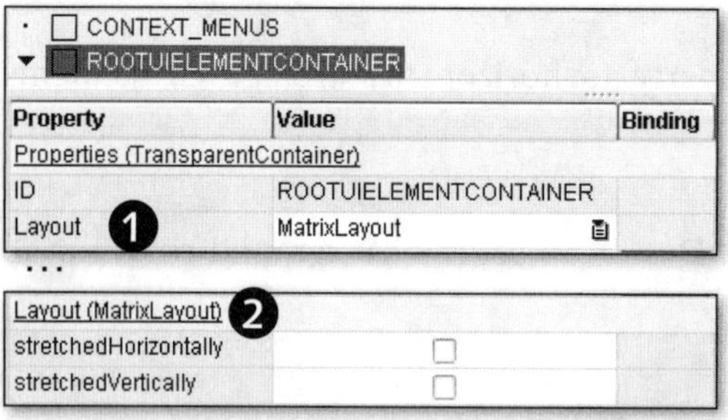

Figure 3.29 MatrixLayout and Its Properties

stretchedHorizontally and stretchedVertically properties

- STRETCHEDHORIZONTALLY
  You use the STRETCHEDHORIZONTALLY property to evenly distribute UI elements horizontally across the width of the container. If the content determines the width of the container, you must deactivate this option.
- STRETCHEDVERTICALLY
  You use STRETCHEDVERTICALLY to evenly distribute UI elements vertically across the height of the container. If the content determines the height of the container, you must deactivate this option.

MatrixData and MatrixHeadData

The lower-level UI elements for the container inherit the layout data property. This property can have the `MatrixHeadData` and `MatrixData` values, as you can see from the example in Figure 3.30.

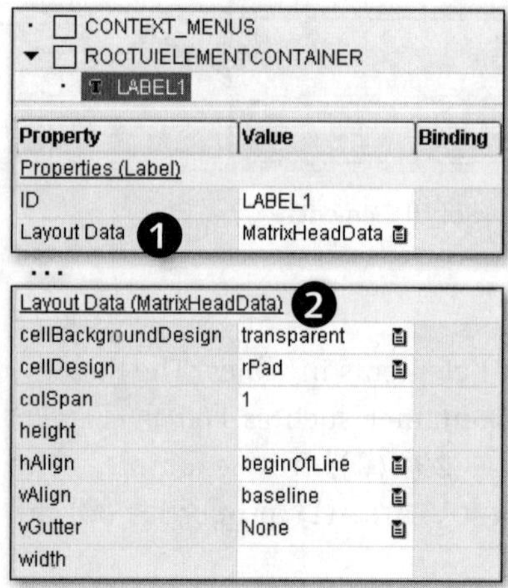

Figure 3.30 Layout Data (MatrixHeadData) for a UI Element

Effects

Setting the MatrixHeadData value in the layout data property causes the row to be wrapped (❶). Like RowData, the effect of the MatrixData value is that the element is placed in the same row as the preceding UI element, but in a new column. If the right-hand border of the displayable area has been reached, the UI element is nevertheless placed.

The number of columns is not defined at the beginning; it instead results from the maximum number of UI elements in a row within the higher-level container. This means that the number of UI elements per row can vary.

The properties for the LAYOUT DATA (❷) enable you to control the cell structure flexibly:

- ROWBACKGROUNDDESIGN
  You use the ROWBACKGROUNDDESIGN property to set the background color for all cells in this row.
- CELLDESIGN
  You use CELLDESIGN to define the spacing of the cell content to the cell border.
- COLSPAN
  You use COLSPAN to define the number of columns a UI element includes in MatrixLayout. You can use this property to position a title across several columns.
- HEIGHT
  You use HEIGHT to define the height of a cell in cascading style sheet (CSS) units of measurement. The units of measurement and corresponding descriptions are listed in Table 3.4.
- HALIGN, VALIGN
  You use HALIGN and VALIGN to define the horizontal and vertical layout of the UI element in the cell.
- VGUTTER
  You use VGUTTER to insert additional spacing for the left-hand cell border, with or without a vertical hyphen.
- WIDTH
  You use WIDTH to define the width of a cell in CSS units of measurement. The units of measurement and corresponding descriptions are listed in Table 3.4.

Unit of Measurement	Type	Description
em	relative	Font size
ex	relative	Height of lowercase letter x in this element (for example, for the width of table columns)
px	absolute	Pixel value. A problem may occur if you change the font size.
%	relative	Percentage value referring to the parent element. Percentage values generally do not work for height values. Percentage values do not work correctly for ScrollContainer and Transparent Container with SCROLLINGMODE not equal to none.

Table 3.4 CSS Units of Measurement

Effects

You can see from Figure 3.31 that the ROWBACKGROUNDDESIGN, WIDTH, and HEIGHT properties are being used.

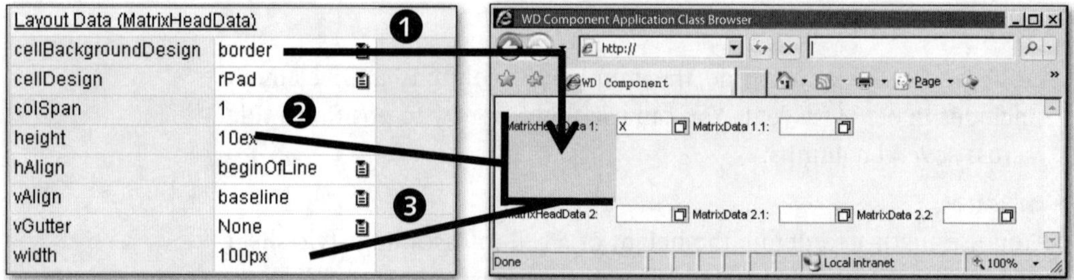

Figure 3.31 Using Layout Data Properties in MatrixLayout and Its Effects

The border value of the ROWBACKGROUNDDESIGN layout data property was used as the background color (❶); therefore, the background is colored gray as a result. The cell height was set to 10EX with the CSS unit of measurement (❷); therefore, the cell height is relative to the height of lower-case letter x of the font in this element. If this font size changes, the cell height will also change. A width of 100PX was specified for the cell width; that is, the WIDTH layout data property (❸). This absolute measurement ensures that the width will not change if the cell content changes.

GridLayout

Layout in tables

GridLayout arranges the layout of UI elements in tables. The GridLayout layout can be assigned to a container such as ROOTUIELEMENTCONTAINER shown in Figure 3.32 (❶), for example.

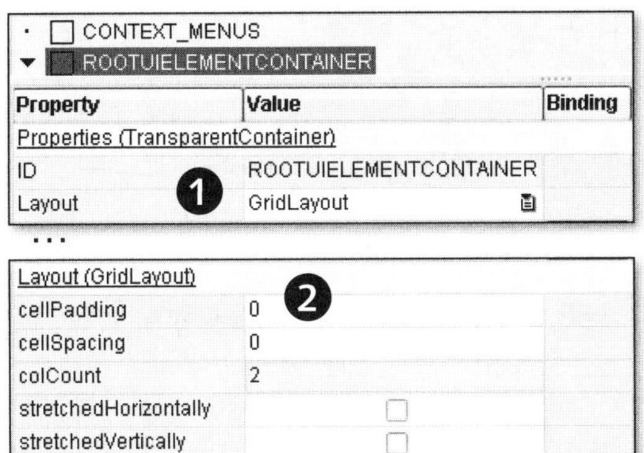

Figure 3.32 GridLayout and Its Properties

GridLayout – properties

Other layout properties you have not yet seen are available for GridLayout (see Figure 3.32, ❷):

- CELLPADDING
  You use the CELLPADDING property to define the cell content spacing for the cell, which is then applied to all GridLayout elements (see Figure 3.33, ❷).
- CELLSPACING
  You use CELLSPACING to define the spacing between cells, which is then applied to all GridLayout cells (see Figure 3.33, ❶).
- COLCOUNT
  You use COLCOUNT to define the number of columns in GridLayout.

No layout data

Unlike other layouts, layout data for UI elements does not exist for elements assigned to the container. This also means that you cannot determine whether an element begins a new row or is displayed in the row.

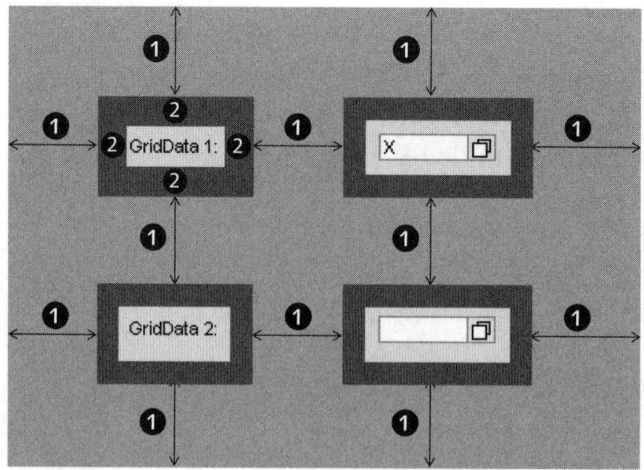

Figure 3.33 Areas of Influence of cellPadding and cellSpacing Layout Data Properties

Defining rows

A new line begins if all of the cells in a row are filled. When you remove an element, the assignment of elements to cells is recalculated. This can cause elements to move. If you want to remove an element, you can replace it with an `InvisibleElement` UI element. Figure 3.34 shows the LAYOUT DATA (GRIDDATA) properties for a UI element (❶).

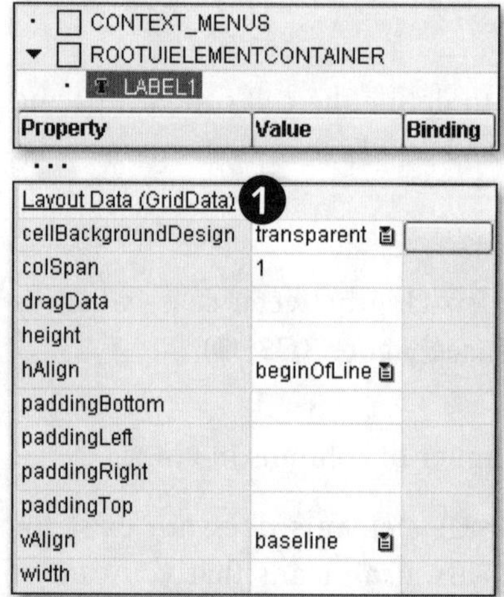

Figure 3.34 Layout Data (GridData) for a UI Element

GridLayout

The (not yet seen by you) properties for the layout data include:

- PADDINGBOTTOM
  You use PADDINGBOTTOM to define the spacing of the cell content to the bottom edge of the cell in CSS units of measurement.
- PADDINGLEFT
  You use PADDINGLEFT to define the spacing of the cell content to the left edge of the cell in CSS units of measurement.
- PADDINGRIGHT
  You use PADDINGRIGHT to control the spacing of the cell content to the right edge of the cell in CSS units of measurement.
- PADDINGTOP
  You use PADDINGTOP to control the spacing of the cell content to the top edge of the cell in CSS units of measurement.

cellPadding and cellSpacing

In Figure 3.35, you can see that the CELLPADDING, CELLSPACING, und COLCOUNT layout data properties are being used. The spacing between the cells has a value of 20 in the CELLPADDING layout property (❶). This setting ensures that a border of 20 pixels is defined around every UI element displayed. The CELLSPACING layout property has a value of 50 (❷) and ensures that there is spacing between all cells. The COLCOUNT property has a value of 2 (❸), which means the elements will be arranged in two columns.

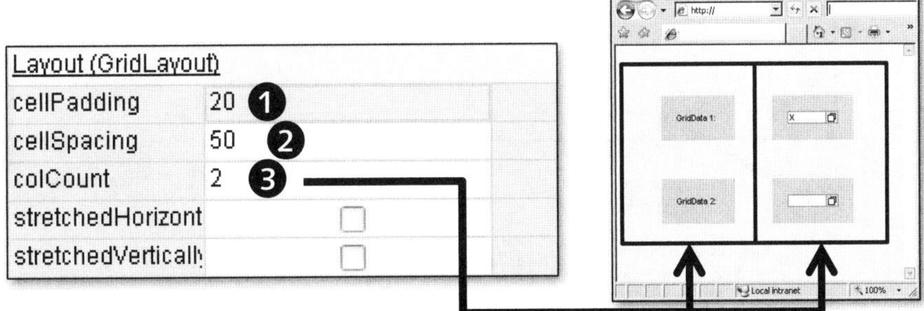

Figure 3.35 Using Layout Properties in GridLayout and Its Effects

3.2.3 Example

V_MAIN_LAYOUT view

It is now time to put what you have learned about the ZWDC_CLASS_BROWSER Web Dynpro component into practice. You will design the V_MAIN_LAYOUT view you created earlier, which will enable you to embed another two views (selection and result). The challenge for you is to arrange these two views in one column and above each other.

This means you will need two ViewContainerUIElement UI elements to let you a) display a *selection view* and b) show the selection result in the form of a *result view*.

1. Switch to the LAYOUT tab of the V_MAIN_LAYOUT view.
2. Assign GridLayout to ROOTUIELEMENTCONTAINER and set the value of the COLCOUNT property to 1 to arrange the subsequent elements all in one column. Assign a value of 5 each for the CELLSPACING and CELLPADDING properties to define spacing of five pixels between the cells and from the UI element to the cell border.
3. Enter VC_CLASS_SELECTION for the ViewContainerUIElement UI element in the selection area (see Figure 3.36, ❶). You can set the CELLBACKGROUNDDESIGN LAYOUT DATA (GRIDDATA) property to border to separate the cells visually.

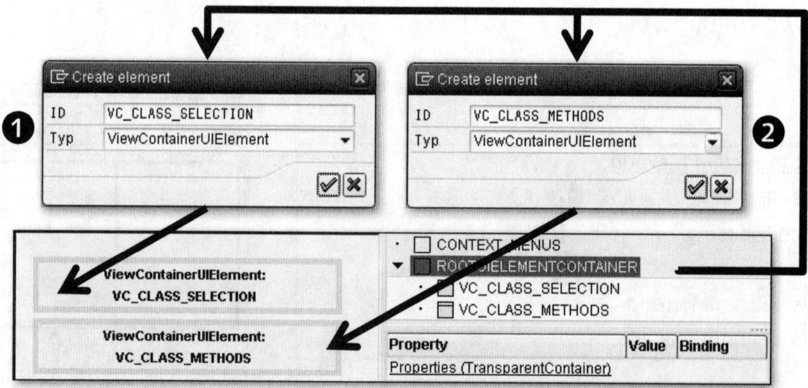

Figure 3.36 Designing the V_MAIN_LAYOUT View

4. In the result area, enter VC_CLASS_METHODS for the ViewContainerUIElement UI element (see Figure 3.36, ❷). After you define

1 as the number of columns, the view container will be placed in a new row.

You have now defined the layout view for this Web Dynpro application and can move on to the next section, where we will cover using view elements. We will introduce and discuss properties and usage options of certain basic view elements.

3.3 Using Important View Elements

So far, we have only discussed designing views from the perspective of arranging areas using containers, for example. Now, we will bring these areas to life to enable the user to input/output data or interact in these areas. Web Dynpro provides an abundance of options for this, which we will now look at in more detail.

Categories

The UI elements provided for designing the UI layout are divided into *categories* and are displayed in the left area of the view editor (see Chapter 2, Web Dynpro Architecture):

- The FAVORITES tab is used to store user-specific view elements.
- The TEXT category contains elements related primarily to texts such as `InputField` or `Label`.
- The ACTION category contains groups of elements that have a range of different actions such as `Button`, for example.
- The elements that provide different selection options such as `CheckBox` or `DropDownByKey` are summarized in the SELECTION category.
- The COMPLEX category contains view elements such as `Table` that are complex due to their structure or content.
- The LAYOUT category contains a collection of elements such as `TransparentContainer`, `ViewContainerUIElement`, `TabStrip`, `Group`, or `Tray`, used to form the layout.
- The GRAPHIC category contains view elements that provide presentation graphics and maps such as `Image`, for example.
- The INTEGRATION category contains view elements that integrate different techniques – such as `InteractiveForm`, `OfficeControl`, and `FileUpload` – into Web Dynpro.

ROOTUIELEMENT CONTAINER

ROOTUIELEMENTCONTAINER is the root node for designing the UI layout. It is a TransparentContainer type. All other UI elements are located at levels below the root node.

Positioning view elements

You can insert UI elements into a container element from UI element categories by using drag-and-drop, or from the hierarchical display by using the INSERT ELEMENT context menu option. The properties for controlling appearance and behavior are available for the UI elements. You can change the display sequence for a UI element using the context menu and UP, and DOWN functions.

Events and data binding

If the user interacts with the layout and triggers a *HTTP roundtrip*, the new or changed data is placed back into the context nodes and attributes. The event handling processing then starts. This means that the event handler operates with the current data. This is similar to the Process After Input (PAI; see Chapter 1, Introduction) event period in classic dynpro programming, where the data from the dynpro is transported into the relevant target structures (communication structures) at the beginning of the PAI processing.

By binding data to correspondingly typed attributes, you can manipulate bound properties. The Web Dynpro runtime makes the relevant types available.

Tip

To conclude this introduction and review, we would like to refer you to an important Web Dynpro application that will help you understand the behavior of view elements. As of SAP NetWeaver 7.0, the WDR_TEST_UI_ELEMENTS Web Dynpro application is available for testing different view elements. You can use this application to manipulate properties of view elements in a user-friendly interface and display the results of changes.

We will now discuss selected view elements as they relate to their area of use and the properties made available.

3.3.1 TextView

Usage and properties

You use the TextView UI element to display texts in a view.

- DESIGN
  You use the DESIGN property to determine the design of the UI element.
- HALIGN
  You use HALIGN to align the content of the UI element horizontally.
- TEXT, TEXTDIRECTION
  TEXT, a *primary property*, inherits the text to be displayed. You use the TEXTDIRECTION property to define the text direction.
- WRAPPING
  You use WRAPPING to control whether the text should be wrapped if it is too wide for the display area.

Tip: UI Element Documentation

Because only the properties for view elements that are used for getting started with Web Dynpro ABAP are discussed here, we recommend that you browse through the UI element documentation. You can easily do so by calling a view element in the view hierarchy from the DISPLAY UI ELEMENT DOCUMENT context menu option. The relevant documentation for the view element is subsequently displayed.

Example

To familiarize you with using the TextView UI element, we will continue with the class browser example (ZWDC_03_CLASS_BROWSER) and display the text for the DESCR_CLASS context attribute from the CLASS_SEL_CRIT context node in a view. You must create the new view and call it V_CLASS_SELECTION. This view will be used as the selection screen in the Web Dynpro application, similar to a *selection screen* in classic ABAP report programming. After you have created the view and expanded the TextView UI element in the view, you will embed the V_CLASS_SELECTION view in the V_MAIN_LAYOUT view and be able to test the Web Dynpro application.

[✎] We will now explain this procedure step by step:

1. Create the V_CLASS_SELECTION view and give it a description (see Section 2.2, View).
2. Map the context of the CLASS_SEL_CRIT context node for the component controller to the local view controller context (see Section 2.4, Context). This will make the context node available with its context attributes for data binding in the view.
3. Select the LAYOUT tab. Use the MatrixLayout to arrange the selection screen in columns. Assign the MatrixLayout value to ROOTUIELEMENTCONTAINER in the LAYOUT property.

TextView UI element

4. Now, create a TextView UI element to display the content of the DESCR_CLASS attribute in the view:
   - ID: TV_DESCR_CLASS
   - TYPE: TextView
5. The layout data property of the TextView UI element was already assigned the MatrixHeadData value and ensures that a new row begins in the display. The TEXT property is still highlighted in red, which means that a *mandatory entry* has not yet been made.

   Display the data from the context. Click on the button in the CREATE BINDING column, next to the input field for the TEXT property, to open the DEFINE CONTEXT BINDING dialog box. There, select the DESCR_CLASS attribute from the CLASS_SEL_CRIT context node for the data binding, and click on the button with the green checkmark to confirm your entry.

Embedding views

6. For the moment, you have completed designing the view. You now have to embed the view in the W_MAIN window to be able to display it. To do so, switch to the window and select the WINDOW tab (see Figure 3.37).
7. Open the W_MAIN node and then V_MAIN_LAYOUT. Assign the V_CLASS_SELECTION (❷) view using the EMBED VIEW (❶) context menu path in the VC_CLASS_SELECTION view container. This results in changing the structure in the window display (❸).

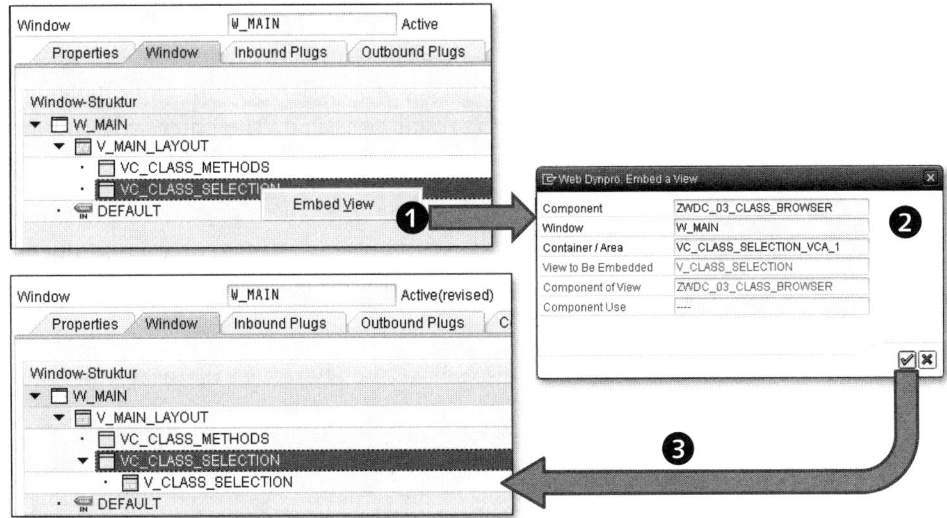

Figure 3.37 Embedding a View in a View Container

8. After activating all changed and new elements, you can test the Web Dynpro application (see Figure 3.38). An ABAP class description will now be displayed for the user.

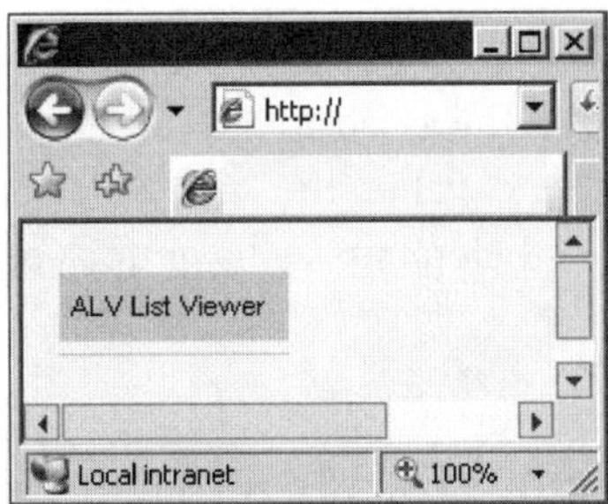

Figure 3.38 TextView UI Element in Action

3.3.2 InputField and Label

Usage and properties

The `InputField` UI element enables the user to edit or display a single row text (input field). An `InputField` can be used to edit all *scalar data (simple type)*. The internal display automatically converts to a visual display and vice versa.

If an error occurs during the conversion, the value is not reset in the context, but is instead kept in the data container. The next time the data is displayed, the input field will have a red border, with the missing value displayed, and an error message will be issued. The entry will only be checked if an HTTP roundtrip has been triggered.

- LENGTH, WIDTH
  You use the LENGTH property to specify the character length of the UI element. The WIDTH property overrides this property.
- PASSWORDFIELD
  You use PASSWORDFIELD to replace the characters the user enters on the screen with asterisks (*).
- READONLY
  You use READONLY to influence the editability of the UI element.
- VALUE
  You use VALUE, a primary property, to display a character string in the UI element. This property must be bound to a context attribute.

Usage and properties

You use the `Label` UI element to label other UI elements – including the `InputField` UI element. This way it is always associated with another UI element. If the assigned UI element in the STATE property has set the `required` value, a red star is displayed next to the `Label` text. This results in a mandatory entry field appearing. If the associated UI element in the ENABLED property has set the `ABAP_FALSE` value, the `Label` is also marked as being inactive. Properties of the UI element we have not yet introduced include:

- LABELFOR
  The LABELFOR property is a mandatory entry field and is used to specify the associated UI element.
- TEXT
  TEXT is an optional property you can use to define the display text for labeling. If the `Label` UI element is associated with another UI element, you use the following procedure to determine the `Label` texts (see Figure 3.39):

Determining text

  - A check is carried out to see whether there is a directly entered text for a `Label` UI element.

- If so, the search for the text is terminated.
- If not, the associated UI element is determined using the value of the LABELFOR property.

Depending on the UI element type, it has a primary property (for example, the VALUE property for the InputField UI element). The data for the primary property is bound to a context node attribute that uses a data element from the ABAP Dictionary for typing. The short text for this data element is found under the field labels and the search is consequently terminated.

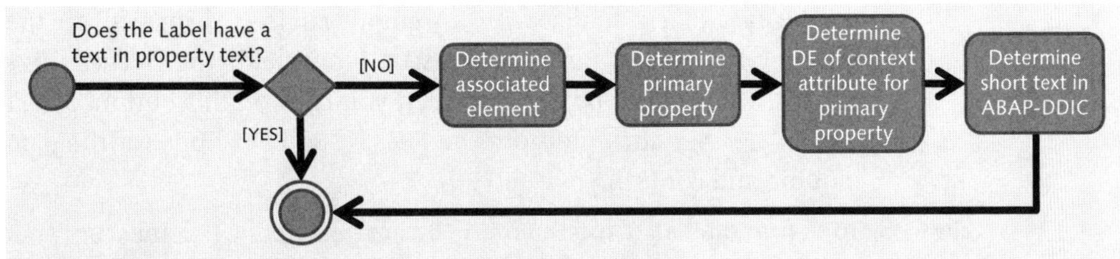

Figure 3.39 Determining Text for a Label

After this overview, let us now take a look at using UI elements in practice. We will continue with our example.

Example

Now, your task is to provide an input field for the NAME_CLASS context attribute of the CLASS_SEL_CRIT context node in the V_CLASS_SELECTION view. You also have to define a Label UI element for InputField so that InputField is labeled and the user can identify which data should be entered in this field. Again, you will proceed step by step to carry out the task: [✎]

1. Create an InputField UI element in the V_CLASS_SELECTION view:
   - ID: IF_NAME_CLASS
   - TYPE: InputField
2. You must change the position of InputField in such a way that it appears in the first position in the row. Use the context menu of the IF_NAME_CLASS UI element in the view hierarchy to move the UI ele- **Positioning**

ment in the hierarchy up using the UP menu option. This will change the display position of the InputField UI element and it will be displayed in the first position (MatrixHeadData).

3. The TV_DESCR_CLASS UI element also appears in the first position, but in the second row. All selection information should be positioned in a row; therefore, change the value of the layout data property for the TV_DESCR_CLASS UI element to MatrixData. This will ensure that TextView is displayed on the right, next to InputField.
4. The VALUE property of the InputField UI element IF_NAME_CLASS is not yet bound to a context attribute. You can tell that this is the case by the fact that a folder with an empty circle is displayed on the button on the right, next to the VALUE input field. The DEFINE CONTEXT BINDING dialog box opens when you click on this button. Select the NAME_CLASS attribute from the CLASS_SEL_CRIT node for the data binding and confirm your entry.

Label

5. To define the Label for InputField, create a new UI element:
   - ID: L_NAME_CLASS
   - TYPE: Label

   Move the Label UI element to the first position in the UI element hierarchy. Adjust the values of the layout data of all UI elements in such a way that all UI elements appear in one row.
6. You still have to associate Label with InputField. To do this, use the dropdown menu of the LABELFOR property and choose the IF_NAME_CLASS entry. This means the field labels of the data element for InputField will be used as the label text. You have now completed designing the view.
7. After you activate all changed and new elements, you can test the Web Dynpro application. The result should correspond to what is displayed in Figure 3.40. L_NAME_CLASS of the Label UI element is in the first position in the UI hierarchy (❶). This means that this element will be displayed as the first element in the view. It is followed by the InputField UI element, IF_NAME_CLASS (❷). Following that is the description, the last of the UI elements (❸) in the row.

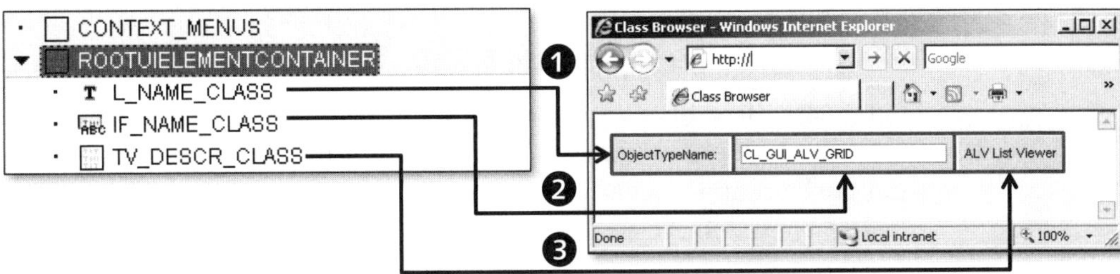

Figure 3.40 Displaying Label, InputField, and TextView UI Elements

After the user has entered the names of the ABAP class to be found, the details for this ABAP class must also be found. The user therefore needs to be able to trigger an HTTP roundtrip and start the search process through the Web Dynpro application. In the following section, we will discuss the option of the `Button` UI element.

Triggering a HTTP roundtrip

3.3.3 Button

Usage and properties

All elements used for actions on the interface are summarized in the ACTION UI element category. One example from this group is the `Button` UI element, which represents a button in the view. By clicking on the button, the user can trigger an action that is then processed by an action handler.

Some of the (not yet discussed) properties included in the `Button` UI element are as follows:

- TOOLTIP
  TOOLTIP lets you display additional text for a MouseOver event.
- IMAGESOURCE
  IMAGESOURCE allows you to define the symbolic name of the image you want to display from the *Multipurpose Internet Mail Extensions (MIME) Repository*, for example. You can also use Transaction ICON to find out the name of an icon.

onAction

You also have to define an event called ONACTION for the `Button` UI element. An action can be assigned to this event; when the user triggers the event, the action creates a coupling to an action handler. This is similar to the event and event handler mechanism in ABAP objects programming.

Example

So far, users of the sample application can view the proposed data (which originates from the default value of the NAME_CLASS context attribute and initialization of the wddoinit( ) method of the component controller) in the selection screen for the Web Dynpro application. They can also enter a new ABAP class name. However, they cannot yet start the search process through a triggered HTTP roundtrip. Likewise, they cannot yet adapt the ABAP class description to a newly entered ABAP class name.

Your job now is to implement these requirements:

Button

1. In the V_CLASS_SELECTION view, create a Button UI element, which you will position after the IF_NAME_CLASS input field:
   - ID: BTN_CLASS_SEARCH
   - TYPE: Button

imageSource

2. The Button UI element is used only to get an icon as its label, preferably a magnifying glass icon. To do this, use the dropdown menu in the IMAGESOURCE property (see Figure 3.41, ❶), which you access using the input help in the input field for the property. A dialog box will open. On the ICON tab, scroll to the icon called TbDetail (❷). Click on this icon to select it. The symbolic name of the icon, ~Icon/TbDetail, is then added to the input field for the ICONSOURCE property (❸).

Action

3. You will find the onAction event in the properties for the Button UI element in the EVENTS section. You can use it to assign an action to this event, and this action will then call an action handler that will implement the search for the ABAP class. Use the button to create the SEARCH_METHODS action.

Action handler method

4. Switch to the source text of the onactionsearch_methods( ) action handler and implement the check to see whether the name entered by the user corresponds to an ABAP class name. To do this, use the is_class( ) method from the component controller. The easiest way to do this is by using the Web Dynpro Code Wizard.

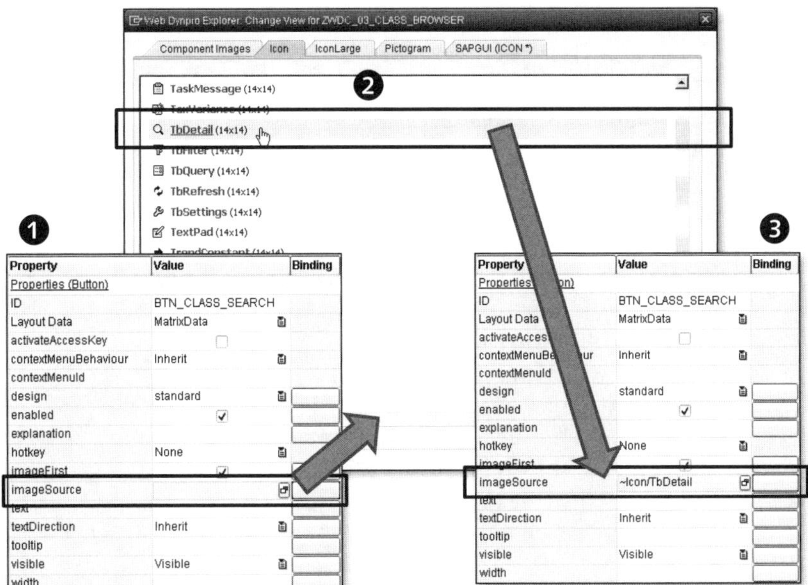

Figure 3.41 Inserting the Symbolic Icon Name

5. Next, determine the description for the ABAP class. To do this, use the `getmodel_class_information( )` component controller method you created in the additional exercise in Section 3.1.3, Creating Context Elements. For illustration purposes, Listing 3.12 shows the complete implementation.

```
METHOD onactionsearch_methods .
* Selection data from context
DATA: lv_rs_value TYPE zst_03_wd_class_sel_crit,
* Existence of class
      ld_exists TYPE abap_bool,
* Meta informations for class
      ls_class TYPE vseoclass.
* Determine selection criteria
lv_rs_value =
wd_comp_controller->getctx_class_sel_crit( ).
* Check if search string is a class name
TRY.
    wd_comp_controller->is_class(
      EXPORTING
        clskey = lv_rs_value-name_class
```

```
          IMPORTING
            ed_exists = ld_exists ).
* If class does exist
      IF ld_exists = abap_true.
* Determine class description
          wd_comp_controller->getmodel_class_information(
                 EXPORTING
                   clskey = lv_rs_value-name_class
                   modif_language = sy-langu
                   version = seoc_version_active
                 IMPORTING
                   class = ls_class ).
* Set description
          lv_rs_value-descr__class = ls_class-descript.
      ELSE. "ld_exists = abap_false
* Handling, info text for users
      lv_rs_value-descr__class = 'Class does not exist'.
      ENDIF.
* Fired by IS_CLASS, class does not exist
CATCH cx_wd_no_handler.
* Handling, info text for users
  lv_rs_value-descr__class = 'Class does not exist'.
ENDTRY.
* Set values back into description
wd_comp_controller->setctx_class_sel_crit(
  is_value = lv_rs_value ).
ENDMETHOD.
```

Listing 3.12 Implementing the onactionsearch_methods( ) Method

Reuse The action handler method is a good example of reusing created methods in controllers. Your goal should always be to define methods in such a way that you can reuse them as often as possible.

With the `onactionsearch_methods( )` method, you have implemented a complex action handler as seen in real Web Dynpro applications. Figure 3.42 shows the current status of the selection screen.

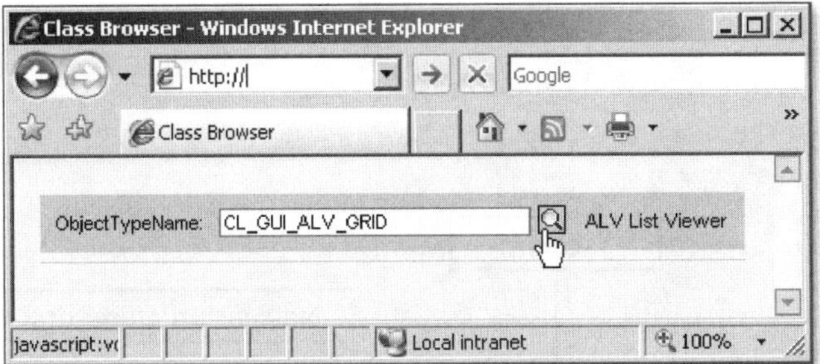

Figure 3.42 Complete Selection Screen

Accessibility of a Web Dynpro Application

We would like to point out that you may get the following message when checking the method:

ACC: Tooltip is not set for element BTN_CLASS_SEARCH.

To make a business application also accessible to users with disabilities who rely on different types of technical support, the Web Dynpro framework enables you to set up accessible applications.

An important prerequisite for *accessibility* is that there is a *tooltip* for every UI element; this is because tooltips can be analyzed using screen reading programs and made accessible to visually-impaired users. You must always maintain the TOOLTIP property for a UI element if:

- The UI element has no title
- A `Label` is not assigned to the UI element
- Elements with a TEXT property have not set or bound this property (for example, a `Button` has no text)

Almost all UI elements also provide the ACCESSIBILITYDESCRIPTION property. You can use this property to add a substitute title if the UI element must not or cannot have a visible title. Behind a label, for example, you can place several input fields to which you cannot assign visible ACCESSIBILITYDESCRIPTION values.

Accessibility checks are performed by default as part of the syntax checks during the design phase. Each component also contains an ACCESSIBILITY CHECKS ACTIVE indicator. If you deactivate this indicator, no accessibility checks from the development environment will be carried out for the corresponding component and their views during the design phase.

3.3.4 TabStrip

Usage

The `TabStrip` UI element enables you to display a `TabStrip` with `Tab` elements, as you can see in Figure 3.43.

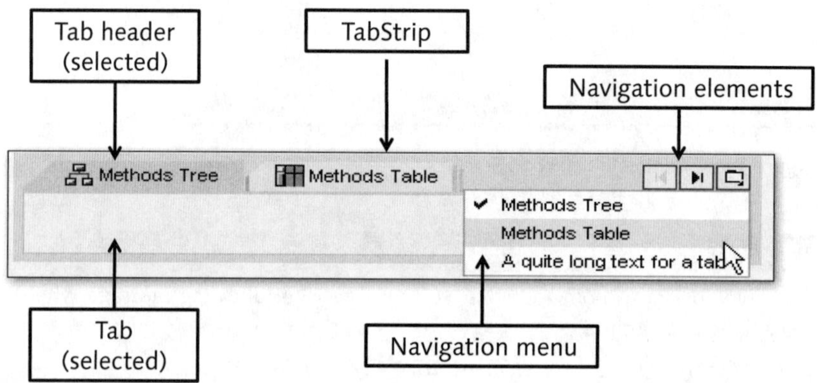

Figure 3.43 TabStrip UI Element with Two View Elements

TabStrip

Users can switch between several tabs by selecting a certain *tab*. If the space in the layout for displaying defined tabs is not sufficient, *navigation elements* are provided in the upper right area of the `TabStrip` UI element that allow you to display the next or the previous tab. You can navigate to a specific tab using the *navigation menu*. The tabs available are listed in this navigation menu and the checkbox for the selected tab is checked. When you choose an entry, the selected tab is displayed and set.

The `Tab` view element is an individual tab within a `TabStrip` UI element. The tab consists of a *tab header*, *tab page (content area)*, and, optionally, a *toolbar*.

Display

To display the content of all tabs, the same window area is used and therefore shared with the other tabs. The user can select the tab to display its content. You design a tab by assigning a UI element to it.

The instances for the properties of the `TabStrip` UI element have different effects. There are no UI element properties that force data to be bound to the context, as you can see in Figure 3.44.

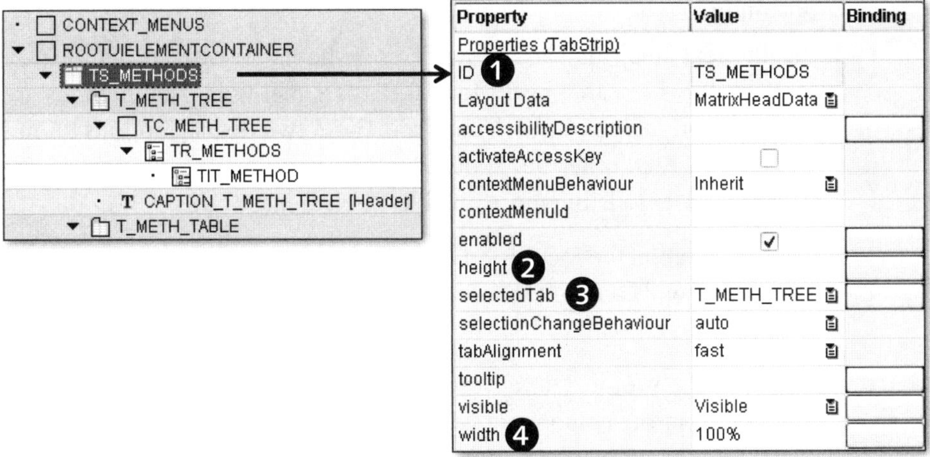

Figure 3.44 Properties for the TabStrip UI Element

TabStrip properties

You assign the `TabStrip` ID (❶) in the usual manner when you create the UI element, or you can change it later. The HEIGHT property (❷) defines the height in CSS value units. If you have not evaluated the SELECTEDTAB property (❸) in the `TabStrip` UI element or if `Tab` specified in SELECTEDTAB in the VISIBLE property has the `ABAP_FALSE` value, the first visible `Tab` is displayed instead when you display `TabStrip` for the first time. To choose the selected tab, you must have already created tabs for `TabStrip`. The WIDTH property (❹) defines the `TabStrip` width in CSS value units. You can, of course, also bind the HEIGHT, SELECTEDTAB, and WIDTH properties to the context, which will be a manipulation option you can use during runtime.

Tab properties

`Tab` view elements are defined for a `TabStrip` and can only be displayed in combination with this tabstrip – this is why it is a view element. A `Tab` has a `caption` view element with a TEXT property for the title and an IMAGESOURCE property for an image. A `tab` can have a `toolbar` that you can set using the INSERT TOOLBAR menu option from the context menu on the tab. The `tab` view element can also have a subelement to display the tab content. This subelement could be a `TransparentContainer` UI element, where you can place any number of other UI elements.

Example

In the next step, the class browser user should be offered two display options for the search result for ABAP class methods. The methods are displayed in *table* or *hierarchical* form. These two display options do not depend on each other but should be displayed in the same area in the layout. `TabStrip` is the most suitable UI element for this.

In this example, the focus is on defining `TabStrip` and `Tab` elements, for which you will carry out the steps that follow. We will discuss designing contents later.

1. Create the `V_CLASS_METHODS` view and map the context of the `METHODS` node from the component controller.

Inbound plug

2. Define the `FROM_CLASS_SELECTION` inbound plug in this view. This plug will take over the handling of the navigation transition from the `V_CLASS_SELECTION` selection view.

Outbound plug

3. Switch to the `V_CLASS_SELECTION` view and define the `TO_CLASS_METHODS` outbound plug. This plug will be needed to trigger the navigation transition to the `V_CLASS_METHODS` results view.
4. Switch to the `W_MAIN` window and embed the `V_CLASS_METHODS` view in `ViewContainerUIElement` – `VC_CLASS_METHODS`.
5. Define the navigation transition from the `TO_CLASS_METHODS` outbound plug to the `FROM_CLASS_SELECTION` inbound plug by using drag-and-drop (see Figure 3.45).

Triggering navigation

6. To trigger the navigation, switch to the `V_CLASS_SELECTION` view and switch from there to the `onactionsearch_methods( )` method that will handle the button action. Trigger the navigation transition using the Web Dynpro Code Wizard (see Listing 3.13).

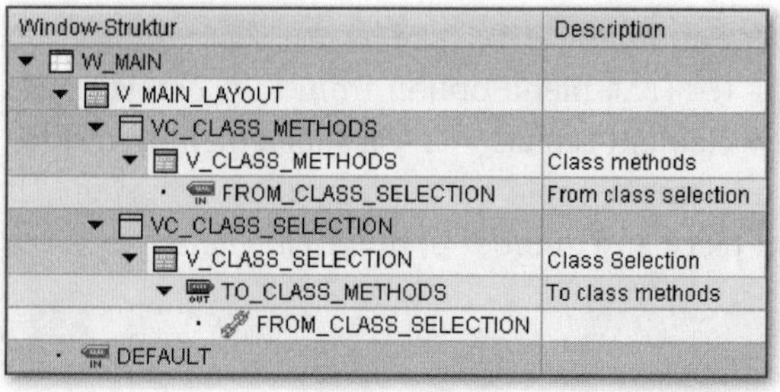

Window-Struktur	Description
W_MAIN	
V_MAIN_LAYOUT	
VC_CLASS_METHODS	
V_CLASS_METHODS	Class methods
FROM_CLASS_SELECTION	From class selection
VC_CLASS_SELECTION	
V_CLASS_SELECTION	Class Selection
TO_CLASS_METHODS	To class methods
FROM_CLASS_SELECTION	
DEFAULT	

Figure 3.45 Window Structure with Navigation Transition

```
* Set values back into description
wd_comp_controller->setctx_class_sel_crit(
  is_value = lv_rs_value ).
* If class exists navigate to result
  wd_this->fire_to_class_methods_plg( ).
```

Listing 3.13 Triggering Navigation Transition from V_CLASS_SELECTION View to V_CLASS_METHODS View

Determining an ABAP class description

7. You determine the ABAP class methods in the `handlefrom_class_selection( )` handler method in the `V_CLASS_METHODS` view. To do this, switch to the handler method. Then, use the Web Dynpro Code Wizard to implement the call for the `getmodel_class_description( )` component controller method (see Section 3.1.3, Creating Context Elements). The result should correspond to the one shown in Listing 3.14.

```
METHOD handlefrom_class_selection .
DATA: ld_exists TYPE abap_bool, "Does class exist?
      ld_not_active TYPE abap_bool. "Active?
* Determine description object for class, store in
* attributes of component controller and integrate
* methods in context.
  wd_comp_controller->getmodel_class_description(
    IMPORTING
      ed_exists = ld_exists
      not_active = ld_not_active ).
ENDMETHOD.
```

Listing 3.14 Handling an ABAP Class Search

Creating a TabStrip

8. Switch to the `V_CLASS_METHODS` view layout. The user should now be offered two views for the methods – one hierarchical, the other tabular. This is visualized using a TabStrip with two tab elements. Assign MatrixLayout for the ROOTUIELEMENTCONTAINER layout and set the stretchedHorizontally property to ABAP_TRUE.
9. Create the TabStrip UI element:
   - ID: `TS_METHODS`
   - TYPE: `TabStrip`
   - WIDTH property: `100%`

Creating a tab

10. Create two tab elements for TabStrip. To do this, use the INSERT TAB menu option from the TabStrip context menu:
    - ID: T_METH_TREE
      The Caption UI element for T_METH_TREE gets the Method Tree value in the TEXT property and ICON_TREE in the IMAGESOURCE property.
    - ID: T_METH_TABLE
      The Caption UI element for T_METH_TABLE gets the Method Table value in the TEXT property and ICON_LIST in the IMAGESOURCE property.
11. In T_METHODS for the TabStrip UI element, set the SELECTEDTAB property to T_METH_TREE to map this tab as the first tab when you display this element for the first time.

You have now created the new V_CLASS_METHODS view and designed a TabStrip with two Tab elements for it, defined the navigation transition from the V_CLASS_SELECTION view, and implemented the handling of the navigation. You have also ensured that methods are determined for an ABAP class if the user triggers the search process using the button. Figure 3.46 shows the V_CLASS_METHODS view designed in this way.

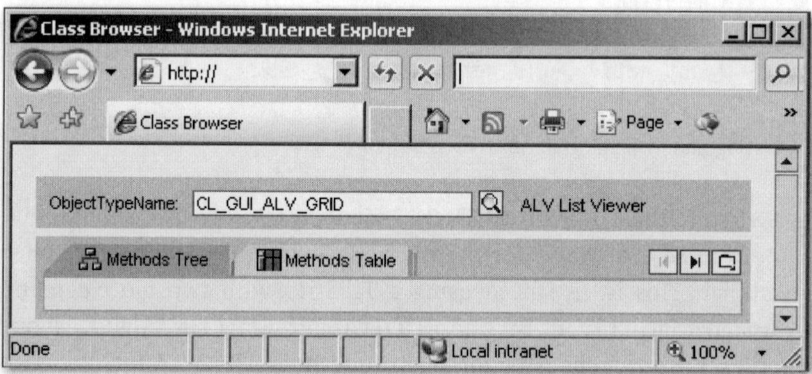

Figure 3.46 TabStrip UI Element of Display for Method Search Results

3.3.5 Tree

Usage

You can use the `Tree` UI element to display hierarchies defined in the context; the hierarchy to be displayed is defined in the context first. Two options are available to describe this context structure:

- At the design phase, you can define a specific number of levels using *non-recursive nodes*.

  An example of *non-recursive nodes* is a context node for methods for an ABAP class with a subnode for parameters of the method. The number of subnodes for the methods is defined and known.

- At the design phase, the number of levels with *recursive nodes* is not yet known.

  An example of a *recursive node* is a context node for ABAP classes with a subnode for inherited ABAP classes. At development time, you do not yet know how deep an inheritance hierarchy can reach because an inherited class can have inherited classes. A subnode therefore repeats the node structure of a supernode – this means this is a recursion.

Recursion

Recursion, a technique in mathematics, logic, and computer science (from the Latin "recurrere" for "run back"), refers to a function that is defined by itself. This means that a function is called that performs a certain task at the given level and is then called again for each of its sublevels, provided sublevels exist.

The relevant sublevel is processed in this new call and the procedure is, in turn, called again for every one of the sublevels found at that (sub)level. This part of the processing ends if no further sublevels are encountered at a level.

Non-Recursive Nodes

Lead selection

The `Tree` UI element is used for displaying hierarchical structures and navigating. You cannot use it to select entries such as the `ItemListBox` UI element; you can only use it for working with the lead selection. Note that although visually this looks like a selection, performance-wise it is a very intensive operation. Therefore, in most scenarios it would be more of a hindrance to use the `Tree` UI element.

Two-tier tree `Tree` nodes and `Tree` leaves belonging to the lead selection are displayed highlighted in the `Tree`, as you can see in Figure 3.47:

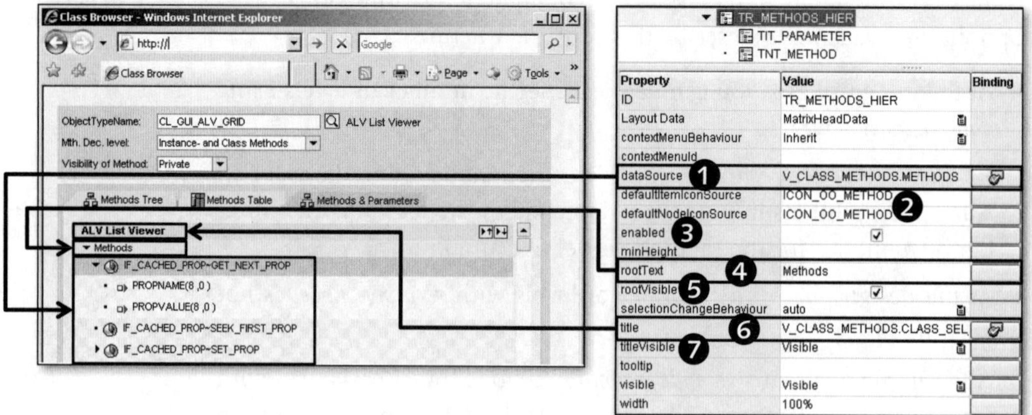

Figure 3.47 Two-Tier Tree

- DATASOURCE
  You can bind the `Tree` UI element to each context node; that is, the uppermost context node you want to be displayed in the tree. The DATASOURCE property is available for this purpose (❶).
- TREENODETYPE and TREEITEMTYPE
  You can display subnodes of this context node as nodes in the tree using the `TreeNodeType` view element. You can display context node subelements as leaves using the `TreeItemType` view element.
- DEFAULTITEMICONSOURCE and DEFAULTNODEICONSOURCE
  You use the DEFAULTITEMICONSOURCE and DEFAULTNODEICONSOURCE properties (❷) to define icons for leaves and nodes that should be used for general display purposes. These default settings can still be overridden subsequently in nodes and leaves.
- ENABLED, ROOTVISIBLE, ROOTTEXT
  You use the ENABLED property (❸) to specify whether the user can interact with the tree, nodes, and leaves. The `Tree` UI element can display a root node if the `ABAP_TRUE` value is set for the ROOTVISIBLE property (❺). If the root is displayed, you can use the ROOTTEXT property (❹) to define the text for the root node.

- TITLE and TITLEVISIBLE
  You can use the TITLE property (❻) to define a title for the `Tree`. Use the TITLEVISIBLE property (❼) to define the visibility of the title and the button for collapsing nodes. As always, you can change the properties during runtime using corresponding data binding.

TreeNodeType view element

After the usage of the `Tree` UI element has been defined and customized, the subelements for `Tree` are created. Subelements have nodes and leaves, which we will now explain in more detail. Figure 3.48 shows a node definition. In this case, the `TreeNodeType` view element is used:

- DATASOURCE
  Selecting a context node as a data source defines which context attributes can be displayed as text or as a tooltip. For this purpose, the DATASOURCE property of the `TreeNodeType` view element (❶) is bound to the corresponding context node.
- EXPANDED
  The EXPANDED property (❷) defines whether the node shown in the `Tree` is displayed open (expanded) or closed (collapsed). If the property is bound to the context, the bound attribute is evaluated for each context element. From an implementation point of view, this means that you can control whether a node is opened at the node level. This property interacts with the HASCHILDREN property (❸).
- HASCHILDREN
  If `ABAP_TRUE` is set for HASCHILDREN, a triangle indicates to the user that this node can be expanded or collapsed and that there is more data under this node at the next hierarchy level. The HASCHILDREN property is only used at runtime for the `TreeNodeType` view element to determine whether children exist. If `ABAP_FALSE` is set for the HASCHILDREN property, the nodes are displayed as leaves.
- ICONSOURCE
  You use the ICONSOURCE property (❹) to influence the way the node is displayed. In addition to the TEXT property (❺), an icon is displayed to the left of the text that – depending on the node – can be omitted individually using data binding. If the ICONSOURCE property is not evaluated, the DEFAULTNODEICONSOURCE property from the `Tree` UI element is used for evaluation purposes.

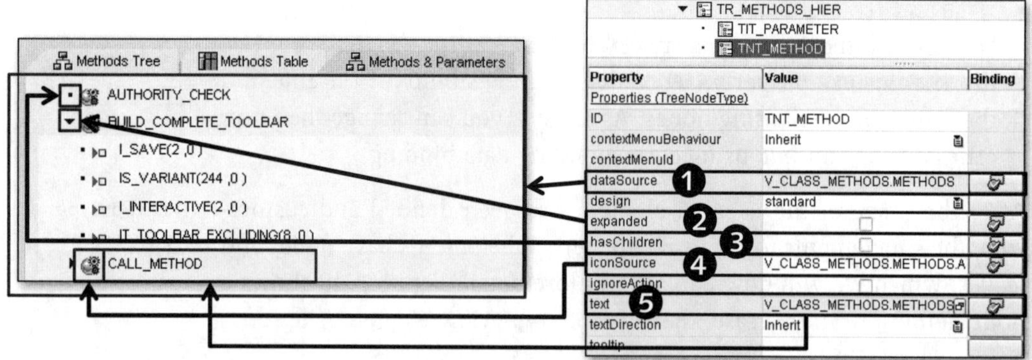

Figure 3.48 TreeNodeType View Element for a Tree

TreeItemType Not only nodes are available for designing the hierarchy in the tree; leaves are as well. They are defined using the `TreeItemType` view element, as you can see in Figure 3.49:

- DATASOURCE
  Like the `TreeNodeType` view element, the DATASOURCE property (❶) defines the data source at context node level and the context attributes that can be used for data binding.
- ICONSOURCE and TEXT
  The ICONSOURCE (❷) and TEXT (❸) properties behave as they do with the `TreeNodeType` view element.

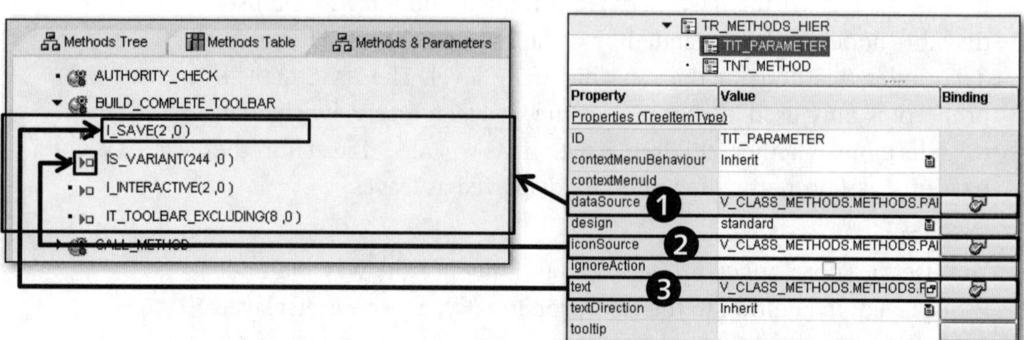

Figure 3.49 TreeItemType View Element for a Tree

TreeItemType elements can never have children and are therefore always displayed as leaves. They are used when it has already been determined at the design phase that the corresponding node does not have any children; in other words, the context node does not have any subnodes.

Caution

The context hierarchy is *not* reflected in the layout design view. All nodes and leaves for the Tree are displayed directly under the Tree in the layout hierarchy, *without* taking into account hierarchy levels.

Context and Tree

None of the hierarchy levels defined in the context can be omitted when the Tree UI element is displayed. All nodes not directly below the context root node must be non-singleton nodes because all elements in a tree should be displayed regardless of the lead selection. Although you can set the SINGLETON property for a context node at development time, this causes a runtime error at execution time.

Singleton

You can apply the SINGLETON property of a context node to use context data memory efficiently. This property controls how often a context node instance is available during runtime. If the SINGLETON property is set to ABAP_TRUE (checked checkbox), only one instance exists for the affected node during runtime.

Context nodes arranged directly below the context root node are always singleton nodes. Subnodes of any context nodes can be customized as singleton or non-singleton nodes.

If subnodes are customized as non-singleton nodes, a subnode instance is created for every supernode element. This means that a buffer is reserved for the subnode and for *each* supernode element. That is the bad news. The good news is that the context data for the subnode elements can be determined, stored, and used later in any way.

If the subnode is customized as a singleton node, *exactly one* subnode instance is created for all supernode elements. The good news is that there is exactly one subnode instance for all elements of the supernode. The bad news is that when the supernode element changes (this is the lead selection), you must determine the data for the subnode elements again. (You will no doubt still remember the supply function you can use specifically for this purpose.)

You can also bind the Tree in such a way that the DATASOURCE for the Tree element binds to a structured 1..1 context node and the element nodes for the Tree element appears below the context node. This is necessary for mapping directory structures, for example. With recursive Tree elements, you can display the recursion against this 1..1 node. As a result, this context node will be skipped during rendering.

onExpandAll

The Tree UI element provides the ONEXPANDALL event, to which you can assign an action. This means that in addition to the COLLAPSE button, the EXPAND button is also displayed in the tree title bar. You can implement the expansion behavior in the event handler for the action. The EXPANDED property for the TreeNodeType view element must be bound to a context attribute for this implementation.

onAction

The TreeNodeType and TreeItemType view elements contain the ONACTION event. If an action is assigned to this event and the user clicks on an entry, an HTTP roundtrip is triggered and the assigned action handler is called. Figure 3.50 shows the contents of the wdevent parameter in the action handler.

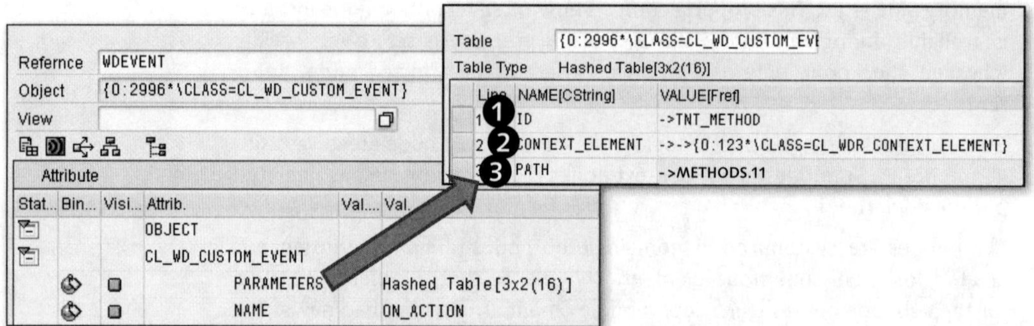

Figure 3.50 Contents of wdevent Parameter During Action Handling

wdevent

You can obtain information for the ONACTION event from the internal parameters table available in the wdevent object. The name of the Tree element to be triggered is stored in the first entry, id (❶), in the parameters table. The reference to the context element belonging to the selected Tree element is stored in the second entry, context_element (❷). The third piece of information provided with path (❸) is the context node name and context element index.

Hook methods

In addition to the action handler being processed, the wddobeforeaction( ) and wddoafteraction( ) hook methods are executed. If the IGNOREACTION property for TreeNodeType and TreeItemType is set to ABAP_TRUE, the action assigned to the ONACTION property is not executed, just like the wddobeforeaction( ) and wddoafteraction( ) hook methods are not executed. However, an HTTP roundtrip can be triggered by clicking on an entry in the tree because the lead selection is set for the integrated context node.

Dynamic loading

You can load node and leave data in the Tree into the context in advance. This was the approach previously taken. It can cause a heavy load on the server and client if a large amount of data has to be stored in memory. An alternative approach involves loading only data for a specific request by the user, for example, by opening a node. We can also refer to data loading in this context as *dynamic loading*.

The ONLOADCHILDREN event is defined for the TreeNodeType UI element in this case. If you assigned an action to the event, an HTTP roundtrip is triggered, the action handler is executed, and the wddobeforeaction( ) and wddoafteraction( ) hook methods are processed. When you close the node, the handling is not executed.

Like with the ONACTION event, the same information from the wdevent parameter can be accessed in the action handler; that is, id, context_element and path. The dependent information is then determined for context_element in the action handler implementation. This can sometimes be time-consuming; therefore, it would be a good idea to use a context attribute to record whether the data was already determined in a previous step. The dynamic data loading approach is particularly interesting for defining and using recursive nodes.

Recursive Nodes

Unknown hierarchy levels

A tree structure may consist of a recursive repetition of nodes for which the hierarchy levels are not known in advance. This means that specific levels can only be defined during runtime, not at development time.

To be able to define a tree with recursive nodes, you need to create a suitable context definition and then define the Tree UI element with its subelements. Figure 3.51 shows the context structure definition based on a simple example of determining superclasses for an ABAP class:

Defining a context structure

- The first step involves creating the nodes in the context that should be repeated; for example, an ABAP class node (❶). You can set up a context structure containing any number of nesting levels; in other words, nodes with subnodes.

Recursion nodes

- In the next step, you create a recursive context node for the context node or nodes that can be repeated. You do this using the RECURSION NODE (❷) menu option from the context menu of the node that can be repeated.
- In the CREATE RECURSION NODE window that opens next, enter a name for the recursion node – in this case SUPERCLASS – and click on the SELECT button to create a reference to the repeating node; you want to repeat the CLASS node. After you confirm your entries, the recursion node appears in the context hierarchy (❸), where its icon differs from the "normal" context nodes.

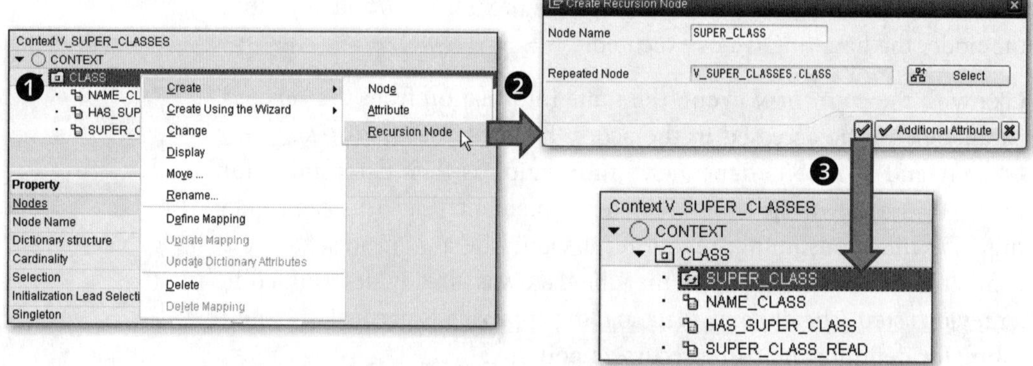

Figure 3.51 Context Definition for a Tree with a Recursive Node

After you have defined the context structure, you can create the `Tree` UI element. Figure 3.52 shows the tree definition with subelements, the data binding to the context, and the result:

dataSource

- The DATASOURCE property (❶) is used to define the context node to be repeated as the data source for the `Tree` UI element and `TreeNodeType` view element. This means that node attributes and subnodes from the context are available for UI element properties.

- You can use the HASCHILDREN property of the `TreeNodeType` UI element to display whether the node is displayed as a leaf or node. You have defined the value for this property using data binding (❷). You will see how to determine or assign this value at runtime. The node text is also defined by data binding to an attribute for the repetition node (❸). The relevant definitions and bindings have now been performed. **TreeNodeType**
- Data is stored in the context at runtime – depending on which node the user opens. The ONLOADCHILDREN (❹) event is available for mapping the reaction to a node being opened. **onLoadChildren**

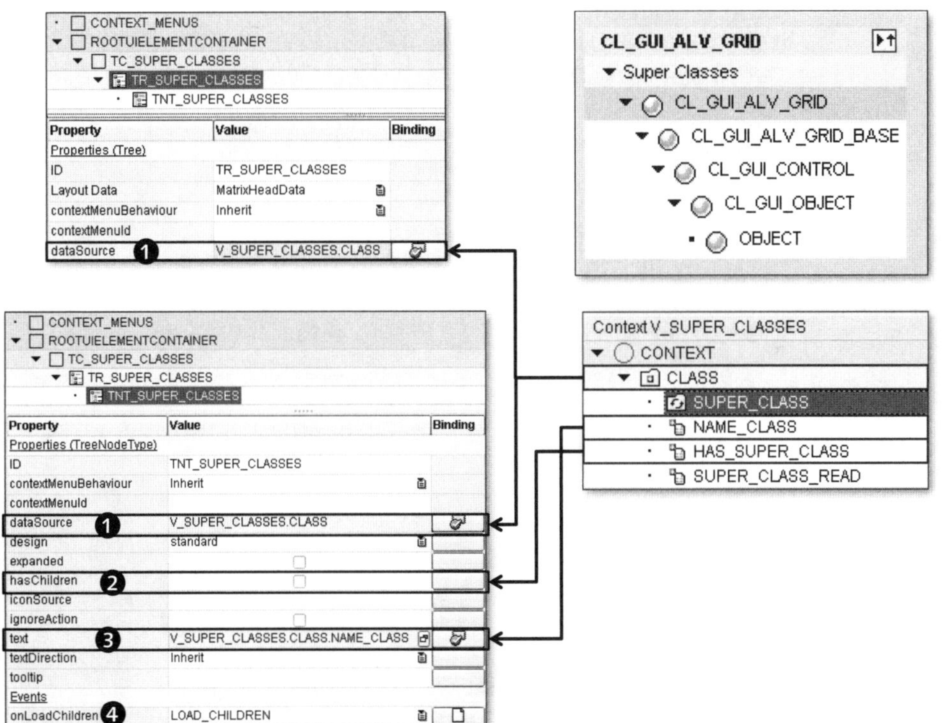

Figure 3.52 Tree UI Element with Recursive Context Node

Listing 3.15 shows the implementation of action handling for the ONLOADCHILDREN event.

```
METHOD onactionload_children .
* Name of superclass for current class
DATA: ld_name_superclass TYPE string,
* RTTI class description
      lo_classdescr TYPE REF TO cl_abap_classdescr,
* Node reference to superclass
      lo_nd_superclass TYPE REF TO if_wd_context_node,
* Data structure for class element
      ls_class TYPE wd_this->element_class,
* Data structure for superclass element
      ls_superclass TYPE wd_this->element_class.
* Determine data of selected element for the class
context_element->get_static_attributes(
  IMPORTING
    static_attributes = ls_class ).
* Check if data for superclass has been read
CHECK ls_class-superclass__read = abap_false.
* Determine data for superclass
TRY.
* Get description object for class via RTTI
    lo_classdescr ?= cl_abap_typedescr=>describe_by_name(
      ls_class-name_class ).
* Read description object for superclass
    CALL METHOD lo_classdescr->get_super_class_type
      RECEIVING
        p_descr_ref           = lo_classdescr
      EXCEPTIONS
        super_class_not_found = 1
        OTHERS                = 2.
* If no superclass exists
    IF sy-subrc <> 0.
* Class does not have a superclass
      ls_class-has_super_class = abap_false.
* But superclass was read
      ls_class-super_class_read = abap_true.
* Set data for the class
      context_element->set_static_attributes(
          EXPORTING
            static_attributes = ls_class ).
* Done
      EXIT.
```

```
    ENDIF.
* Determine name of superclass
  ld_name_superclass = lo_classdescr->get_relative_name( ).
* Determine subnodes for current class context node
  lo_nd_superclass = context_element->get_child_node(
         'SUPER_CLASS' ).
* Collect data for element
* Name of superclass
    ls_superclass-name_class = ld_name_superclass.
* Assume that superclass also has a superclass
    ls_superclass-has_super_class = abap_true.
* Create new element for superclass, that is, subnode
    lo_nd_superclass->bind_structure( ls_superclass ).
* Set data for class
* You have found superclass for class
    ls_class-has_super_class = abap_true.
* You have read the data for superclass
    ls_class-super_class_read = abap_true.
* Set data for class in context
    context_element->set_static_attributes(
        EXPORTING
          static_attributes = ls_class ).
CATCH cx_root.
* Class does not have superclass
    ls_class-has_super_class = abap_false.
* Superclass was not read
    ls_class-super_class_read = abap_false.
* Set data for class
    context_element->set_static_attributes(
        EXPORTING
          static_attributes = ls_class ).
  ENDTRY.
ENDMETHOD.
```

Listing 3.15 Action Handler for Opening a Recursive Node

Description

The main implementation approach involves first checking whether the ABAP superclass data has already been read for the current ABAP class. This information is contained in the SUPERCLASS_READ context attribute. If the data has already been read, you do not need to determine it again and you can exit the method.

You then implement the business logic; this means the RTTI description object was determined for the current ABAP class whose name you know from the context element attributes (context_element parameter), and the RTTI description object for the ABAP superclass was consequently defined (get_super_class_type( ) method). As a result, you can use this reference to determine the superclass name (get_relative_name( ) method).

Copying context nodes

If the ABAP superclass is found, a new context subnode must be created for this ABAP class. This is done using the following statement:

```
lo_nd_superclass = context_element->get_child_node( 'SUPER_
CLASS' ).
```

This means a new subnode is created for the entry the user selected, represented by the context_element parameter. The node to which the recursion node points is structurally copied at runtime. The copy process also relates to the recursion node and is triggered by the get_child_node( ) method. After you have determined the data for the superclass, you can store it in the new node for the ABAP superclass. This completes the action handler implementation.

This implementation can be difficult; therefore, we recommend that you review our explanations carefully before putting them into practice. You will next implement a simple example of using a non-recursive Tree UI element.

Example

[✎] You will use the ZWD_03_CLASS_BROWSER Web Dynpro component again when implementing this practical example. You previously stored the ABAP class methods found from the selection view in the METHODS context node created in one of the previous examples. You are now going to display the context node contents using a Tree UI element. This will also involve mapping individual methods as TreeItemType view elements; in other words, as leaves in the tree.

1. Switch to the V_CLASS_METHODS view layout.
2. Add a TransparentContainer UI element to the T_METH_TREE tab with MatrixLayout. You may need this UI element to display scrollbars if there are too many entries in the tree. Enter 400PX as the value for the HEIGHT property and set the SCROLLINGMODE property to auto. In the LAYOUT section, set the STRETCHEDHORIZONTALLY property to ABAP_TRUE to ensure the Tree UI element stretches across the entire width of the displayable area.

   Designing tabs
3. Insert a Tree UI element into TransparentContainer with the ID TR_METHODS. Bind the DATASOURCE property for the tree to the METHODS context node. This defines the data source for the TreeItemType view element still to be defined.
4. Assign the ICON_OO_METHOD value to the DEFAULTITEMICONSOURCE and DEFAULTNODEICONSOURCE properties. Store the "Methods" value for the ROOTTEXT property and set the ROOTVISIBLE property to ABAP_TRUE. For the TITLE property it makes sense to describe the class, which you can determine through context mapping from the CLASS_SEL_CRIT component controller context node. Bind the DESCR_CLASS attribute for the CLASS_SEL_CRIT node to the TITLE property. You must set the TITLEVISIBLE property to visible so that the title can be displayed.
5. Use the INSERT NODE TYPE context menu option to insert the TreeItemType-type TIT_METHOD for the TR_METHODS Tree UI element.

   Inserting TreeItemType
6. Bind the DATASOURCE property to the METHODS context node for TIT_METHOD of the TreeItemType UI element. Bind the TEXT property to the NAME attribute of the METHODS context node.

You have now completed defining the data. After you activate all inactive elements, you can test the Web Dynpro application. After you have performed the example successfully, the display for your Web Dynpro application should look like the one shown in Figure 3.53.

Alternative to a tree

Use a hierarchical table instead of a Tree if you want to display a tree structure that is suitable for entry purposes and also enables you to scroll. We will discuss the Table UI element for this in more detail in the following section.

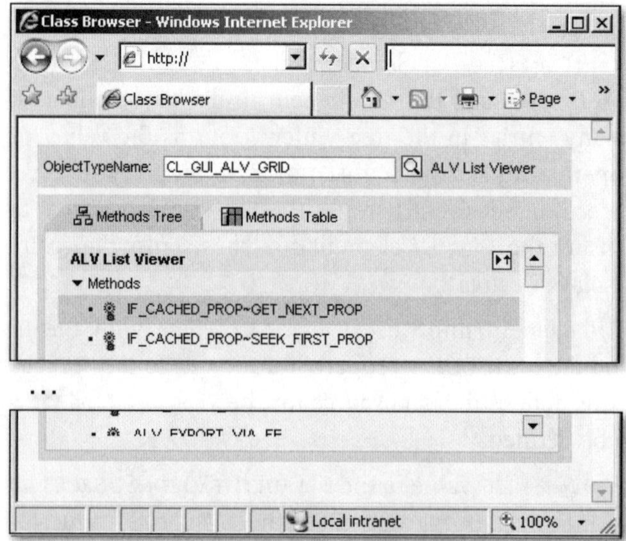

Figure 3.53 Tree Display for ABAP Class Methods

3.3.6 Table

Usage

In this section, we will explain the basic properties of a complex UI element that you can use flexibly: the `Table` UI element. You use this UI element to display data two-dimensionally in table cells arranged in rows and columns. Figure 3.54 shows an example of a simple table.

Table structure

A table has an optional *header* that can consist of a text and an image. Under the header, you can insert an optional *toolbar* where you can call user-specific *functions*. *Data rows* are displayed in columns in the detail area of the table. Individual *columns* have optional headers to which you can assign an image.

The user has the option of selecting no data rows, individual data rows, or several data rows through the *selection column*. The user can also use a *scrollbar* to change the content of the displayable area. When the user scrolls through the table, a tooltip is shown indicating which *data row area* will be displayed after the user releases the mouse button (*table scrolling*).

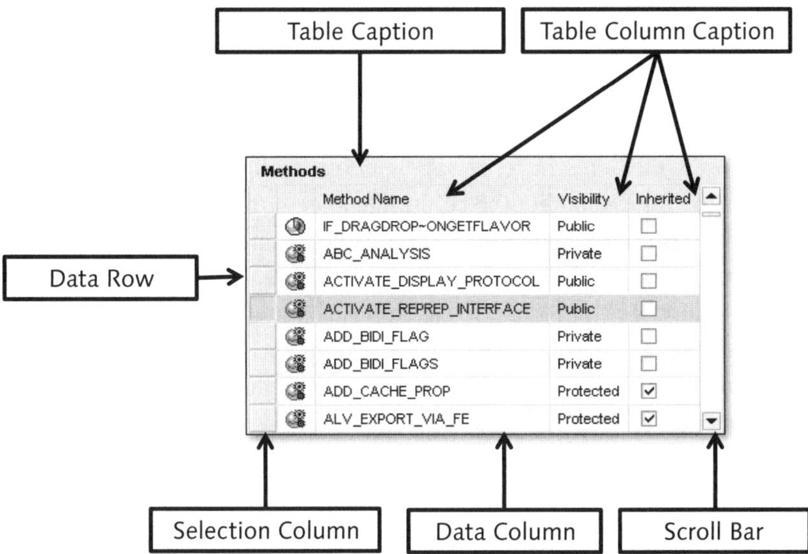

Figure 3.54 Simple Table

Like the `Tree` UI element, the `Table` UI element belongs to *composite UI elements*. Composite UI elements are displayed hierarchically in the view designer (see Figure 3.55).

Composite UI element

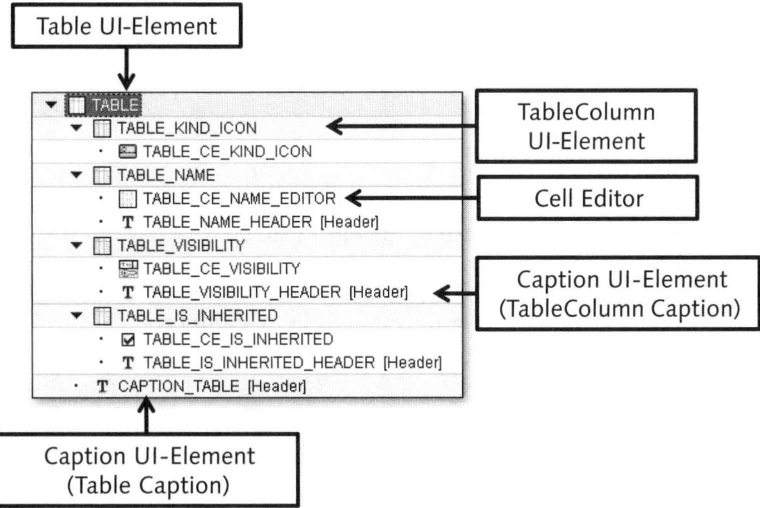

Figure 3.55 View Element Hierarchy for a Table

View element hierarchy for a table

The highest element in the hierarchy is the `Table` UI element. As a lower-level element, it can have a `Caption` view element for displaying a table header. The `Table` UI element also contains other composite view elements such as `TableColumn` view elements, for example. These `TableColumn` view elements have, as subelements, an optional `Caption` that is responsible for displaying the column header, and a *cell editor*. The term *cell editor* represents several UI elements you can use for displaying cell contents. Which cell editor you choose will depend on the type of information you want to display; for example, text (`TextView` UI element), a selection list (`DropDownByKey` UI element), or image information (`Image` UI element). The issue of input readiness can also influence which UI elements you choose.

Methods for creating tables

There are three methods you can use to create a table, two of which you carry out during development time; the third is carried out during runtime:

- **Manually**
  With this method, you define the table and all of its subelements manually in the view designer.
- **Web Dynpro Code Wizard**
  With this method, you create the table using the Web Dynpro Code Wizard (TABLE template). Here, you bind the data by selecting a context node in the wizard. The columns are created in accordance with the attributes.
- **Method**
  Using the public static `cl_wd_dynamic_tool=>create_table_from_node( )` method, you can create a simple table dynamically; in other words, so that it can be created during runtime.

In Chapter 4, Dynamic Web Dynpro Application, we will discuss in more detail how to create a table dynamically. Next, we will take a closer look at creating a table manually.

Cardinality

Before you can begin creating a table manually, you must define an adequately customized node in the context, an example of which is shown in Figure 3.56. By "adequately," we mean that the CARDINALITY property (❶) has the instance `0..n` or `1..n`. As already mentioned, this property controls the number of possible elements for a node. As a result, every element corresponds to a data row in the table to be displayed.

Selection

The SELECTION property (❷) is another customization for the context node we have not used yet. This property has the same instances as the CARDINALITY property (`0..1`, `1..1`, `0..n` and `1..n`) and controls how many entries the user can and must select in the table.

Selecting rows

The lead selection determines the row the user selects because the relevant data row for this is highlighted in the table. This is especially true if the INITIALIZATION LEAD SELECTION (❸) was set. However, the user can also use the `Shift` or `Ctrl` keys and click on different data rows to select them. The selection the user makes will be displayed in one or more highlighted row(s).

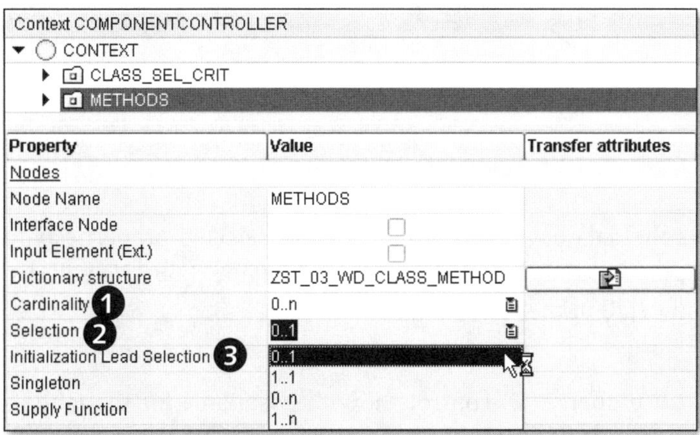

Figure 3.56 Context Node Customizations for the Table

Table

After you have configured and checked the context settings, you can create the table in the view designer. You do this the same way as with other UI elements: In the view designer, you create a new `Table` UI element using the context menu of a container element. The result of the UI element you create is shown in Figure 3.57.

- The `Table` UI element (❶) you inserted from the context menu (you can also transfer it from the COMPLEX category by using drag-and-drop) is generated with the `Caption` table header (❷). The header is optional and you can remove it. If you do use it, you can define a header text (TEXT property) and a header image (IMAGEFIRST and IMAGESOURCE properties).

- A quick look at the properties of the `Table` UI element shows that multiple setting options and properties are available for this UI element. We will explain the most basic ones. The main property you must set to let `Table` know which context node contains the data to be displayed is DATASOURCE (❸). Here, data binding is used to create the reference to the context node.

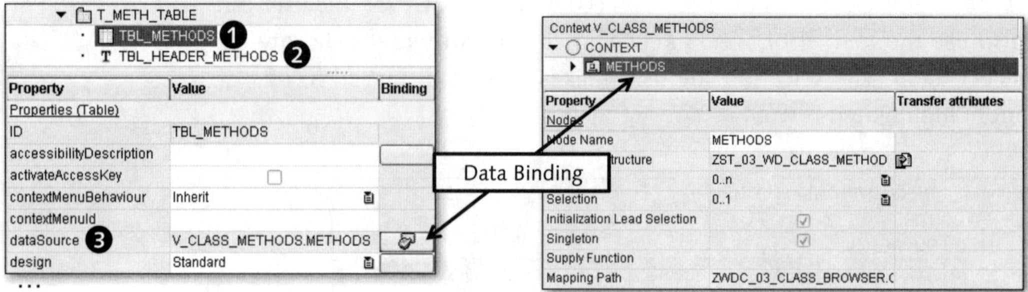

Figure 3.57 Creating a Table UI Element

Properties

This defines the data basis for the table. Other selected properties you can set for the `Table` UI element are shown in Figure 3.58. We will discuss them in detail in the following list:

- DESIGN
  The DESIGN property (❶) controls how the data area for the table is displayed; for example, whether it is displayed with alternating row colors (`alternating` value) or without grid lines. The `alternating` instance is only effective if the READONLY property has the `ABAP_FALSE` value.
- VISIBLEROWCOUNT
  The VISIBLEROWCOUNT property (❼) controls how many rows are displayed for the user in the table. This is why the height of the data area is defined in rows.
- DISPLAYEMPTYROWS
  The DISPLAYEMPTYROWS property (❷) has the following functions:
  - The `ABAP_TRUE` value ensures that a fixed number of rows is always displayed, even if the number of rows with content is smaller than the value specified in the VISIBLEROWCOUNT (❼) property.

- The ABAP_FALSE value ensures that only rows with content are displayed, regardless of the value stored in the VISIBLEROWCOUNT (❼) property. This can cause the height of the data area in the table to be reduced.

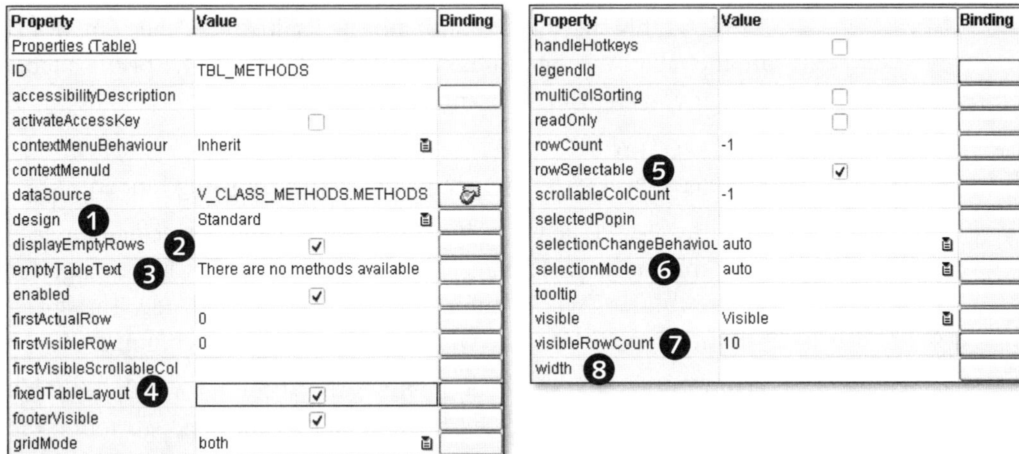

Property	Value	Binding
Properties (Table)		
ID	TBL_METHODS	
accessibilityDescription		
activateAccessKey	☐	
contextMenuBehaviour	Inherit	
contextMenuId		
dataSource	V_CLASS_METHODS.METHODS	
design ❶	Standard	
displayEmptyRows ❷	☑	
emptyTableText ❸	There are no methods available	
enabled	☑	
firstActualRow	0	
firstVisibleRow	0	
firstVisibleScrollableCol		
fixedTableLayout ❹	☑	
footerVisible	☑	
gridMode	both	

Property	Value	Binding
handleHotkeys	☐	
legendId		
multiColSorting	☐	
readOnly	☐	
rowCount	-1	
rowSelectable ❺	☑	
scrollableColCount	-1	
selectedPopin		
selectionChangeBehaviou	auto	
selectionMode ❻	auto	
tooltip		
visible	Visible	
visibleRowCount ❼	10	
width ❽		

Figure 3.58 Selected Properties for the Table UI Element

Figure 3.59 shows the interaction of these different properties.

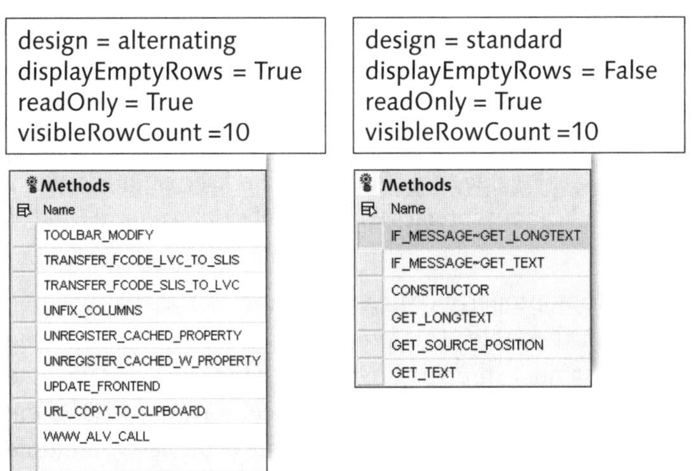

Figure 3.59 Interaction of Table UI Element Properties

- EMPTYTABLETEXT

  The EMPTYTABLETEXT property (❸) defines the text that will be displayed if there is no data to display.

- WIDTH

  The WIDTH property (❽) controls the table width. The table is at least as wide as this specification, but adjusts itself so that the content fits into the table. We therefore recommend that you only specify a table width if you are using percentage column widths.

- FIXEDTABLELAYOUT

  The FIXEDTABLELAYOUT property (❹) has the following functions:

  - For the ABAP_TRUE value, it defines that the width specified for each column in the table is fixed and that content that is too large for these columns will be truncated on the right-hand side. This specification results from the widths set for individual columns.
  - For the ABAP_FALSE value, it defines that a column width is exactly the size that was specified for it. If there is not enough room, the column width corresponds to the width of the widest cell editor.

- ROWSSELECTABLE

  The ROWSELECTABLE property (❺) requires binding data to a context attribute for each WDY_BOOLEAN context node element, and has the following functions:

  - For the ABAP_TRUE value, it defines that the user can select a row. The interaction with the selection column for this row is enabled for this purpose.
  - For the ABAP_FALSE value, it defines that the user cannot select a specific row and cannot interact with the selection column.

- SELECTIONMODE

  The SELECTIONMODE property (❻) controls how many data rows the user can select in the table. This property is directly related to the SELECTION context node property, which is connected through the Table property for DATASOURCE, as you can see in Figure 3.60. If the 0..1 instance is stored in the SELECTION context property, multiple selections *cannot* be defined in the SELECTIONMODE UI property.

Handling selectionMode

The SELECTIONMODE property requires further attention. The user can select an individual row (`auto`, `single`, `singleNoLead`) or a number of rows (`auto`, `multi`, `multiNoLead`) using the left mouse button or the keyboard and selection column.

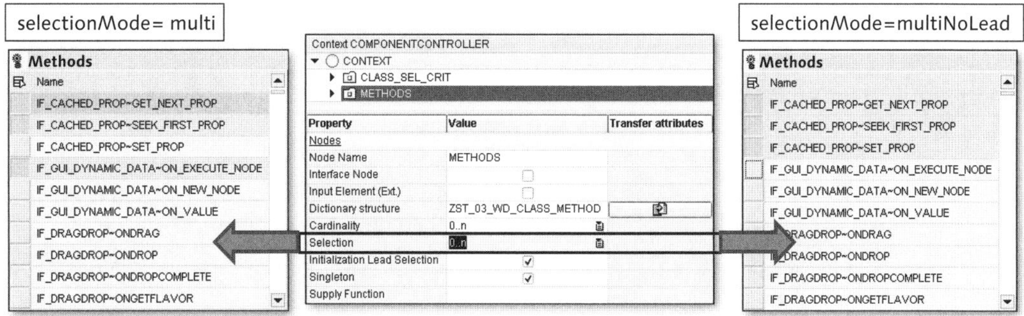

Figure 3.60 Effects of selectionMode Property for Table UI Element

The lead selection generally changes based on what the user chooses, except for the `singleNoLead` and `multiNoLead` instances. In these cases, although the selection is adjusted, the lead selection does not change.

In the case of `multi` and `auto` settings (`0..n` or `1..n` cardinality), the user handles the SELECTIONMODE property as follows:

- If the user holds down the `Shift` key and at the same time clicks the left mouse button to select a row (`Shift` + click), all rows from the lead selection to the selected row are included and highlighted in the selection (*area selection*). The lead selection is highlighted with a different color intensity. If another selection had already been made, it is deleted.
- If the user holds down the `Ctrl` key and at the same time clicks the left mouse button to select a row (`Ctrl` + click), the new row is included in the selection (*individual selection*) in addition to the existing selection. The lead selection is highlighted with a different color intensity.

As an alternative to clicking on the mouse, the user can also use the keyboard (`Shift` + `space bar`) or (`Ctrl` + `space bar`) and arrow keys to navigate among the table rows. Table 3.5 contains a list of SELECTION-

MODE instances; in this table, LL stands for the lower limit of the SELECTION context node property and UL for the upper limit.

Value	Selection Lower Limit	Selection Upper Limit	Triggers HTTP Roundtrip	Sets Lead Selection
auto	LL (SELECTION)	UL (SELECTION)	Yes	Yes
single	LL (SELECTION)	1	Yes	Yes
multi	LL (SELECTION)	UL (SELECTION)	Yes	Yes
none	0	0	No	No
singleNoLead	LL (SELECTION)	1	No	No
multiNoLead	LL (SELECTION)	UL (SELECTION)	No	No

Table 3.5 Effects of the selectionMode Property

get_selected_elements( )

The IF_WD_CONTEXT_NODE node interface makes the get_selected_elements( ) method available to return the selected elements to an internal table. When the method is called, the user can determine whether the lead selection element – if selected – should appear in the results.

onLeadSelection

If an action is still assigned to the ONLEADSELECTION event of the Table UI element, the wddobeforeaction( ) and wddoafteraction( ) methods and action handler are still executed, in addition to the lead selection being changed.

The data is displayed in rows and columns in the table. To display data, the Table UI element needs at least one TableColumn view element that is bound to one of the attributes for the table context node. For this, every attribute with a scalar type can be used.

A TableColumn view element must be inserted hierarchically under the Table UI element for every column to be output (see Figure 3.61).

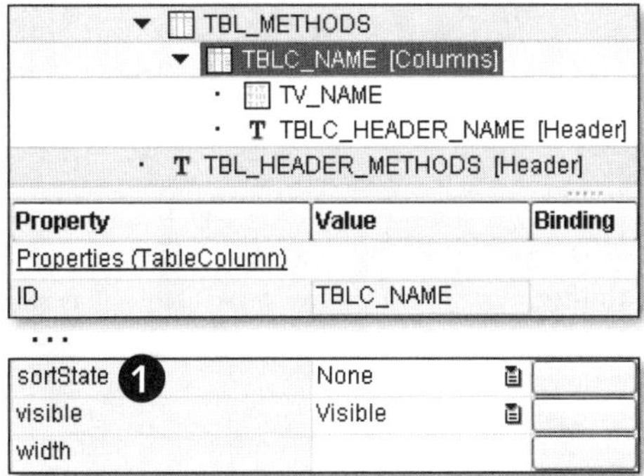

Figure 3.61 TableColumn View Element

Creating TableColumn

You can create `TableColumn` easily in the view designer using the context menu for the `Table` UI element. The INSERT TABLE COLUMN menu option takes care of creating `TableColumn` and an optional `Caption` column header. Typical steps after creating a column include changing the ID for `TableColumn` and `Caption`. You can assign a text and an image to the `Caption`.

sortState

The SORTSTATE property is especially worth mentioning (see Figure 3.61, ❶). This property describes how a column is sorted. For this purpose, an action needs to be stored for the ONSORT `Table` UI element. In this case, an icon illustrating the sort direction is displayed for the user in the column. The sorting must be programmed and is not performed automatically.

Sorting Table Content

The way content is sorted in the `Table` UI element depends on the underlying Support Package in SAP NetWeaver Application Server 7.0.

Through Support Package Stack (SPS) 12, you must program sorting as follows:

- Determine the column and sort direction: You usually do this in the event handler method for the ONSORT event using the `col` and `direction` parameters.
- Transport the context node content in an internal table (`if_wd_context_node=>get_static_attributes_table( )`).
- Determine possible selected rows and the lead selection (`if_wd_context_node=>get_selected_elements( )`).

- Sort the internal table (SORT).
- Place the sorted table back in the context node and delete the old data (if_wd_context_node=>bind_table( )).
- Select the relevant rows again and reset the lead selection (if_wd_context_node=>set_selected( ), lead_selection( )).

The sorting algorithm has been simplified considerably as of SAP NetWeaver Application Server 7.0 SPS 13 and higher. A service method is available for carrying out the sorting.

- You determine the reference for the affected Table UI element: The best way to do this is in the wddomodifyview( ) view hook method using the following call:
- <TABLE_REF> = VIEW->GET_ELEMENT(Id = <Id>)
- You determine the service object through the UI element reference using the <table_ref>->_method_handler attribute and downcasting on a <table_service> help reference of the IF_WD_TABLE_METHOD_HNDL type.
- You store the <table_service> service object help reference in the view attributes (<go_table_service>) for later sorting actions.
- You must perform the sorting in the event handler method for the ON-SORT event for the table. You do this using the service object reference (wd_this-><go_table_service>->apply_ sorting( )).

Cell editor

A *cell editor* is responsible for displaying data in a column. This cell editor, in turn, is a subelement of the TableColumn view element. The cell editor type depends on the specific requirement to be fulfilled by the column: Should the user be able to change the data? How should the user interact with the data? How should the data be displayed for the user?

Figure 3.62 shows the steps for mapping context attributes to UI elements in the table.

- **Creating a cell editor**

  You use the context menu of the TableColumn view element to create a cell editor. When you use the INSERT CELL EDITOR menu option, the known window for creating view elements opens, containing a subset of view elements you can use as cell editors. In general, you can use the TextView UI element (❷) to display text and the Image UI element (❹) to display images.

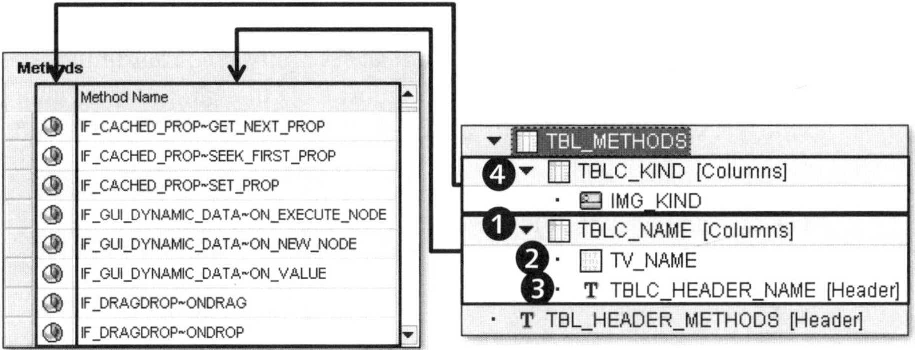

Figure 3.62 Cell Editors and Column Headers in the Table UI Element

- **Properties**
  After you have defined the cell editor, you must bind the data from the context to the cell editor using data binding. You can do this for the `TextView` UI element using the TEXT property. In the usual manner, bind the UI property to an attribute for the context node you defined as a data source for the table.

- **Table header**
  As already mentioned, the header is optional. A table header was not defined for `TableColumn`, which has the `Image` UI element (❹) as a cell editor. You can tell that this is so because no text or icon is displayed above the column.

- **Determining text**
  A header (❸) that is also displayed was defined for `TBLC_NAME` (❶) of the `TableColumn` view element. The header content was either stored explicitly in the TEXT property of the `Caption` view element or by the reference to the `TextView` UI element (❷). The reference results because `Caption` is assigned to the same `TableColumn` as `TextView`.

  If a data element from the ABAP Dictionary types the context attribute for `TextView`, the field labels can be transferred from this data element. You must repeat the manual definition of the table columns for all required context node attributes needed for display.

Example

As you can see, creating a table manually is pretty time-consuming. The Web Dynpro framework developers must have thought the same thing, which is why they made a template available in the Web Dynpro Code Wizard ([Ctrl] + [F7]).

For the sample application, we will now look more closely at the way the wizard works:

1. Switch to the V_CLASS_METHODS view layout. Open the TabStrip called TS_METHODS and below this, the Tab called T_METH_TABLE. In this Tab, you will create a Table UI element for displaying ABAP class methods.
2. Click on the WEB DYNPRO CODE WIZARD button or use the [Ctrl] + [F7] key combination to create the table automatically. The TEMPLATE GALLERY opens, where you will find the TABLE entry.
3. By double-clicking on the TABLE entry, you open the definition window where you define the data binding, column definitions, and cell editors for the table to be created. Figure 3.63 shows the definition window for the table with the defined context attributes.
   Creating a table
4. Click on the CONTEXT button (❶) and select the METHODS context node from the context. Selecting the context node defines the data source for the table and provides the number of context attributes (❹) of the context node as candidates for possible columns. The context path for the context node is displayed in the CONTEXT NODE field.
   Context node as a data source

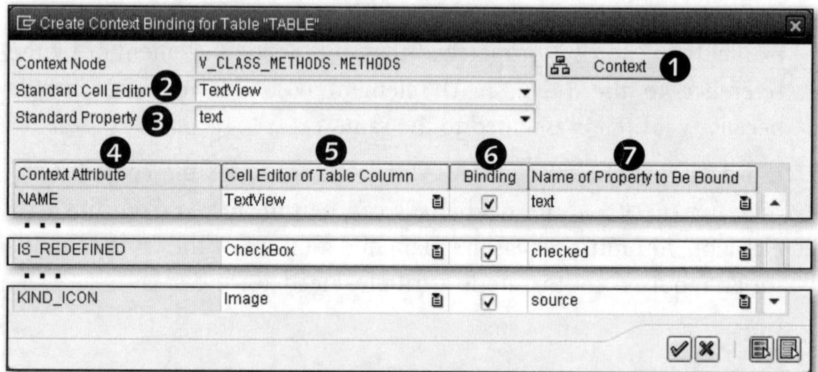

Figure 3.63 Table Definition with the Web Dynpro Code Wizard

5. The STANDARD CELL EDITOR field (❷) lets you define a default cell editor for all attributes, whereby the cell editor (UI element) property to which the attribute content should be bound can be defined using the STANDARD PROPERTY input field (❸). If desired, you can then individually override the settings for each particular attribute.

Selecting column attributes

6. The list of attributes (❹) represents the possible candidates for table columns. You use the BINDING (❻) column to select the attributes relevant for you as columns. For this example, choose the NAME, IS_REDEFINED and KIND_ICON attributes to define a table with these three columns.

Defining a cell editor

7. The way the columns are displayed depends on the cell editor you choose (❺).
   - Text output should also be used for the first NAME table column of the method. You can therefore keep the TextView STANDARD CELL EDITOR with the TEXT standard property.
   - The second table column, IS_REDEFINED, represents a *Boolean value*, which can be output as text. However, the display as a CheckBox is more compact and visually more familiar for the user. Select the CheckBox cell editor in the CELL EDITOR OF TABLE COLUMN column (❺). This selection changes the property in the NAME OF PROPERTY TO BE BOUND column (❼) to CHECKED, thereby defining the data binding on this property.

   Use an Image cell editor for displaying the KIND_ICON column; this will change the property name to SOURCE.

8. You have now completed defining a cell editor and can transfer your definition by clicking on the button with the green checkmark. The result of the definition steps you took are shown on the left in Figure 3.64.

Adjusting IDs manually

9. After you automatically created the table with its subelements, partly non-descriptive IDs are generated for the view elements. We recommend that you adjust these IDs because under some circumstances in dynamic programming, UI elements can be accessed specifically. This was already done for this example.

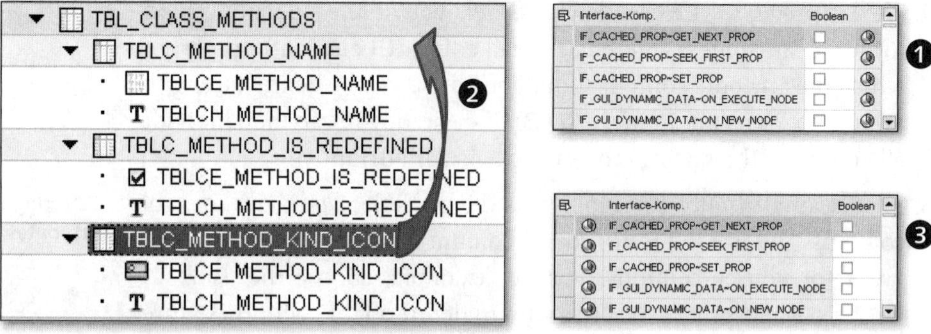

Figure 3.64 Moving TableColumn View Elements

Changing the column sequence

10. We will now discuss moving columns. After you create the table, the columns appear in the same sequence as the sequence specified in the definition (❶) where you were not able to change it. To do this retroactively, switch to the UI hierarchy of the `Table` and move a column to the position you want by using drag-and-drop. In this example, the `TableColumn` called `TBLC_METHOD_KIND_ICON` and its subelements will be moved to the first position; therefore, drag the `TBLC_METHOD_KIND_ICON` column to the `TBLC_METHOD_NAME` column (❷). This places `TBLC_METHOD_KIND_ICON` into the first position and `TBLC_METHOD_NAME` into the second position. See (❸) for the result of this move.
11. You can also still set the input readiness for checkboxes to `ABAP_FALSE` and change the BOOLEAN header on your own text.

Sorting columns

12. As an example of using events for a table, this mechanism is used as of SAP NetWeaver Application Server SPS 13 to implement column sorting. We already described the main process in the Sorting Table Content box.
13. Switch to the list of view attributes. Here, you must create an object reference for the service object to be able to call the sorting later through this object. Call the attribute `go_tbl_class_methods`, and type it as an `IF_WD_TABLE_METHOD_HNDL` object reference (`RefTo`).

14. Next, switch to the methods list for the V_CLASS_METHODS view and then to the wddomodifyview( ) method, and implement this method as shown in Listing 3.16. In Chapter 4, Dynamic Web Dynpro Applications, we will analyze in detail the programming for the wddomodifyview( ) method. At this point, we will only discuss the essential points:
    - You determine the reference to the Table UI element through the view reference using the get_element( ) method. Make sure to spell the name (ID) of the Table UI element correctly because a runtime error will occur if the Web Dynpro framework cannot find the UI element.
    - You determine the service object reference through the UI reference and store it in the go_tbl_class_methods view attribute.

```
METHOD wddomodifyview .
* Reference to UI element Table
DATA lo_wd_table TYPE REF TO cl_wd_table.
* Is the method called for the first time?
CHECK first_time = abap_true.
* Determine reference to UI element Table
lo_wd_table ?= view->get_element(
  'TBL_CLASS_METHODS' ).
* Determine service object handler
wd_this->go_tbl_class_methods ?=
  lo_wd_table->_method_handler.
ENDMETHOD.
```

Listing 3.16 Determining the Service Object Reference for Sorting a Table

Using the onSort event

15. After you have completed implementing the column sorting, switch to the V_CLASS_METHODS view layout and then to the events for the TBL_CLASS_METHODS table.
16. Create the SORT_METHODS action for the ONSORT event (see Figure 3.65). By setting the TRANSFER UI EVENT PARAMETERS option, you also generate UI event parameters in the handler method interface. This is not necessary for this implementation but is relevant for the second sorting option.

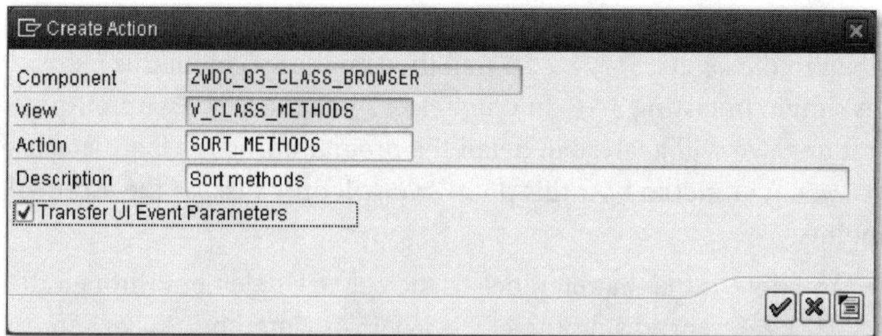

Figure 3.65 Creating the SORT_METHODS Action for the onSort Event of the Table UI Element

Implementing sorting

17. Forward navigate to switch from the action to the handler method where you will implement sorting. This is easy to do, as you can see from Listing 3.17: Use the service object reference to call the `apply_sorting( )` method, which sorts the contents of the column the user selected.

```
METHOD onactionsort_methods .
* Apply sorting
wd_this->go_tbl_class_methods->apply_sorting( ).
ENDMETHOD.
```

Listing 3.17 Sorting the Column the User Selected

Testing

You have now completed implementing the sorting and can test the Web Dynpro application. When sorting a column, you will notice that the sort direction is displayed on the upper right of the column header (see Figure 3.66).

3.3.7 FileUp/Download

In Web Dynpro applications, users frequently need information that was displayed in the client (for example, a list) to be loaded onto the client as a file for file sharing purposes. Functions for uploading files are also needed to be able to store files on the server. The two `FileDownload` and `FileUpload` UI elements from the INTEGRATION UI category are available in Web Dynpro for this purpose.

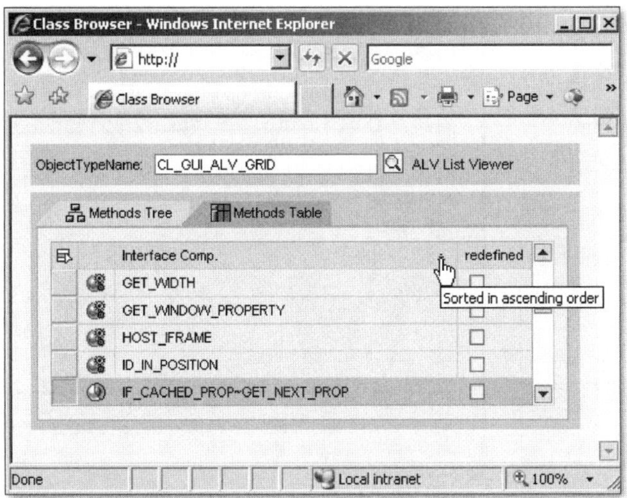

Figure 3.66 Sorting a Table Column

FileDownload

You use the `FileDownload` UI element to download data from the server to the client. Figure 3.67 shows the definition aspects for this UI element. Usage

The data format of the download content specified using the MIMETYPE property (❺) is defined by the MIME (Multipurpose Internet Mail Extensions) type. Properties

MIME Types

MIME is an Internet standard for describing the content type of a message. The official MIME standards are provided by the *Internet Engineering Task Force (IETF)*.

MIME messages can contain texts, images, audio files, videos, and application-specific data. Table 3.6 shows some examples.

Type/Subtype	Extension	Explanation
text/plain	txt	Simple Textfile
application/vnd.ms-excel	xls	MS-Excel Data

Table 3.6 Examples for MIME types

You can refer to a list of valid MIME types in the `SDOKFEXT` table in the SAP system.

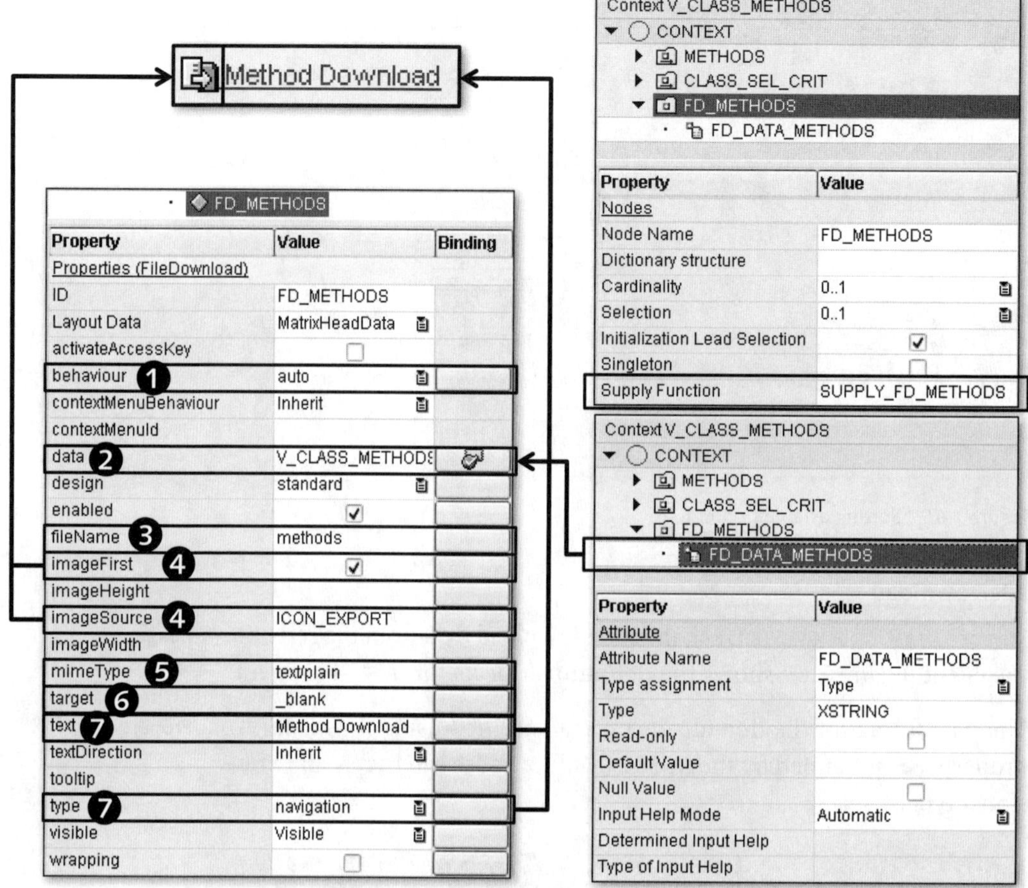

Figure 3.67 Definition of FileDownload UI Element

data and target

The DATA property (❷) of the `FileDownload` UI element determines the data source in the view context. The TARGET property (❻) defines the target window ID in the browser. Either the user defines the value for this property or it has a special `_blank` instance that ensures an external, unnamed window is opened.

imageSource, text, and data

Data for a `FileDownload` UI element is accessed when the user clicks on the displayed link. The IMAGESOURCE (see Figure 3.67, ❹) and TEXT properties (❼) define the link display. This access procedure requires binding the DATA property for the `FileDownload` UI element to a context node that meets the following criteria:

- The node has a supply function.
- The node only has one attribute with the XSTRING type.

This ensures that the supply function is only called when the user requests the data. To avoid unnecessary data in the context, the FileDownload node is invalidated after the download. However, this only happens if the node was not provided before the download. This way, no data will be lost.

In Listing 3.18, you can see the implementation for creating the content for the context attribute. In this listing, the CL_ABAP_CONV_OUT_CE ABAP class – an important service class in this context – is used for converting the data.

```
METHOD supply_fd_methods .
* Reference to context node for download
DATA: ls_fd_methods TYPE wd_this->element_fd_methods,
* Export converter reference
      lo_converter TYPE REF TO cl_abap_conv_out_ce,
* Exception reference
      lo_root TYPE REF TO cx_root,
* All methods from context node
      lt_methods TYPE wd_this->elements_methods,
* One method from context
      ls_method LIKE LINE OF lt_methods,
* Auxiliary string, prepare for XSTRING conversion
      ld_method_string TYPE string.
* Determine methods from context
lt_methods = wd_comp_controller->getctx_methods( ).
* Conversion
TRY.
* Instance converter
    lo_converter = cl_abap_conv_out_ce=>create( ).
* Formatting logic for export data
    LOOP AT lt_methods INTO ls_method.
      CONCATENATE
        ld_method_string
        cl_abap_char_utilities=>cr_lf
        ls_method-name INTO ld_method_string.
    ENDLOOP.
* Execute conversion
    lo_converter->convert(
```

```
          EXPORTING
            data = ld_method_string
          IMPORTING
            buffer = ls_fd_methods-fd_data_methods ).
CATCH cx_root INTO lo_root.
* Determine exception text
  ld_method_string = lo_root->get_text( ).
* Execute conversion for exception text
  lo_converter->convert(
    EXPORTING
      data = ld_method_string
    IMPORTING
       buffer = ls_fd_methods-fd_data_methods ).
  ENDTRY.
* Place result in context node
node->bind_structure(
  new_item             =  ls_fd_methods
  set_initial_elements = abap_true ).
ENDMETHOD.
```

Listing 3.18 Example of a Supply Function for Filling the Context Attribute for the FileDownload UI Element

Data conversion The data for the methods is read from the context. The data converter is then instantiated using the static `cl_abap_conv_out_ce=>create( )` method. A text concatenation (`CONCATENATE`) sets up the `ld_method_string` string variable as the conversion input.

However, there is a restriction with this: only the method names are concatenated to a string, separated by *carriage return* and *line feed* (`cl_abap_char_utilities=>cr_lf`). This ensures that a new row is output. The `convert( )` instance method for the conversion object copies the string transformation to an `XSTRING`-type text that is then bound to the context.

Browser display After you click on the corresponding UI element, the relevant URL is generated for this data stream and the result is displayed in a browser window. The kind of display depends on the MIME type that is specified in more detail using the MIMETYPE property (see Figure 3.67, ❺).

behavior

Whether you have an individual file or several files, you have the same display and save options. You define these using the BEHAVIOR property (❶):

- The allowSave instance defines that a SAVE dialog box appears. If the user saves the data as a file, the value of the FILENAME property (❸) is used as the file name.
- The openInplace instance opens the data in the browser depending on the MIME type and its associated program. The auto instance lets the browser decide how the data will be opened. The browser behavior is based on the file type A dialog box for displaying or saving the file.

Figure 3.68 shows an example of how displays differ depending on the MIME type:

- In the first case, the value used for the BEHAVIOR property is auto, for MIMETYPE it is text/plain, and for TARGET it is _blank. These value instances ensure that the attribute content in the context node is displayed as text in a new browser window.
- In the second case, the value used for the BEHAVIOR property is openInplace, for MIMETYPE it is application/vnd.mx-excel, and for TARGET it is _blank. These value instances ensure that the attribute content in the context node is displayed in a new browser window using the Microsoft Excel plug-in. The name of the Excel sheet where the content is displayed is derived from the FILENAME property.

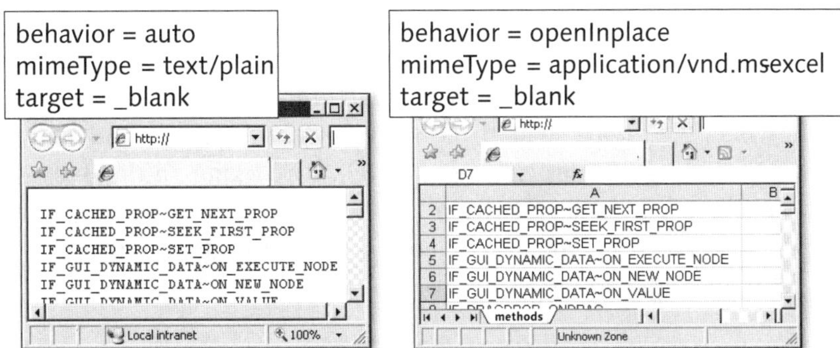

Figure 3.68 Different Data Displays Based on the MIME Type

Alternatives

An alternative to the FileDownload UI element is the static attach_file_to_response( ) method of the CL_WD_RUNTIME_SERVICES ABAP class for the file export. This method lets you attach any number of files to a response. The method parameters listed in Table 3.7 are available for this purpose.

Name	Description	Optional
i_filename	File name	
i_content	File content as XSTRING	
i_mime_type	MIME type in normal Web format	
i_in_new_window	Boolean parameter that specifies whether the file should be displayed in a new window (default is ABAP_FALSE)	X
i_inplace	Boolean parameter that specifies whether the file replaces the content of the current window (default is ABAP_FALSE). If this parameter is ABAP_FALSE, a SAVE AS dialog box is displayed.	X

Table 3.7 Formal Parameters for the cl_wd_run time_services=>attach_file_to_response( ) Method

Note that you cannot use the i_inplace parameter if you want to display several files at the same time in the current window. In this case, all files are displayed in a new window.

FileUpload

Usage

You use the FileUpload UI element to upload files from the client to the server. The interface element is displayed with an InputField UI element where the directory path and file name are displayed, and a Button for browsing for files (see Figure 3.69). By clicking on the BROWSE button, the search dialog box from the browser opens to enable you to browse for a file. After you have selected a file, the absolute path appears in the input field.

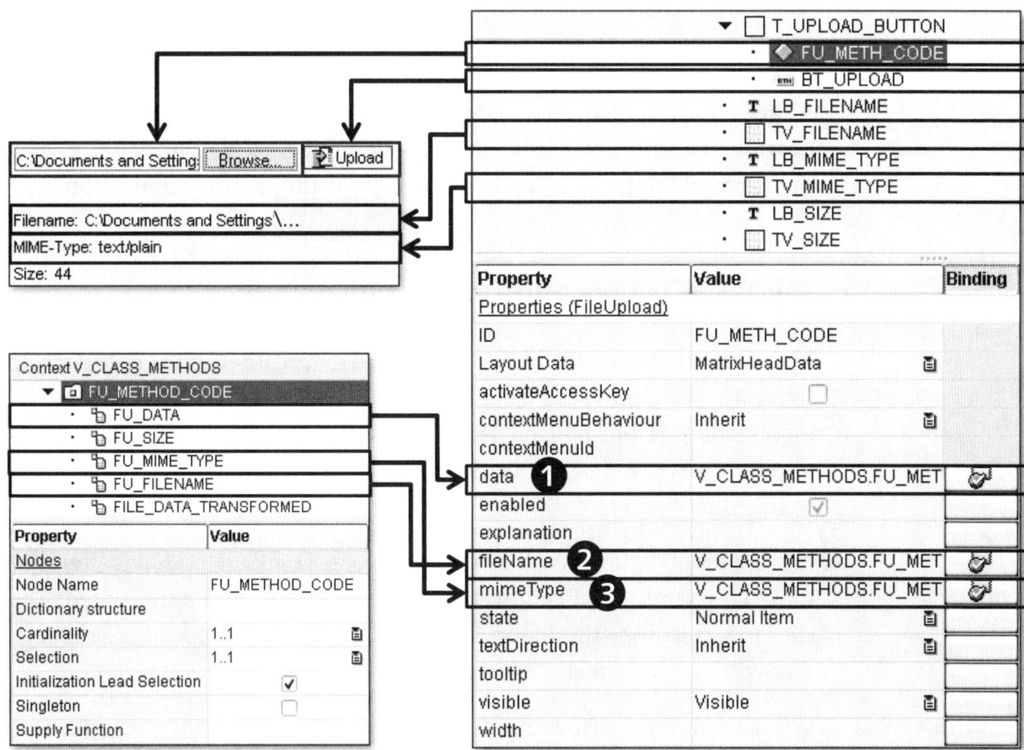

Figure 3.69 FileUpload UI Element

Because of browser restrictions, on which Web Dynpro ABAP has no effect, clicking on a `FileUpload` UI element may cause the previously specified file path (❶), name (❷), and type (❸) to disappear. With newer browser versions, you therefore cannot enter the file name in the input field again. The field always remains empty.

data, fileName and mimeType

There is no event in the properties for the `FileUpload` UI element to which you can assign an action for uploading files. We generally recommend that you use a dedicated screen or dialog box for the upload because an upload is triggered for every user interaction that requires an HTTP roundtrip – even scrolling through a table, for example – and this may be irritating to the user.

No event

Read the context data to check whether data was uploaded for every action. Then, delete the data directly from the context. Otherwise, the file is kept in memory until the context is removed or a new upload is triggered.

Although we have not worked on an explicit example for the upload and download options, we will leave it up to your creativity to develop your own area of application for UI elements for the sample application.

3.4 Messages and Internationalization

The *internationalization* (I18N) of Web Dynpro applications relates to the feature of displaying texts in a specific target language, generally the logon language of the user. Texts can be displayed for the user in many different ways, for example as `Labels`, as a selection option in a `DropDown`, or as *messages*.

Internationalization involves defining each language-relevant literal in the Web Dynpro application in such a way that it can be translated. The user logon defines the logon language used and therefore the language that will be used for displaying data.

Internationalization techniques

We have not yet discussed defining translation-relevant texts, but we have already come across a few areas where they would have been relevant – table titles, for example. Different techniques are available for defining translatable texts:

- Online Text Repository (OTR)
- Text symbols in ABAP classes
- Texts in the ABAP Dictionary

Issuing messages

These texts are displayed for the user in the UI or as messages. Even more options are available as message sources for outputting messages:

- Messages from the `T100` table
- Assistance class for the Web Dynpro application
- Messages from exception classes

In this section, we will therefore look at options for internationalizing texts. We will begin with the ABAP Dictionary, then discuss OTR, and also look more closely at using the assistance class. Our second focus aside from texts will be on outputting messages to the user and you will learn basic techniques and uses.

3.4.1 Texts from the ABAP Dictionary

Field labels

You can define texts for data elements in the ABAP Dictionary. They are called *field labels* and have four different lengths: SHORT, MEDIUM, LONG, and HEADING. Figure 3.70 shows the field labels for the SEOCLSNAME data element.

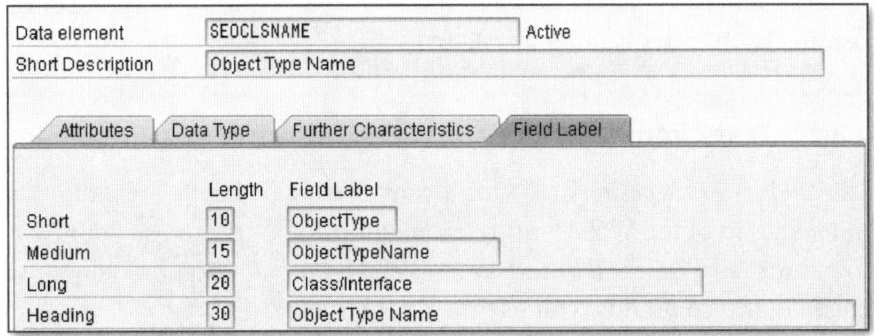

Figure 3.70 Field Labels for a Data Element

You can translate text symbols into the required target languages using Transaction SE63.

Using field labels in the UI

When you create view elements such as Label, Caption, and TableColumn, a reference to another view element is created that allows you to enter or display data. For example, through the LABELFOR property, the Label UI element can create a reference to an InputElement UI element.

Through data binding, this other view element has a reference to a context attribute. If this has been typed with an ABAP Dictionary data element, the Medium field label is used as the *label text*. For this example, this means that the Medium field label is used as the label value.

Explicitly defining a data element

In addition to this (from the perspective of Label, Caption, and TableColumn) indirect use of data element texts, you can also reference data elements directly. Do this using the button in the CREATE BINDING... column, next to the property for a view element. You already know this button from defining data binding on context nodes or context attributes. When you click on the button, the context view opens. Instead of selecting a node or an attribute (as we did before), select the DDIC BINDING TO/FROM button. This enables you to define the data element name explicitly and choose the relevant text length, thereby defining the text selection. You remove the definition by clicking on the DDIC BINDING TO/FROM button again.

RTTI classes and CL_TEXT_IDENTIFIER

Access classes on ABAP Dictionary definitions are another option for using texts from the ABAP Dictionary. For example, RTTI provides classes to determine texts for DDIC definitions. Another class you can use for reading DDIC texts is `CL_TEXT_IDENTIFIER`.

3.4.2 Texts from the Online Text Repository

OTR short texts

The *Online Text Repository (OTR)* is a central storage area for texts that is independent of the Web Dynpro framework. To be able to use your own *short texts* (also called *alias texts*) in a Web Dynpro application, you must create them. To do this, you use the OTR browser.

> **Online Text Repository**
>
> The OTR is a central storage area for texts and provides services for editing and managing these texts.
>
> It differentiates between short texts up to 255 characters long and texts of any length. Each text is stored only once per package. General, frequently occurring texts are included in the OTR basic vocabulary and can be used across all packages.
>
> Internally, the texts are identified by unique numbers. A number indicates a concept that not only includes other spellings for the text (such as abbreviations and length variations), but also its translations and possibly its localization-specific (specific to industry, country, or customer) instances.

If you are in the display or edit area of a controller, view, or window, you will find this browser in the menu under the GOTO • ONLINE TEXT REPOSITORY BROWSER option. If you are in display mode, only the OTR contents are displayed, without the option to create new OTR alias texts.

Setting up the browser

Alias texts are grouped by packages in the OTR browser (see Figure 3.71). The standard package for texts is `SOTR_VOCABULARY_BASIC` (❶) which contains commonly used texts provided by SAP. If you need your own texts, you must create your own OTR alias texts. The functions for this are available in the application toolbar (❹). When doing so, you must specify the ALIAS NAME (❸) for the OTR alias text. It consists of the package where the text is stored, and an identifier. For example, the `abstract` text has been defined under the `$TMP/ABSTRACT` alias name in the `$TMP` package (❷).

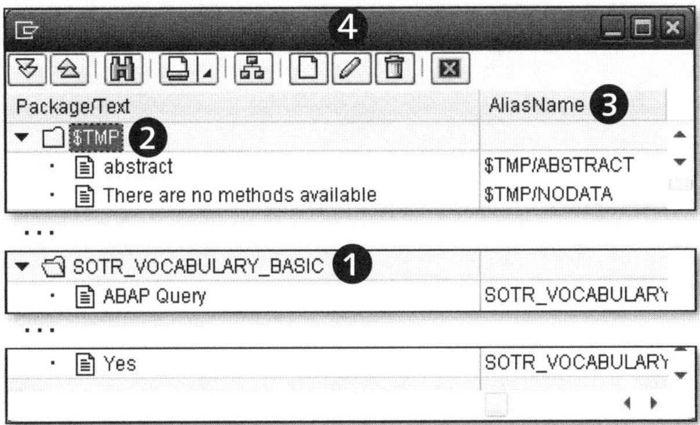

Figure 3.71 OTR Browser

Other functions the OTR browser provides include searching for texts that have already been created, translating texts, and the where-used list of texts. You can use Transaction SOTR_EDIT as an alternative for creating OTR alias texts.

Forward navigation

If you are in a view element definition, you can also create OTR alias texts directly by forward navigating out of a view element property (see Figure 3.72).

Creating OTR alias texts by forward navigating

The display text for a `Label` UI element is defined using the TEXT property (❶). Here, you can either access already defined OTR alias texts using the input help, or you can create new texts. To create an OTR alias text, enter a name for the text that must correspond to the generic `$OTR:<package>/<alias>` name structure. The name in this example is `$OTR:$TMP/NAMECLASS`. When you press the [Enter] key, an intermediate dialog box for confirming whether you want to create the OTR alias text (❷) opens. Click on YES to confirm that you do.

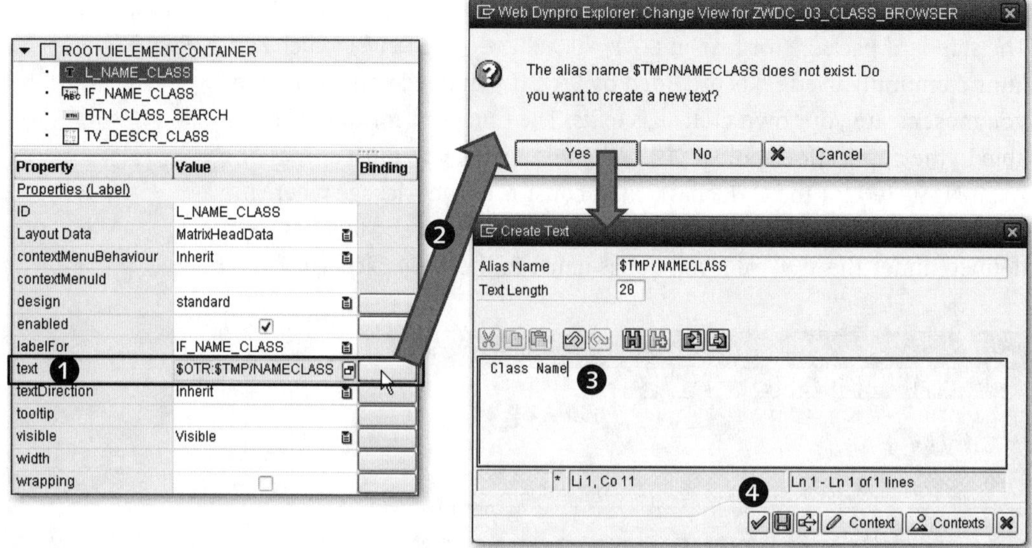

Figure 3.72 Creating an OTR Alias Text by Forward Navigating

Maintaining an OTR alias text

The window for creating the OTR alias text then opens. The alias text name has already been transferred from the properties. The text length is calculated from the entry in the text editor but you can also manually change it; for example, it can be changed to have more characters available for translations. Because you have entered the text for the OTR alias text (❸), click on CHECKMARK (❹) to confirm your entry. You have now completed the creation process, and can use the new OTR alias text anywhere in your Web Dynpro application.

Read access to Online Text Repository with the CL_WD_UTILITIES ABAP class

You can also access OTR alias texts through an implementation. To do this, use the `get_otr_text_by_alias( )` method from the `CL_WD_UTILITIES` ABAP class to access text according to language using the OTR alias. An example of this is shown in Listing 3.19.

```
DATA: ld_otr_alias_text TYPE string.
ld_otr_alias_text = cl_wd_utilities=>get_otr_text_by_alias(
  alias      = '$TMP/NAMECLASS'
  language   = sy-langu ).
```

Listing 3.19 Implementing Read Access to an OTR Alias Text

OTR is a central medium to define reusable and translatable texts for Web Dynpro applications.

3.4.3 Texts from the Assistance Class

Assistance class

You know from programming *executable programs* and *module pools* that *text symbols* summarized in a *text pool* can be defined for these programs. This technique is not immediately available for Web Dynpro components and Web Dynpro applications; however, a mechanism was created using an ABAP class (the *assistance class* that was already the subject of Chapter 2, Web Dynpro Architecture) to define text symbols and be able to use them in a Web Dynpro component. Let us look at an example of this:

1. Switch to the editing area of the `ZWDC_03_CLASS_BROWSER` Web Dynpro component and then change to the properties of the Web Dynpro component. [✎]
2. Create the assistance class, calling it `ZCL_03_A_CLASS_BROWSER`.
3. Navigate to the assistance class. When you switch to the class methods, you see the inherited `if_wd_component_assistance~get_text( )` method that will enable texts to be read.
4. You can now define texts by selecting the GOTO • TEXT ELEMENTS menu option. Assign a three-digit ID for a text and then the text that can be translated into a target language when you select the GOTO • TRANSLATION menu option.

   Creating a text element

   Figure 3.73 shows an example of the text definition:

   - Assign a three-digit ID (❶) for the text. This ID must not contain any spaces. You will use it later to determine the text symbol.
   - Create the text (❷). It can contain placeholders that can be replaced when you call the `get_text( )` method. You can specify a maximum of four placeholders called `&PARA1&` to `&PARA4&` that are written in uppercase spelling and limited by `&`.
   - The defined length (❸) results from what you enter and is calculated.
   - You can define the maximum length (❹). It must at least correspond to the defined length and can contain a maximum of 132 characters. You will generally change the maximum length; other-

wise, as a result of the defined length, too few characters may be available for translating into a target language.

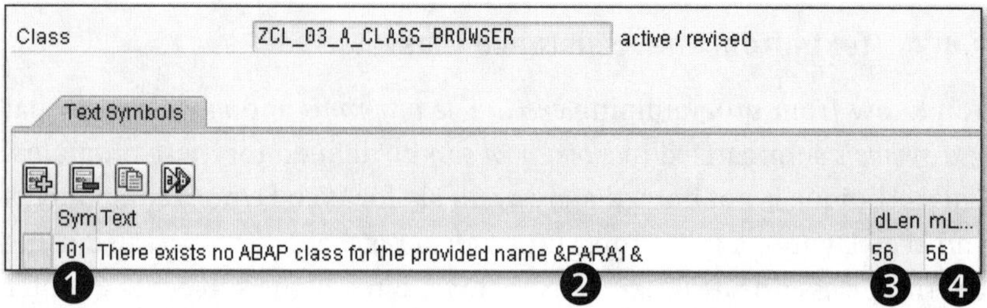

Figure 3.73 Creating a Text Symbol

Creating constants for a text element

5. Use the BACK button (F3 key) to switch to the assistance class definition. On the ATTRIBUTES tab, you can define constants that have the text symbol ID as a value. By creating constants, you can create descriptive IDs for text symbols that, as a result of the name, are more meaningful than the three-digit IDs (see Figure 3.74):
   - Give the constant for the text symbol (❶) a meaningful name.
   - The reference type to be used for this type of constant is `WDR_TEXT_KEY` (❷).
   - The INITIAL VALUE for the constant (❸) corresponds to the three-digit ID for the text symbol from the definition.

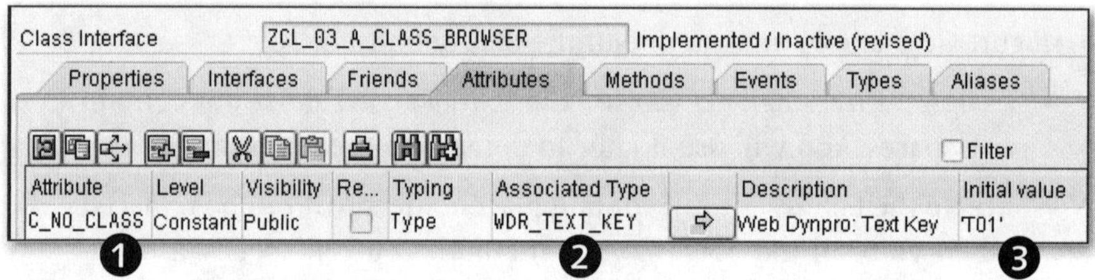

Figure 3.74 Defining Constants for Text Symbols in an Assistance Class

Activating

6. All of the relevant definitions have now been configured for the text in the assistance class. After you activate the assistance class and all dependent objects, you can use it in the Web Dynpro component.

Due to the assistance class being assigned to the Web Dynpro component, the Web Dynpro framework automatically creates the wd_assist attribute for accessing the assistance class in all controllers of the Web Dynpro component.

Example of improvement

We will now discuss accessing the previously defined text element in the assistance class. In the Web Dynpro component example, the user can enter a text for an ABAP class for which he can then determine the ABAP class methods by clicking on the use BTN_CLASS_SEARCH button. The onactionsearch_methods( ) method in the V_CLASS_SELECTION view was defined as an action handler. If an ABAP class is not found, a text is issued for the user in the TV_DESCR_CLASS UI element for TextView. Listing 3.20 shows an extract of the current implementation.

```
* Selection data from context
DATA: lv_rs_value TYPE zst_03_wd_class_sel_crit.
* Handling, info text for users
lv_rs_value-descr_class = 'Class does not exist'.
* Set values back into description
wd_comp_controller->setctx_class_sel_crit(
 is_value = lv_rs_value ).
```

Listing 3.20 Extract of Action Handling for ABAP Class Search

Neglecting of language

The following statement sets the information text for the user – in German:

```
lv_rs_value-beschr_klasse = 'Klasse existiert nicht'.
```

If the user is logged on in English and cannot speak German, this will present a problem when using the Web Dynpro application.

Web Dynpro Code Wizard

To overcome this shortcoming, you use the assistance class to determine the texts for a specific target language and then make the assignment. We have already discussed how to define the text you want to be output. Now, we will look at reading the text. The Web Dynpro Code Wizard provides support for determining defined texts from the assistance class (see Figure 3.75).

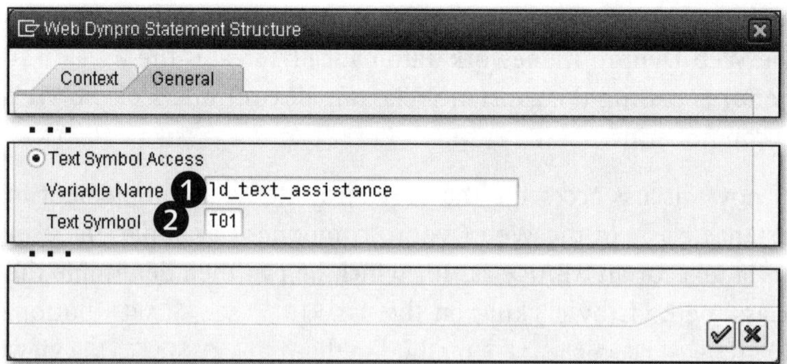

Figure 3.75 Reading a Text Symbol from the Assistance Class Using the Web Dynpro Code Wizard

1. After you have placed the cursor in the appropriate place in the source text, call the Web Dynpro Code Wizard (`Ctrl` + `F7` key combination).

Text symbol access

2. Switch to the GENERAL tab and select the TEXT SYMBOL ACCESS option. The `get_text( )` method from the assistance class returns a string value as the result. You can save this value in an already defined method variable or create a new variable. In this example, use the already defined `ld_text_assistance` (❶) variable. In the TEXT SYMBOL input field (❷), you define the text symbol you want to read. Input help is available for the text symbols defined in the assistance class.

Generating source text

3. After you have made your entries, confirm them to generate the source code. Listing 3.21 shows the produced source text.

```
METHOD onactionsearch_methods .
* Selection data from context
  DATA: lv_rs_value TYPE zst_03_wd_class_sel_crit,
* Texts from assistance class
        ld_text_assistance TYPE string.
** Variant 1 **
* Created by Web Dynpro Code Wizard and left unchanged
*ld_text_assistance =
*wd_assist->if_wd_component_assistance~get_text( 'T01' ).
** Variant 2 **
* Created by Web Dynpro Code Wizard and enhanced manually
 ld_text_assistance =
   wd_assist->if_wd_component_assistance~get_text(
     key =  wd_assist->c_no_class
```

```
      para1 = lv_rs_value-name_class ).
  * Assign text from assistance class
  lv_rs_value-descr_class = ld_text_assistance.
  ENDMETHOD.
```

Listing 3.21 Determining Text Using the Assistance Class

Automatically generated source code

In the `Variant 1` section in Listing 3.21 you see the `get_text( )` method call as it was created by the Web Dynpro Code Wizard. The `ld_text_assistance` variable was specified to transfer the return value of the method. The `T01` text literal transfers the ID for the text to the method. The placeholder is not replaced in the text because no value for the placeholder is transferred to the method. You would have to use alternative options to do this when using this call variant; for example, by sending a message to the user.

Manually adjusted source code

`Variant 2` contains a second call variant that has resulted from manual changes to the created source text. The literal text was replaced by the descriptive `wd_assist->c_no_class` constant. The replacement value for the placeholder in the text element was also transferred to the `para1` importing parameter. This replaces the placeholder with the value of the actual parameter, `lv_rs_value-name_class`.

3.4.4 Messages

ABAP MESSAGE statement

Using the `MESSAGE` statement to notify users in ABAP programs should be nothing new to you:

```
MESSAGE E041(OO) WITH `CX_ROOT`.
* Could not repair class pool for class &1
```

You should be familiar with the call syntax; however, we will nevertheless repeat it in an example to discuss using messages in Web Dynpro components.

- **Message type**
  A message is initiated by the `MESSAGE` statement. One addition is the *message type*, whose functions include specifying how, where, and when the message is displayed, and the effect the message will have on the runtime behavior of the program. Values available for the message type include `E` for error or `I` for information.

- **Message number and message class**
  The three-digit *message number* specifies which message should be read from the T100 table. For this, you still have to specify the *message class* from which the message texts are determined. The message number within a message class is unique. Preferably use Transaction SE91 (message maintenance) to determine a list of all messages in a message class.
- **Placeholder**
  If the message text has placeholders of which a maximum of four can be defined in the short text and four in the long text, you must specify the replacement values for the MESSAGE statement with the WITH addition.

After this brief discussion, we will look at how to map the described aspects of the MESSAGE statement in Web Dynpro components.

Message Area

Message area

You need a message area to be able to display messages. Two options are available for this in Web Dynpro development.

Standard message area

The first option involves using a predefined message area. This is known as the *standard message area* and can be used as shown in Figure 3.76. The standard message area is shown in the page header, and the message text is displayed (❶).

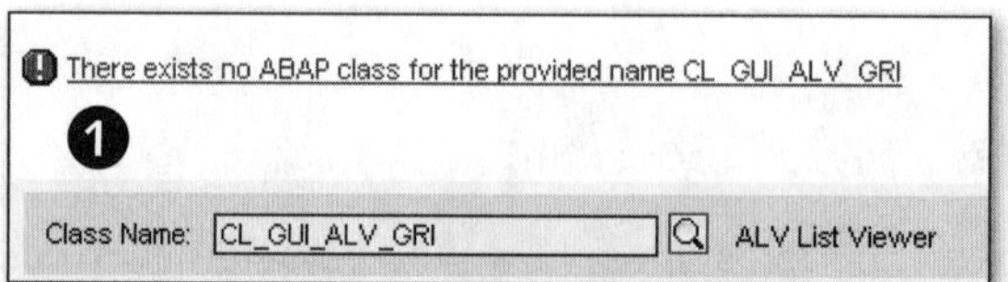

Figure 3.76 Standard Message Area

Display

You can determine whether you want the message area to always be shown or to only be shown as required. To implement this setting, you must switch to the PROPERTIES of the corresponding Web Dynpro application, as you can see in Figure 3.77.

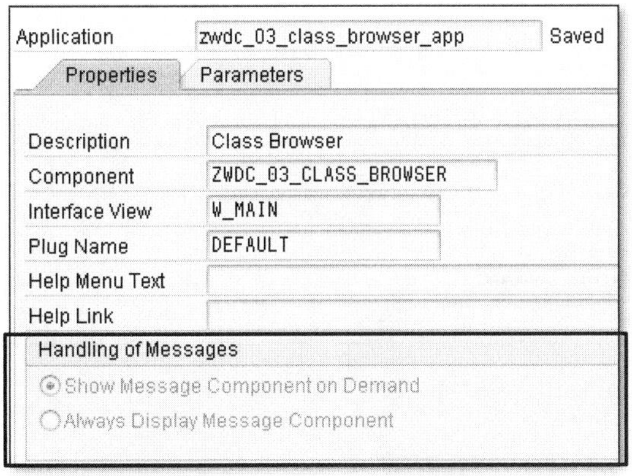

Figure 3.77 Message Area Display

In the HANDLING OF MESSAGES property group, you can specify whether you want the message area to only be shown as required or to always be displayed. If you choose the SHOW MESSAGE COMPONENT ON DEMAND option, when a message is issued, the displayed view elements move downward by the amount of space required for this. If there is no message to issue, the message area is not displayed and the view elements will be displayed according to the layout definition.

MessageArea UI element

A second option for displaying the message area is to use the `MessageArea` UI element. Using it means you can issue the messages anywhere in the layout. If you use this UI element, you must ensure (particularly when reusing Web Dynpro components) that you only use it once per window in the entire Web Dynpro application; otherwise, runtime errors will occur.

Customizing the message area

Regardless of whether you use the first or second option for displaying the message area, you can influence the appearance of the message area. To do this, you must customize the message area in a suitable place – for example, in the `wddoinit( )` method of a window. Figure 3.78 shows an example of the results of customizing the message area.

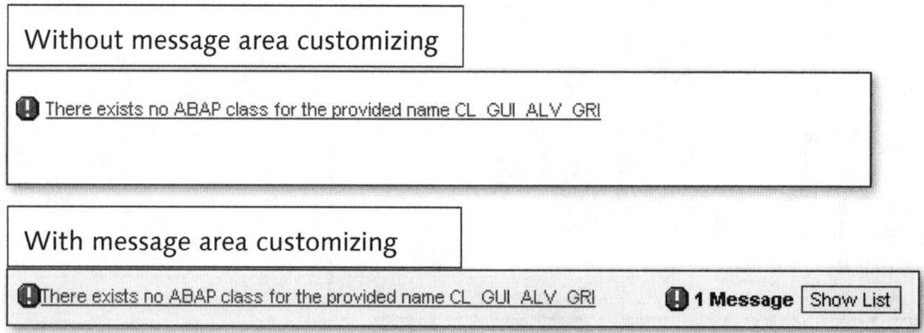

Figure 3.78 Result of Customizing the Message Area

> **Note**
>
> The design for message area messages has changed with SAP NetWeaver 7.0 SPS 11. However, you can switch back to the old design by customizing the message area.

Effects of customizing

Without customizing, the message area is displayed with a white background and a list of all messages. With customizing, the message area can have different appearances and functions. In the example from Figure 3.78, only the first message is displayed, with additional information about how many messages there are. The SHOW LIST button is also made available to display the list of messages.

Listing 3.22 shows the source text for customizing the message area.

```
METHOD set_message_area .
* API of window controller
DATA: l_api_mycomp TYPE REF TO if_wd_window_controller,
* Message Area
        l_wd_message_area TYPE REF TO if_wd_message_area.
* Determine window API
l_api_mycomp ?= wd_this->wd_get_api( ).
* Determine message area
l_wd_message_area = l_api_mycomp->get_message_area( ).
* Set message area attributes
l_wd_message_area->set_display_attributes(
"Display current messages only
  i_for_all_instances = abap_false
"Simultaneously visible messages with expanded log
  i_msg_lines_visible = '3'
```

```
"Message area can toggle between text line and list
  i_use_toggle_area = abap_true
"Sets attributes for all message area instances
  i_show_only_current = abap_false ).
ENDMETHOD.
```

Listing 3.22 Customizing the Message Area

Encapsulating customizing

The message area customizing in the `set_message_area( )` window controller method was encapsulated to be able to call it easily in the `wddoinit( )` method of the window controller.

To be able to customize the message area, you must first determine the reference to the *window API*. The API provides the `get_message_area( )` access method for determining the reference to the message area. The appearance and functions of the message area are controlled by supplying interface parameters of the `set_display_attributes( )` methods for the message area reference. Table 3.8 contains a list of what the parameters mean.

Parameter	Value	Effect
i_use_toggle_area	SPACE	Shows new message area design (default).
	X	Shows old message area design.
i_msg_lines_visible	0	All messages are displayed (default).
	greater than 0	Only x messages can be displayed and the remaining messages can be accessed by scrolling.
i_show_only_current	X	A message log is not displayed if the I_USE_TOGGLE_AREA parameter has the X value.
	SPACE	If the I_USE_TOGGLE_AREA parameter has the X value, a link to show the message log is displayed.

Table 3.8 set_display_attributes( ) Method Parameters

Message Manager

Tasks

The *Message Manager* is available to let you send messages to the user. You can obtain it from the current controller API. The Message Manager is the central object for managing and handling messages and provides methods to retrieve texts from different sources and place them in the message area with the relevant translation.

To work efficiently with the Message Manager in the Web Dynpro component, we recommend that you determine the reference to the Message Manager in an initialization step and store this reference in such a way that all controllers can access it. The reference type made available by the Web Dynpro runtime is `IF_WD_MESSAGE_MANAGER`. If a message has to be issued in a controller, this globally available reference is used, and the corresponding method is called using the Message Manager reference. Let us look at an example of this.

Defining a global attribute for the Message Manager

1. Switch to the component controller of the Web Dynpro component.
2. In preparation of determining the reference to the Message Manager, create the global `go_mm` attribute of the `IF_WD_MESSAGE_MANAGER` reference type in the `Component Controller` (see Figure 3.79).

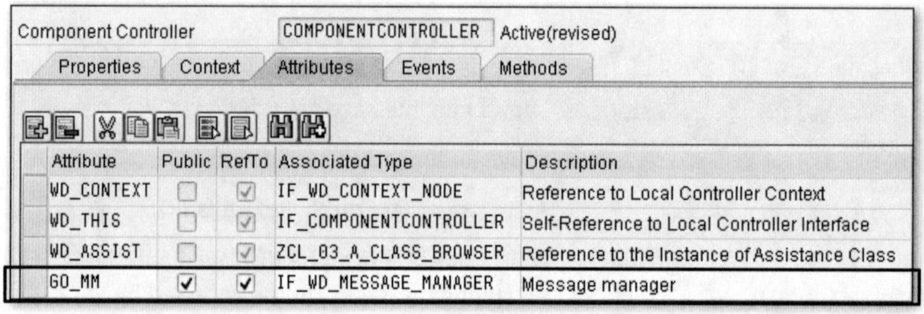

Component Controller | COMPONENTCONTROLLER | Active(revised)

Properties | Context | Attributes | Events | Methods

Attribute	Public	RefTo	Associated Type	Description
WD_CONTEXT	☐	☑	IF_WD_CONTEXT_NODE	Reference to Local Controller Context
WD_THIS	☐	☑	IF_COMPONENTCONTROLLER	Self-Reference to Local Controller Interface
WD_ASSIST	☐	☑	ZCL_03_A_CLASS_BROWSER	Reference to the Instance of Assistance Class
GO_MM	☑	☑	IF_WD_MESSAGE_MANAGER	Message manager

Figure 3.79 Message Manager Reference

By creating the Message Manager reference as a global attribute in the component controller, you ensure that all other controllers in the Web Dynpro component can access this reference. This is because all controllers in the Web Dynpro component have access to the component controller.

3. Next, you have to determine the reference to the Message Manager. This access is encapsulated in the get_message_manager( ) component controller method to enable it to be subsequently called in the wddoinint( ) method of the component controller. Listing 3.23 shows how the reference to the Message Manager is determined.

   Determining the Message Manager reference

```
METHOD get_message_manager .
* Reference component controller API
DATA lo_api_controller  TYPE REF TO if_wd_controller.
* Determine component controller API
lo_api_controller ?= wd_this->wd_get_api( ).
* Determine Message Manager
wd_this->go_mm =
  lo_api_controller->get_message_manager( ).
ENDMETHOD.
```

   Listing 3.23 Determining the Message Manager Reference

   The get_message_manager( ) component controller method encapsulates determining the Message Manager reference. In the first step, the component controller API is determined using the wd_get_api( ) method. The API reference is used to call the get_message_manager( ) method, which returns the reference to the Message Manager. You store this reference in the previously defined global go_mm attribute, making it available to other controllers.

4. You still have to call the get_message_manager( ) component controller method in the wddoinit( ) component controller method. By doing so, you ensure that the global go_mm attribute is allocated a valid reference and can be used by other controllers.

   Integrating determining the Message Manager

The next step involves actually using the Message Manager. However, before you get to that, we will explain the different text sources the Message Manager may issue.

Message Categories

Text sources

The texts for issuing messages can come from different text sources such as the assistance class T100 message table, or ABAP OO exception objects. These sources (or message categories) are displayed in Figure 3.80.

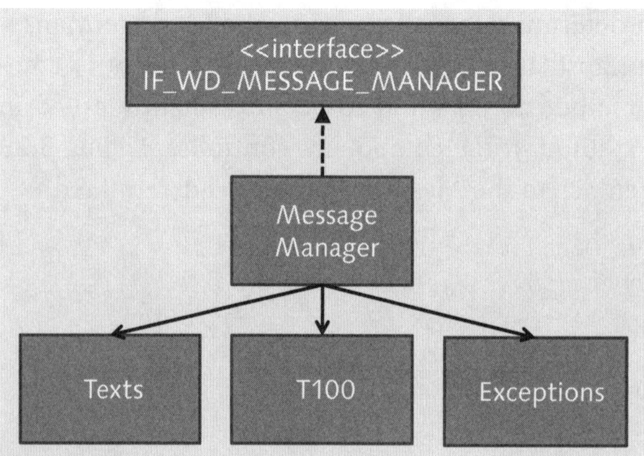

Figure 3.80 Message Categories

IF_WD_MESSAGE_MANAGER

Because the Message Manager implements the IF_WD_MESSAGE_MANAGER interface, methods for issuing messages are available that can use texts from different sources. These sources are split into categories we will now describe in detail:

- **Texts**
  The Texts category enables you to use any texts. For example, texts can be short texts from the OTR, text symbols from the assistance class, or texts from the ABAP Dictionary. We have already discussed the options for accessing these texts.
- **T100**
  Texts are saved according to language and grouped in message classes in the T100 table. For each message, you can create a long text that provides the user with additional information about the message. You can use placeholders in the message and long text to merge information into the texts during runtime.
- **Exceptions**
  Exceptions are a part of the exception mechanism in ABAP Objects and are defined using ABAP classes. Exception classes are created in the Class Builder (Transaction SE24) and are derived from the CX_ROOT ABAP class. These exceptions are triggered by the RAISE EXCEPTION TYPE <exception class> ABAP statement. When an exception is triggered, it can define which exception text in the exception object should be used.

Exceptions that occur must be handled, meaning the exception must be responded to accordingly. The statement sequence shown in Listing 3.24 is available in ABAP for handling exceptions.

```
DATA: LO_EXCEPTION TYPE REF TO <exception class>.
TRY.
* Critical area in which an exception can occur,
* for example the call of a method that triggers an
* exception
CATCH <exception class> INTO LO_EXCEPTION.
* Handling occurs here, for example message output
* through the Message Manager
ENDTRY.
```

Listing 3.24 Exception Handling for Exceptions

Access to exception objects

The interesting thing about messages being issued is that when exceptions occur, you can save the exception objects in object reference variables. The following segment is relevant for this:

```
CATCH <exception class> INTO LO_EXCEPTION.
```

Because the exception object can be addressed using the object reference, the Message Manager can determine and issue the text from the exception object.

Placeholders and linking

The Message Manager methods for the TEXT and T100 categories provide parameters that enable you to replace placeholders with values in texts. The methods for all categories allow you to create a reference from the message to a UI element to let the user know the reason for the message. This linking of the message with a UI element also supports the navigation from the message to the UI element. The UI element and its content are highlighted in a relevant color.

Issuing Messages

The Web Dynpro Code Wizard supports you in issuing a message. After you have placed the cursor in the relevant place in the source text, call the Web Dynpro Code Wizard. Then, choose the GENERATE MESSAGE option (see Figure 3.81).

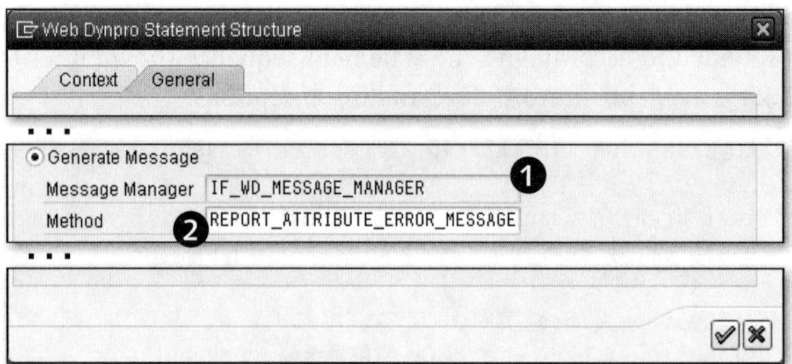

Figure 3.81 Generating a Message Using the Web Dynpro Code Wizard

The `IF_WD_MESSAGE_MANAGER` interface is displayed in the MESSAGE MANAGER field (❶) for information purposes only. All Message Manager methods are provided in the METHOD field through input help (❷). You can choose the relevant method depending on the application. Next, we will show you examples of applications based on message categories.

Text category To send a message from the TEXT category, you must first determine the message text. This text may have placeholders you will have to replace. You must also decide whether you need to link the message to a UI element.

Listing 3.25 contains the call for the `report_attribute_error_message( )` Message Manager method to issue a message with a reference to a UI element.

```
* Selection data from context
DATA: lv_rs_value TYPE zst_03_wd_class_sel_crit,
* Texts from assistance class
      ld_text_assistance TYPE string,
* Determine element
 lo_nd_class_sel_crit TYPE REF TO if_wd_context_node,
 lo_el_class_sel_crit TYPE REF TO if_wd_context_element.
* From <CONTEXT> to <CLASS_SEL_CRIT> via lead selection
lo_nd_class_sel_crit = wd_context->get_child_node(
  name = wd_this->wdctx_class_sel_crit ).
* get element via lead selection
lo_el_class_sel_crit =
  lo_nd_class_sel_rit->get_element( ).
* Determine text from assistance class
```

```
ld_text_assistance =
  wd_assist->if_wd_component_assistance~get_text(
    key =  wd_assist->c_no_class
    para1 = lv_rs_value-name_class ).
* Create message
wd_comp_controller->go_mm->report_attribute_error_message(
  message_text             = ld_text_assistance
  element                  = lo_el_class_sel_crit
  attribute_name           = 'NAME_CLASS' ).
```

Listing 3.25 Issuing a Message for the Text Category

Text and placeholders

To issue the message, a message text is first determined using the assistance class, and the placeholder is replaced with the user input value in the selection view. If an ABAP class for the user entry is not found in the repository, the `report_attribute_error_message( )` Message Manager method sends the error message to the user.

In addition to the message text, the reference to the context node element and the name of the context attribute to which the UI element is linked with the incorrect entry are transferred to the method. As a result, the error message can provide a link to the UI element so that the user can branch more easily to his entry to correct it. The UI element is also highlighted in color.

Replacing placeholders with a parameter table

The method also provides the `params` parameter to which you can transfer an internal table with placeholder names and replacement values. This means the placeholders in the message text can be exchanged with replacement values during runtime.

You must declare and populate an internal `WDR_NAME_VALUE_LIST` table type for this and transfer it to the method. Listing 3.26 shows the parameter table variant.

```
* With parameter table
DATA: lt_params TYPE wdr_name_value_list,
      ls_param LIKE LINE OF lt_params.
* Created by Web Dynpro Code Wizard and enhanced manually
ld_text_assistance =
   wd_assist->if_wd_component_assistance~get_text(
     key =  wd_assist->c_no_class ).
* Fill parameters
ls_param-name = 'PARA1&'.
```

```
ls_param-value = 'Manual entry'.
APPEND ls_param TO lt_params.
* Create message
wd_comp_controller->go_mm->report_attribute_error_message(
  message_text               = ld_text_assistance
  element                    = lo_el_class_sel_krit
  attribute_name             = 'NAME_CLASS'
  params                     = lt_params ).
```

Listing 3.26 Issuing a Message for the Text Category with a Parameter Table

Parameter table

First, declare the internal table for the parameters with reference to the `WDR_NAME_VALUE_LIST` table type and a work structure to set up the parameter table content. The parameter table has two columns: `name` and `value`. The `name` column contains the name of the parameter to be replaced in the message text. The placeholder name in this example is `¶1&`. The closing `&` is required due to placeholders being replaced through the `get_text( )` method of the assistance class.

For placeholders, you generally only need the opening `&`, as you will already know from messages from the `T100` table. To replace the `¶1&` placeholder in the `report_attribute_error_message( )` method now, the name of the placeholder to be exchanged is `para1&`. The `value` column contains the replacement text.

The parameter table populated row by row (meaning placeholder by placeholder) is then transferred to the Message Manager method. Figure 3.82 shows the message to the user if an ABAP class is not found in the repository.

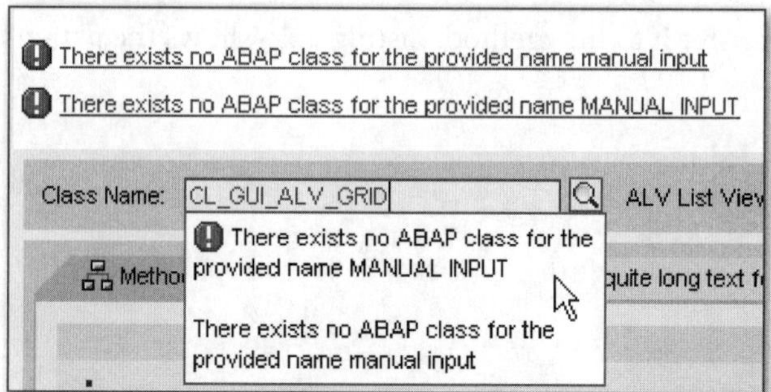

Figure 3.82 Text Category Message Issued by the report_attribute_error_message( ) Message Manager Method

An ABAP class could not be found in the repository for the name the user entered, which is why the message was issued. The message is issued in the message area in the window header area and provides a link to easily navigate to the UI element to correct the ABAP class name entered. Table 3.9 contains additional methods assigned to the TEXT category.

Method Name	Parameter Table	Linking with a UI Element
`report_success( )`	+	–
`report_warning( )`	+	–
`report_message( )`	+	–
`report_attribute_message( )`	+	+
`report_error_message( )`	+	–
`report_fatal_error_message( )`	+	–
`report_attribute_error_message( )`	+	+
`report_element_error_message( )`	+	+

Table 3.9 Message Manager Methods for the Text Category

Three Message Manager methods are available for issuing texts from the `T100` table. You must at least transfer the *message number*, *message class*, and *message type* to all three methods. T100 category

Like TEXT messages, `T100` message texts may also contain placeholders that are subsequently replaced with values that are transferred to methods. Table 3.10 shows a summary of methods for issuing messages based on Table `T100`.

Method Name	Parameter Table	Linking with a UI Element
`report_t100_message( )`	+	–
`report_attribute_t100_message( )`	+	+
`report_element_t100_message( )`	+	+

Table 3.10 Message Manager Methods for T100 Category

In Listing 3.27, you can see that two methods from this category are used. Note the different method parameters provided.

```
* Message structure
DATA: ls_msg TYPE symsg,
      lo_element TYPE REF TO if_wd_context_element.
* Issue message
* 041 = Could not repair class pool for class &1
wd_comp_controller->go_mm->report_t100_message(
  msgid                      = '00'
  msgno                      = '041'
  msgty                      = 'E'
  p1                         = 'CX_ROOT' ).
* Fill message structure
ls_msg-msgid = '00'.
ls_msg-msgno = '041'.
ls_msg-msgty = 'E'.
ls_msg-msgv1 = 'CX_ROOT'.
* Issue message
wd_comp_controller->go_mm->report_attribute_t100_message(
  msg                        = ls_msg
  element                    = lo_element
  attribute_name             = 'NAME_CLASS' ).
```

Listing 3.27 Issuing a Message for the T100 Category

Tranferring message information

The main difference in using both methods is in the message information transferred. The `report_t100_message( )` method provides individual parameters for the message class, message number, message type, and a maximum of four parameters for placeholder replacements.

In contrast, the `report_attribute_t100_message( )` method expects a `SYMSG`-type structure to transfer the message information. The structure fields correspond to the `report_t100_message( )` method parameters.

Exceptions category

You can use the exception text in the exception object to issue messages. In this case, you cannot replace placeholders with specific values. Table 3.11 contains the methods for the EXCEPTIONS category.

Method Name	Parameter Table	Linking with a UI Element
report_exception( )	–	–
report_fatal_exception( )	–	–
report_attribute_exception( )	–	+
report_element_exception( )	–	+

Table 3.11 Message Manager Methods for T100 Category

Link to element

In Listing 3.28, you can see that the `report_element_exception( )` method is used. The difference to the Message Manager methods we have discussed so far is that messages are linked with view elements.

```
* Exception object
DATA: lo_exception TYPE REF TO cx_root,
* Select attributes
      lt_attributes TYPE string_table,
* One attribute
      ls_attribut LIKE LINE OF lt_attributes.
TRY.
* Check if search string is a class name
  wd_comp_controller->is_class(
   EXPORTING
     clskey = lv_rs_value-name_class
   IMPORTING
     ed_exists = ld_exists ).
* Fired by IS_CLASS, class does not exist
CATCH cx_wd_no_handler INTO lo_exception.
* Fill attribute table
  ls_attribut = 'NAME_CLASS'.
  APPEND ls_attribut TO lt_attributes.
* Message with reference to output
  wd_comp_controller->go_mm->report_element_exception(
    message_object          = lo_exception
    element                 = lo_el_class_sel_crit
    attributes              = lt_attributes ).
ENDTRY.
```

Listing 3.28 Issuing a Message for the Exceptions Category

Defining the color highlighting

The `report_element_exception( )` method is called in the `CATCH` section of the `TRY` statement. The caught exception object and reference to the context element are transferred to this method. A table with attributes from the context node belonging to the context element is also transferred. This attribute table controls which UI elements are highlighted in color if the message is displayed. If no attributes are transferred to the method, all UI elements linked to a context attribute for the element are highlighted.

Now that we have discussed the different message categories using examples, we will next explain the navigation behavior when messages are called.

Messages and Navigation Behavior

Messages are generally issued as a reaction to checks. In the previous examples we showed you, the Message Manager was also used to send the user a message after an exception occurred in the action handler method. You could ask yourself a few questions at this stage:

- Is it inefficient for the same checks to be run in different action handler methods? Is there an efficient way to summarize checks?
- When a message is issued, you sometimes need to cancel the program processing and instruct the user to make a new entry. How do you do this?

Look at the answers provided for these questions in the Web Dynpro framework. We will discuss the first question about an efficient check first.

wddobeforeaction( ) hook method

The `wddobeforeaction( )` hook method provides an alternative period for performing checks for each view. You activate this method before you call one of the action handler methods. If a window contains several views, all `wddobeforeaction( )` methods are activated before one of the action handler methods of the views involved is called.

Applying the mandatory entry field check

Let us take a look at an option for using the `wddobeforeaction( )` method. We want to check whether the user has made all of the entries for mandatory entry fields. Because the Web Dynpro framework does not provide any direct support for this, you must explicitly implement this check. To do this, proceed as follows:

1. To show the user that a specific field is a mandatory entry field, you must set the value for the STATE property to `required` in the UI element properties. As a result, a red asterisk appears in front of the UI element, indicating that the subsequent UI element is a mandatory entry field. However, this is only a display option without functional features. You must create these features manually.

state property

2. To do this, switch to the `wddobeforeaction( )` method of the view and use the `CL_WD_DYNAMIC_TOOL` ABAP class to perform the check on mandatory entry fields. Listing 3.29 gives an example of implementing the `wddobeforeaction( )` method in relation to mandatory entry fields.

Check

```
METHOD wddobeforeaction .
* API of view controller
DATA lo_api_controller TYPE REF TO if_wd_view_controller,
* Reference to action
     lo_action TYPE REF TO if_wd_action.
* Determine API of view
lo_api_controller = wd_this->wd_get_api( ).
* Determine current action
lo_action = lo_api_controller->get_current_action( ).
* Evaluate action
IF lo_action IS BOUND.
  CASE lo_action->name.
    WHEN 'SEARCH_METHODS'.
      cl_wd_dynamic_tool=>check_mandatory_attr_on_view(
        EXPORTING
          view_controller  = lo_api_controller ).
  ENDCASE.
ENDIF.
ENDMETHOD.
```

Listing 3.29 Implementing the wddobeforeaction( ) Method in a Mandatory Entry Field Check

3. The API for the current view is determined first to establish the current action. This is provided by the `get_current_action( )` API method. The `name` public instance attribute for the action contains the name of the action that will subsequently be analyzed by a `CASE` statement.

check_mandatory_attr_on_view( )

4. In this example, additional checks are only to be performed for the SEARCH_METHOD action. If the user has actually triggered the methods search, the check_mandatory_attr_on_view( ) method from the CL_WD_DYNAMIC_TOOL class will be used to execute the check for all mandatory entry fields. Figure 3.83 shows the check result for an empty entry field:
   - By setting the value for the STATE property to required in the UI element properties, the red asterisk appears in front of the input field for the class name (❶).
   - If the user does not enter a value in the input field and starts the search, the mandatory entry field check finds the missing entry at the wddobeforeaction( ) point and sends the message to the user (❷). At the same time, possible navigation to another view is prevented, and the other processing actions are cancelled.

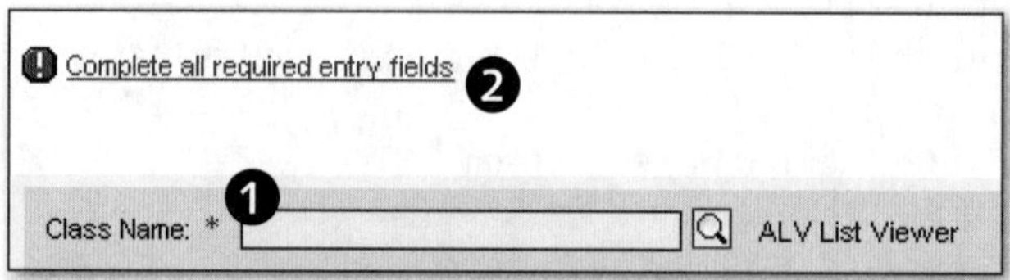

Figure 3.83 Message for Empty Mandatory Entry

Canceling navigation

Now, let us look at the question about navigation behavior in Web Dynpro. As you saw in the previous example, the mandatory entry fields check resulted in the processing being canceled and an error message being issued. Here, the action type an action has is one of the determining factors. You can set ACTION TYPES for every action on the ACTIONS tab in a view. The standard (as the default value) and validation-independent values are available for this. You must look at the effect of the action type in combination with the message type, especially error messages.

Types of error messages

Error messages in Web Dynpro can affect the phase model process flow. We differentiate between two error message types in this context:

- **Error messages with a context reference**
  These messages affect the phase model process flow. If an error message with a context reference is issued, standard actions will not be executed. Any possible pending navigation and the wddomodifyview( )

method will not be executed either. However, validation-independent actions are executed if error messages are issued. In addition, navigation to this type of action is subsequently made and the wddomodifyview( ) method is executed.

- **Error messages without a context reference**
  Just like warnings and success messages, these messages do not affect the phase model process flow.

cancel_navigation and is_validation_independent parameters

The cancel_navigation parameter is available for all Message Manager methods for issuing messages. You can use it to cancel navigation. Another parameter is is_validation_independent, which is available for all methods with a context reference.

Additional Information About Messages

Message types

We generally differentiate between two message types in Web Dynpro:

- **Standard messages**
  These messages are deleted before an action is executed by the Web Dynpro runtime and therefore have to be created again as required in each HTTP roundtrip.
- **Permanent messages**
  These messages are not automatically deleted before an action is executed. You can define the lifecycle of a permanent message by specifying a scope. Possible scopes include: COMPONENT, CONTROLLER, and CONTEXT ELEMENT. If you want a message to be permanent, you must identify it as is_permanent when you generate it.

Other methods

The Message Manager provides other useful methods. Some of these are summarized in Table 3.12.

Method Name	Description
is_empty( )	Checks whether there are messages.
clear_messages( )	Deletes all existing messages.
remove_message( )	Removes a message.
get_messages( )	Reads all messages from the Message Manager.

Table 3.12 Selected Message Manager Methods

3.5 Summary

In this chapter, you developed your first major Web Dynpro application (Figure 3.84).

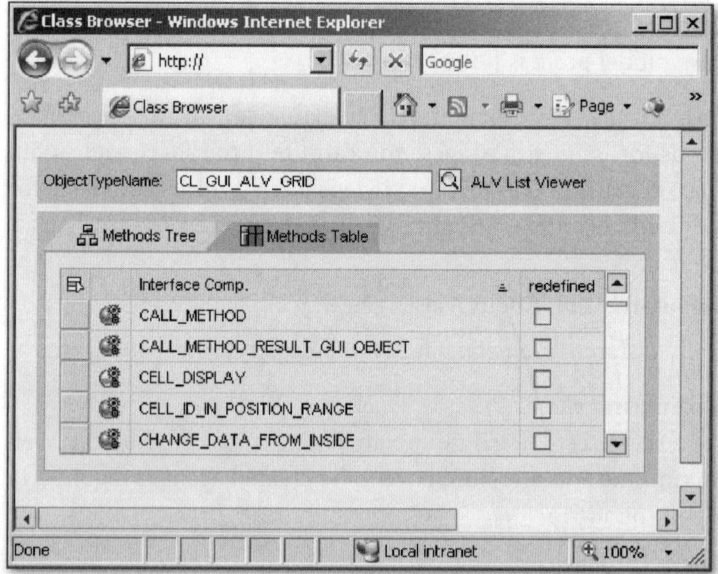

Figure 3.84 The Created Web Dynpro Application

You have learned about many different areas in the course of developing the Web Dynpro application:

- Context programming showed you how you can read data from the context, store data in the context, and manipulate and delete this data. The `IF_WD_CONTEXT_NODE` and `IF_WD_CONTEXT_ELEMENT` ABAP interfaces were extremely important for this purpose. Some of the things for which you used context programming included transferring the user entry in the object type name (ABAP class name) and providing search results in the context so that they could then be displayed in a tree or table.
- The sections about layouts, containers, and UI elements showed you how you can arrange and group data for display. You used different layouts to create appealing views that enable the user to enter data

efficiently. You also learned about UI elements as complex as tabs, trees, and tables in the available display options.

- Language-dependent messages to the user are a must for every professional Web Dynpro application. You integrated these messages into your Web Dynpro application with reference to the various message sources, thereby also influencing the navigation behavior of your Web Dynpro application.

In Chapter 4, Dynamic Web Dynpro Applications, you will learn about options for dynamically programming Web Dynpro applications.

How can you respond to information that is not yet known during development and integrate it into Web Dynpro components? Read this chapter to learn the basic options for programming Web Dynpro applications dynamically.

4 Dynamic Web Dynpro Applications

Integrating information during runtime

Previously developed Web Dynpro applications supported requirements and information that were fully known during the development phase; however, this does not always have to be the case. Information that will affect the controller context structure, view layouts, and the assignment of actions to view elements may only be available during runtime.

For example, let us assume you want to display a `TabStrip` with one `Tab` each for implemented ABAP interfaces of the ABAP class in the *Class Browser* Web Dynpro application from Chapter 3, Developing Web Dynpro Applications (see Figure 4.1). An ABAP class the user is looking for (❶) may not implement any ABAP interfaces or (❷) may implement one or several ABAP interfaces. Information about the number of ABAP interfaces is only available at runtime and determines the context structure because the data for the ABAP interface or interfaces must be stored there. The view structure is also affected in this case because a `Tab` has to be displayed for each ABAP interface (❸). If methods are defined for the ABAP interface, they are mapped in a table with a column for the name (❹) and a table will only be displayed if methods actually exist.

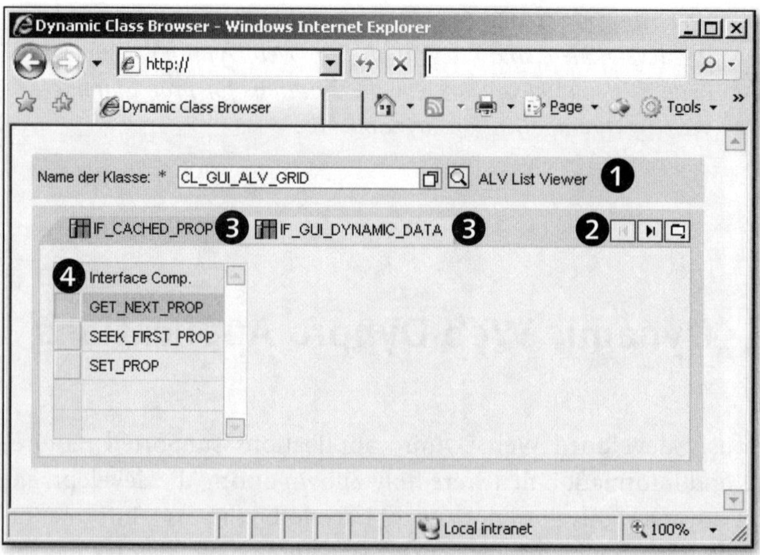

Figure 4.1 Sample Application for Dynamic Programming

We will be covering several topics in this chapter. First, we will discuss the advantages and disadvantages of dynamic programming. Then, after looking at the options provided by dynamic programming, we will describe in detail how to adjust the context structure during runtime. Next, we will explain in depth the techniques for creating and customizing context nodes and context attributes.

Another focus area will be adjusting the user interface during runtime. You will learn the necessary basics to generate user interfaces dynamically with containers, layouts, and view elements. We will also show you how to assign action handlers to UI elements dynamically.

Topics Discussed

We will discuss the following topics in this chapter:

- Types of dynamic changes
- Adjusting the context at runtime
- Adjusting the user interface at runtime

4.1 Advantages and Disadvantages of Dynamic Programming

Defining context during the development phase

The procedure we previously used for defining context was to define it in the development phase and specify or statically define the property values for a view element through data binding to the context attributes or nodes. With data binding, changing the context attribute contents can influence view element properties such as the visibility of a view element (see Figure 4.2).

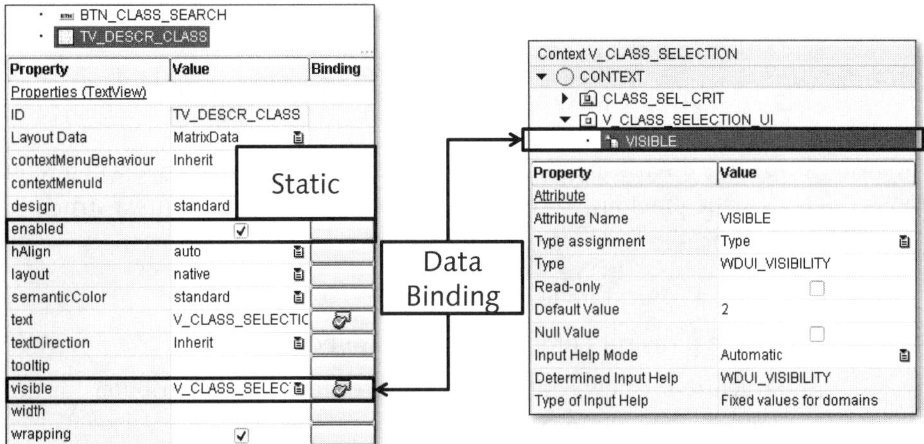

Figure 4.2 Statically Defining View Element Properties vs. Data Binding

Reasons against using dynamic programming

In general, you should always try to influence view element properties through data binding rather than through dynamic programming and make use of this function as much as possible. The reasons for this are as follows:

- Dynamic programming is complex.
- Dynamic programming generates extensive source code.
- Dynamically programmed applications are more difficult to maintain than statically programmed applications.
- Dynamically programmed applications are sometimes slower than statically programmed applications. This is a factor that often plays a role, especially when implementing the `wddomodifyview( )` method.

Reasons in favor of dynamic programming

You should not use dynamic programming to manipulate statically defined values of view element properties. Instead, use dynamic programming under the following circumstances:

- If the data structure is only known during runtime
- If generic applications have to be developed
- If the structure for views is generic

In the next section, you will learn about the options available to you if you have taken these recommendations into account and then still have to use dynamic programming.

4.2 Types of Dynamic Changes

Previously used procedure in Web Dynpro development

Before we discuss the different types of dynamic changes, we will briefly review the previously used procedure for defining the context structure and views during development:

1. Create a context node in a controller.
2. Set the properties of this new context node.
3. Structure the new context node by creating context attributes for the context node and/or subnodes.
4. Set the properties of the new context attributes.
5. Perform the context mapping for the relevant context nodes.
6. Define a view layout using view elements.
7. Define the data binding of the view element properties to the context nodes and attributes.
8. Define or use actions and their action handlers for view element events and assign the actions to the events.

Types of dynamic changes

Different types of dynamic changes are available in Web Dynpro that allow you to carry out each of these steps dynamically. The explanations we will provide focus on the following most important basic options:

- **Dynamic context manipulation**
  You can create, change, and delete context nodes and context attributes when manipulating context dynamically.

- **Dynamic layout manipulation**
  You can create, change, and delete view elements when structuring the layout during runtime.
- **Dynamically assigning actions to view elements**
  You can also bind events against existing actions or manipulate the parameter mapping of event parameters.

We will discuss these different types of dynamic adjustments in detail in the sections that follow. We will use numerous examples to help you understand how to use these dynamic programming options.

4.3 Adjusting Context at Runtime

Sample application

To illustrate manipulating context at runtime, we will use the class browser from Chapter 3, Developing Web Dynpro Applications. We will remodel it here as a *dynamic class browser*.

As mentioned previously, you can determine whether and how many ABAP interfaces are implemented by an ABAP class only at runtime. If an ABAP interface is not implemented, no context structures are required for ABAP interface data. If an individual ABAP interface is implemented, or if several ABAP interfaces are implemented, you will need context structures whose property values may have different characteristics.

We will examine this in detail in the examples. Figure 4.3 shows the context structure to be created.

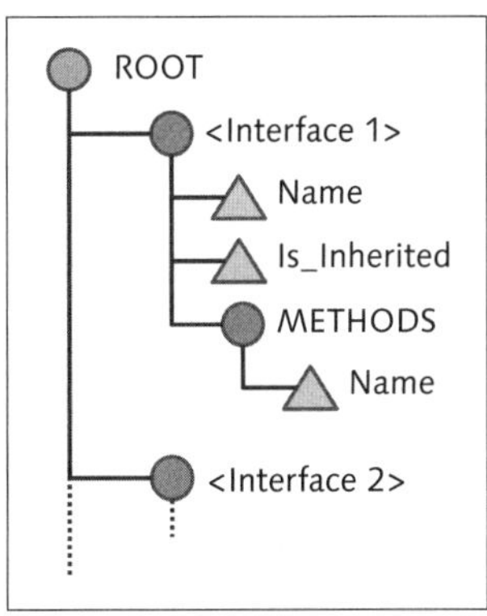

Figure 4.3 Context Structure for the Dynamic Class Browser

Creating context dynamically

One context node is created under the context root for every interface found. The node name called `<Interface 1>`, `<Interface 2>`, and so on, corresponds to the ABAP interface name. This context node has two attributes:

- `NAME`
  This attribute includes the ABAP interface name.
- `IS_INHERITED`
  This attribute indicates whether the ABAP interface was inherited from a superclass.

If the ABAP interface has methods, the `METHODS` subnode is created under the `<Interface i>` interface node. This context node only has the `NAME` attribute. For this reason, it has the names of all of the methods for the ABAP interface.

Procedure for changing context dynamically

You may have different reasons for dynamically manipulating context nodes. For example, one reason might be that the number of nodes in generic components is unknown at development time. Even if the context nodes are known, you may only be able to determine a node structure during runtime.

The procedure for dynamically changing the context is easy to describe:

1. The context root node is always available and cannot be changed or deleted.
2. Determine the reference to the context node under which you want to create a node or change its structure.
3. Use the reference to the context node to determine the *description object* (alternative names are *meta information object* or *information object*) for the context node.
4. Use the description object to extend the new context node or change the structure of an existing context node.

The following sections will describe the outlined procedure to manipulate context during runtime. However, before we proceed with more explanations, you will copy the existing Web Dynpro component:

1. Copy the ZWDC_03_CLASS_BROWSER Web Dynpro component to the new ZWDC_04_CLASS_BROWSER Web Dynpro component.
2. Create the new V_CLASS_INTF view and embed the view in the W_MAIN window in the VC_CLASS_METHODS view container. You can delete the other views in the view container (see Figure 4.4).

Window Structure	Description
W_MAIN	
V_MAIN_LAYOUT	
VC_CLASS_METHODS	
V_CLASS_INTF	Class interfaces
FROM_CLASS_SELECTION	From class selection
VC_CLASS_SELECTION	
V_CLASS_SELECTION	Class selection
TO_CLASS_INTF	To class interfaces
FROM_CLASS_SELECTION	
TO_CLASS_METHODS	To class methods
DEFAULT	

Figure 4.4 Window Structure for the Web Dynpro Application of the Dynamic Class Browser

3. Define a navigation transition from the V_CLASS_SELECTION view to the V_CLASS_INTF view. (Do not forget to define the plugs beforehand.) You should implement the transition handling in the same way as for the V_CLASS_METHODS view.
4. Switch to the onactionsearch_methods( ) method of the V_CLASS_SELECTION view and implement the method for the transition to the V_CLASS_INTF view, as shown in Listing 4.1.

   IS_NEW_SEARCH

   You still have to create the public is_new_search component controller attribute and type it using WDY_BOOLEAN. Subsequently, it will always be set when the user triggers a new search. You will use this attribute later to find out whether you have to create the view layout again.

```
* A new search is performed
wd_comp_controller->is_new_search = abap_true.
* If the class exists, navigate to the result
wd_this->fire_to_class_intf_plg( ).
ENDMETHOD.
```

Listing 4.1 Transition from the Selection Screen to the View for the ABAP Interfaces

Testing

5. Create a Web Dynpro application, activate all inactive elements of the ZWDC_04_CLASS_BROWSER Web Dynpro component, and test the Web Dynpro application.

After you have triggered the search, you see nothing – this is how it should be. The missing visualization still has to be added. You have now completed the preparations and can focus on dynamically changing the context. The first step toward dynamically programming context involves determining the description object for a context node.

4.3.1 Determining a Description Object (Meta Information) for a Context Node

All context nodes to be created dynamically need a higher-level context node. The ever-present context node that cannot be deleted or changed is the context root node.

Determining the description object

You can use the root node or other existing nodes to create a subnode. To do this, you need to determine the description object of the context node for which you want to create a subnode. You can easily do this using the reference to the context node. When you have determined the reference to the context node (using the wd_context controller attribute in the root node example), use this node reference to call the get_node_info( ) method and get the description object for the context node.

We will look at the procedure by way of an example where you will create the createctx_interfaces( ) method. In this method, you will perform all of the implementations for dynamically changing the context.

The listings we will show you will result in the createctx_interfaces( ) method being fully implemented. The beginning and end of a control structure or loop may be distributed across different listings; however, do not worry about this.

1. Switch to the V_CLASS_INTF view and select the METHODS tab.

Determining the description object

2. Create the createctx_interfaces( ) method and implement the description object determination of the context root node, as shown in Listing 4.2:
   - Define the lo_nd_info_root object reference variable for the IF_WD_CONTEXT_NODE_INFO description object.

- Due to the wd_context attribute, the reference to the context root node is already available and does not have to be determined explicitly. If you need a subnode reference to the context root node, use the wd_context->get_child_node( ) method.
- Call wd_context->get_node_info( ) to determine the description object for the context root node, which you store in the lo_nd_info_root reference variable.

```
METHOD createctx_interfaces .
* Root node description node
DATA: lo_nd_info_root TYPE REF TO
        if_wd_context_node_info.
* Determine information object for root node
lo_nd_info_root = wd_context->get_node_info( ).
```

Listing 4.2 Determining the Description Object for the Context Root Node

You will now have the description object for a context node. Having determined the information object for the node, you can now create subnodes in the context.

4.3.2 Creating and Adding Context Nodes

add_new_child_node( )

IF_WD_CONTEXT_NODE_INFO, the ABAP interface you learned about when determining a node information object, includes the add_new_child_node( ) method for creating a new context node, which creates a hierarchy one level lower. We will use this method in this example to define a context node for every ABAP interface found (see Figure 4.5).

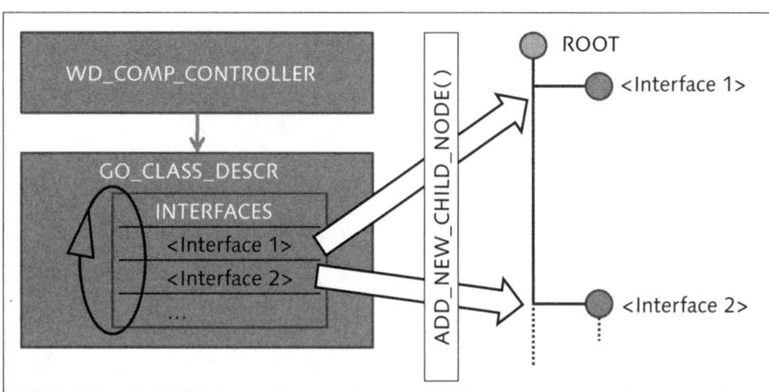

Figure 4.5 Creating Context Nodes for each ABAP Interface

ABAP class – description object

The global go_class_description attribute is stored in the component controller, which you can access using the wd_comp_controller reference. This attribute has an internal table with the implemented ABAP interfaces of the ABAP class. The add_new_child_node( ) method is used to create a context node for every interface (see Listing 4.3).

```
* The name of the interface from the class RTTI object
DATA: ls_interface LIKE LINE OF
wd_comp_controller->go_class_description->interfaces,
* For converting the interface name type to text
      ld_intf_name TYPE string,
* The information object of the interface node
      lo_nd_info_intf TYPE REF TO if_wd_context_node_info.
* If interfaces exist for the searched for class,
* a node is created for each interface
LOOP AT
  wd_comp_controller->go_class_description->interfaces
  INTO ls_interface.
** Option 1: Create context node and attributes individually **
* Convert name type to string
    ld_intf_name = ls_interface-name.
* Create new child node
    lo_nd_info_intf = lo_nd_info_root->add_new_child_node(
      name                          = ld_intf_name
      is_mandatory                  = abap_true
      is_multiple                   = abap_false
      is_mandatory_selection        = abap_true
      is_multiple_selection         = abap_false
      is_singleton                  = abap_true
      is_initialize_lead_selection = abap_true
*     static_element_type          =
*     static_element_rtti          =
*     attributes                   =
        is_static                     = abap_false ).
```

Listing 4.3 Creating a Context Node

Creating a context node for each ABAP interface

A context node is created directly below the context root node for every entry in the internal interfaces table. The lo_nd_info_root description object of the context root node previously determined can be used to call the add_new_child_node( ) method to create a subnode for the context root node. Calling the method results in a description object being returned for the newly created context node with properties that are set using the method parameters.

Importance of add_new_child_node( ) method parameters

Figure 4.6 shows the relationship between the method parameters and context node properties. This figure is shown for illustration purposes because this context node is created at runtime and is not displayed in the context structure.

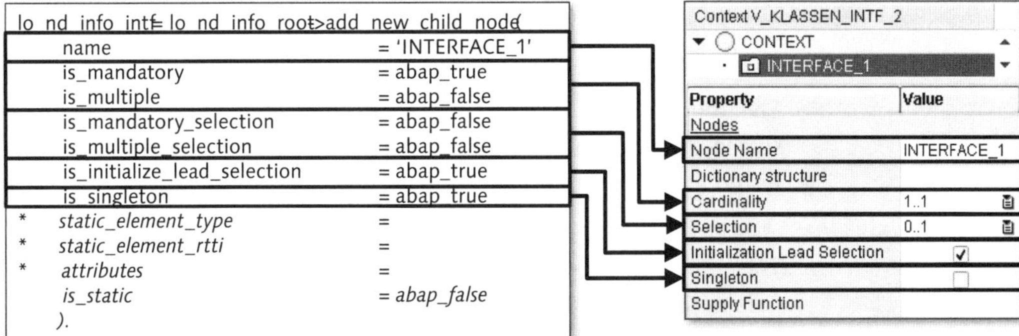

Figure 4.6 Defining Property Values for a Context Node Using the add_new_child_node( ) Method

You can use the following importing parameters when calling the `add_new_child_node( )` method:

- `name` = node ID
  The context nodes in this example have the same names as the interfaces.
- `is_mandatory`, `is_multiple` = cardinality
  `is_mandatory` stands for the cardinality's lower limit, where `ABAP_TRUE` corresponds to `1` and `ABAP_FALSE` corresponds to `0`. `is_multiple` stands for the cardinality's upper limit, where `ABAP_TRUE` corresponds to `n` and `ABAP_FALSE` corresponds to `1`.
- `is_mandatory_selection`, `is_multiple_selection` = selection
  The selections correspond to those of the cardinality.
- `is_singleton` = singleton
  The singleton property for a context node is set to the `ABAP_TRUE` default setting in the example because the new ABAP interface context node is created directly under the root node.

- `is_initialize_lead_selection` = lead selection initialization
  In the example, the lead selection is set to the `ABAP_TRUE` default setting.
- `is_static` = can the node be deleted at runtime?
  This very important property for dynamic programming controls whether the node can be deleted during runtime:
  - The node can be deleted if the value for the parameter is set to `ABAP_FALSE`.
  - The node cannot be deleted if the `ABAP_TRUE` value is set.

  The node will have to be deleted at a later stage if the user runs a new search, for example; therefore, the `ABAP_FALSE` value will be transferred for the parameter.
- `static_element_type`, `static_element_rtti` and `attributes`
  The `static_element_type`, `static_element_rtti`, and `attributes` parameters are used for transferring information to context node attributes. In the following sections, we will show you how you can use these parameters.

Defining attributes with a flat structure type

The new subnode was created at runtime by calling the `add_new_child_node( )` method. The question is now: How can you define attributes? This can be done in several ways.

The easiest way is to use a flat structure type from the ABAP Dictionary (structure, transparent table, or view) and specifically transfer it to the `static_element_type` interface parameter. In this case, all structure fields become context node attributes (see Figure 4.7).

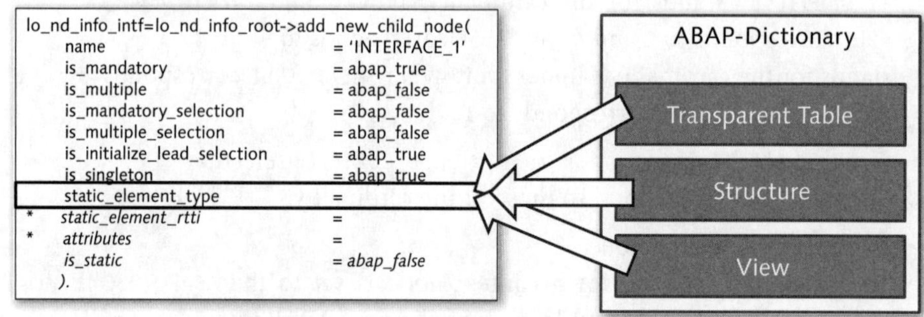

Figure 4.7 Using the static_element_type Formal Parameter for Defining Attributes

However, individual attributes that are not necessarily part of a structure type often have to be added during runtime, or types from an ABAP Dictionary type group have to be used. We will discuss both of these scenarios in the following section.

4.3.3 Creating and Adding Context Attributes Individually

Creating attributes individually

If you created a context node with a DDIC structure in the design phase, or if you want to define general node attributes, you can create these attributes dynamically (see Figure 4.8).

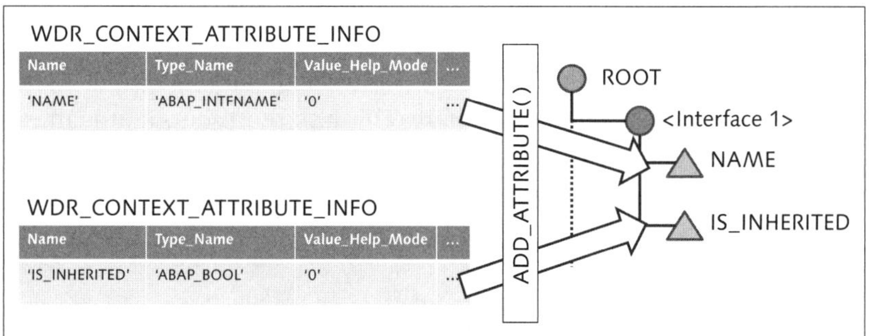

Figure 4.8 Dynamically Creating Individual Attributes Using the add_attribute( ) Method

add_attribute( )

For this purpose, the `IF_WD_CONTEXT_NODE_INFO` ABAP interface contains the `add_attribute( )` method. However, a `WDR_CONTEXT_ATTRIBUTE_INFO` structure must first be filled for this and transferred to the method. Listing 4.4 shows how the method is used.

```
* Context node attributes
DATA: ls_attribute TYPE wdr_context_attribute_info.
* Create context attribute for interface context node
* Attribute for interface name
ls_attribute-name = 'NAME'.
ls_attribute-type_name = 'ABAP_INTFNAME'.
ls_attribute-value_help_mode = '0'.
* Add attribute for name
lo_nd_info_intf->add_attribute(
  attribute_info = ls_attribute ).
* Attribute for inheriting the interface
ls_attribute-name = 'IS_INHERITED'.
```

```
ls_attribute-type_name = 'ABAP_BOOL'.
ls_attribute-value_help_mode = '0'.
* Add attribute for inheritance
lo_nd_info_intf->add_attribute(
  attribute_info = ls_attribute ).
```

Listing 4.4 Defining Attributes for a Context Node Using an Individual Definition

In addition to other fields, the `WDR_CONTEXT_ATTRIBUTE_INFO` structure contains the following:

- `name`
  This is the attribute name.
- `type_name`
  This is the field type name. Both ABAP Dictionary types and types from a type group can be used here. This also represents a fundamental difference to defining the context during development. In the development phase, you cannot use any types from type groups for typing attributes. This can only be done in dynamic programming.
- `value_help_mode`
  This is the value help mode. The `0` value is set because the value help will be found automatically. You can determine possible field values easily using the ABAP Dictionary. Forward navigate from the `WDR_CONTEXT_ATTRIBUTE_INFO` structure to the interesting data elements first, and then navigate to the domains. The fixed values for the domains show you the possible field values.

Alternative Options for Determining Values: Constants for View Element Properties

Alternatively, you can use constants in the implementing view element classes (details about ABAP classes follow in Section 4.4, Adjusting the User Interface at Runtime). For example, the `TabStrip` UI element is implemented by the `CL_WD_TABSTRIP` class. Constants containing property values are defined in this class. These constants follow the `E_<property>` name structure (E stands for enumeration).

In the Class Builder (Transaction SE24), you will find the `E_VISIBLE` constant on the ATTRIBUTES tab in the `CL_WD_TABSTRIP` ABAP class. This constant is defined as a structure with the `blank`, `none`, and `visible` fields. One of these constant fields – for example, `none` – can be addressed as follows in the programming:

```
cl_wd_tabstrip=>e_visible-none.
```

The preferred option in programming is to use constants rather than absolute values because constant names do not depend on absolute values and will therefore not be affected by changes to absolute values.

Transferring a filled structure

After values have been collected and set for an attribute, the filled structure is transferred to the `add_attribute( )` method and consequently, the attribute is defined. The structure must be filled and the method called for every attribute. Two attributes are created for the context node in this example: The ABAP interface `name` and an `is_inherited` Boolean value that specifies whether the interface was inherited from a superclass. If there are now a large number of attributes, the source code may be quite long.

4.3.4 Creating and Adding Context Attributes in Bundles

attributes

The `add_new_child_node( )` method provides the `attributes` parameter to transfer an internal table with attribute descriptions. This option is similar to the option for creating an attribute individually in that you must fill a `WDR_CONTEXT_ATTRIBUTE_INFO` description structure for each attribute to be created, as you can see in Figure 4.9.

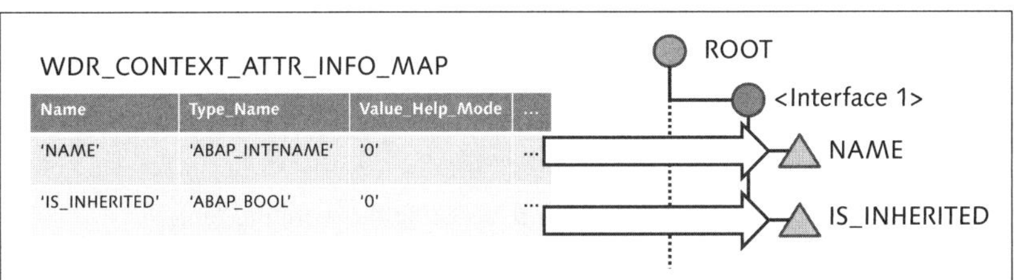

Figure 4.9 Dynamically Creating Attributes Using the Attributes Formal Parameter

Attribute table

In this case, the description structures are collected in an internal `WDR_CONTEXT_ATTR_INFO_MAP` table and then transferred to the `attributes` parameter. Another difference to creating attributes individually is that the internal table must be filled with attribute information before the method for creating the context node is called. Let us now look at this option as an alternative to the previous example. The implementation option using the attribute table is shown in Listing 4.5.

```
* Context node attributes
DATA: ls_attribute TYPE wdr_context_attribute_info,
* Table of context node attributes
      lt_attributes TYPE wdr_context_attr_info_map.
** Option 2: Create nodes and attributes using a table **
* Attribute for interface name
ls_attribute-name = 'NAME'.
ls_attribute-type_name = 'ABAP_INTFNAME'.
ls_attribute-value_help_mode = '0'.
INSERT ls_attribute INTO TABLE lt_attributes.
* Attribute for inheriting the interface
ls_attribute-name = 'IS_INHERITED'.
ls_attribute-type_name = 'ABAP_BOOL'.
ls_attribute-value_help_mode = '0'.
INSERT ls_attribute INTO TABLE lt_attributes.
* Create node for interface
ld_intf_name = ls_interface-name.
lo_nd_info_intf = lo_nd_info_root->add_new_child_node(
  name                         = ld_intf_name
  is_mandatory                 = abap_true
  is_multiple                  = abap_false
  is_mandatory_selection       = abap_true
  is_multiple_selection        = abap_false
  is_singleton                 = abap_true
  is_initialize_lead_selection = abap_true
  attributes                   = lt_attributes
  is_static                    = abap_false ).
```

Listing 4.5 Defining Context Node Attributes Using the Attribute Table

The way the parameters are supplied is identical to the first option although the `attributes` parameter is used here. Furthermore, a method does not need to be called separately to define an attribute. However, using this option does not mean you have exhausted every alternative. You can also use an RTTI description object.

static_element_rtti

The `add_new_child_node( )` method provides the `static_element_rtti` parameter to which an RTTI structure description object can be transferred – in other words, an object that describes a structure and encapsulates this description. Look at Listing 4.6 as an example of this option.

```
* RTTI description object for structure
DATA: lo_intf_rtti TYPE REF TO cl_abap_structdescr.
** Option 3: Creating nodes, RTTI **
* Generate RTTI description object for structure
lo_intf_rtti ?= cl_abap_typedescr=>describe_by_name(
  'ABAP_INTFDESCR' ).
* Create nodes for interface
ld_intf_name = ls_interface-name.
lo_nd_info_intf = lo_nd_info_root->add_new_child_node(
  name                          = ld_intf_name
  is_mandatory                  = abap_true
  is_multiple                   = abap_false
  is_mandatory_selection        = abap_true
  is_multiple_selection         = abap_false
  is_singleton                  = abap_true
  is_initialize_lead_selection = abap_true
  static_element_rtti           = lo_intf_rtti
  is_static                     = abap_false ).
```

Listing 4.6 Defining Context Node Attributes Using an RTTI Description Object

Creating an RTTI description object

The RTTI description object in this example is created by calling the public static method `cl_abap_typedescr=>describe_by_name( )`. The actual parameter type will determine which description object type – on which casting can be performed – is returned.

In this example, the `ABAP_INTFDESCR` structure type defined in the `ABAP` type group is transferred to the `describe_by_name( )` method. Due to the `ABAP_INTFDESCR` type, a `CL_ABAP_STRUCTDESCR` description object is delivered, which can then be transferred to the `static_element_rtti` parameter of the `add_new_child_node( )` method.

You have now learned about all of the options for defining attributes for a context node. However, the context requires an additional change in this example: For every ABAP interface context node, a subnode must be created in the context for existing ABAP interface methods.

4.3.5 Other Methods for Dynamic Context Manipulation

Creating subnodes

In this example, a context node with two attributes has already been created for each ABAP interface for an ABAP class. We now also want to store the possibly defined interface-methods in the context for the ABAP interfaces, to be able to display them to the user. This means that if methods exist for the interface, we must set up a subnode under every interface context node (see Figure 4.10).

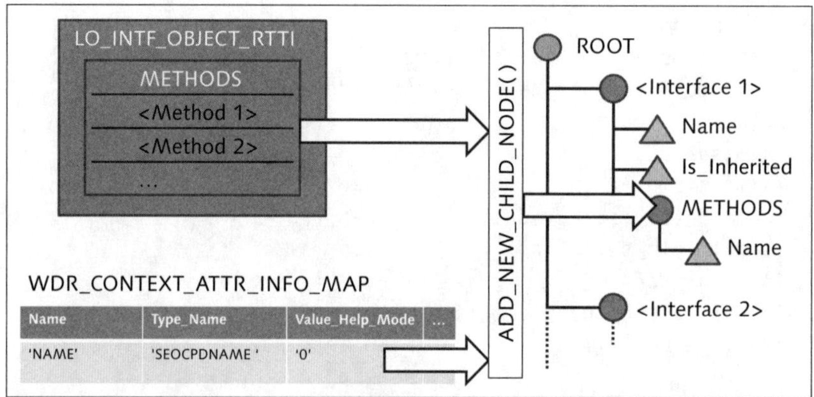

Figure 4.10 Dynamically Creating the METHODS Node with the NAME Attribute

The `lo_intf_object_rtti` RTTI description object for the ABAP interface determines whether methods are defined for the ABAP interface. The internal `methods` table in the RTTI description object is used for this purpose. If methods are defined, the `name` attribute is transferred to the `add_new_child_node( )` method using the attribute table. Listing 4.7 contains the implementation for creating the `METHODS` context node with the `NAME` attribute.

```
* The reference to the interface node
DATA: lo_nd_intf TYPE REF TO if_wd_context_node,
* The RTTI description object for an interface
      lo_intf_object_rtti  TYPE REF TO cl_abap_intfdescr,
* The reference to the context node
      lo_nd_interface_methods
        TYPE REF TO if_wd_context_node,
* Table of context node attributes
      lt_attributes TYPE wdr_context_attr_info_map.
* Put data in the generated interface node
* First, determine the reference to the node
lo_nd_intf = wd_context->get_child_node(
  name = ld_intf_name ).
```

```
* Bind the data to the node
lo_nd_intf->bind_structure( ls_interface ).
* If methods exist for the interface, display them
* Determine the description object for the interface
lo_intf_object_rtti ?= cl_abap_typedescr=>describe_by_name(
  ld_intf_name ).
* If the interface has methods
IF LINES( lo_intf_object_rtti->methods ) > 0.
* Attribute for the name of interface methods
  ls_attribute-name = 'NAME'.
  ls_attribute-type_name = 'SEOCPDNAME'.
  ls_attribute-value_help_mode = '0'.
  CLEAR lt_attributes.
  INSERT ls_attribute INTO TABLE lt_attributes.
* Create nodes for interface methods
  lo_nd_info_intf->add_new_child_node(
    name                          = 'METHODS'
    is_mandatory                  = abap_true
    is_multiple                   = abap_true
    is_mandatory_selection        = abap_false
    is_multiple_selection         = abap_false
    is_singleton                  = abap_true
    is_initialize_lead_selection = abap_true
    attributes                    = lt_attributes
    is_static                     = abap_false ).
* Store the method names in the context node
* Determine nodes for methods
  lo_nd_interface_methods = lo_nd_intf->get_child_node(
        'METHODS' ).
* Put the methods in the node
  lo_nd_interface_methods->bind_table(
    lo_intf_object_rtti->methods ).
    ENDIF.
  ENDLOOP.
ENDMETHOD.
```

Listing 4.7 Defining the METHODS Subnode for the Context Node Interface

We will now discuss the relevant parts of the implementation:

Storing data in the context

- At the beginning, an element is created for the interface context node. The reference to the interface context node is determined first; then, the element is created using the `bind_structure( )` method.

Filling an attribute table

- The attribute table contains exactly one attribute, the name of the method in the interface. The SEOCPDNAME data element was used for the typing because field labels that are available as column headers are also defined for this data element.

Storing data in the context

- If the subnode has been defined for the methods, the data for the node still has to be set. After the reference to the node for the interface methods has been determined with the get_child_node( ) method, the bind_table( ) method can be used to create the table of interface methods – which are used as elements – in the METHODS context node.

The createctx_interfaces( ) method has now been implemented. The method is best called at the end of the handlefrom_class_selection( ) method to structure the context for the search result.

What you have to keep in mind here, however, is that with every positive search result, a node is created in the context for each interface for the many different ABAP classes. This is a waste of resources, and runtime errors may occur if a context node had already been created for an interface.

Deleting context nodes

This means that the existing context nodes in the context must be deleted before new context nodes can be created. The IF_WD_CONTEXT_NODE_INFO interface provides additional methods to do this, which we will describe by way of an example.

[✎]

1. Switch to the V_CLASS_INTF view and select the METHODS tab.
2. Create the deletectx_interfaces( ) method and implement the deletion of all context nodes (see Listing 4.8).

```
METHOD deletectx_interfaces .
* Node information of root node
DATA: lo_nd_info_root TYPE REF TO
        if_wd_context_node_info,
* The child nodes of the root node
      lt_nodes TYPE wdr_context_child_info_map,
* One child node of the root node
      ls_node LIKE LINE OF lt_nodes.
* Determining the node description of the root node
lo_nd_info_root = wd_context->get_node_info( ).
* Determining all child nodes of the root node
```

```
lt_nodes = lo_nd_info_root->get_child_nodes( ).
* Delete all child nodes of the root node
LOOP AT lt_nodes INTO ls_node.
  lo_nd_info_root->remove_child_node(
    name = ls_node-name ).
ENDLOOP.
ENDMETHOD.
```

Listing 4.8 Deleting Context Nodes

Process flow

In this example, the `wd_context->get_node_info( )` method determines the information object for the context root node. This information object can be used with the `get_child_nodes( )` method to determine all context child nodes.

Call the `remove_child_node( )` method of the supernode information object for each of these context child nodes and transfer the context subnode name. This removes all context nodes and their subnodes from the context. The `deletectx_interfaces( )` method should be called before the context is created.

4.3.6 Conclusion

Context node information

In this section, you learned about the key importance of the `IF_WD_CONTEXT_NODE_INFO` interface. The most important methods provided by the `IF_WD_CONTEXT_NODE_INFO` interface are listed in Table 4.1.

After now having defined the context structure and stored the data from the search results in the context, you can turn your attention to the visualization.

Method	Description
`add_new_child_node( )`	Creates a new node one hierarchy level lower.
`add_attribute( )`	Creates an attribute for a node.
`get_attributes( )`	Returns the meta data of all attributes for a node.
`get_attribute( )`	Returns the meta data of one attribute for a node.

Table 4.1 Selected IF_WD_CONTEXT_NODE_INFO Interface Methods

Method	Description
get_child_nodes( )	Returns the meta data of all child nodes for a node.
get_child_node( )	Returns the meta data of one child node for a node.
get_parent( )	Returns the meta data of a higher-level node for a node.
remove_attribute( )	Deletes a node attribute.
remove_child_nodes( )	Deletes all child nodes for a node.
remove_child_node( )	Deletes one child node for a node.

Table 4.1 Selected IF_WD_CONTEXT_NODE_INFO Interface Methods (Cont.)

4.4 Adjusting the User Interface at Runtime

A final warning

In principle, dynamically manipulating the layout (just like dynamically manipulating the context) should only be done if a Web Dynpro component cannot be created in a declarative way at development time.

wddomodifyview()

If you need to do this, you must make the changes to a view layout structure in the `wddomodifyview( )` method or in a method called in it. Only in this method can the view element hierarchy be accessed by the `view` parameter reference. Another particularly important parameter is `first_time`. This parameter contains information about whether the `wddomodifyview( )` method is executed for the first time during the lifecycle of the view controller. This controls whether the view layout has already been created dynamically.

If the view has to be created several times while the Web Dynpro application is being executed, you must define a separate parameter that indicates whether the view layout has to be created again. The view layout structure for this example is as shown in Figure 4.11.

View structure in the example

Each dynamically generated context node for an ABAP interface stands for a `Tab` view element in a `TabStrip` UI element. The `Tab` name, implemented as a `Caption` view element, is derived from the `NAME` attribute of the interface context node. A `TransparentContainer` UI element that includes a `Table` UI element for the ABAP interface methods is placed within the `Tab` view element. However, the `Table` UI element is only generated if the `METHODS` context node actually exists. The table only has one `TableColumn` view element for the method names.

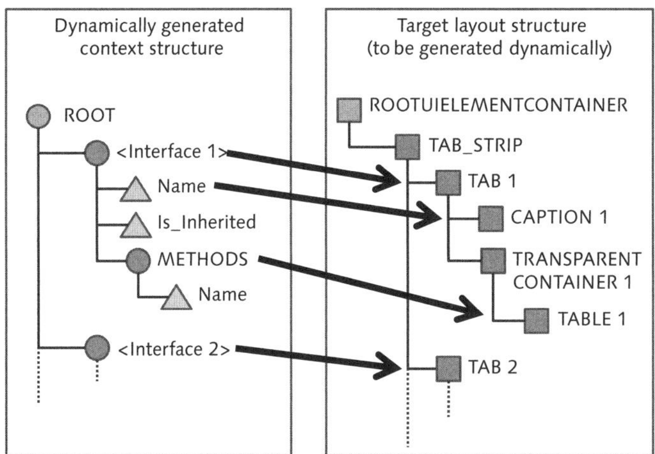

Figure 4.11 View Layout to be Dynamically Generated

4.4.1 Adding a View Element to a Container

You will now change the basic structure of the view layout. You must perform the following steps if you want to add a new view element to a view container:

- You must determine the view element type.
- You must create a reference to the container element where you want to add the new view element. The `view->get_root_element( ).` method is available for accessing `ROOTUIELEMENTCONTAINER`.
- You must specify the area in the container layout where you want to put the new element. For this purpose, you must create relevant layout data for the newly created UI element.

Class Hierarchy for View Elements

There are many different view elements you can use for defining a view. These view elements are represented by ABAP classes and you must have knowledge of ABAP classes for dynamic programming. The ABAP classes are arranged in an inheritance hierarchy.

The simplified inheritance hierarchy for selected view elements is displayed in Figure 4.12. Don't panic: Although many ABAP classes are displayed, the structure is not complicated. The view elements used in this example have a gray background.

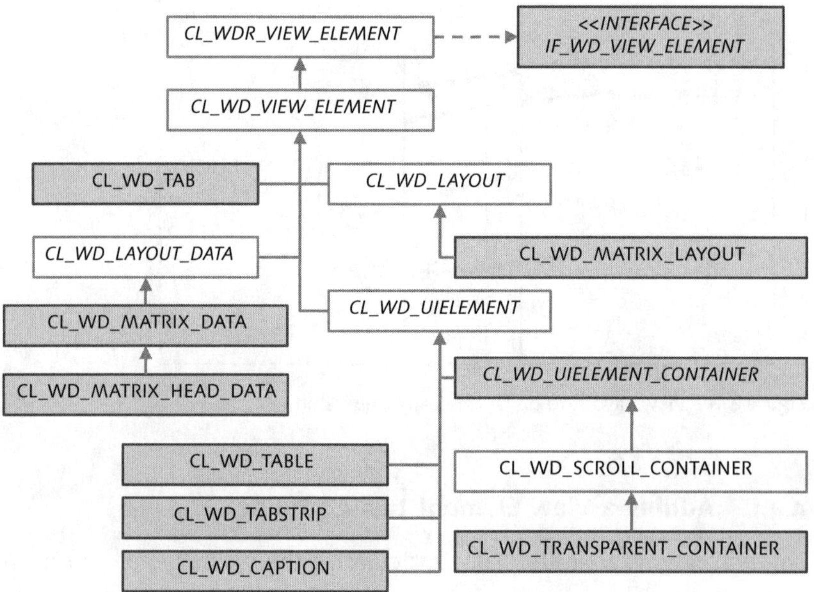

Figure 4.12 Inheritance Hierarchy for Selected View Elements

Basic class for view elements

The CL_WDR_VIEW_ELEMENT class is the basis for all view elements. This class may also be referred to as the highest or most general class in the inheritance hierarchy. One of the attributes contained in the class is a public String attribute called id. You will have frequently seen this id in the view element properties in the view designer, where you will have assigned the name, or even this id, as a view element name. The CL_WDR_VIEW_ELEMENT class also implements the IF_WD_VIEW_ELEMENT interface, which – due to inheritance – is available for all subclasses.

By defining inheritance at the next level, which is represented by the CL_WD_VIEW_ELEMENT class, the id attribute is also available for this class. This passing on of attributes is a basic inheritance property.

Two of the subclasses that appear under the CL_WD_VIEW_ELEMENT class in the inheritance hierarchy are the CL_WD_UIELEMENT and CL_WD_TAB classes. The CL_WD_TAB class ends an inheritance branch and is the Tab subelement of the composite TabStrip UI element. This UI element is represented by the CL_WD_TABSTRIP class, which is a subclass of the CL_WD_UIELEMENT class.

Inheritance hierarchy in the Class Builder

You can view the full inheritance hierarchy in the Class Builder (Transaction SE24). By displaying the object list for an ABAP class ([Ctrl] + [Shift] + [F5] key combination), you can navigate through the inheritance hierarchy of the SUPERCLASSES and SUBCLASSES directories.

Superclasses and subclasses

When you access the Class Builder, select the name of an ABAP class that represents a view element (see Figure 4.13, ❶). If they exist, folders for SUPERCLASSES (❷) and SUBCLASSES (❸) will appear in the object list. The subclasses for the CL_WD_LAYOUT_DATA ABAP class are displayed in the figure. One of them is the CL_WD_MATRIX_DATA ABAP class. This, in turn, has the CL_WD_MATRIX_HEAD_DATA subclass.

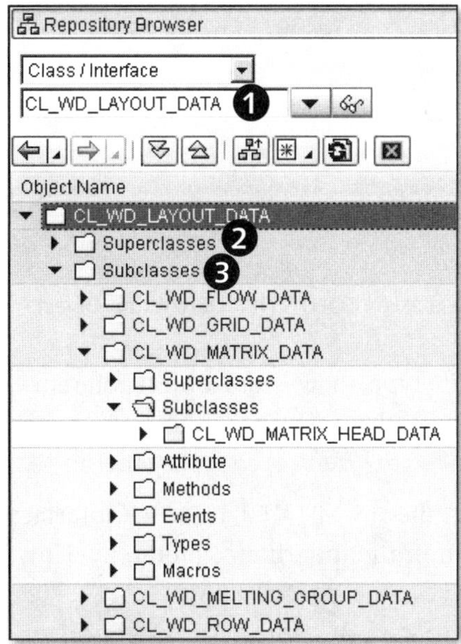

Figure 4.13 Analyzing the Inheritance Hierarchy for View Elements

wddomodifyview( ) Method

Now that you have some basic knowledge about view and UI elements, we can discuss the different areas of use and defining aspects of view elements in detail. The listings we will show you will result in the wddomodifyview( ) method being fully implemented.

[✎]

1. Switch to the V_CLASS_INTF view and select the METHODS tab.
2. Switch to the source text of the wddomodifyview( ) method. All other implementations are made in this method.

ROOTUIELEMENT CONTAINER

3. Implement access to the ROOTUIELEMENTCONTAINER element to set up the layout hierarchy. The view method parameter returns the get_element( ) or get_root_element( ) access methods to enable you to determine the description object (see Listing 4.9).

```
METHOD wddomodifyview .
* The reference to the view root node
DATA: lo_ui_root TYPE REF TO if_wd_view_element,
* The cast view root node reference
      lo_container TYPE REF TO cl_wd_uielement_container.
* Determine the root reference
** Option 1 **
* lo_ui_root = view->get_element(
* id = 'ROOTUIELEMENTCONTAINER' ).
** Option 2 **
lo_ui_root = view->get_root_element( ).
* Perform down cast on container
lo_container ?= lo_ui_root.
```

Listing 4.9 Determining the ROOTUIELEMENTCONTAINER Description Object

- Define the IF_WD_VIEW_ELEMENT-type lo_ui_root object reference. This reference variable contains the reference returned by the view->get_element( ) or view->get_root_element( ) method.
- As you saw in Figure 4.12, the IF_WD_VIEW_ELEMENT interface appears in the highest position in the inheritance hierarchy. However, because you have to access the special ROOTUIELEMENTCONTAINER properties, you need to cast this interface reference to a CL_WD_UIELEMENT_CONTAINER reference. To do this, you need to define the second object reference of type CL_WD_UIELEMENT_CONTAINER, lo_container.

- You can choose between two options to determine the description object for ROOTUIELEMENTCONTAINER: view->get_element( ) and view->get_root_element( ). Regardless of the option on which you decide, you must then cast the reference to be able to access the special ROOTUIELEMENTCONTAINER properties.

Properties and Layout

After you have determined the description object for ROOTUIELEMENTCONTAINER, you use it to begin setting the properties and layout for ROOTUIELEMENTCONTAINER (see Listing 4.10).

```
* If the method is called for the first time
IF first_time = abap_true.
* Set MatrixLayout
  cl_wd_matrix_layout=>new_matrix_layout(
    container = lo_container ).
* Set width to 100  %
  lo_container->set_width( value = '100%' ).
ENDIF.
```

Listing 4.10 Customizing ROOTUIELEMENTCONTAINER

first_time importing parameter

You should only set the layout and properties for ROOTUIELEMENTCONTAINER when you start the Web Dynpro application. These settings will subsequently remain unchanged. The first_time method parameter provides the answer to the question of whether the wddomodifyview( ) method is executed the first time. This has the ABAP_TRUE value if the method is being processed for the first time; otherwise, it has the ABAP_FALSE value. You use the parameter in the implementation and thereby ensure that the layout and properties are only changed once.

Creating a layout

Each container has a layout assigned to it. You will use MatrixLayout for ROOTUIELEMENTCONTAINER. The static cl_wd_matrix_layout=>new_matrix_layout( ) method is available for this. The way you use this method is worth mentioning because it expects the reference to the container as an actual parameter. Furthermore, you can specify for all of the view elements that a public static new_<view element>( ) method will always be available to create a class runtime object.

SET and GET methods for properties

Public set_<property>( ) methods are provided to set properties for a view element description object. The ROOTUIELEMENTCONTAINER width in this example is set to 100% by the set_width( ) method (see Figure 4.14).

The properties and layout for ROOTUIELEMENTCONTAINER are now set to the necessary values and you can begin creating view elements.

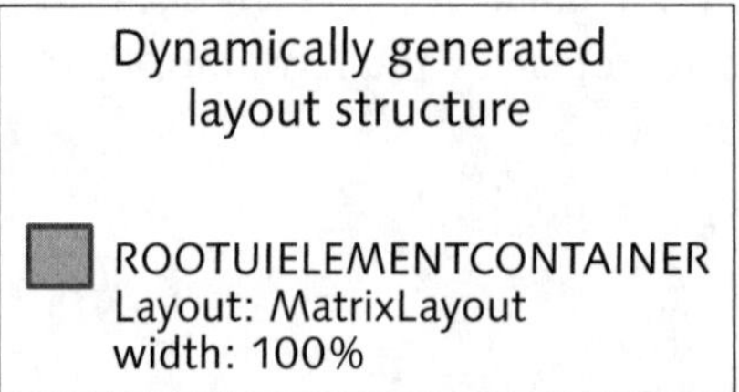

Figure 4.14 Result of Changing Properties for ROOTUIELEMENTCONTAINER

Creating a TabStrip

View Elements

One of the requirements of the application is to create a Tab view element for every ABAP interface. However, the Tab view element needs a higher-level TabStrip UI element. This is created in the next step (see Listing 4.11).

```
* The Tabstrip reference
DATA: lo_tabstrip TYPE REF TO cl_wd_tabstrip.
* Was a new search run?
CHECK wd_comp_controller->is_new_search = ABAP_TRUE.
* Allocate variable
wd_comp_controller->is_new_search = ABAP_FALSE.
* Delete tabstrip and all other elements
lo_container->remove_all_children( ).
* Structure of tabstrip with a tab for each interface
* Check whether the description of the searched class and
* at least one interface exists
IF wd_comp_controller->go_class_description IS BOUND
AND LINES(
  wd_comp_controller->go_class_description->interfaces
  ) > 0.
* Create tabstrip
  lo_tabstrip = cl_wd_tabstrip=>new_tabstrip(
    id = 'TS_INTERFACES' ).
```

```
* Set layout data on MatrixHeadData
  cl_wd_matrix_head_data=>new_matrix_head_data(
    element = lo_tabstrip ).
* Add to view hierarchy
  lo_container->add_child( the_child = lo_tabstrip ).
```

Listing 4.11 Generating the TabStrip UI Element

Optimizing performance

As already mentioned, generating the layout at runtime is time-consuming. You can counteract view elements being generated unnecessarily by performing a check that detects whether a new search is being performed. The public `is_new_search` component controller attribute is set to `ABAP_TRUE` in the action handler method of the search in the `V_CLASS_SELECTION` view (see Listing 4.1). If `is_new_search` has `ABAP_TRUE` as its value, the generation of the view layout is resumed and it is assigned the `ABAP_FALSE` value. If `is_new_search` has the `ABAP_FALSE` value, the generation of the view layout is skipped.

Before the generation of the view layout begins, you must remove already existing view elements and set certain properties for `ROOTUIELEMENTCONTAINER`. You can use the `remove_all_children( )` method of the `ROOTUIELEMENTCONTAINER` description object to remove all view elements from the view hierarchy. This sets the ground for restarting a full generation of the view hierarchy.

A check is first run to see whether a valid description object exists for an ABAP class and whether this ABAP class implements ABAP interfaces. If not, you should not create any view elements. To set up the `TabStrip` UI element, you call the static `cl_wd_tabstrip=>new_tabstrip( )` method and transfer the `TabStrip` `id` to the `id` importing parameter.

Setting Layout Data

Creating layout data

The `TabStrip` UI element should be placed as the first element in the `ROOTUIELEMENTCONTAINER` layout. The relevant layout data is assigned to `TabStrip` for this purpose. Calling the `cl_wd_matrix_head_data=>new_matrix_head_data( )` method ensures that the relevant layout data is assigned.

Extending UI Subelements

The settings for TabStrip have now been implemented and you can assign it to ROOTUIELEMENTCONTAINER. To do this, call the add_child( ) method using the description object for ROOTUIELEMENTCONTAINER, which will enable you to extend the view element. Figure 4.15 shows the result after you have added TabStrip to the view layout.

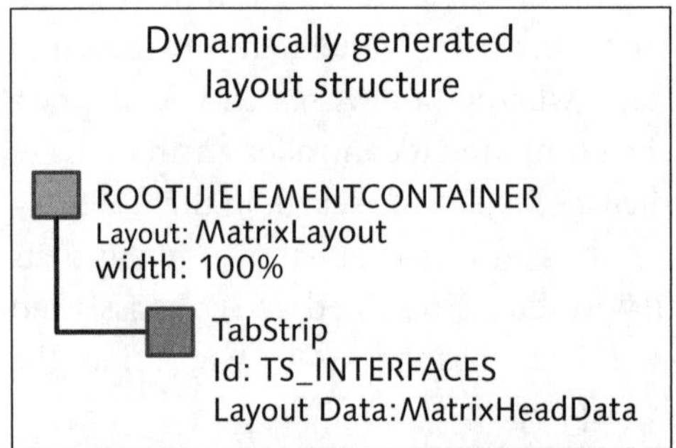

Figure 4.15 Added TabStrip in the View Layout

Extending tab view elements

You will now create a Tab view element for every ABAP interface context node. Listing 4.12 shows the implementation for this.

```
* Description object for the context root node
DATA: lo_nd_info_root TYPE REF TO if_wd_context_node_info,
* All child nodes of the root node
      lt_nodes TYPE wdr_context_child_info_map,
* One child node
      ls_node LIKE LINE OF lt_nodes,
* The tab reference
      lo_tab TYPE REF TO cl_wd_tab.
* Create a tab for each interface
* Description information of context root node
lo_nd_info_root = wd_context->get_node_info( ).
* All child nodes of root node
lt_nodes = lo_nd_info_root->get_child_nodes( ).
* Each child node = Interface = Tab
LOOP AT lt_nodes INTO ls_node.
* Create new tab per interface context node
  lo_tab = cl_wd_tab=>new_tab(
    id = ls_node-name
    view = view ).
```

```
* Extend tab in TabStrip
  lo_tabstrip->add_tab( the_tab = lo_tab ).
```

Listing 4.12 Generating the Tab View Element

Creating a tab and assigning it to TabStrip

You determine the number of ABAP interface context nodes using the `get_child_nodes( )` method of the description object for the context root node. A `Tab` is created for each node; that is, for each ABAP interface. The name of the method for creating the tab is `cl_wd_tab=>new_tab( )`. The new `Tab` is assigned to `TabStrip` using the `add_tab( )` method. The result is displayed in Figure 4.16.

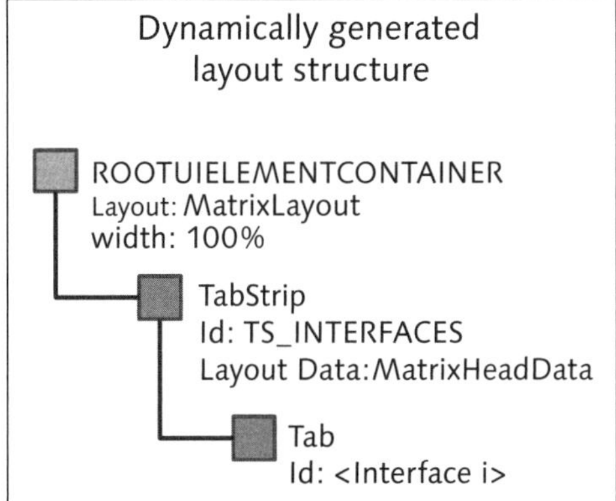

Figure 4.16 Added Tab in the View Layout

Extending Caption and Transparent Container

You will need a `Caption` UI element and `TransparentContainer` for the `Tab` content for the `Tab` view element. You create them as shown in Listing 4.13.

```
* The tab caption reference
DATA: lo_tab_caption TYPE REF TO cl_wd_caption,
* The TransparentContainer reference
      lo_transparent_container TYPE REF TO
        cl_wd_transparent_container,
* The data binding path for the tab caption
      ld_tab_caption_binding TYPE string,
* The reference to the interface context node
      lo_nd_intf_methods TYPE REF TO if_wd_context_node,
* The data binding path to the interface method subnode
      ld_intf_methods TYPE string.
```

```
* The data binding path for the tab caption
CONCATENATE
  ls_node-name '.NAME' INTO ld_tab_caption_binding.
* Generate the caption with data binding
lo_tab_caption = cl_wd_caption=>new_caption(
* text = ls_node-name "Alternative = static
  bind_text = ld_tab_caption_binding ).
* Add caption to tab
lo_tab->set_header( the_header = lo_tab_caption ).
* Read methods and display table for interface
* Set the path for the interface method context node
CLEAR ld_intf_methods.
CONCATENATE
  ls_node-name '.METHODS' INTO ld_intf_methods.
* Determine the reference to the interface context node
TRY.
  lo_nd_intf_methods = wd_context->path_get_node(
    ld_intf_methods ).
CATCH cx_root.
  CLEAR lo_nd_intf_methods.
ENDTRY.
* Could a reference be determined?
IF lo_nd_intf_methods IS BOUND.
* Set the caption icon because methods were found
  lo_tab_caption->set_image_source( 'ICON_LIST' ).
* Create TransparentContainer as content for tab
  lo_transparent_container =
  cl_wd_transparent_container=>new_transparent_container(
    view = view ).
* Set MatrixLayout for TransparentContainer
  cl_wd_matrix_layout=>new_matrix_layout(
    container = lo_transparent_container ).
* Add TransparentContainer to tab
  lo_tab->set_content(
    the_content = lo_transparent_container ).
```

Listing 4.13 Generating the Caption and TransparentContainer UI Elements

It is worth mentioning at this point that the `bind_text` parameter is used when the static `cl_wd_caption=>new_caption( )` method is called. This parameter can be used to define the data binding from the UI property to the context attribute. The path for the context attribute is determined based on the `<node name>.<attribute name>` syntax. As an alternative, you can also transfer a static text to the method using the `text` parameter. The `Caption` UI element is also transferred to the `Tab` view element using the `set_header( )` method.

Determining a context node using a path

The next implementation step involves determining the `METHODS` subnode for the ABAP interface context node. This can be done using the `wd_context->path_get_node( )` method. The path for the node is transferred to this method as a string parameter. The path in this case must be created according to the `<node name>.<node name>` syntax. If a node cannot be found for the specified path, an object-oriented exception will be thrown, which will be handled with a `TRY. CATCH. ENDTRY.` block in the program.

If the `METHODS` node has been found in the context, the title of the `Tab` view element should already signify to the user that methods exist for this interface. You indicate this by using an icon in the `Tab` title. You use the `lo_tab_caption->set_image_source( )` method to set this icon in the `Caption` UI element.

A `Tab` view element can only include one subelement. If you want to display several view elements in the tab, you can do this by using a `TransparentContainer` UI element assigned to the `Tab`. You create this in the next step using the public static `cl_wd_transparent_container=>new_transparent_container( )` method. You also set the layout to `MatrixLayout` for the container. To end, you assign `TransparentContainer` to the `Tab` with the `lo_tab->set_content( )` method. The result of the discussed implementation steps is shown in Figure 4.17.

If you do not specify an `id` when creating a view element using the `new_<view element>( )` method, the Web Dynpro framework automatically generates one. In the figure, the automatic `id` generation is indicated by the text ID: AUTO.

The only thing left to do now is to generate the table for displaying the ABAP interface method names. If you think back to Chapter 3, Section 3.4, Messages and Internationalization, where we discussed the `Table` UI element, you will remember how time-consuming it was to create a table manually. The Web Dynpro code wizard is available for the static definition and can be used to create tables.

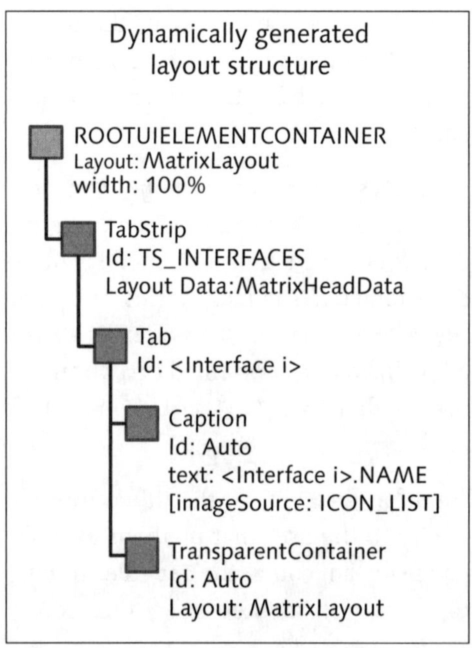

Figure 4.17 Added Caption and the TransparentContainer in the View Layout

Dynamically Generating a Table

CL_WD_DYNAMIC_TOOL service class

The CL_WD_DYNAMIC_TOOL service class is available for dynamic programming. It provides the create_table_from_node( ) method to generate the composite Table UI element with the relevant subelements. Here, to generate the table, you only have to call the cl_wd_dynamic_tool=>create_table_from_node( ) method and supply method parameters (see Listing 4.14).

```
* The table ID
DATA: ld_table_id TYPE string,
* The table reference
      lo_table TYPE REF TO cl_wd_table.
* Create table in TransparentContainer
* Generate the table name
CONCATENATE
  ls_node-name '_METHODS' INTO ld_table_id.
* Create the table dynamically
lo_table = cl_wd_dynamic_tool=>create_table_from_node(
  ui_parent      = lo_transparent_container
```

```
  table_id          = ld_table_id
  node              = lo_nd_intf_methods ).
ENDIF.
ENDLOOP.
ENDIF.
ENDMETHOD.
```

Listing 4.14 Generating the Table UI Element

create_table_from_node( )

The `id` of the `Table` UI element is generated first and transferred to the `cl_wd_dynamic_tool=>create_table_from_node( )` method. In addition, the reference to the `TransparentContainer` is transferred to the table as a UI parent of the `Table` UI element, and the `METHODS` context node is transferred as a data and definition source. The table is now generated. The result of this addition is shown in Figure 4.18.

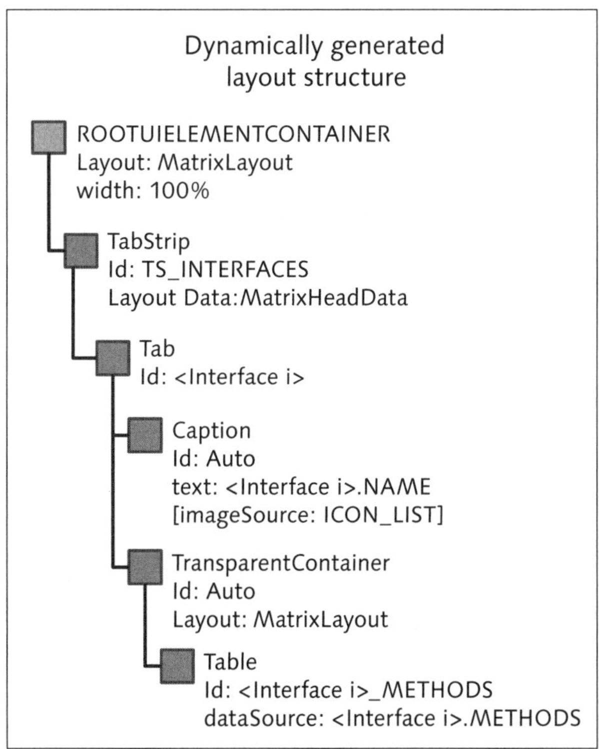

Figure 4.18 Added Table UI Element in the View Layout

This completes the dynamic programming of contexts and views. However, we still have one type of dynamic change left to discuss: Assigning existing actions to view element events.

4.4.2 Assigning Actions to View Element Events

Event, action, and action handler

Some view elements can trigger events in clients, as is the case with the `TabStrip` UI element when you select a `Tab`. The Web Dynpro component can respond to these types of events with an assigned action and its associated action handler method. We have already used this mechanism several times but actions were always assigned during the development phase. However, actions can also be assigned to events during runtime, whereas actions and action handlers cannot be generated dynamically during runtime.

on_<event> class attribute

Every view element you can use to trigger an event in a client has a corresponding `on_<event>` class attribute. When the `new_<view element>` method creates a view element dynamically, the `on_<event>` method parameter can specify the action name. The `set_on_<event>` also exists to assign an action to an existing view element.

wdevent importing parameter

All action handlers have a `wdevent` parameter that is filled by the Web Dynpro runtime if an event is triggered in a client. In Figure 4.19, you can see that the content of the `wdevent` parameter is displayed in the ABAP Debugger.

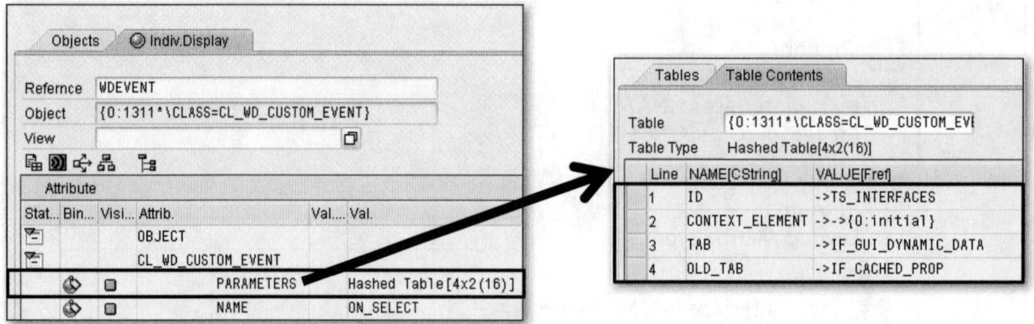

Figure 4.19 Attributes and PARAMETERS Table of the WDEVENT Object

To be able to view the object content in the ABAP Debugger, you set a breakpoint in the action handler method. By triggering an event in a client, the action handling is activated and the ABAP Debugger is started. In the debugger, select the OBJECTS tab and enter the `wdevent` value in the REFERNCE input field on the INDIV.DISPLAY subtab. The object attributes are displayed after you confirm your entry by pressing the Enter key. You get the content of the internal `parameters` table by double-clicking the `parameters` attribute.

The `wdevent->name` attribute contains the event name. The internal `wdevent->parameters` table contains additional information about the view element. The table has two columns: `name` and `value`. The `id` of the view element that has triggered the event is always available as an entry in the table. Additional name/value pairs may exist, depending on the view element type.

Handling a tab selection

In this example, the Web Dynpro component should respond to the user selecting a `Tab` and follow-up actions should be triggered to determine additional information for an interface.

[✎]

1. Select the ACTIONS tab in the `ZWDC_04_CLASS_BROWSER` Web Dynpro component.

Creating an action

2. On this tab, create the `select_tab` action with the `standard` action type. By creating the action, the `onactionselect_tab( )` action handler method is automatically created.

Implementing the action handler

3. Double-click the name of the action. This will take you to the implementation of the action handler method. Implement the method as shown in Listing 4.15:
   - The `wdevent->name` attribute contains the name of the event in the client. In this example for `TabStrip`, this is `ON_SELECT`.
   - The `wdevent` object provides auxiliary methods to determine the contents of the `parameters` table. The `get_string( )` method was used to read the entries.

```
METHOD onactionselect_tab .
* Old tab
DATA: ld_old_tab TYPE string,
* New Tab
      ld_new_tab TYPE string,
```

```
* The TabStrip ID
      ld_id      TYPE string,
* The message to be issued
      ld_message TYPE string.
* Checks to see whether the action handler is triggered by
* The ON_SELECT event
IF wdevent->name = 'ON_SELECT'.
* Determining the PARAMETERS parameter using GET_STRING( )
  ld_old_tab = wdevent->get_string( name = 'OLD_TAB' ).
  ld_new_tab = wdevent->get_string( name = 'TAB' ).
  ld_id      = wdevent->get_string( name = 'ID' ).
* Generating the message
  CONCATENATE
    'You have switchedfrom tab' ld_old_tab
    'to tab' ld_new_tab
    'in TabStrip' ld_id INTO ld_message separated by space.
* Issue message using the message manager
  wd_comp_controller->go_mm->report_success(
    message_text = ld_message ).
ENDIF.
ENDMETHOD.
```

Listing 4.15 Handling the ON_SELECT Event

wddomodifyview()

4. Switch to the implementation of the `wddo-modifyview( )` method and navigate to the generation point of the `TabStrip` UI element.
5. Assign the `SELECT_TAB` value to the `on_select` formal parameter of the `new_tabstrip( )` method; that means, with the name of the action you previously defined and implemented (see Listing 4.16).

```
* Create TabStrip
lo_tabstrip = cl_wd_tabstrip=>new_tabstrip(
  id = 'TS_INTERFACES'
  on_select = 'SELECT_TAB' ).
```

Listing 4.16 Assigning the SELECT_TAB Action to the select Event of the TabStrip UI Element

6. Activate all inactive objects and test the `ZWDC_04_CLASS_BROWSER_APP` Web Dynpro application. Your result should correspond to the one shown in Figure 4.1.

4.4.3 Conclusion

Important methods

In this section, you have learned about the key importance of `CL_WD_<view element>` ABAP classes. The most important methods of these classes are listed in Table 4.2.

Method	Description
All view elements	
`get_<property>( )`	Returns the property value.
`set_<property>( )`	Sets the property to the transferred value.
`bind_<property>( )`	Binds the property value to a context attribute/node.
`bound_<property>( )`	Returns the context attribute/node to which the property is bound.
View Elements with an Event	
`set_on_<event>( )`	Binds the action to the `on<event>` property.
`get_on_<event>( )`	Returns the name of the action bound to the `on<event>` property.
Container Elements	
`get_child( )`	Returns the subelement.
`get_children( )`	Returns all subelements.
`remove_child( )`	Removes a subelement.
`remove_all_children( )`	Removes all subelements.
`add_child( )`	Adds an element.

Table 4.2 Selected Methods of the CL_WD_<view element> ABAP classes

4.5 Summary

The dynamic programming of Web Dynpro applications is used to integrate information determined during runtime into the structure of the Web Dynpro application. Some of the available dynamic programming options are summarized here:

- You can create, change, and delete context nodes and context attributes when manipulating context dynamically. It is important to determine the meta information for a node for which you want a subnode to be dynamically generated or for which you want the properties changed. The `get_node_info( )` method called using the node reference returns this `IF_WD_CONTEXT_NODE_INFO` object description.
- You can create, change, and delete view elements when changing the layout during runtime. `CL_WD_<view element>` ABAP classes instantiated in the `wddomodifyview( )` method or in a method called there are key factors for this.
- You can bind events against existing actions or manipulate the parameter mapping of event parameters. Note that actions and action handler methods are not generated during runtime. Only existing actions can be used.

Chapter 5, Web Dynpro Standard Components, discusses using several Web Dynpro components for a Web Dynpro application. This means that we will be moving our focus to aspects of reuse.

The Model View Controller architecture pattern allows for applications to be based on any number of models, views, and controllers. You can create complex Web Dynpro architectures by binding and reusing existing Web Dynpro components.

5 Web Dynpro Standard Components

In the previous chapters, we have been looking only at small, self-contained Web Dynpro components. For example, in Chapter 2, Web Dynpro Architecture, you created a component with one window and two views. This type of development with only one Web Dynpro component may be sufficient for smaller projects. However, you will quickly reach its limits when you work in a team of developers.

Multi-component architectures

Therefore, it is often useful to create multiple, semantically related Web Dynpro components. Section 5.1, Multi-Component Architectures, describes how you can reuse Web Dynpro components. Based on simple examples, you will learn step by step how to embed external components into your own component, how to call methods of an external controller, and how to map context nodes across different components.

Standard components

After you have been introduced to the basic principles of developing multi-component applications, the subsequent sections will cover standard components. SAP provides a small set of useful reusable components and the following list provides an overview of the most important standard components available:

- **SAP List Viewer**
  The ALV table used also in the dynpro environment enables you to display complex tables in Web Dynpro.
- **Personal Object Work Entity Repository (POWER) list**
  The POWER list provides a useful framework that is based on the ALV and allows for creating and storing queries.

- **Select Options**
  These are the `SELECT OPTIONS` used also in the dynpro environment.
- **Other components**
  In addition, other small components exist such as the object value selector component for developing input helps. Both the object value selector component and the `SELECT OPTIONS` component are discussed in detail in Chapter 6, Input Helps and Semantic Helps.

Topics Discussed

This chapter discusses the following topics:

- Usage scenarios for reusable components
- Examples of reusable components
- Defining and instancing component usages
- Using the interface controller
- Normal and external mapping
- Using and configuring the SAP List Viewer
- POWER list and Easy-POWL

5.1 Multi-Component Architectures

Web Dynpro components are reusable building blocks that can be combined into complex applications with rather little effort. This chapter describes the basic principles of programming cross-component architectures. For this purpose, this section covers the following aspects:

- Reusing components through controller usages
- Accessing the controller of an external component
- Mapping the context across different components

Sample components

Before we enter into our discussion of the technical details of implementing components, we will give you a few suggestions and ideas concerning the division of components into semantic blocks:

- **Address management component**
  The address component is the classic component among the reusable Web Dynpro components. Because addresses are required at several

points within an application landscape, there is an obvious need for developing an address component.

- **Business partner component**
  Whether for customers, suppliers, or partners, it is often useful to develop a central component for business partners. Potential particularities of individual business partner roles can be implemented in the business partner component.
- **Frame/toolbar component**
  To reduce the amount of maintenance work and to standardize the user interface in more complex applications, it is advisable to create a kind of frame component containing fundamental generic blocks of your applications such as a toolbar, general settings, and so on. You can then use this component as a basic structure for all other user interfaces of your components. The exercise in the next section will guide you through the process of creating this type of frame component.

Performance Tip

Multi-component architectures provide a range of options. However, you should always try to establish a sound mixture between the number of components and the advantages of storing a UI in a separate, new component. At runtime, the process of instancing a component entails both longer runtimes and increased memory requirements.

5.1.1 Component Usages

Component usages

To be able to use an external component within another component, the external component must be made known to the using component. For this, you must first enter a *component usage* for the external component into the using component. Component usages can be entered in the header area of the using component and consist of a combination of a usage and a component name. The usage name must be unique because the external component will be accessed through this usage. After you have defined a component usage, you can access the interface controller objects of the external component.

Sample usage

Figure 5.1 illustrates a sample component usage taken from the exercise in this section. In this exercise, you will create two new components,

ZWDC_05_MAIN and ZWDC_05_NATIONS. The NATIONS component usage allows you to integrate the window of the ZWDC_05_NATIONS component into the main component (note that the window will be referred to as an interface view from here on). You can access the interface view, context, methods, and events of the integrated component via the interface controller.

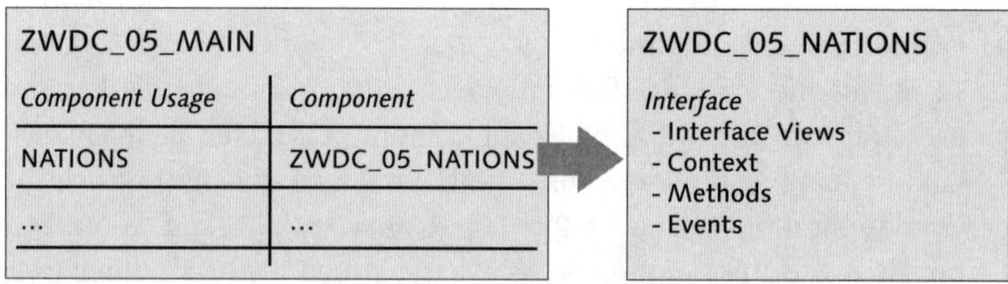

Figure 5.1 Defining Component Usages

In the first part of the exercise, you will create the components, ZWDC_05_MAIN and ZWDC_05_NATIONS. In this context, the main component serves as a frame for the remaining components of the chapter. The nations component will be used to display the database table, T005T. This system table contains a list of all countries/nations maintained in the system in the available languages.

Communication between components

Based on these two components and the nations text table (T005T), you will learn about the basic principles of multi-component architectures. For this, you will create a method that determines the output language for the nations table in the nations component. Then, you will practice establishing a cross-component mapping between the nations table and both components.

Multiple Instances of a Component

You can define any number of component usages for an external component. As a result, the same number of instances of the external component can be instanced at runtime. This allows you, for example, to simultaneously display an interface view (window) of a generic component multiple times in one view.

[✎] We will now begin with the exercise. In the first part, you will create the two components ZWDC_05_MAIN and ZWDC_05_NATIONS and connect them with each other:

1. Create a new component called ZWDC_05_MAIN. Assign the names W_MAIN and V_MAIN to the window and view, respectively.
2. Go to the V_MAIN view. Later in the exercise, the view will be used as a frame for all other UI elements and views. Therefore, it makes sense to define a header for this view. To do so, the PageHeader UI element is the best solution. Insert this element into the view and enter the following value into the TITLE property: Chapter 5: Country list.

   Creating a PageHeader
3. Add a tabstrip (UI element TabStrip) under the PageHeader in the view. Create a tab. To do so, right-click on the tabstrip and select INSERT TAB from the context menu. Select the CAPTION on the new tab and enter "Form view" as the TEXT property.

   Creating a tab
4. Insert a new view container into the tabstrip. To do so, right-click on the tab and select ADD ELEMENT TO TAB from the context menu. Then, select the ViewContainer type in the dialog box that opens. Your view should now look like the one shown in Figure 5.2.

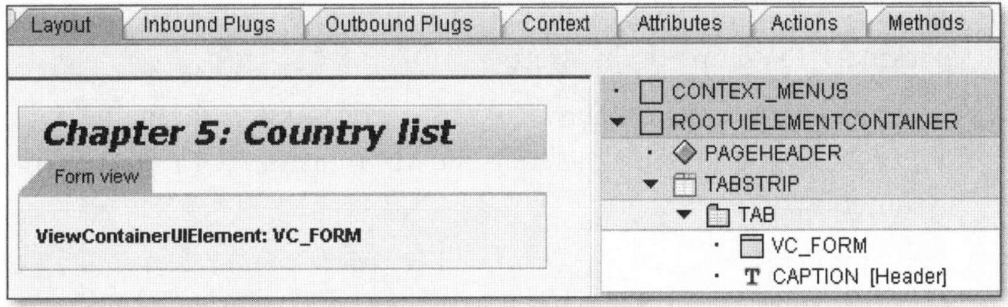

Figure 5.2 V_MAIN after Completion

5. Create a new application. You can copy the system default value, zwdc_05_main for this. Save the application and activate and test the component. Figure 5.3 shows the result of this test.

   Testing the application
6. Next, create the second component, ZWDC_05_NATIONS. Assign the names W_NATIONS and V_NATIONS to the window and view, respectively.

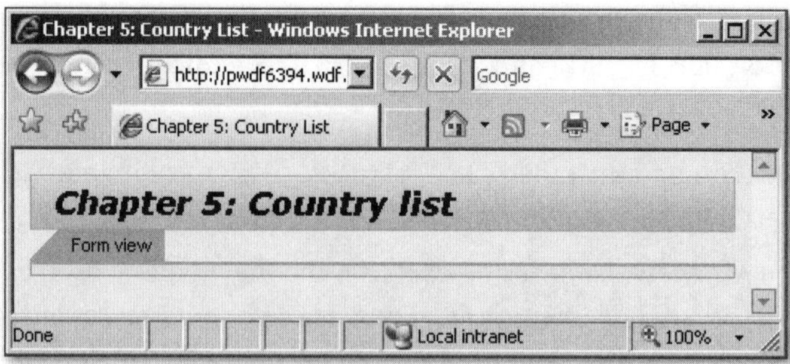

Figure 5.3 Current Status of the Exercise

Creating the T005T node

7. Then, go to the component controller within the new component. Select the CONTEXT tab and create the `T005T` node. Define it as an interface node. You will need this property at a later stage for the purpose of cross-component mapping. Use the `T005T` ABAP DICTIONARY STRUCTURE and CARDINALITY `0..n`. Leave all other default settings unchanged and finish your entries by clicking on ADD ATTRIBUTE FROM STRUCTURE.

8. In the window that opens, you can now select individual components from the structure and copy them into the context node. Select all fields except for the `MANDT` field and click on the button with the green checkmark to complete this step.

Supply function

9. Create a supply function for the `T005T` node. Assign the name `supply_t005t` to it and enter the code shown in Listing 5.1 into the supply function.

```
DATA lt_t005t TYPE wd_this->elements_t005t.
SELECT * FROM t005t INTO TABLE lt_t005t
  WHERE spras = 'E'
  ORDER BY land1.
* Bind internal table to context node
node->bind_table(
  new_items
  set_initial_elements = abap_true ).
```

Listing 5.1 Supply Function supply_t005t( )

Mapping

10. Define a mapping between the respective contexts of the component controller and the `V_NATIONS` view for the `T005T` node. You will

need this mapping to be able to display the data of the node in the view.

11. Display the attributes `LAND1`, `LANDX50`, and `NATIO50` of the `T005T` node in the view:

    Creating a form in the view

    - Select the `DropDownByIndex` UI element for the `LAND1` attribute. Bind the TEXT property of the UI element to the node attribute `LAND1`. Create an empty action for updating the display after an element has been selected in the dropdown list. By creating an empty event handler, you can make sure that the UI is updated every time a user selects an element.
    - Use a `TextView` for the other two UI elements and bind the TEXT property of either UI element to the node attributes `LANDX50` and `NATIO50`.
    - Finally, add the `TextView` labels using the UI element `Label`. Then, bind the LABELFOR property of these labels to the respective `TextView` element. Overwrite the label that was automatically used by the `LANDX50` attribute with the text "Country."

    Your view should now look like the one shown in Figure 5.4. The layout used was the `MatrixLayout`. To allow the dropdown list to extend the width of the label, its COLSPAN property was assigned the value `2`.

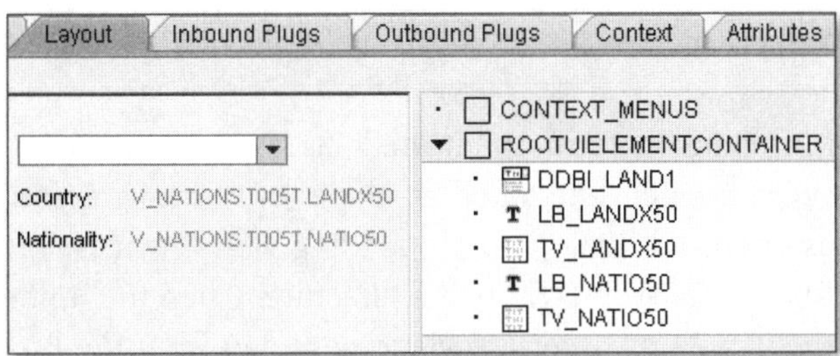

Figure 5.4 V_NATIONS after Completion

12. Activate the component. Because this component will later be used exclusively through a component usage, you do not need an application for it.

    Activating

Going through the exercise so far has refreshed existing knowledge for you. In the next part of the exercise, you will learn how to connect the ZWDC_05_MAIN and ZWDC_05_NATIONS components using a component usage:

Entering component usages

1. Return to component ZWDC_05_MAIN. Select the root in the object list of the component and enter the NATIONS component usage for Web Dynpro component ZWDC_05_NATIONS on the USED COMPONENTS tab.
2. After you have confirmed your entry by pressing the [Enter] key, the COMPONENT USAGES node displays in the object list of the component. By entering the usage, you get access to the windows and all interface controller objects of the external component. Figure 5.5 shows the exercise with the entered usage of the nations component.

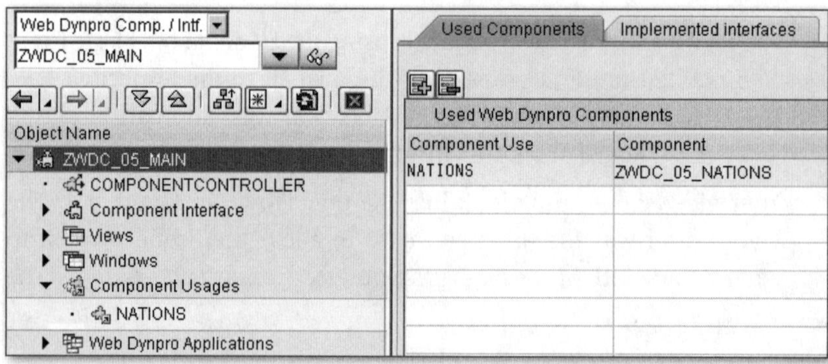

Figure 5.5 Entering Component Usages

Integrating a window

3. Modify the W_MAIN window. Then, open the V_MAIN node and right-click on the view container integrated in the V_MAIN view. Select EMBED VIEW. This opens the dialog for embedding views, which you already used in Chapter 2, Web Dynpro Architecture. Open the input help and select the W_NATIONS interface view (window) from the list, as shown in Figure 5.6.

   It makes no difference in a window whether the integrated object is a local view or an external window, also referred to as an interface view. However, if you integrate an interface view, you can only access the plugs of the view that are integrated in the interface. In this case, the internal structure of the window that originates from the external component remains hidden.

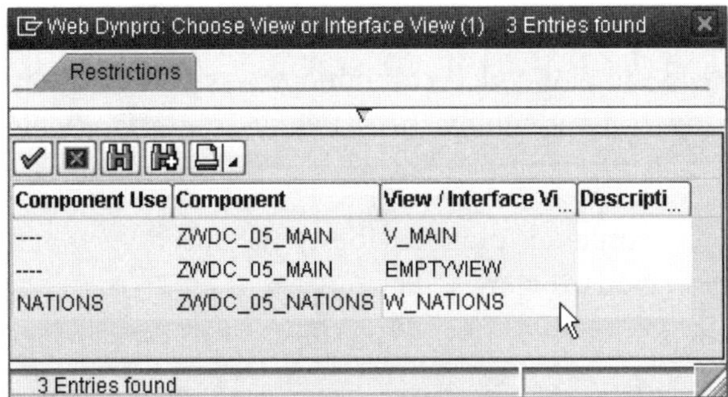

Figure 5.6 Embedding the W_NATIONS Window

Testing the application

4. Activate the `ZWDC_05_MAIN` component and test the application. Select a country identifier from the dropdown list to display the name of the associated country and the respective nationality (see Figure 5.7).

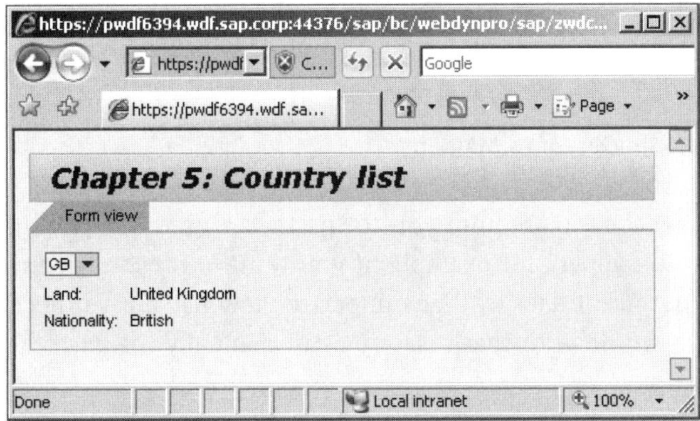

Figure 5.7 Testing the Multi-Component Application

Comment on the exercise

You have now developed your first multi-component architecture. The `ZWDC_05_NATIONS` component is reused by the `ZWDC_05_MAIN` component. However, at this stage, the two components are self-sufficient and there are no controller interfaces between them. Therefore, it would theoretically be no problem to operate the nations component by simply creating an application without the main component.

However, you need powerful interfaces when developing complex architectures. Therefore, the following sections describe step by step how you can use the interface controller of a component on the basis of real-life examples.

Instancing Components

Automatic Instancing

In the previous exercise, the embedded component was automatically instanced by the window. A window instances a view or interface view every time this view:

- Is integrated in a view container of a previously instanced view and has been defined as a standard view.
- Is addressed via a plug.

In the previous exercise, the W_NATIONS interface view in the VC_FORM view container was defined as a standard view (see Figure 5.8). Therefore, you did not need to bother with instancing the external component.

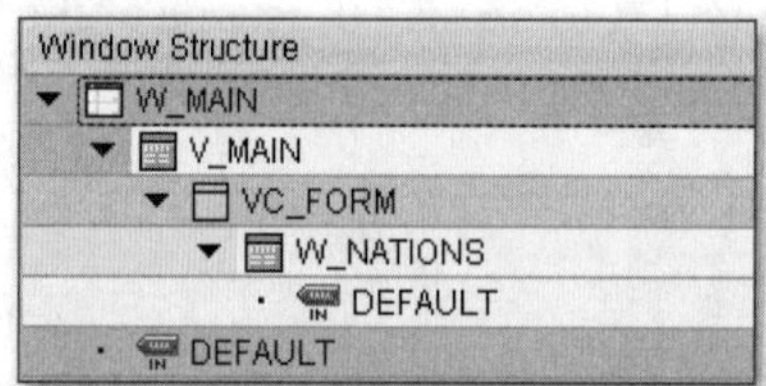

Figure 5.8 Window Structure of W_MAIN

Manual instancing

However, certain scenarios require you to instance a used component manually. This can happen, for example, if you want to prepare a component for the output of data while its interface view has not yet been instanced by the window. In that case, you can manually instance the component upfront.

In general, you instance an external component manually from within any controller of the using component. However, you should note that to be able to do so, you must first copy the component usage that has been entered in the properties of the component into the respective controller. The subsequent instancing process can be divided into the following two steps:

1. The wd_this->wd_cpuse_<component usage> ( ) method enables you to obtain a reference to the respective component usage. The type of this component usage is always IF_WD_COMPONENT_USAGE, irrespective of the name of the external component.

This interface provides methods for managing the external component. For example, you can use the methods `create_component( )` and `delete_component( )` to instance the relevant component and delete it after using it.

2. You must then instance the external component via the `create_component( )` method. Before you can do so, you must use the `has_active_component( )` method to check whether the component has already been instanced. If so, another instancing process would cause the application to abort.

[✎] In the following exercise, you will instance the nations component manually in the `wddoinit( )` method of the component controller of the using component. In the subsequent section, this will enable you to access the interface controller of the nations component.

Entering the component usage

1. Go to the PROPERTIES tab of the component controller of the main component. Click on the CREATE CONTROLLER USAGE button located directly above the USED CONTROLLERS/COMPONENTS table.
2. This opens a dialog box with a list of available component usages. As shown in Figure 5.9, select the `ZWDC_05_NATIONS` component by double-clicking on it. After you have selected this component, the component usage is entered in the table of used controllers/components.

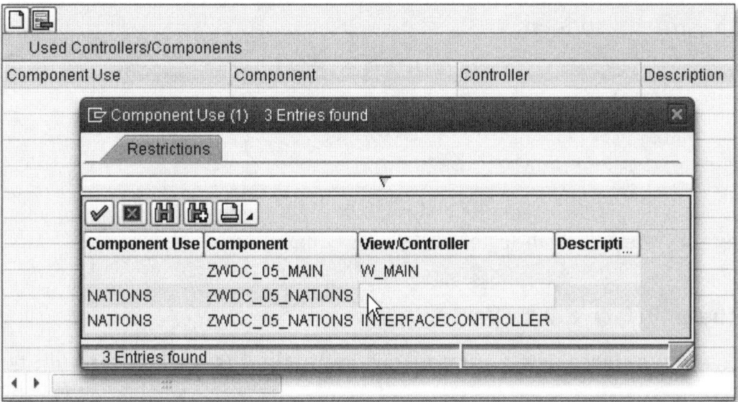

Figure 5.9 Component Controller – Creating a Component Usage

Instancing a component manually

3. The nations component can now be instanced from within the component controller. Open the `wddoinit( )` method and instance the nations component. The easiest way to do this is to use the Code Wizard. Thus, launch the Code Wizard and select the GENERAL tab. Click on INSTANTIATE USED COMPONENT and enter `NATIONS` in the associated input field (see Figure 5.10). Click on the button with the green checkmark to terminate the Code Wizard.

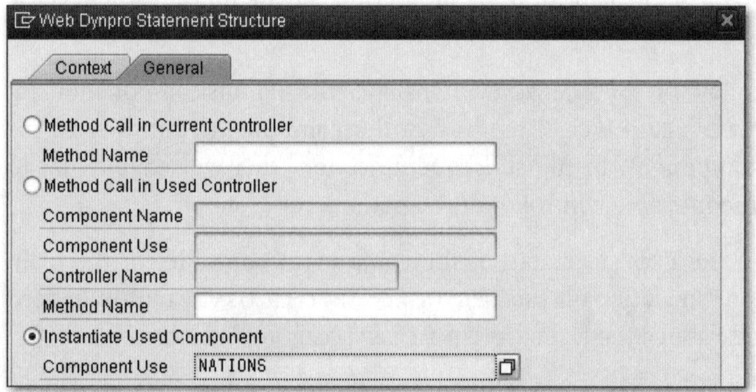

Figure 5.10 Instancing the Nations Component

4. At this stage, the wizard has generated the coding needed for instancing the component (see Listing 5.2). Carry out a syntax check and activate the component.

```
DATA lo_cmp_usage TYPE REF TO if_wd_component_usage.
lo_cmp_usage = wd_this->wd_cpuse_nations( ).
IF lo_cmp_usage->has_active_component( ) IS INITIAL.
  lo_cmp_usage->create_component( ).
ENDIF.
```

Listing 5.2 Manual Instancing of the Nations Component

Using the Interface Controllers

So far, we have described how you can manually instance components. After the instancing process is finished, you can access the external component via the respective interface controller. For example, you can register for external events or call methods of the external component.

External events

Registering for external events is pretty easy. The only thing you need to do is enter a usage for the external component in the properties of the relevant controller; you already did that in the previous exercise. Then, when you define a new event handler, the list of available events will also contain the objects of the external component.

External methods

The process of calling an external method, on the other hand, is slightly different. Similar to local controller usages, you must obtain a reference to the interface controller first. This reference will then allow you to access the methods of the external component. You can obtain the interface controller of the external component using the `wd_this->wd_cpifc_<component usage>( )` method. This method returns the interface controller of the `IWCI_<component usage>` type.

Controller Interfaces in Web Dynpro

Web Dynpro provides up to three different interfaces for each controller. The following list is intended to help you categorize these interfaces and keep track of them:

- `IF_<controller name>`
  This interface is only visible within the respective controller and can be used for programming purposes within the controller. The `wd_this` self-reference, which is contained in every controller, is always based on this data type.
- `IG_<controller name>`
  You can use this interface for the purpose of cross-controller programming within a component. Note that concerning usage and visibility, the same rules described in Chapter 2, Web Dynpro Architecture, apply. Accordingly, this interface is not available for views, for example. The `wd_this->get_<controller name>_ctr( )` enables you to obtain a reference to the external controller.
- `IWCI_<component name>`
  This interface can be used only for cross-component programming and represents a portion of the interface controller. Because you can only integrate component controller methods in the interface controller, the interface represents a kind of subset of the component controller. The `wd_this->wd_cpifc_<controller usage>_ctr( )` enables you to obtain a reference to the external interface controller.

Exercise In the following exercise, you will create the `set_language( )` method in the nations component and call that method from within the main controller via the interface controller. This new method will allow you to set the output language for the list of countries.

Preparing the nations component

1. Open the ATTRIBUTES tab in the component controller of the nations component. Enter the `gv_spras` attribute with data type `SPRAS` into the table.
2. Go to the METHODS tab and create the `set_language( )` method. Define the method as an INTERFACE METHOD (see Figure 5.11).

SET_LANGUAGE	Method	☑	Set language
	Method	☐	

Figure 5.11 set_language( ) Method

3. Open the method body and create an import parameter called `iv_spras` with data type `SPRAS`. Enter the value of import parameter `iv_spras` (`wd_this->gv_spras = iv_spras.`) into the controller attribute `gv_spras`.
4. Modify supply function `supply_t005t( )`. Replace the `WHERE` condition in the `SELECT` statement with the new condition `WHERE spras = wd_this->gv_spras`. Carry out a syntax check and activate the component.

Entering the interface controller usage

5. Return to the component controller of the main component. Select the PROPERTIES tab and enter a component usage of the interface controller of the nations component (see Figure 5.9). The USED CONTROLLERS/COMPONENTS table on the PROPERTIES tab should then appear, as shown in Figure 5.12.

Used Controllers/Components

Component Use	Component	Controller	Description
NATIONS	ZWDC_05_NATIONS		
NATIONS	ZWDC_05_NATIONS	INTERFACECONTROLLER	

Figure 5.12 Component Usage of Nations Component

6. Open the component controller method, wddoinit( ). After instancing the component, you want to call the set_language( ) method of the nations component using the method discussed just now and the parameter iv_spras = 'E' (for English). For this, you first need a reference to the interface controller of the nations component. Then, you can call the method via the interface controller in the external component. Listing 5.3 shows the coding for this method call.

Calling the external component

```
DATA lo_nations TYPE REF TO ziwci_wdc_05_nations.
lo_nations = wd_this->wd_cpifc_nations( ).
lo_nations->set_language( iv_spras = 'E' ).
```

Listing 5.3 Calling the External set_language( ) Method

7. Carry out a syntax check and activate the component. Then, test the component. Go ahead and play around a little. For example, you can change the iv_spras parameter to sy-langu to bind the output language to the logon language.

In this section, you have learned how to use external events and methods via the interface controller. The following section describes the remaining aspect of developing multi-component architectures – cross-component mapping.

5.1.2 Cross-Component Mapping

You already learned about the options of cross-controller mapping in Chapter 2, Section 2.4.3, Mapping. In addition to cross-controller mapping, Web Dynpro also provides the option of cross-component mapping. This kind of mapping allows you to exchange data that is stored in context nodes across the boundaries of separate controllers. Cross-component mapping can be carried out at any time after you have defined the component usage for the interface nodes of an external component.

Simple and external mapping

Cross-component mapping distinguishes between simple and external context mapping. Whereas simple mapping involves the flow of data from the context of the external component to the context of the using component, in external mapping, the data flows in the opposite direction. At this point, the term dataflow refers only to the primary node, which is responsible for calling supply functions, for example.

The two exercises in this section will provide you with the details of the simple and external context mapping processes. For this purpose, the T005T node created earlier will be integrated in the component interface. Then, you will define a mapping between the main and nations components and display data from the nations component in the main component. In the external mapping exercise, you will then reverse the flow of data.

Simple Mapping

With simple context mapping, the primary node is located in the external component. If the external component contains a supply function, this function provides the mapped node in the using component with data. For simple mapping to function properly, both nodes must be based on the same structure.

Figure 5.13 shows a simple mapping based on the example taken from the next exercise. In this exercise, you will define a mapping for node T005T from the nations component to the main component. In this scenario, the nodes will continue to be provided with data from the nations component via the supply function. In the final part of the exercise, you will integrate a text field for the display of data from the T005T node of the nations component into the main component.

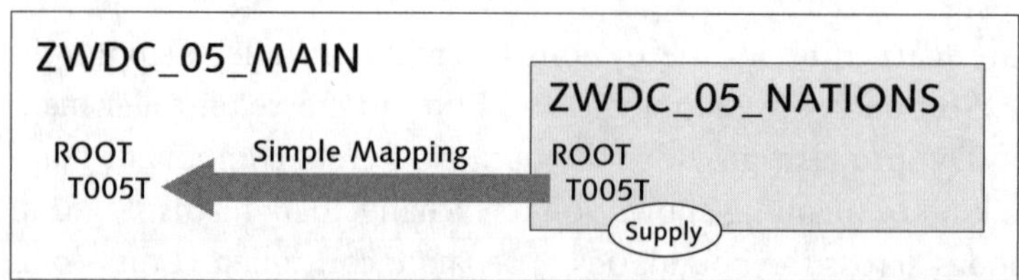

Figure 5.13 Simple Mapping

Flagging as interface node

1. Open the CONTEXT tab of the component controller of component ZWDC_05_NATIONS. Mark the T005T node. Activate the checkmark next to the INTERFACE NODE property (see Figure 5.14). The INTERFACE NODE property is available only for nodes of the component controller; by setting this property, you ensure that the node is integrated into the component interface.

Property	Value
Nodes	
Node Name	T005T
Interface Node	☑
Input Element (Ext.)	☐

Figure 5.14 Defining an Interface Node

Defining a mapping

2. Go to the component controller of the main component and select the CONTEXT tab. The external context of the nations component should now display on the right. Drag the context node `T005T` from the external component and drop it into the local context (see Figure 5.15). When you do this, the system automatically creates a copy of the external node.

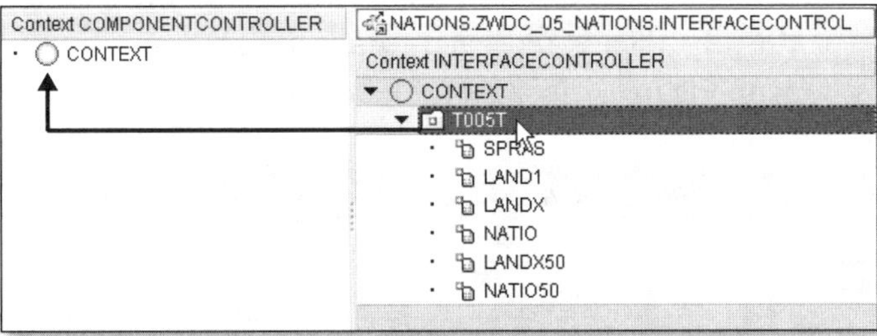

Figure 5.15 Creating a Cross-Component Mapping

Mapping between controller and view

3. Go to the `V_MAIN` view and copy the mapping of the `T005T` node from the component controller into the context of the `V_MAIN` view.

Note

In the previous two steps of the exercise, you defined a mapping from the interface controller of the external component to the component controller and from there to the `V_MAIN` view in the main component. Theoretically, you could also enter a component usage in the view to create a direct mapping between the external context and the `V_MAIN` view. However, you will need the detour via the component controller in the external mapping exercise.

Adding the header area

4. Select the LAYOUT tab and right-click on the `PageHeader` element in the element hierarchy. Select INSERT AREA. The `PageHeader` then provides a header (`PAGEHEADERAREA`) you can use to insert additional UI elements.

5. Insert a new TextView element into the PAGEHEADERAREA and bind the TEXT property of the UI element to the node attribute LANDX50. The view should appear, as shown in Figure 5.16.

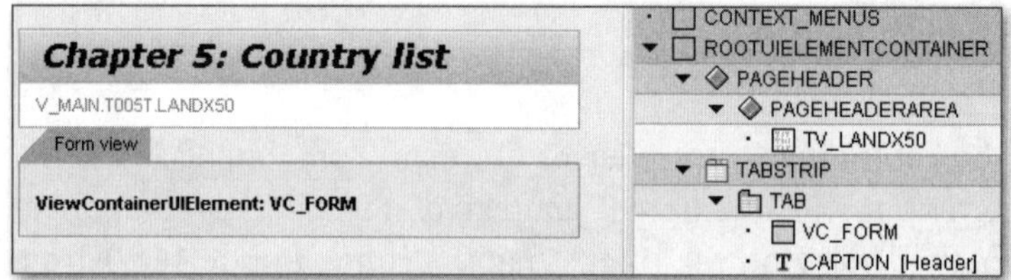

Figure 5.16 V_MAIN after Adding the TextView Element

Testing the application

6. Activate the inactive objects and test the application. The header area of the main component now displays the country currently selected in the list. For this, the data is retrieved from the T005T node of the nations component. Figure 5.17 shows the final application.

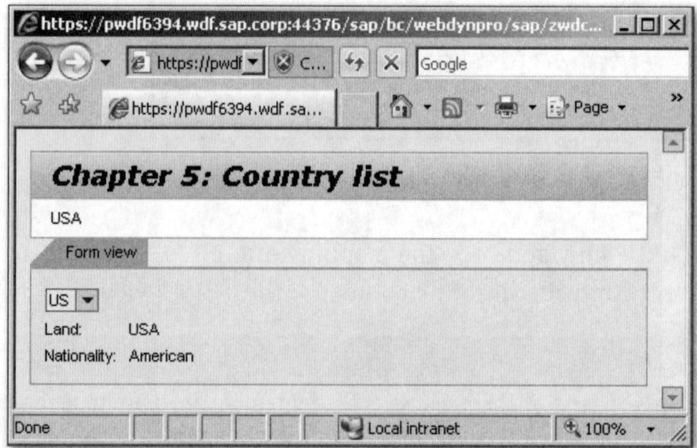

Figure 5.17 Testing the Simple Context Mapping

External Mapping

Compared to simple mapping, in an external mapping scenario, the data flows in the opposite direction. Thus, the local node of the using component acts as the primary node instead of the external node. The primary node can be filled with data in the using component using a supply function.

Specifics of external mapping

In addition, you should take note of certain specific aspects of external mapping. For example, you do not need to type the node of the using component that you want to map externally. If you leave it untyped, the node will receive its entire typing through the context node for which you will define a mapping to the external node. However, note also that if you create a node in this way, you can only program dynamically against it in the associated controller because its structure is unknown at design time (see Chapter 4, Dynamic Web Dynpro Applications).

Simple vs. External Mapping

In principle, there is not a big difference between simple and external mapping. Therefore, in many cases, you can achieve the required result via both external and simple mapping, provided you modify the design of the application in question accordingly.

- If your architecture provides for a central data exchange component, it is advisable to map the external nodes to the nodes of the using components using the simple mapping method.
- However, if you intend to use a generic component for displaying data from a local component, the external mapping method is often the better choice. In that case, you can leave the node of the external component untyped.

In the end, the kind of mapping you use is your decision.

In the following exercise, you will change the previously defined simple mapping from node `T005T` into an external mapping. For this, you will define the `T005T` node in the nations component to be mapped externally and copy the supply function into the main component. Figure 5.18 illustrates the data flow in an external mapping scenario; also, take a moment to compare Figure 5.18 with Figure 5.13.

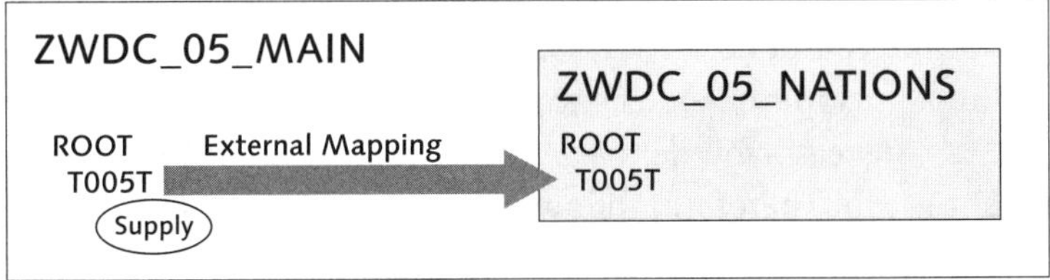

Figure 5.18 External Mapping

Activating the external mapping

1. Open the component controller in the `ZWDC_05_NATIONS` component. Select the CONTEXT tab and open the property dialog of the `T005T` node. Activate external mapping by selecting the INPUT ELEMENT (EXT.) property (see Figure 5.19).

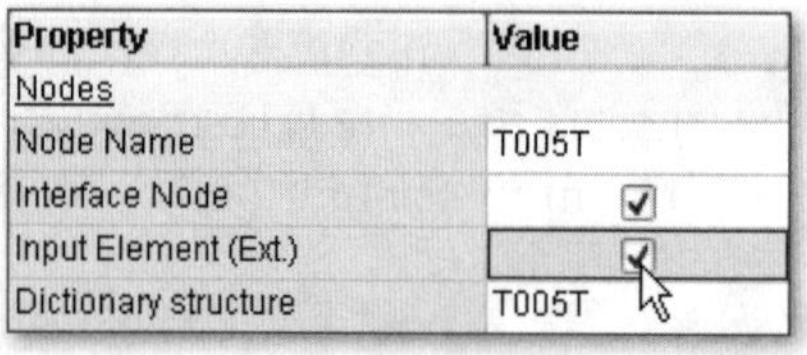

Property	Value
Nodes	
Node Name	T005T
Interface Node	☑
Input Element (Ext.)	☑
Dictionary structure	T005T

Figure 5.19 Activating External Mapping

2. Copy the content of supply function `supply_t005t( )` to the clipboard and remove the supply function entry from the node properties.

Deleting the simple mapping

3. Leave the nations component and go to the component controller of the main component. Select the CONTEXT tab. Right-click on the `T005T` node and select DELETE MAPPING from the context menu to delete the simple mapping you defined in the previous exercise.
4. Create a supply function for the `T005T` node. Navigate to the body of the supply function and paste the coding of the previous supply function from the clipboard. Adapt the `SELECT` statement to the main component by replacing `wd_this->gv_spras` in the `WHERE` condition with `'E'`.
5. Open the properties of the `ZWDC_05_MAIN` component. Delete the component usage of the nations component and re-enter it from scratch into the table. This way, you update the interface property of the component usage. Without this update, the nations component would continue to be regarded as a component with normal mapping (not with external mapping).

Navigation to the component usage

6. Navigate to the component usage of the nations component. In contrast to simple mapping, you cannot define external mapping on the CONTEXT tab; instead, you define it in the interface controller of the component usage. Therefore, follow the path, COMPONENT USAGES • `NATIONS` and select `CONTROLLER_USAGE` (see Figure 5.20).

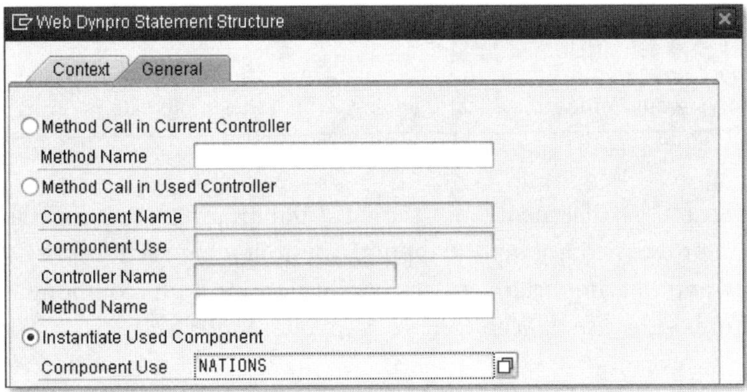

Figure 5.20 Opening the Component Usage

Creating the external mapping

7. Define the external mapping for node T005T between the local component controller and the interface controller of the external component. To do this, you must first enter a component usage for the local component controller. For this, click on the CREATE CONTROLLER USAGE icon on the PROPERTIES tab. Select the local component controller and close the dialog box.
8. Then, go to the CONTEXT tab and create the external mapping. Drag the local node T005T from the right-hand area of your screen and drop it on the interface controller on the left (see Figure 5.21).

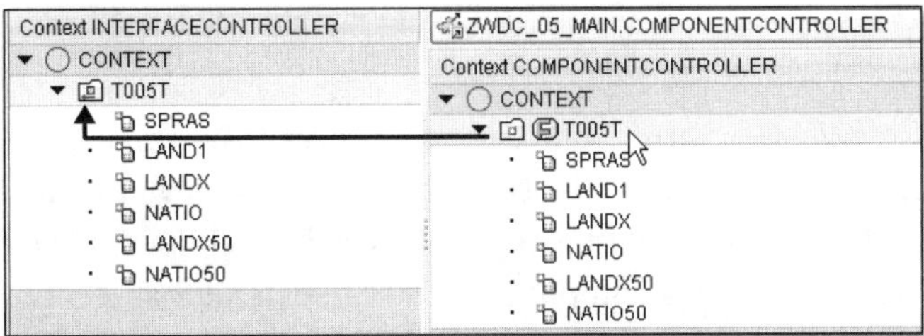

Figure 5.21 Creating an External Mapping

Testing the application

9. Activate the components and test the application. The application should behave in the same way as during the previous test. However, in contrast to the previous exercise, you are now using external mapping.

Note

You cannot create both simple and external mapping for the same controller usage. This would entail a cyclical mapping, which inevitably causes errors during runtime.

In this section, you learned about the most important aspects and the variations of cross-component mapping. The following section briefly discusses another important aspect of developing multi-component architectures – the use of Web Dynpro component interfaces.

5.1.3 Component Interfaces

Component interfaces

Imagine the following scenario: You are part of a team of developers who are developing a complex Web Dynpro architecture, and you want each individual team member to develop a single component. Every time a component has been completely developed, it should be integrated into the architecture of existing components that have already been finished.

During the development phase, you quickly realize that each developer on your team has a different understanding of the concept of interfaces. This can result in a proliferation of different types of interfaces among individual components, which is increasingly difficult to undo as the project continues. When you reach this point, you should consider standardizing your component interfaces.

You can compare Web Dynpro component interfaces to normal ABAP class interfaces. For example, as is the case in ABP Objects, you can also define interface methods for component interfaces in Web Dynpro. By implementing an interface in a component, you can extend that component by the methods and other objects defined in the interface. Thus, in addition to methods, you can define events, context nodes, and interface views in the component interface.

Creating and implementing component interfaces

To create a component interface, you must enter the name of the interface to be created in the input field below the object list selection and press [Enter]. Then, select Web Dynpro Component Interface in the dialog box that opens. After you have created the interface, you can use it in any number of components. To do so, go to the properties of your component and enter the interface into the table on the IMPLEMENTED INTERFACES tab (see Figure 5.22).

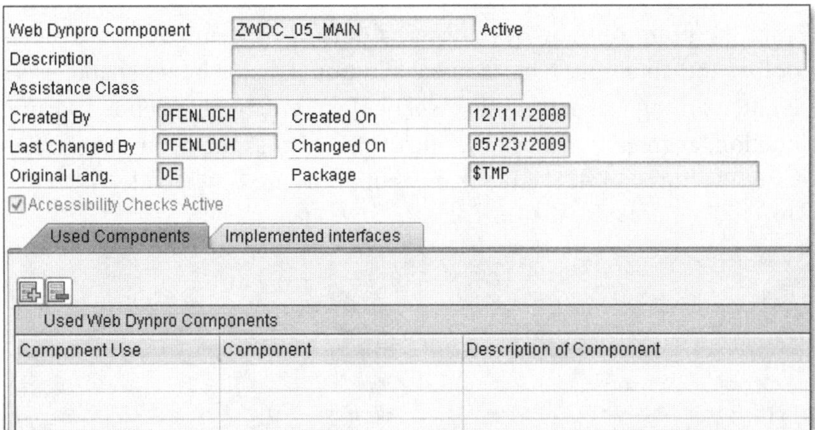

Figure 5.22 Implementing Component Interfaces

Because this book is intended for Web Dynpro beginners, an extensive description of component interfaces would go beyond its scope. However, they are an integral part of the Web Dynpro framework and must not be left out. Therefore, you have been made aware of this topic in this section and have learned about the basic principles you need for continued self-study.

5.2 SAP List Viewer

You already learned about developing and using tables in Web Dynpro back in Chapter 3, Developing Web Dynpro Applications. In addition to those rather simple tables, Web Dynpro also provides the SAP List Viewer (ALV), which you may know from the classic dynpro environment. This is a very flexible and powerful tool for displaying lists and table-like structures.

> **Note**
>
> As of release 4.6C, the ABAP List Viewer (ALV) was renamed to SAP List Viewer. However, its short name, ALV, is still commonly used among developers, as well as in all technical SAP List Viewer objects.

Appearance of ALV tables

From the point of view of the user, a default ALV output consists of a toolbar and an output table. Several additional dialog boxes enable users to enter settings related to the display of columns, the extended sorting function, aggregation, and other functions such as the print output. Figure 5.23 shows an ALV table that is bound to the `T005T` node.

View [Standard View] | Print Version | Export | Filter | Settings

Name	Nationality	Long name	Nationality
Paraguay	Paraguayan	Paraguay	Paraguayan
Qatar	Qatari	Qatar	Qatari
Reunion	French	Reunion	French
Romania	Rumanian	Romania	Rumanian
Russian Fed.	Russian	Russian Federation	Russian
Rwanda	Rwandan	Rwanda	Rwandan

Figure 5.23 Node T005T Displayed in ALV Table

Features

From a technical point of view, a Web Dynpro ALV table consists of the UI element `Table`, which is wrapped by a component. This is why many properties of the `Table` element are supported such as different cell editors, background colors, and dimensions. Moreover, the ALV component provides the following additional options, among others:

- Sorting, filtering, and calculation of column values
- Showing/hiding of columns via the column set
- Definition and saving of settings; for instance, to the column set, as a view and by the user
- Usage of a toolbar with standard ALV functions, such as Excel export and any other buttons

Implementing ALV tables

In Web Dynpro, a fundamental difference exists between the implementation phase of ALV tables and that of simple tables. For example, when implementing simple tables, you can access the UI elements of those tables in the view designer, whereas the implementation of ALV tables in the view designer allows you only to use a view container to integrate the ALV component. Consequently, you only have the ALV component interface available to configure ALV tables.

A look ahead and exercise

Based on practical examples, the following sections describe how you can implement ALV tables. For this, you will integrate an ALV component in the main component to display the T005T node as a table. The subsequent sections will cover the extended configuration of ALV tables. Among other things, you will learn how to manipulate table columns and how to program the ALV toolbar in theory and practice.

5.2.1 Integrating ALV

Integrating ALV tables in components is a simple matter. To do so, you must perform the following steps:

1. Define a component usage for ALV component SALV_WD_TABLE.
2. Create an external mapping between the local node to be displayed and the DATA node in the ALV component; alternatively, you can also do this dynamically at runtime (see the following exercise).
3. Integrate a view container for displaying the ALV table in the required position, and then integrate the ALV interface view TABLE in the local window in the view container.

In the following exercise, you will integrate an ALV component in the main component to display the T005T node as a table.

1. Enter a component usage for the ALV component in the main component. To do this, go to the properties of component ZWDC_05_MAIN. Enter a component usage called ALV_T005T for ALV component SALV_WD_TABLE into the table.
2. **Preparing V_MAIN** Integrate the ALV table in V_MAIN. To do so, open the V_MAIN view and insert a new tab (INSERT TAB) under the TABSTRIP UI element. Select CAPTION_1 on the new tab, and enter the text "ALV table" for the TEXT property.

   Then, add a view container to the Tab. To do so, right-click on the tab and select INSERT ELEMENT IN TAB. The view should now appear as shown in Figure 5.24.

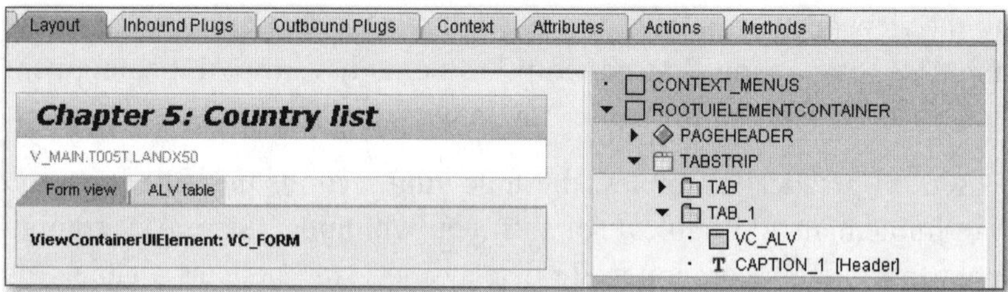

Figure 5.24 V_MAIN after Integrating the ALV Table

Enhancing the window

3. Integrate the ALV interface view TABLE in the W_MAIN window. Open the V_MAIN node and right-click on the view container you created for the ALV table. Select EMBED VIEW and open the input help in the corresponding dialog box that appears. Select the TABLE interface view of the ALV_T005T component usage from the list.

   In addition to the TABLE interface view, the ALV component provides two more interface views: SERVICE and CONTROL_VIEW. You can use the SERVICE interface view to change the position of the settings dialog, which allows users to make changes to the column display, sorting, filters, and so on, and which normally displays above the table.

Creating an external mapping

4. Finally, you must create an external mapping between the local node T005T and the ALV component. For this, the ALV component provides the DATA node. Open the path COMPONENT USAGE • ALV_T005T • INTERFACECONTROLLER_USAGE in the component object list and enter a component usage for the component controller into the table. Then, go to the CONTEXT tab and drag the T005T node from the right onto the DATA node in the ALV component.

Dynamic Mapping

In the current exercise, you have bound the DATA node of the ALV component statically to the local T005T node using external mapping. However, in your daily work, you will see that static mapping is often rather inflexible or that it cannot meet specific requirements.

Therefore, the ALV component also allows you to modify the data source of the component dynamically at runtime. To modify or set the data source, you can use the set_data( ) method of the interface controller of the ALV component. The described method provides the r_node_data parameter of the IF_WD_CONTEXT_NODE type for this.

Testing the ALV table

5. At this stage, the ALV table has been completely integrated into the main component. Activate the component and go to the ALV TABLE tab to test the application. Here, the ALV table containing the data of the T005T node displays instead of the view container (see Figure 5.25).

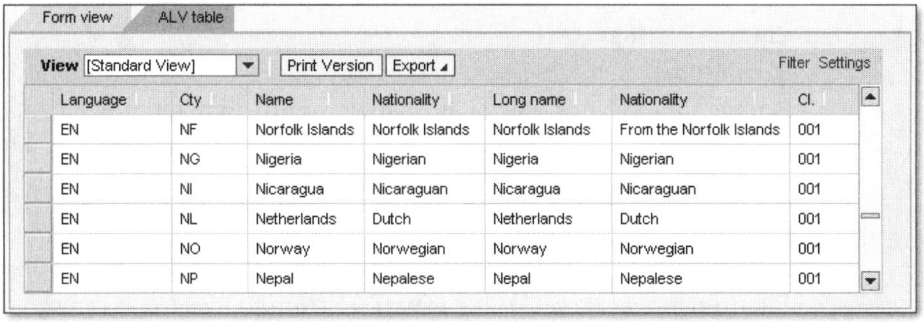

Form view | ALV table

View [Standard View] | Print Version | Export | Filter Settings

Language	Cty	Name	Nationality	Long name	Nationality	Cl.
EN	NF	Norfolk Islands	Norfolk Islands	Norfolk Islands	From the Norfolk Islands	001
EN	NG	Nigeria	Nigerian	Nigeria	Nigerian	001
EN	NI	Nicaragua	Nicaraguan	Nicaragua	Nicaraguan	001
EN	NL	Netherlands	Dutch	Netherlands	Dutch	001
EN	NO	Norway	Norwegian	Norway	Norwegian	001
EN	NP	Nepal	Nepalese	Nepal	Nepalese	001

Figure 5.25 Testing the ALV Table

This exercise was based on several assumptions that do not often occur in real life. For example, in the table, the ALV component simply displays all fields of the table structure of T005T. The column names are also copied automatically from the data elements of the structure. However, because in your daily work you will often want to display only a portion of the fields of a structure and because the field names can be misleading, the following sections describe how you can configure ALV tables and their table columns.

5.2.2 ALV Configuration Model

The *configuration model* represents the core of the ALV component. It is based on an object with the type CL_SALV_WD_CONFIG_TABLE. Each ALV component contains exactly one configuration model. This model enables you to configure every single detail of an ALV table, from the table header to its individual columns. The following list provides an overview of the areas that can be configured in the configuration model:

- **Table settings**
  These settings primarily include output settings such as two-dimensional tables or characteristics hierarchies, and display color schemes, table headers, and so on.

- **Field settings**
  Fields describe the data that is used in the ALV output. The name of a field corresponds to the name of an attribute in a context node. Thus, each context attribute has a field representative of the same name in the configuration model. The relevant field settings allow you to sort, filter, and aggregate data.
- **Column settings**
  At runtime, each table column is represented by a column object. Among other things, this object allows you to configure the column header, the column sequence, and the column editor (text field, input field, dropdown list, and so on).
- **Settings for standard ALV functions**
  ALV provides a number of standard functions, such as the sort and filter functions, as well as the export function to Excel. You can show and hide these functions according to your requirements via specific methods of the configuration model.
- **Settings for application-specific functions**
  You can store custom buttons in the toolbar of an ALV table, which will allow you to respond to events triggered via the interface controller.

Fetching the configuration model

The `get_model( )` interface controller method enables you to obtain a reference of type `CL_SALV_WD_CONFIG_TABLE` to the respective configuration model of an ALV component. After you have done this, you can use the methods of the object to configure the ALV table according to your requirements. At this stage, you should take a look at the methods available in the configuration model.

[✎] In the following exercise, you will obtain a reference to the configuration model and store this reference as an attribute in the component controller of the main component. This exercise is rather short and is intended to prepare you for the subsequent exercise.

1. Create a reference variable to the ALV configuration model in the component controller. To do this, select the ATTRIBUTES tab in the component controller of the ZWDC_05_MAIN component. Enter the attribute go_alv_t005t with reference type CL_SALV_WD_CONFIG_TABLE into the attribute table. Define the attribute as PUBLIC.

2. Then, instance the ALV component. For this, select the PROPERTIES tab and enter a component usage for the interface controller of the ALV component. Then, go to the METHODS tab and open the wddoinit( ) method. Instance the ALV component manually and get a reference to the interface controller of this component. Your coding should now appear as shown in Listing 5.4.

Instancing the ALV

```
DATA: lo_cmp_usage_alv TYPE REF TO if_wd_component_usage,
      lo_ifc_alv_t005t TYPE REF TO iwci_salv_wd_table.
* Instance ALV component
lo_cmp_usage_alv = wd_this->wd_cpuse_alv_t005t( ).
IF lo_cmp_usage_alv->has_active_component( ) IS INITIAL.
  lo_cmp_usage_alv->create_component( ).
ENDIF.
* Get interface controller
lo_ifc_alv_t005t = wd_this->wd_cpifc_alv_t005t( ).
```

Listing 5.4 Instancing the ALV Component

3. Get the configuration model and store a reference to it in the go_alv_t005t attribute. For this, you must add the following line at the end of the method:

Fetching the configuration model

```
wd_this->go_alv_t005t = lo_ifc_alv_t005t->get_model( ).
```

Carry out a syntax check and activate the component.

You just obtained a reference to the configuration model of the ALV component. The following sections and exercise will require you to use this reference for the configuration of the ALV table.

Important methods of the configuration model

Irrespective of the exercises, Table 5.1 provides a list of the most important general methods of the configuration model, which can be used for customizing ALV tables.

Method	Description
`if_salv_wd_table_settings~create_header( )`	Creates an object for the table title. This object allows you to design a table header.
`if_salv_wd_table_settings~set_edit_mode( )`	Defines whether the mass data mode is enabled or disabled. If it is enabled, the end of the ALV output contains a page with empty rows, ready for the input of data.
`if_salv_wd_table_settings~set_fixed_table_layout( )`	Defines that the width of the ALV output does not depend on the width of the column content.
`if_salv_wd_table_settings~set_read_only( )`	Defines whether the ALV output is read-only or can be edited.
`if_salv_wd_table_settings~set_visible_row_count( )`	Defines the height of the ALV output in table rows.
`if_salv_wd_table_settings~set_width( )`	Defines the width of the ALV output.

Table 5.1 General Configuration Model Methods

5.2.3 Methods and Events of the Interface Controller

In Section 5.2.2, ALV Configuration Model, the `get_model( )` method enabled you to take a first look at the interface controller of the ALV component. In addition to this method, the ALV component contains several other methods and events that enable communication with the using components. While the greater part of the ALV component methods serves to configure the table, events are used for interaction purposes. They notify the using component about user actions such as the modification of the lead selection, for example.

The following sections describe the most important methods and events of the ALV component. The next section begins with the major events of the ALV; the subsequent section deals with the most important methods of the ALV component. This part of the chapter does not contain an exercise but you will need this information later on in the book.

Events of the ALV Component

Table 5.2 provides a list of the most important events of the ALV component:

Event	Description
ON_CLICK	This event is triggered when the user clicks on a button or LinkToAction in an ALV table cell.
ON_DATA_CHECK	This event is triggered when data is checked in an editable ALV table after the data has been modified.
ON_FUNCTION	This event is triggered when the user selects a custom button in the toolbar (see Section 5.2.5, Changing the Toolbar).
ON_LEAD_SELECT	This event is triggered when the user changes the lead selection in the table.

Table 5.2 Events of the ALV Component

ON_SELECT Event

Whereas the ON_LEAD_SELECT event is triggered only when the lead selection changes, SAP NetWeaver 7.0 EhP 2 and later versions also provide the ON_SELECT event, which is activated when the lead selection or any other selection changes. In the configuration model of the ALV component, you can define which of the two events you want to have triggered. (This can be activated in the configuration model of the ALV component.)

R_PARAM parameter

Each of the events listed in Table 5.2 contains the importing parameter r_param with interface class type IF_SALV_WD_TABLE_<event name> (without the ON_ prefix of the event). The interfaces provide detailed information about the respective event.

For example, the data type of the event handler parameter is IF_SALV_WD_TABLE_LEAD_SELECT for the ON_LEAD_SELECT event. The interface contains the index and old_index attributes, which are filled with the index value of the new and old lead selection. If a user changes the lead selection, you can read the index value in the event handler via r_param->index.

set_data( ) Method

The options provided by the `set_data( )` methods were already mentioned in Section 5.2.1, Integrating ALV. This method allows you to bind an ALV component dynamically to any context node. For this, the method provides the `r_node_data` parameter of the `IF_WD_CONTEXT_NODE` type.

get_model_extended( ) Method

By default, the ALV component transfers all attributes of a context node into the column set of the ALV table. If the node is based on a dictionary structure, then the ALV component even transfers all fields of the structure into the column set.

However, it frequently happens that you only want to transfer a portion of the node attributes into the column set of the ALV table. This is the case, for example, if the attribute is a technical attribute that does not provide added value to the user.

At this point, you should take another look at Figure 5.25. On the far left of the screen, you can see the technical column LANGUAGE (`SPRAS` attribute), whereas the CLIENT column appears on the far right. These are two typical examples of columns that are usually not relevant to users.

get_model( ) vs. get_model_extended( )

When using the `get_model( )` interface controller method, which you saw earlier, the configuration model automatically transfers all attributes of the node into the column set of the table. However, if you use the `get_model_extended( )`method instead of `get_model( )`, the importing parameter `s_param-default_columns` enables you to decide whether you want to have all node attributes transferred automatically into the column set.

Benefits of get_model_extended( )

But what is the benefit of `get_model_extended( )` if this method does not automatically transfer the node attributes into the column set? The answer is quite simple: It allows you to achieve better system performance. For example, the instancing of unused columns that are deleted after the instancing process takes time and requires storage space. This does not much matter if only a small number of columns is affected but if it affects between five and ten technical columns or more, you should start using the `get_model_extended( )` method.

data_check( ) Method/Event

Context of ALV tables

In contrast to normal Web Dynpro tables, in ALV tables the data is not displayed directly from within the context of the own component but from within a separate context in the ALV component. The ALV component constantly synchronizes the data between its own context and the table context used in the view. Figure 5.26 illustrates this data check process on the basis of Table T005T.

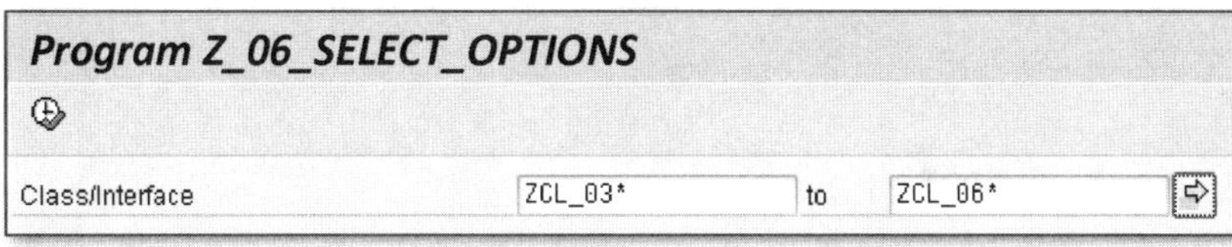

Figure 5.26 Data Check of the ALV Component

Data synchronization via data_check( )

This synchronization process, which can be compared to the process of mapping different nodes, usually occurs without you noticing it. For example, the transport of data from the ALV component context to the view context is carried out automatically. The transport of data in the opposite direction, from the table context to the component's own context, is carried out via the `data_check( )` method. During the data check process, the accuracy of the data is checked for the first time (data type and format, etc.). Therefore, it only makes sense to manually call `data_check( )` if the table is in change mode.

Calling time of data_check( )

Depending on the settings in the configuration model, the `data_check( )` method is called automatically by the ALV component every time you press the `Enter` key in a table cell, or when you click on the CHECK button in the toolbar of the ALV table. In addition, you can start the `data_check( )` method manually at any time. This can be necessary, for example, if a user triggers the automatic data check and you want to make sure that the component's own context node contains the current dataset of the table context.

ON_DATA_CHECK event

After the data check has been completed, the `ON_DATA_CHECK` event provides information about the changes that have been carried out in the context. For this, the attributes of the `r_param` parameter with data type

IF_SALV_WD_TABLE_DATA_CHECK create a table with a list of all changes carried out in the component's own context.

5.2.4 Changes to the Column Set

Now that you have learned about the most important events and methods of the ALV component, you should return to more practical topics. Therefore, the following sections will describe how you can add, delete, and modify columns in ALV tables and how you can manipulate their arrangement.

Deleting Columns

The if_salv_wd_column_settings~delete_column( ) method of the configuration model allows you to delete individual columns from ALV tables. Columns to be deleted are transferred with the ID parameter.

[✎] In the following exercise, you will create a new method for the configuration of the ALV table. Then, you will delete the short text columns LANDX and NATIO, as well as the client column in the method, from the column set.

1. Open the ZWDC_05_MAIN component and create the init_alv_t005t( ) method in the component controller. Go to the body of wddoinit( ) and call the new method at the end (wd_this->init_alv_t005t( )).

Deleting a column

2. Double-click on the method name to navigate to the new method and delete the MANDT. column. To do this, enter the following line in the method:

```
wd_this->go_alv_t005t->if_salv_wd_column_settings~delete_
column( id = 'MANDT' ).
```

Then, delete the LANDX and NATIO columns.

Testing the application

3. Activate the component and test the application. The ALV table should no longer contain the last column for the client. The column set (SETTINGS • COLUMN SELECTION) of the table no longer contains this column.

Configuring Columns

Changes to ALV table columns can be implemented very easily. For example, you can get a column object of type CL_SALV_WD_COLUMN by calling the if_salv_wd_column_settings~get_column( ) method. This column object allows you to configure the column per your requirements. Table 5.3 provides an overview of selected methods for column configuration.

Method	Description
set_width( )	Defines the column width.
set_visible( )	Shows or hides the column.
set_position( )	Defines the position of the column in the ALV output.
get_header( )	Returns the object of the column header.

Table 5.3 List of Selected Methods for Column Configuration

Changing a column header

To be able to change a column header, you must obtain a column header object of type CL_SALV_WD_COLUMN_HEADER by using the get_header( ) method. After you have done this, you can use the set_text( ) method to change the column header.

DDIC Binding of Column Headers

For table columns that are based on DDIC objects, the ALV component automatically uses the header stored in the DDIC. You can use the set_prop_ddic_binding_field( ) method to bind the column header to other DDIC field labels as well (short, medium, long).

If you want to be able to set the column header of a column with DDIC binding manually via the set_text( ) method, you must first release its DDIC binding.

[✎] In the following exercise, you will learn how to work with columns and column headers. In the first step, you will ensure that the SPRAS and LANDX50 columns are hidden by default (note that you are not going to delete them). Then, you will use your own values to overwrite the headers of columns that are based on LANDX and LANDX50.

1. Activate change mode and open the `init_alv_t005t( )` in the component controller of the main component.

Hiding columns

2. Hide the `SPRAS` column. To do this, get the associated column object from the configuration model and call the `set_visible( )` method in this object. To hide the column, you must fill the `value` importing parameter with a value of type `CL_WD_ABSTR_TABLE_COLUMN=>T_VISIBLE`. To do so, you must use the constant `cl_wd_uielement=>e_visible-none`.

Changing the DDIC column header binding

3. Currently, the column header of the `LANDX50` attribute contains the text "Long description." To change the label to "Country," use the `get_header( )` method to obtain the column header object from the column and release the DDIC binding of the column header by calling the `set_prop_ddic_binding_field( )` method. Then, use the `set_text( )` method to change the header to "Country." Listing 5.5 contains the solution to this exercise.

```
DATA: lo_column          TYPE REF TO cl_salv_wd_column,
      lo_column_header TYPE REF TO cl_salv_wd_column_header.
* Get SPRAS column
wd_this->go_alv_t005t->if_salv_wd_column_settings~
get_column(
  EXPORTING
    id = 'SPRAS'
  RECEIVING
    value = lo_column ).
* Hide SPRAS column in column set
lo_column->set_visible( cl_wd_uielement=>
e_visible-none ).
* Get LANDX50 column
wd_this->go_alv_t005t->if_salv_wd_column_settings~
get_column(
  EXPORTING
    id = 'LANDX50'
  RECEIVING
    value = lo_column ).
* Get column header from LANDX50
lo_column_header = lo_column->get_header( ).
* Release DDIC binding
lo_column_header->set_prop_ddic_binding_field(
  property = if_salv_wd_c_ddic_binding=>bind_prop_text
```

```
    value    = if_salv_wd_c_ddic_binding=>ddic_bind_none ).
  * Change the column title of LANDX50
    lo_column_header->set_text( 'Land' ).
```

Listing 5.5 Changing Table Columns

Testing the application

4. Carry out a syntax check and activate the component. Then, test the application. The ALV table should now appear, as shown in Figure 5.27.

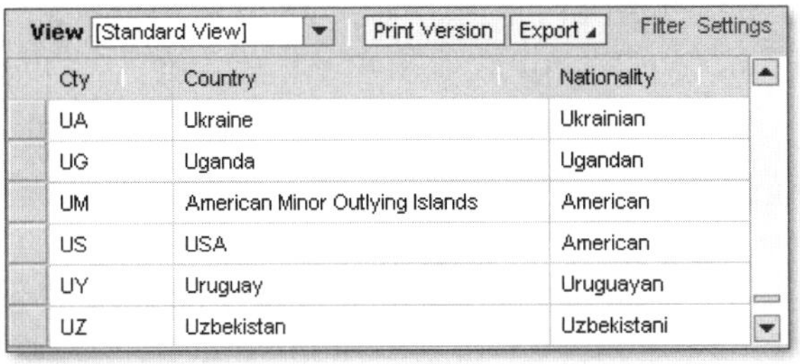

View [Standard View] | Print Version | Export | Filter Settings

Cty	Country	Nationality
UA	Ukraine	Ukrainian
UG	Uganda	Ugandan
UM	American Minor Outlying Islands	American
US	USA	American
UY	Uruguay	Uruguayan
UZ	Uzbekistan	Uzbekistani

Figure 5.27 ALV Table After Table Column Change

Creating columns

If you chose to use the `get_model_extended( )` method and need to create all columns explicitly, you can do so via the `if_salv_wd_column_settings~create_column( )` method of the configuration model. After you have called this method, you will obtain a column object that you can configure like any other column.

Changing the cell editor

Finally, you should also know how to replace the cell editor of columns. The ALV component provides a large number of cell editors such as simple input fields, checkboxes, and dropdown lists. You can change a cell editor by calling the `set_cell_editor( )` for the column object. Then, you must transfer a cell editor object of type `CL_SALV_WD_UIE_<editor type>` to the method. Listing 5.6 shows how you can replace the cell editor of column `LANDX50` by enhancing it with the coding from Listing 5.5.

```
DATA: lo_input_field TYPE REF TO cl_salv_wd_uie_input_field.
* Create an input field of type cell editor
CREATE OBJECT lo_input_field
  EXPORTING
    value_fieldname = 'LANDX50'.
* Change the cell editor of column LANDX50 to input field
```

```
lo_column->set_cell_editor( lo_input_field ).
* Deactivate read-only mode of the ALV table
wd_this->go_alv_t005t->if_salv_wd_table_settings~set_read_only(
  abap_false ).
```

Listing 5.6 Changing the Cell Editor of a Column

5.2.5 Changing the Toolbar

Standard functions

By default, ALV tables contain a toolbar, which provides a set of standard functions such as the export of data to Excel. You can enable and disable these standard functions according to your requirements via the configuration model.

Custom functions

In addition, the configuration model allows you to integrate any number of custom functions into the toolbar. Functions can be mapped through simple buttons, links, or even input fields, among other things. If, for example, a user clicks on a custom button, this button triggers the `ON_FUNCTION` event of the ALV component, and in doing so, notifies the user about the execution of the associated toolbar function.

You can create a new function by calling the configuration model method `if_salv_wd_function_settings~create_function( )`. This method returns an object of the `CL_SALV_WD_FUNCTION` class. However, the function does not yet have an editor, which you must assign to it via the `set_editor( )` method.

All editors are based on the class `CL_SALV_WD_FE<editor type>`. If the user clicks on the toolbar button now, the ALV component triggers the `ON_FUNCTION` event.

[✎] In the following exercise, you will create a new function with a button.

1. Activate change mode and open the `init_alv_t005t( )` in the component controller of the main component.
2. Create a new function with the `MY_BUTTON` ID at the end of the method.

Creating a button

3. Then, generate a button object from within the `CL_SALV_WD_FE_BUTTON` class and use the button as an editor for the function. Use the

set_text( ) method of the button to label it with the text "My Button." Listing 5.7 contains the solution.

```
DATA: lo_function TYPE REF TO cl_salv_wd_function,
      lo_button   TYPE REF TO cl_salv_wd_fe_button.
* Create a new button
CREATE OBJECT lo_button.
lo_button->set_text( 'My Button' ).
* Create MY_BUTTON function
lo_function =
  wd_this->go_alv_t005t->if_salv_wd_function_settings~
    create_function(
      id = 'MY_BUTTON' ).
* Use a button as editor
lo_function->set_editor( lo_button ).
```

Listing 5.7 Creating Functions

4. Create an on_function( ) method with type EVENT HANDLER in the component controller. Register this method for the ON_FUNCTION event of the ALV component. Within this method, you can query the ID of the function by reading r_param->id and responding to it.

Creating an event handler

5. Carry out a syntax check and activate the component. Then, test the application. The ALV table now contains a button called MY BUTTON, as shown in Figure 5.28. When you click on this button, the on_function( ) event handler method is called in the main component.

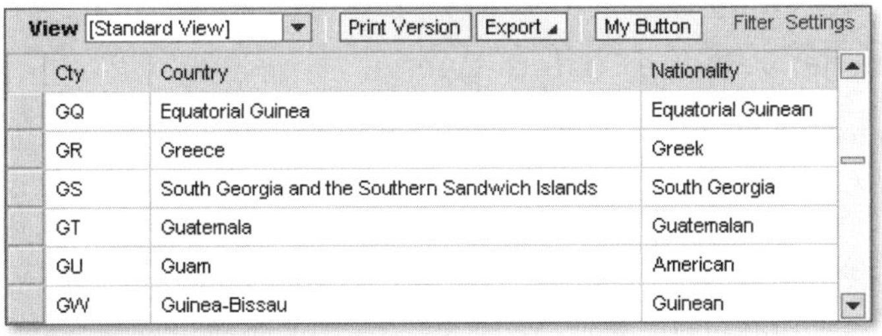

Testing the application

View [Standard View] | Print Version | Export | My Button | Filter Settings

Cty	Country	Nationality
GQ	Equatorial Guinea	Equatorial Guinean
GR	Greece	Greek
GS	South Georgia and the Southern Sandwich Islands	South Georgia
GT	Guatemala	Guatemalan
GU	Guam	American
GW	Guinea-Bissau	Guinean

Figure 5.28 ALV Table with My Button

In this section, you learned how to integrate ALV tables in your component and how to configure these tables according to your requirements. For example, you can now show and hide columns, change the associated column header, and create your own functions or buttons. The basic

ALV knowledge you have acquired so far is the ideal preparation for you to effortlessly delve into other areas of the ALV component.

5.3 POWER List

The *Personal Object Work Entity Repository List*, generally known as *POWER list* and previously referred to as *POWL (Personal Objects Worklist)*, represents a comprehensive and flexible Web Dynpro framework for managing queries with results lists that are based on any kind of data. You can create the queries either in the Customizing section of the POWER list or directly from within the POWER list. The data is transferred for display in a POWER list via interfaces that are implemented in the system.

Examples of use

You can use the POWER list for searching any data and for displaying data in a table. For example, you could use it to list all sales orders that exist in a system. Transactional users can use different pre-defined queries to view open orders in the system, orders that are currently to be picked, or closed orders. In addition, transactional users can create custom queries with more sophisticated search criteria for the sales orders.

The following sections describe the functions of the POWER list in the system so that you can identify potential ways of using them in your own projects. (Note that we deliberately avoided covering the technical details of the POWER list framework.)

5.3.1 Example: Defining Custom Queries

Readers who have already participated in an SAP training will be familiar with the SAP flight data model and the `SFLIGHT` database table. This table contains flight connections, including departure times, airfares, and aircraft types. The following example uses the `SFLIGHT` table for demonstrating the usage options of the POWER list. For this, SAP provides the demo component `POWL_EASY_DEMO`.

After you have started the `powl_easy_demo` sample application of the `POWL_EASY_DEMO` component, an empty POWER list appears, as shown in Figure 5.29. With a little bit of customizing, you can also easily display previously defined queries.

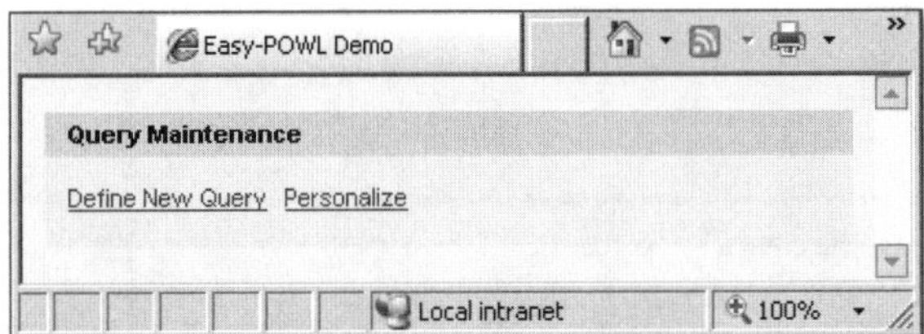

Figure 5.29 Empty POWER list

Step 1 – define query

Click on DEFINE NEW QUERY to create a new query. A roadmap opens that consists of three steps to define the query. In the first step, you must select an object type. The object type indicates on which data source – that is, on which *feeder class* – the new query should be based. The available object types are stored in the Customizing section of the POWER list. In our example, as shown in Figure 5.30, we selected the only available object type, EASY-POWL DEMO. This type is based on a query of the `SFLIGHT` database table.

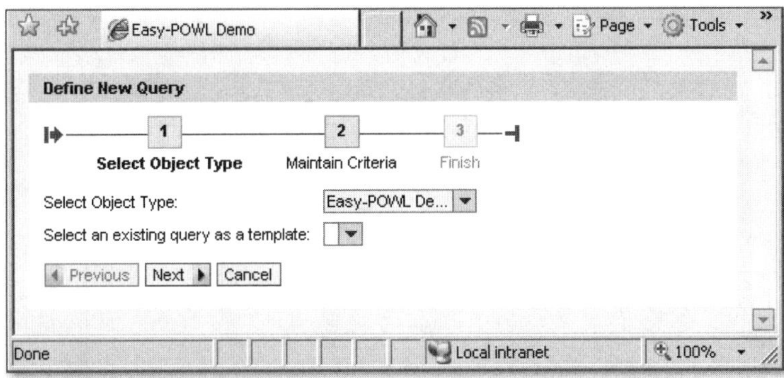

Figure 5.30 Selecting an Object Type

Step 2 – maintain search criteria

Click on NEXT to configure the search criteria of the query. The available criteria can be stored in the Customizing section of the POWER list. Figure 5.31 shows the criteria maintenance for object type EASY-POWL DEMO. Here, you can configure AIRLINE, CONNECTION NUMBER, and FLIGHT DATE. Click on CALCULATED DATA to maintain rolling date horizons for date fields (for example, the next three days).

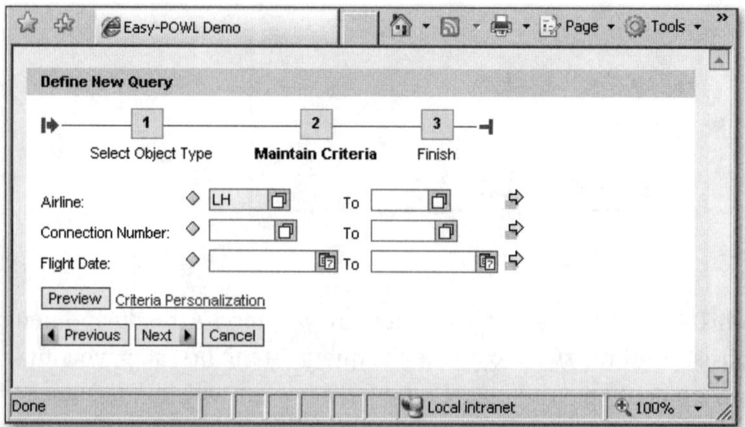

Figure 5.31 Defining Custom Queries

Step 3 — finish query

In the final step, you can enter a description for the new query and also categorize it. Figure 5.32 shows the almost completed LUFTHANSA query, which should be integrated in the newly created MY FAVORITES category. Click on FINISH to save the new custom query.

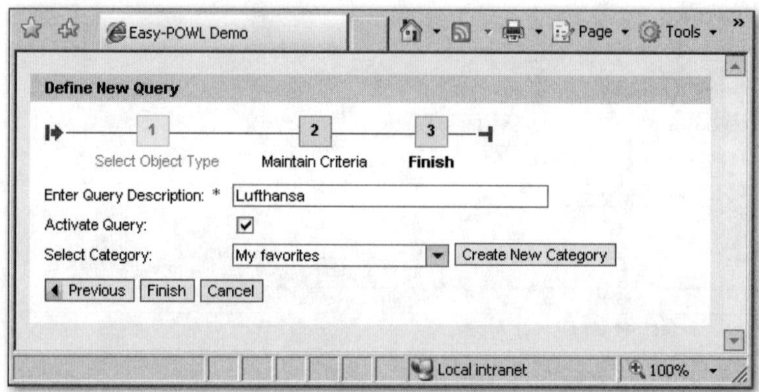

Figure 5.32 Finishing the Query

Main view of the POWER list

Next, the system returns you to the main area of the POWER list, where the upper area now displays the list of available queries (see Figure 5.33). Currently only one item is available because you defined only one query. The lower area displays the results table of the POWER list. This is a fully functional ALV table. You can now configure additional POWER-list-specific settings between the list of available queries and the ALV table. For example, you can retroactively change the search criteria of the query or modify the layout of the POWER list.

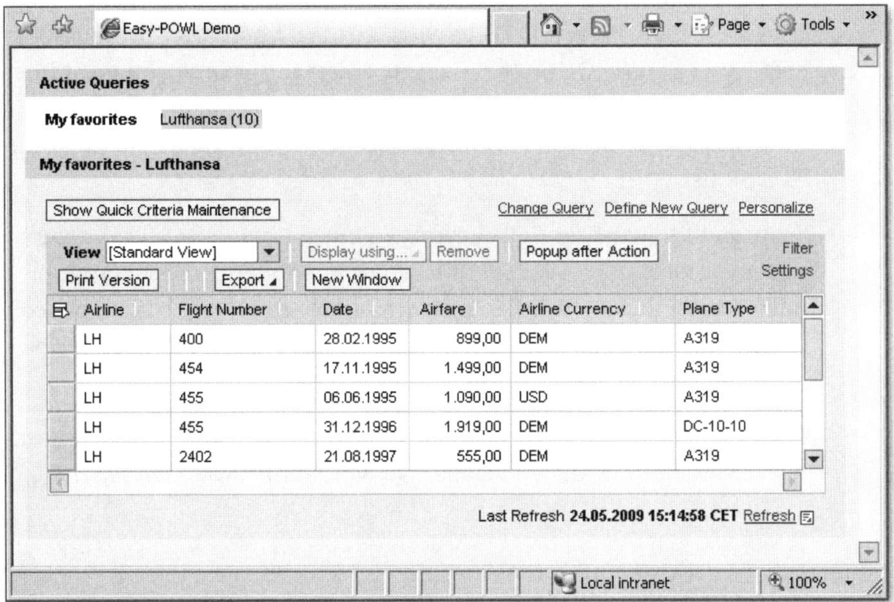

Figure 5.33 Lufthansa Flights Displayed in a POWER List

POWL vs. Easy-POWL

The sample application used here is based on what is called the *Easy-POWL*. The Easy-POWL is a POWER list extended by additional Customizing for the table columns and toolbar buttons. It facilitates the maintenance and programming of queries considerably. Therefore, it is advisable to always use the Easy-POWL when you want to use the POWER list.

Updating the data

Finally, you should be aware of the following important aspect: POWER lists are based on queries that can be executed at firmly defined points in time. Thus, they always indicate the status of the data source at a specific point in time. You can trigger an update of a query at any time by clicking on REFRESH below the table on the right.

5.3.2 Additional Information

Technial details – POWER list

The POWER list is based on the POWL_UI_COMP component, and all administration of the POWER list takes place via Customizing. The most important transactions for implementing the POWER list are POWL_TYPE, POWL_QUERY, POWL_CAT, as well as the two transactions POWL_TYPER and POWL_QUERYR. To create a database query, you must integrate the IF_POWL_FEEDER interface into your implemented classes. This interface enables all communication between your application and the POWER list.

Technical details – Easy-POWL

If you want to use Easy-POWL, you can integrate the POWL_EASY component instead of POWL_UI_COMP into your components. Easy-POWL provides Transaction POWL_EASY, which allows for configuring table columns and toolbar buttons. The IF_POWL_EASY_FEEDER interface enables your applications to communicate with Easy-POWL.

You can find additional information about using and implementing POWER lists in the SAP Developer Network (*http://www.sdn.sap.com*).

5.4 Summary

This chapter has comprehensively covered the topic of multi-component architectures and standard components. You should now be able to establish a network between your components using component usages. Moreover, you have learned about the SALV_WD_TABLE component, which enables you to display nodes in tables.

Chapter 6, Input Helps and Semantic Helps, will describe input helps and semantic helps, along with the different options that are available to implement input helps. Other important aspects discussed in this chapter include the Object Value Selector (OVS) and SELECT-OPTIONS components.

Input help for a Web Dynpro application is crucially important for accepting and reducing incorrect entries made by the user. Web Dynpro provides a broad range of input help. This chapter therefore deals with implementing available input help concepts and semantic help in Web Dynpro.

6 Input Help and Semantic Help

Usage

Input help in a Web Dynpro application has many different effects for a user. It improves user-friendliness, increases operating speed, decreases input errors made by the user, and reduces hotline support costs. Web Dynpro provides a broad range of options for implementing input help, grouped into two large categories:

- **Selection options**
  Selection options provide the user with a predefined number of selectable values. This number of values may originate from the ABAP Dictionary or may be created by the developer at runtime. The user can only choose from this predefined set of values. The range of values is generally very low.
- **Input help**
  Input help, in contrast, represents complex selection methods. The number of values is significantly higher than for selection options. For this reason, a multilevel selection procedure is also used. The most well-known help in the input help category is *search help*.

Semantic help

When choosing values, under certain circumstances, the user must be supported by help texts and additional information. Web Dynpro provides many different technical options to offer the user support in the form of content, ranging from brief help texts to detailed documentation texts. We will introduce these different *semantic help* options in this chapter.

We will use examples to present our explanations on the different options. Our first focus will be on implementing selection options. This will involve discussing known dropdowns, radio buttons, checkboxes, list boxes, and the less well-known `TriStateCheckBox` element. For the input help, we will show you how to set the input help mode to be used when working with context attributes. We will also explain which technical tools you will need for implementing a mode. We will pay particular attention to the *Object Value Selector* and *Select Option*, which are both provided by reusable Web Dynpro components. We will end this chapter by discussing the use of semantic help for providing additional information while using the Web Dynpro application.

You can use the dynamic class browser (the Web Dynpro component from Chapter 3, Developing Web Dynpro Applications) for the practical exercises.

Topics Discussed

We will discuss the following topics in this chapter:

- Selection options
- Input help
- `SELECT-OPTIONS`
- Semantic help

6.1 Implementing Selection Options

UI elements

In this section, we will present the options available in Web Dynpro applications for providing the user with a set of values and being able to display them. We will describe the following UI elements:

- `DropDownByIndex/DropDownByKey`
- `RadioButton/RadioButtonGroupByIndex/RadioButtonGroupByKey`
- `CheckBox`
- `CheckBoxGroup`
- `ItemListBox`
- `TriStateCheckBox`

6.1.1 DropDown

1 from n

DropDown UI elements are the first category to make predefined selection options available to users. They offer a list of values from which one entry can be selected. This type of selection is known as *1 from n* because one entry must be selected from a set of values. This also means that in any situation, one of the entries is selected.

A DropDown list consists of the following graphical components: a text field, a button, and a selection list. An already selected list entry is displayed in the text field. The list of all possible values is displayed when the user clicks on the button.

DropDownByIndex, DropDownByKey

Two versions of DropDown selection options are available, as follows:

- DropDownByIndex
- DropDownByKey

These two options do not differ in the way they are displayed but in the way they are integrated into the context.

DropDownByIndex

In the case of the DropDownByIndex UI element, the UI element is bound to a context attribute in a context node containing a number of elements (n cardinality upper limit). The elements define the entries in the DropDown list. The selected element corresponds to the lead selection of the node and the lead selection changes when the user selects an entry. We already defined ice cream flavors in this manner in Chapter 2, Web Dynpro Architecture. Therefore, we have kept the descriptions in this chapter brief.

onSelect event

One more comment: selecting a value does not necessarily result in an HTTP roundtrip. This happens only if an action was defined for the ONSELECT event. The data stored in the context does not change when the user selects a value.

DropDownByKey

Selection list values are determined for the DropDownByKey UI element using attribute information in the node information; you have already seen this in Chapter 4, Dynamic Web Dynpro Applications. The node information you can determine for a node describes this node. This description contains all of the information specified when the context node was defined. This naturally also includes attribute information.

The list of values can be generated in two ways:

- Domain fixed values
- Implementation

DropDownByKey with domain fixed values

If the attribute was typed using a reference to an ABAP Dictionary data element with domains, the texts for the domain fixed values are displayed.

The following example shows you how you can use the `DropDownByKey` UI element to arrange selection options. The user can choose the visibility of ABAP class methods. A suitable data element for this is `SEOEXPOSE`, which references the `SEOEXPOSE` domain with fixed values of `0` (Private), `1` (Protected), and `2` (Public).

The context requirement to be able to use the `DropDownByKey` UI element is an attribute with an ABAP Dictionary reference to a data element that references a domain with fixed values. This means that you have to create an attribute for a context node; for example, `CLASS_SEL_CRIT`. This is typed with the `ZST_03_WD_CLASS_SEL_CRIT` ABAP Dictionary structure. To learn how to add an attribute to an ABAP Dictionary structure and copy new additions into the context of the Web Dynpro component, you will now change a structure:

1. Add the `SEOEXPOSE`-type `VISIBILITY_METHOD` to the `ZST_03_WD_CLASS_SEL_CRIT` structure. Use the ABAP Dictionary (Transaction SE11) to do this. Do not forget to activate the structure.

Including a new attribute in the context node

2. Switch to the component controller of the `ZWDC_03_CLASS_BROWSER` Web Dynpro component and include the new component from the structure as an attribute in the `CLASS_SEL_CRIT` context node. In the context node properties, a button for inserting new attributes from the structure is available on the right-hand side, next to the input field

for the Dictionary Structure property (see Figure 6.1, ❶). Click on this button to display the dialog box for selecting components.

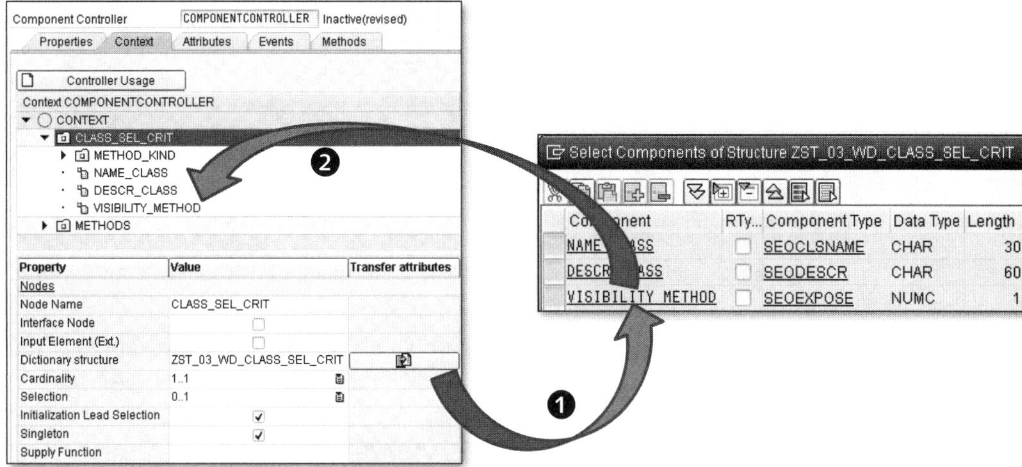

Figure 6.1 Changing an ABAP Dictionary Structure and Copying the Change to the Context

3. Copy the VISIBILITY_METHOD component. Select the component row to do this and click on the button with the green checkmark to confirm your entry. This makes the VISIBILITY_METHOD attribute available in the CLASS_SEL_CRIT node for further use (❷).

4. Update the mapping for the CLASS_SEL_CRIT context node in the V_CLASS_SELECTION view so that the new attribute can also be used there.

Updating mapping

5. Switch to the Layout tab for the V_CLASS_SELECTION view. You can display the selection options by creating a DropDownByKey UI element. Call this new UI element DDBK_VIS_METH. Bind the SELECTEDKEY property to the VISIBILITY_METHOD attribute of the CLASS_SEL_CRIT node, as you can see in Figure 6.2 (❷). Also, set the MatrixData value for the Layout Data property (❶). This makes the texts for domain fixed values available as selection options.

Creating the DropDownByKey UI element

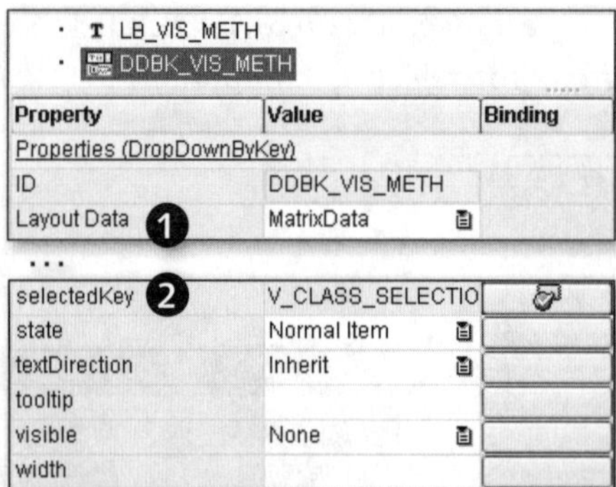

Figure 6.2 Label and DropDownByKey UI Element

Testing

6. Activate all changed objects and test the Web Dynpro application. Your result should correspond to the one shown in Figure 6.3.

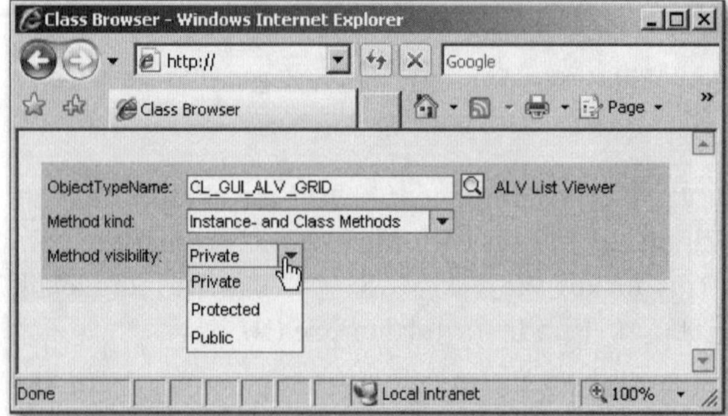

Figure 6.3 Expanded DropDownByKey UI Element

When using this technique, you must make sure that selecting a value in the `DropDown` list only results in an HTTP roundtrip if an action was bound to the ONSELECT event. Unlike `DropDownByIndex`, the lead selection does not change when you select a value. The element data stored in the attribute is overwritten by the key value relating to the selection.

Implementation for DropDownByKey

As already mentioned, selection list values can also be generated by implementation during runtime. Listing 6.1 shows the implementation for this option:

get_child_node()

- The first step involves determining the reference to the context node containing the attribute for which the set of values should be set.

- The get_node_info( ) method then determines the information node using the context node reference from the previous step. **get_node_info( )**
- The values to be displayed are compiled in an internal table with the WDR_CONTEXT_ATTR_VALUE row type. In this example, the internal lt_value_set table was defined using TYPE TABLE OF WDR_CONTEXT_ATTR_VALUE and then populated row by row with the required values.
- Finally, the attribute values are set with the set_attribute_value_set( ) method using the node information reference. When the method is called, the name of the attribute and of the internal table must be transferred. **set_attribute_value_set( )**

```
METHOD setctx_view_meth .
* Reference to the node
DATA: lo_nd_class_sel_crit TYPE REF TO
        if_wd_context_node,
* Reference to the node information
      lo_nd_class_sel_crit_info TYPE REF TO
        if_wd_context_node_info,
* Values to the selection option as an internal table
        lt_value_set TYPE TABLE OF wdr_context_attr_value,
* Work structure
        ls_value_set LIKE LINE OF lt_value_set.
* Navigate to <CLASS_SEL_CRIT> via lead selection
lo_nd_class_sel_crit = wd_context->get_child_node(
  name = wd_this->wdctx_class_sel_crit ).
* Retrieve the information for the node
lo_nd_class_sel_crit_info =
  lo_nd_class_sel_crit->get_node_info( ).
* Set the value
* All
ls_value_set-value = '3'.
ls_value_set-text  = 'All'.
APPEND ls_value_set TO lt_value_set.
...
* Set the value set in the description object
lo_nd_class_sel_crit_info->set_attribute_value_set(
    name      = 'VISIBILITY_METHOD'
    value_set = lt_value_set ).
ENDMETHOD.
```

Listing 6.1 Defining Sets of Values for an Attribute Through an Implementation

The result of the implementation is shown in Figure 6.4. Note that we used the same attribute as before but in this case, the information object for setting values was used.

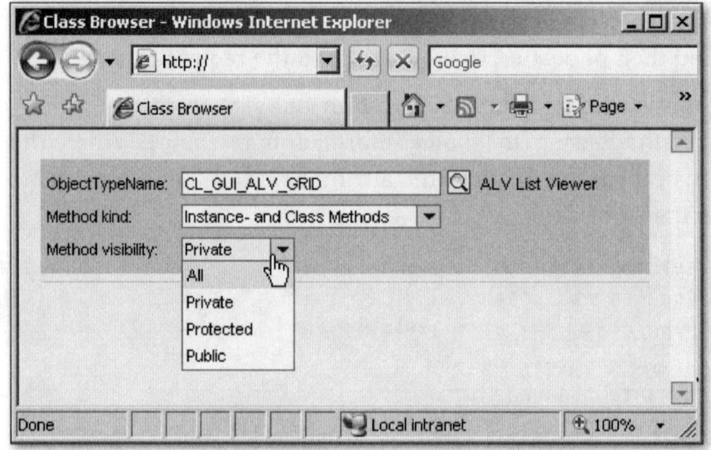

Figure 6.4 Expanded DropDownByKey UI Element with Dynamic Values

6.1.2 RadioButton

Usage A `RadioButton` UI element represents a UI element with two statuses that can be displayed using a set button or an empty button. An example of a group of `RadioButton` elements is shown in Figure 6.5. To group the elements visually, a `Group` UI element was used into which four `RadioButton` UI elements were placed.

The grouping of these `RadioButton` elements is the result of data binding on the context attribute used before, for which the SELECTEDKEY `RadioButton` property was used (❷). You set the `RadioButton` if the SELECTEDKEY property value contains the value of the key belonging to this selection button, which was defined using the KEYTOSELECT (❶). The TEXT property determines the text for the `RadioButton` (❸).

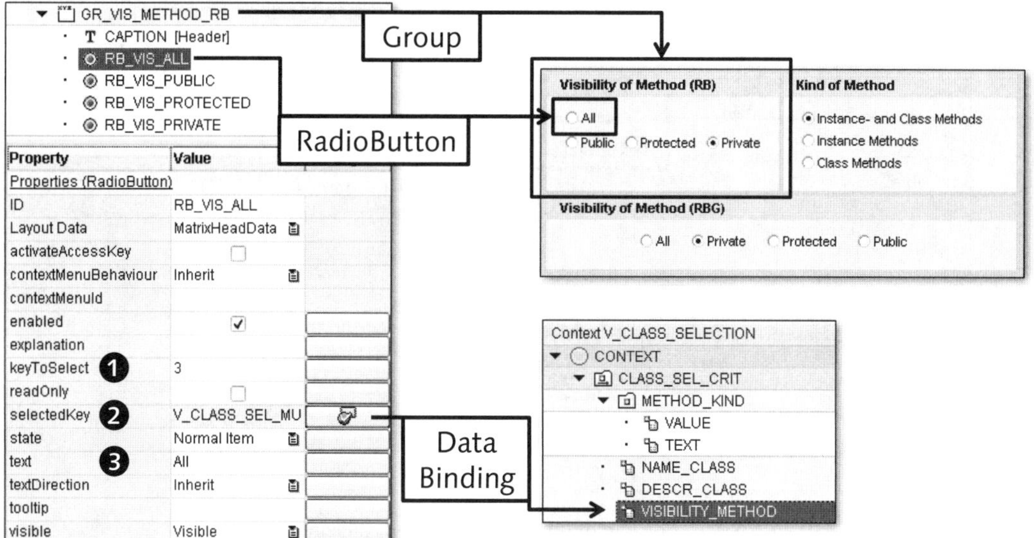

Figure 6.5 Group of RadioButton Elements

Layout of RadioButton elements

A maximum of only one element can be selected (*1 from n*) from a group of `RadioButton` elements. Unlike the `RadioButtonGroupByIndex` and `RadioButtonGroupByKey` UI elements, where `RadioButton` elements are arranged in rows and columns, you can place individual `RadioButton` elements anywhere in the layout. Figure 6.5 shows that the ALL `RadioButton` is displayed in the first row and the three other radio buttons are displayed in the second row.

RadioButton GroupByIndex

The `RadioButtonGroupByIndex` UI element represents a set of `RadioButton` elements in rows and columns. `RadioButton` UI elements are arranged in one column in Figure 6.6. This is controlled by the COLCOUNT property (❶).

The user can choose exactly one element from this set of `RadioButton` elements. Through data binding, the TEXTS property of the UI element (❷) is bound to an attribute in a node containing a cardinality with `n` as its upper limit. A `RadioButton` is displayed for every node element for `RadioButtonGroupByIndex`. The lead selection of the context node is used in context programming to determine the selected `RadioButton`.

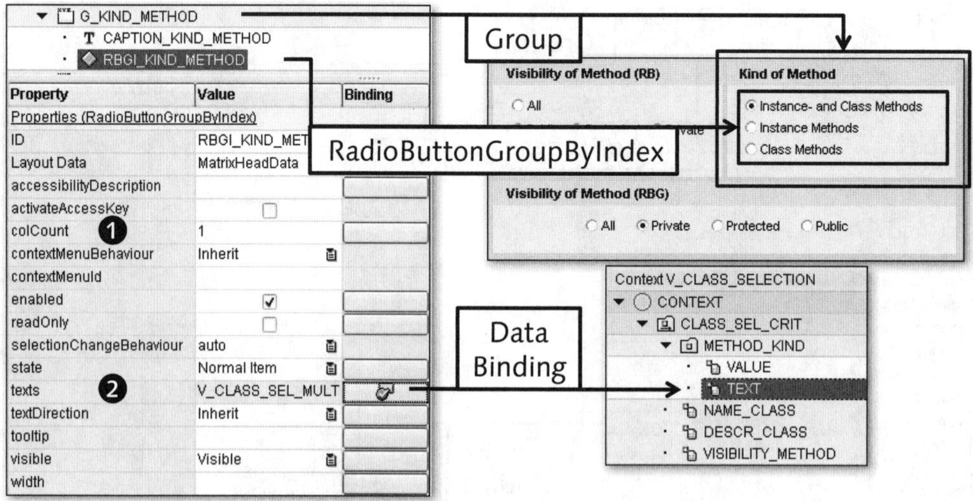

Figure 6.6 Using RadioButtonGroupByIndex UI Elements

RadioButton GroupByKey

As you can see in Figure 6.7, the SELECTEDKEY property for a `RadioButtonGroupByKey` UI element is bound to a context attribute (❷) containing a set of values, for example, domain values from the ABAP Dictionary.

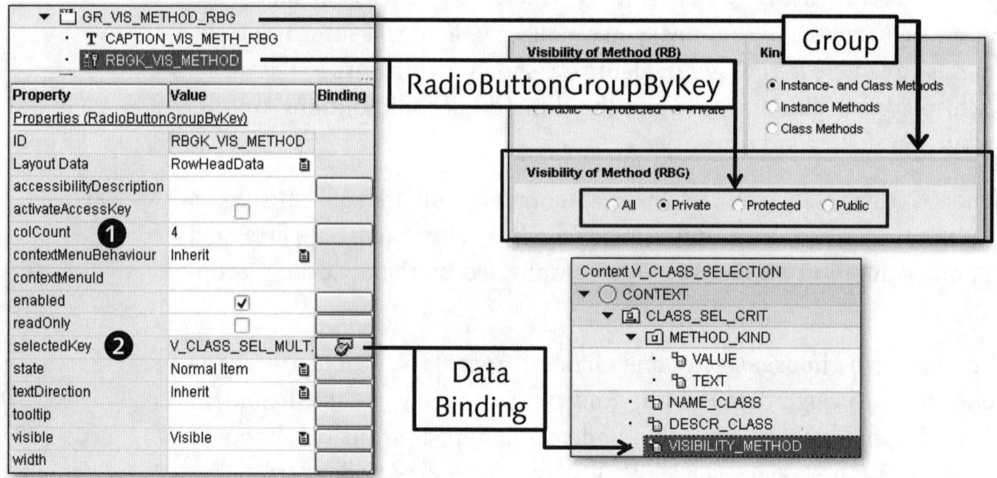

Figure 6.7 Using RadioButtonGroupByKey UI Elements

For a RadioButtonGroupByKey, a RadioButton corresponding to the layout defined in the COLCOUNT property (❶) is then displayed for every individual key. If a RadioButton is selected, the relevant value is returned to the context attribute and can be determined using context programming.

6.1.3 CheckBox

You use a CheckBox UI element to implement the concept of an individual on/off switch in the form of a checkbox. A CheckBox enables the user to select a Boolean value, whereby the set CheckBox represents the ABAP_TRUE value and the unset CheckBox represents the ABAP_FALSE value. The CHECKED property is used for binding data to a context attribute (see Figure 6.8, ❶).

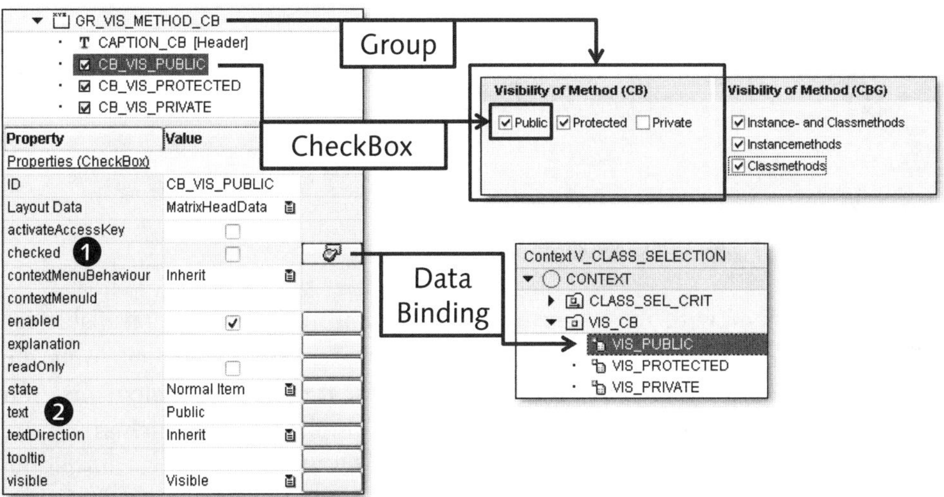

Figure 6.8 Group of CheckBox Elements

The UI element consists of a graphic with relevant text that you can determine using the TEXT property (❷). A checkmark in the graphic indicates that the option was selected and the value set to ABAP_TRUE. The selection made by the user is stored in the bound context attribute, which you type using the WDY_BOOLEAN type, for example.

Text and graphic

6.1.4 CheckBoxGroup

m from n

The `CheckBoxGroup` UI element enables the user to select an element from a set of predefined alternatives by ticking a checkbox. This is referred to as an *m from n selection*. The `CheckBoxGroup` UI element arranges the individual *CheckBox elements in one or more columns in a table* (see Figure 6.9).

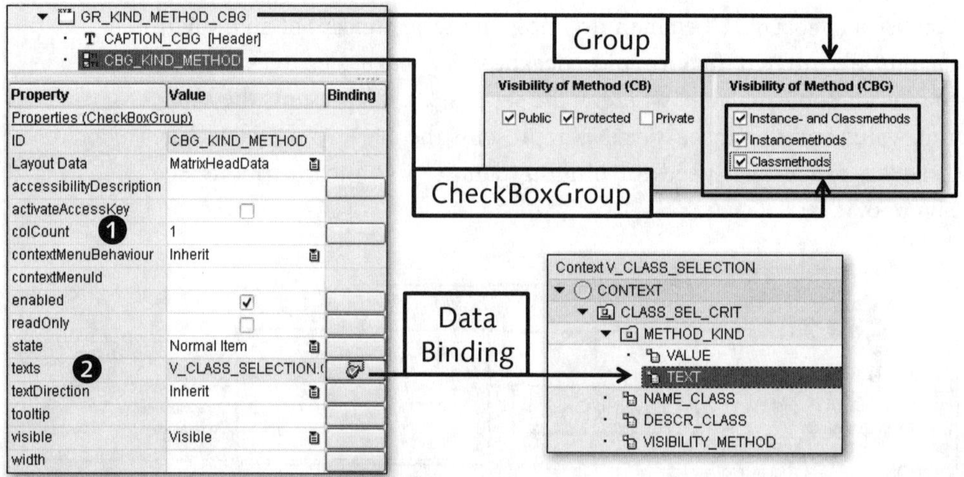

Figure 6.9 Using CheckBoxGroup UI Elements

A node with the `n` cardinality upper limit must be made available for a `CheckBoxGroup`. One of the context node attributes bound using the TEXTS property (❷) returns the texts for the `CheckBox` elements. You can standardize the attribute with any simple data type such as `String`, `int`, and so on. You can define the layout of the checkboxes using the COLCOUNT property. It controls how many checkboxes are displayed per row.

You can choose from two options to set a `CheckBox` in a `CheckBoxGroup`. The first option uses the reference to the context node; the second the reference to a context element.

set_selected( )

- You use the `set_selected( )` method from the `IF_WD_CONTEXT_NODE` interface to influence the status of `CheckBox` elements in the group through the context node reference. An example of this method is shown in Listing 6.2.

```
* Node reference
DATA lo_nd_<node> TYPE REF TO if_wd_context_node.
* Determine node reference
lo_nd_<node> =
  wd_context->path_get_node( path = <path> ).
* Delete the selection using the lead selection
lo_nd_<node>->set_selected(
  flag    = ABAP_FALSE
  index   = if_wd_context_node=>USE_LEAD_SELECTION ).
* Set the selection using the index
lo_nd_<node>->set_selected(
  flag    = ABAP_TRUE
  index   = 2 ).
```

Listing 6.2 Setting a CheckBox Using the Node Reference

You determine the context node reference using the `path_get_node( )` method. The `CheckBox` belonging to the lead selection is deselected the first time the `set_selected( )` method is called. The second time the `set_selected( )` method is called, the element on index position `2` is marked as selected. This results in a set `CheckBox` being displayed.

- **set_selected( )** To set the status of a `CheckBox` using an element reference, you use the `set_selected( )` method of the `IF_WD_CONTEXT_ELEMENT` interface for the relevant context element.

Reading the selection status There are also two options available for reading selected `CheckBox` elements: the `get_selected_elements( )` method of the `IF_WD_CONTEXT_NODE` interface – this method is used on node references – and the `is_selected( )` method of the `IF_WD_CONTEXT_ELEMENT` interface – this method is used for the element reference.

6.1.5 ItemListBox

The `ItemListBox` UI element is similar to the classic GUI concept of a selection list with single and multiple selection (list box; see Figure 6.10).

A list of text entries is displayed in a box of a fixed size (VISIBLEITEMS property, ❺) through which you can also scroll, if required. For the values, one column (TEXT property, ❹), two columns (DESCRIPTIVETEXT property), and perhaps also a column for icons (ICONSOURCE property, ❷) are displayed before the value column.

Behavior In the case of a single selection (MULTIPLESELECTION property set to ABAP_FALSE, ❸), the selected entry is determined by the lead selection of the context node integrated by the DATASOURCE property (❶). The SELECTIONCHANGEBEHAVIOR property is adhered to when the user changes a selection. With a multiple selection (MULTIPLESELECTION property = ABAP_TRUE), the selected entries are determined by selecting the DATASOURCE property only; SELECTIONCHANGEBEHAVIOR is ignored in this case.

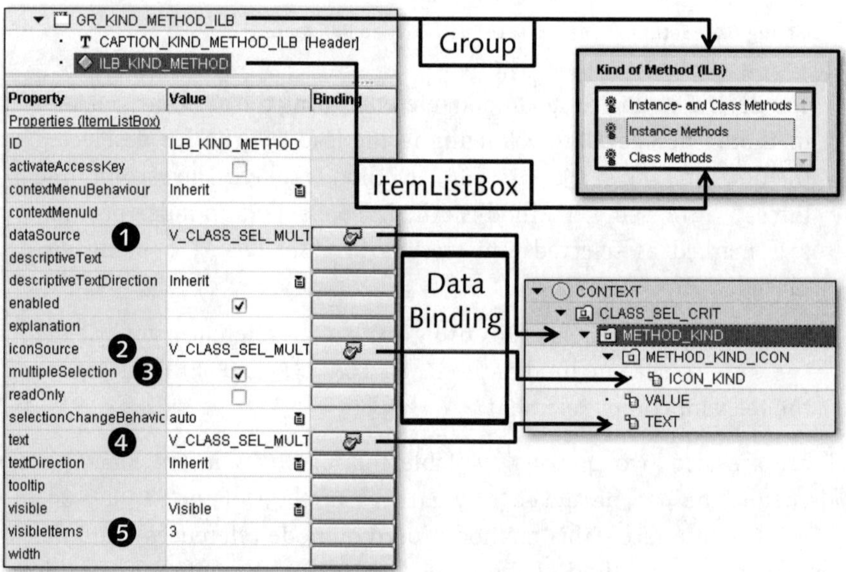

Figure 6.10 Using an ItemListBox UI Element

Selection The user can select several entries from the list by holding down the [Shift] or [Ctrl] key and clicking the required entry.

6.1.6 TriStateCheckBox

The TriStateCheckBox UI element is similar to a CheckBox but differs in that the clicked status is variable (see Figure 6.11).

TriStateCheckBox can have three statuses:

- CheckBox can be activated (selected). With this, a checkmark is displayed in the checkbox for the user.
- CheckBox cannot be activated (selected). With this, an empty checkbox is displayed for the user.
- CheckBox is unspecified. With this, the user can decide whether to set this CheckBox. A normal checkbox does not know this third status and an asterisk is displayed in the checkbox for the user.

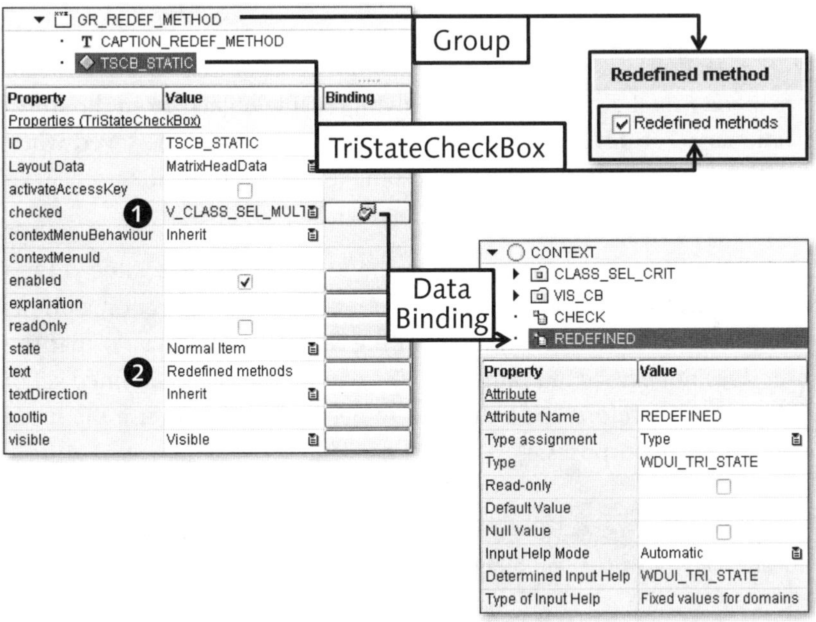

Figure 6.11 Using a TriStateCheckBox UI Element

You bind the UI element to a context attribute using the CHECKED property (❶). You can type the context attribute using the WDUI_TRI_STATE runtime type in Web Dynpro. This data element references the

Typing

WDUI_TRI_STATE domain with the following three fixed values, which can be used for analysis purposes in context programming:

- 00
  for undecided
- 01
  for true
- 02
  for false

Like CheckBox, you specify the name for TriStateCheckBox in the UI using the TEXT property.

6.2 Input Help

In this section, we will discuss one of the greatest assets of Web Dynpro, *input help*. Its strength lies mainly in reusing objects from the ABAP Dictionary. For developers, this means a lot of time can be saved when implementing requirements. At the same time, it affords the user maximum convenience.

Differentiation with selection options

The idea of input help is to enable the user to choose a value from a number of possible values. The difference with the selection options discussed in Section 6.1, Implementing Selection Options, is that the user does not *have to* but rather *is able to* choose from a predefined set of values. It is therefore up to the user to decide whether to use the input help for entry purposes.

Note

Search help or *F4 help* are other terms used for the term "input help."

Types of input help

If the user is not restricted to selecting one value from a set of values, but is instead supposed to be able to enter values as he wishes, the InputField UI element is the correct choice as the input medium. The input help must be integrated on this field. The different types of input help available for input fields are:

- Search help
- Check table
- Domain fixed values and fixed value area
- Date selection
- Self-programmed input help

Input help mode

In the INPUT HELP MODE property in the context attribute properties, you can implement which input help setting should be used (see Figure 6.12). Five different values are available for the INPUT HELP MODE property. We will discuss these in detail in the following sections. Selecting a particular mode will influence which additional fields will be provided for entering or displaying data.

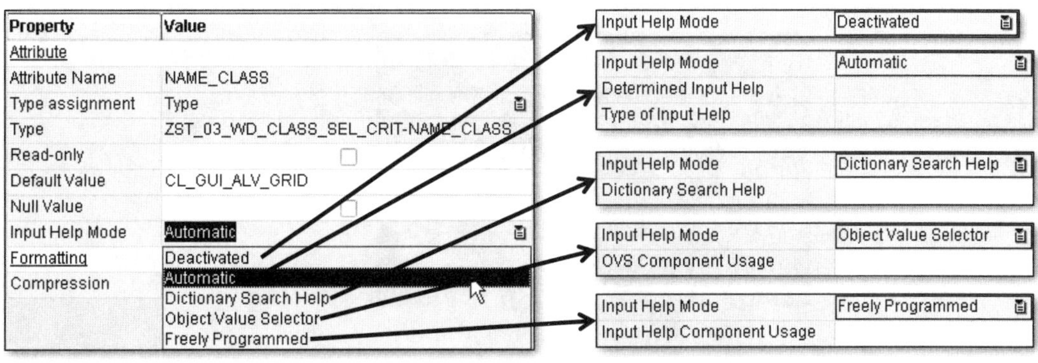

Figure 6.12 Different Input Help Modes

Activating help

As a result of the mode selected for the corresponding `InputField`, the Web Dynpro framework automatically generates and implements the specific icon the user will have to use for calling the input help at runtime. At the same time, the F4 key is also automatically available for calling the input help.

The icon to show that search help exists (see the Search Help box) is always the same, regardless of whether the help is search help from the ABAP Dictionary, *OVS search help* (Object Value Selector), or *freely programmed search help*.

(ABAP Dictionary) Search Help

An *input help* mechanism known as *search help* is provided at the input field level in the ABAP Dictionary. This search help is an encapsulated function used for selecting and finding values, as you can see in Figure 6.13.

In this case, values entered by the user into an input field (also using * and + wildcard characters) can be transferred to the search help through the import parameter. Based on the selection method defined in the search help (transparent table or view), the data in the database system is selected and presented to the user as a hit list. If the hit list exceeds a certain number of hits (100), an intermediate value selection dialog can be shown through search help customizing.

If the user selects a specific value, it is placed into the input field(s) by the export parameter.

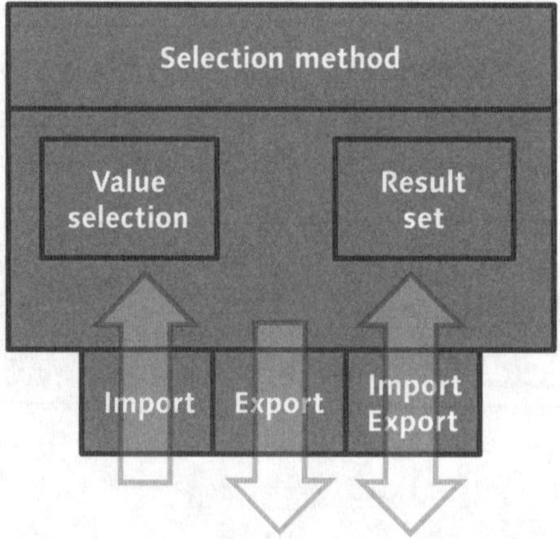

Figure 6.13 Structure of ABAP Dictionary Search Help

6.2.1 Input Help Mode: Deactivated

As the name suggests, the input help is deactivated. An `InputField` without any indication of input help – in other words, no icon or F4 key function – is provided for the user.

6.2.2 Input Help Mode: Automatic

In the AUTOMATIC input help mode, the Web Dynpro framework decides which input help should be used. The search for input help is run at development time. The search algorithm used here is developed as follows:

Integrating search help

1. If the context attribute was standardized using a field from a structure type and search help integration exists for this field in the ABAP Dictionary, this search help is used (see Figure 6.14):
   - The NAME_CLASS attribute was typed with a component from an ABAP Dictionary structure (❶).
   - This ABAP Dictionary component has an explicit search help integration that is found by the AUTOMATIC input help mode (❷) (SFBECLNAME, ❸) and is classified correctly as search help by the Web Dynpro framework (❹).
   - The input help type found controls that an input help icon is displayed for the InputField UI element that binds the NAME_CLASS attribute through data binding (❺).
   - By selecting the icon or pressing the F4 key, the user can activate the search help (❻), search for a value, and select the found value to place it into the InputField (❼).

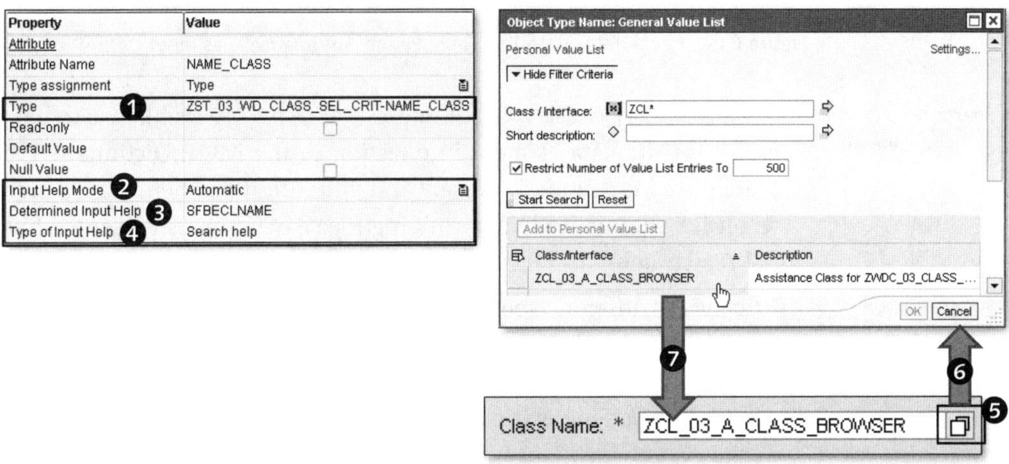

Figure 6.14 Search Help Found Automatically as Input Help

Check table

2. If search help was not found, the Web Dynpro framework checks whether a foreign key check was defined for the component or a field from the ABAP Dictionary. If one was defined, the Web Dynpro

framework checks whether search help exists for the check table. If so, this search help is displayed; otherwise, the key fields of the check table are displayed with descriptions if a text table was defined for the check table.

Figure 6.15 shows how the NAME_CLASS attribute was typed with a component from an ABAP Dictionary structure (❶). This ABAP Dictionary component has a foreign key check that was found by the AUTOMATIC input help mode (❷) (SEOCLASS, ❸) and classified correctly as a check table with a text table by the Web Dynpro framework (❹).

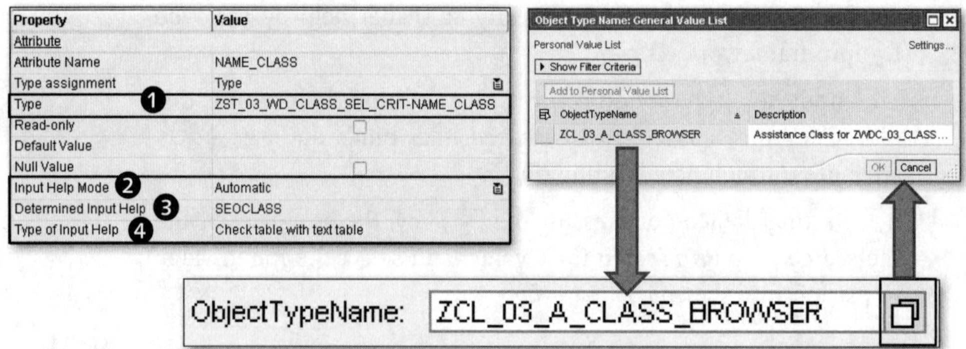

Figure 6.15 Check Table with Text Table Found Automatically as Input Help

Search help for a data element

3. If a foreign key check was not found, a search for possible search help is run for the data element in question in the ABAP Dictionary. If a search help is found, it is used to define the input help. The search result for automatically determining the search help is presented like the search help for fields.

   What is the difference between search help at the field level and at the data element level? If search help is integrated at the field level, other structure fields can be taken into account by the search help import and export parameters; data can be included in the search help and delivered to fields. This is known as *search help context* and is not possible if search help is bound to the data element.

Default values

4. With the next search option, the Web Dynpro framework checks whether fixed values or fixed value areas exist for the domain in ques-

tion. In Figure 6.16, the VISIBILITY_METHOD attribute was typed with a component from an ABAP Dictionary structure (❶). This ABAP Dictionary component has an ABAP Dictionary domain that was found by the AUTOMATIC input help mode (❷) (SEOEXPOSE, ❸) and classified correctly as FIXED VALUES FOR DOMAINS by the Web Dynpro framework (❹).

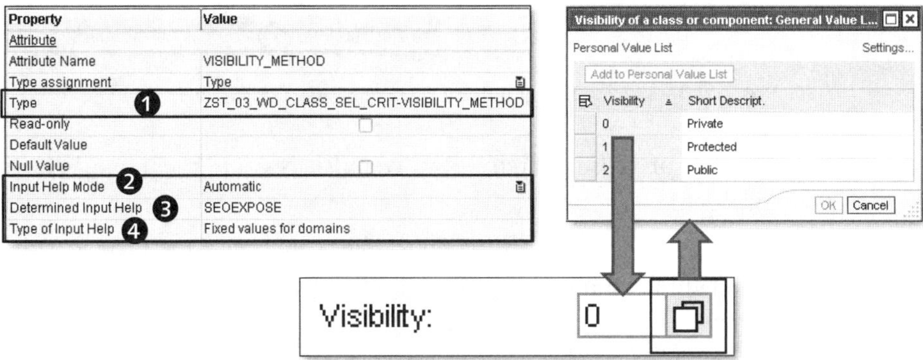

Figure 6.16 Fixed Values for Domains Found Automatically as Input Help

DATS data element or TIMS for typing

5. The next check in the automatic search for input help examines the attribute typing. If the DATS or TIMS data element was used for the typing, the calendar help or clock help is found, as you can see for the DATS data element in Figure 6.17:
   - The DATE attribute was typed with the DATS ABAP Dictionary data element (❶).
   - This ABAP Dictionary data element has the CALENDAR HELP input help type that was found by the AUTOMATIC input help mode (❷, ❸) and classified correctly as CALENDAR HELP by the Web Dynpro framework (❹).
   - The found input help type controls that a date icon is displayed for the input help for the InputField UI element that binds the DATE attribute through data binding (❺).
   - By selecting the icon or pressing the F4 key, the user can activate the search help, search for a value, and select the found value to place it into the InputField (❻).

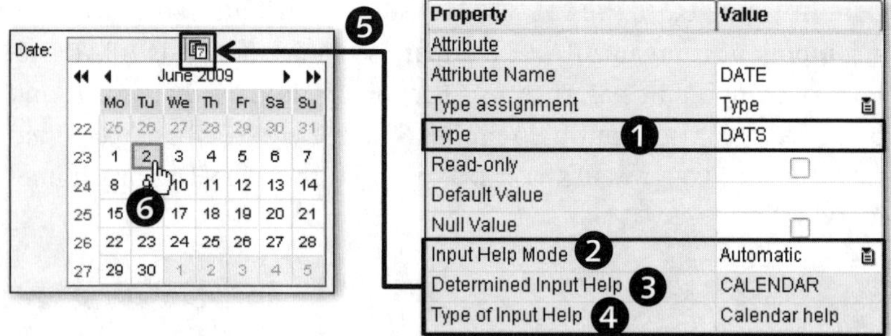

Figure 6.17 Input Help Found Automatically for DATS Data Element

No help

6. If none of these search steps were successful, no input help is displayed.

The algorithm seems quite complicated at first glance, but is actually a very natural approach if you want to use definitions from the ABAP Dictionary.

6.2.3 Dictionary Search Help

Manual specification

An automatic search for input help sometimes does not yield the required result. In this case, you can use the DICTIONARY SEARCH HELP input help mode to specify search help from the ABAP Dictionary by directly making an entry in the DICTIONARY SEARCH HELP field.

Test this direct allocation as follows: Use the predefined SFBECLNAME search help for the NAME_CLASS context attribute in the CLASS_SEL_CRIT context node of the component controller. You will see that the check table with the text table found using the automatic input help mode is now no longer provided for the input field; instead, the search help you specified is available as input support for the user.

6.2.4 Object Value Selector

Usage

You can use the OBJECT VALUE SELECTOR (OVS) input help if you cannot use ABAP Dictionary resources to run a search; for example, for determining the set of values in the Web Dynpro application. Like with integrating search help into components or at the field level, the other benefit of OVS is that you can fill several fields at once in a corresponding implementation (for instance, the two fields for the name of the ABAP class and its description).

WDR_OVS Web Dynpro component

OVS input help is implemented using the provided WDR_OVS Web Dynpro component that can be used by every Web Dynpro component. We already covered the basics for using Web Dynpro in Chapter 5, Web Dynpro Standard Components. After OVS input help has been entered for a context attribute, it is automatically available for every InputField bound to this context attribute. At runtime, an active instance is always created automatically for the OVS component when a user presses the F4 key for a selected InputField, or clicks the input help icon next to the InputField. The dialog box also automatically appears on the screen at this time.

Integrating input help into a context attribute

To integrate OVS input help into a context attribute, you need to carry out the following steps, which we will illustrate by way of an example. OVS input help is defined for the IF_NAME_CLASS InputField of the V_CLASS_SELECTION view.

1. Switch to the ZWDC_03_CLASS_BROWSER Web Dynpro component shown in Figure 6.18, and enter the USAGE_OVS component usage (❶) for the WDR_OVS OVS component (❷) on the USED COMPONENTS tab.

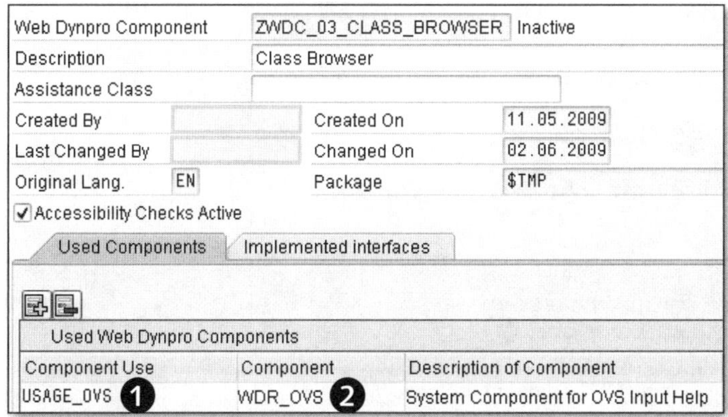

Figure 6.18 Declaration of Use of the WDR_OVS Web Dynpro Component

Defining the use

2. Also define this use on the PROPERTIES tab of the V_CLASS_SELECTION view, as shown in Figure 6.19. Click the CREATE CONTROLLER USAGE button (❶) to copy the OVS use (❷).

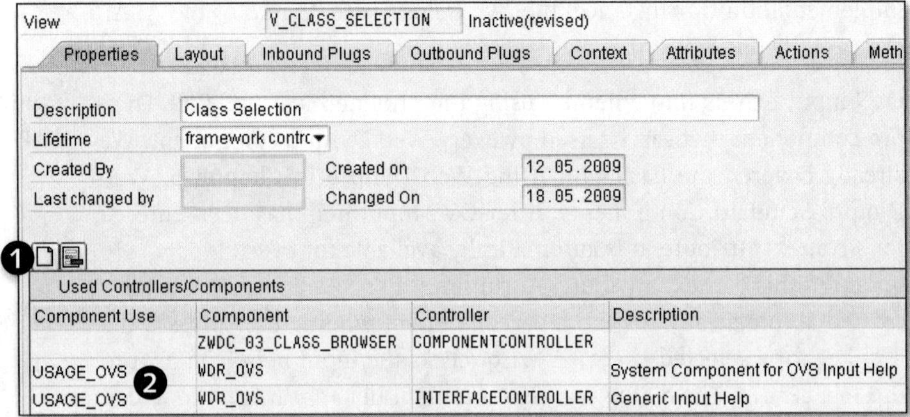

Figure 6.19 Declaration of Use of the OVS Input Help in the View

Setting the Input Help Mode property

3. Switch to the component controller context and then to the NAME_CLASS attribute in the CLASS_SEL_CRIT node. In the properties table (see Figure 6.20) of the NAME_CLASS context attribute (❶), you can now select the OBJECT VALUE SELECTOR entry in the INPUT HELP MODE row (❷). In the new OVS COMPONENT USAGE row in the properties table, you must enter the component usage provided for the input help. Input help is available for this in this row – select the USAGE_OVS input help (❸).

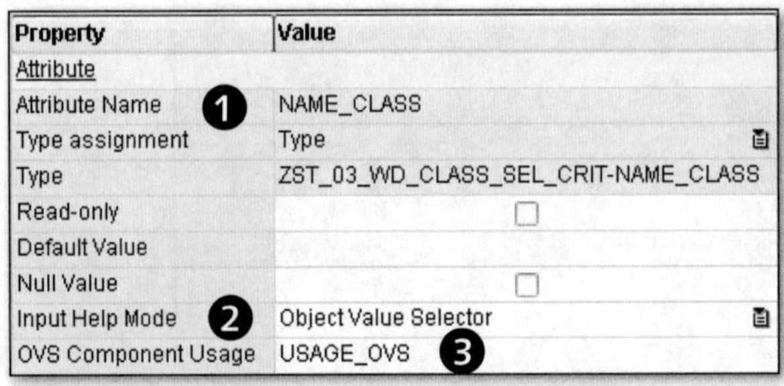

Figure 6.20 Assigning OVS Component Usage

Creating an event handler method

4. For the V_CLASS_SELECTION view, you must create an event handler for the OVS event of the USAGE_OVS OVS component being used. To do this, switch to the METHODS tab of the V_CLASS_SELECTION view (see Figure 6.21). Enter the name on_ovs for the event handler method

(❶). Using the input help, choose Event Handler (❷) as the entry for Method Type. Select the OVS (❸) event from the Component Usage input help. You have now completed the registration of the on_ovs( ) event handler method for the OVS event.

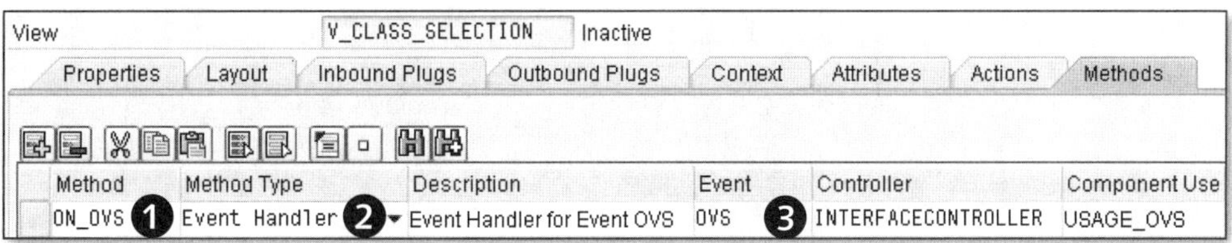

Figure 6.21 Defining the OVS Event Handler

You are provided considerable support when implementing the event handler method because a source code structure is already generated by assigning the handler method to the OVS event. To be able to understand the source code structure, you must first consider the internal structure and the interaction behavior of the OVS component.

The WDR_OVS component provides an event view where search results are displayed as a table. The component also contains a selection view you can use to restrict search results. The input fields for the selection view, as well as the structure and contents of the table for the search result view resulting from this restriction, are defined by the using application component. Therefore, at a suitable time based on user interaction, the OVS component has to communicate again with the using Web Dynpro component.

OVS phase model

Communication with the using component is achieved using the OVS event for the OVS component. This event is triggered automatically four times in succession and transfers the ovs_callback_object parameter to the corresponding event handler in the using Web Dynpro. An example of the *phase model* for the OVS component is illustrated in Figure 6.22.

We will explain the phase model in detail in the following sections. The explanations are based on the interaction cycle between the using component (ZWDC_03_CLASS_BROWSER) and the component being used (WDR_OVS).

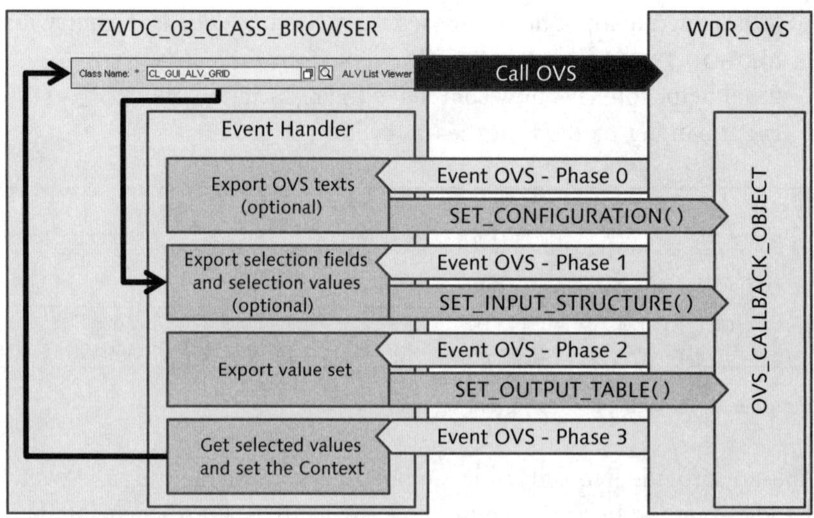

Figure 6.22 Phase Model for an OVS Component

Calling the Object Value Selector

The user activates the `OVS` input help by clicking the input help icon or the F4 key on an input field. This results in the `OVS` component being initialized. The `OVS` component triggers the `OVS` event, which causes the event handler in the using component (in this example, the `ZWDC_03_CLASS_BROWSER` component) to be called.

The event handler contains the `ovs_callback_object` importing parameter, which has the public `ovs_callback_object->phase_indicator` instance attribute. You use this to find out which `OVS` phase contains the `OVS`. The phase count begins at `0`, whereby the constants `if_wd_ovs=>co_phase_[0|1|2|3]` are defined for the different phases. It is now up to the event handler to implement the reactions to the events.

Object Value Selector: Phase 0 Event

Configuration

You can configure the `OVS` component in the phase 0 period. This means, for example, that you can define the window title, header, or column header for the event table. The different layout options for `OVS` views are displayed in Figure 6.23.

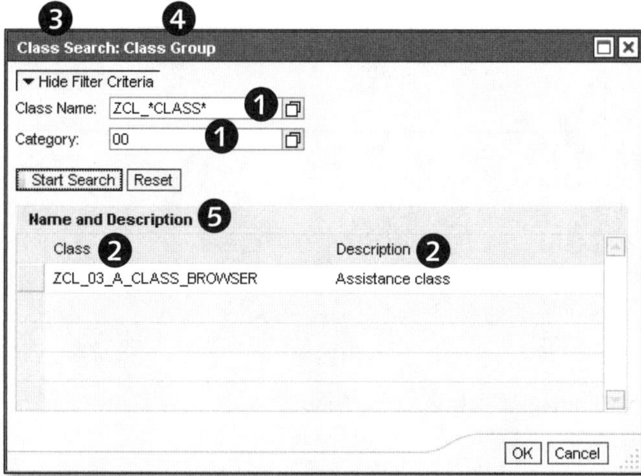

Figure 6.23 OVS View Layout

You can specify the input fields for the selection view and their labels (❶), the number of display columns and rows for the result view (hit list), and a header for every column (❷). You can also specify a group header for the hit list (❺), and create a window header and group header for the windows that display the `OVS` component (❸, ❹).

set_configuration( )

At this time, you can also implement a setting to specify whether one or more rows can be selected from the result table. The `ovs_callback_object` event parameter provides the `set_configuration( )` method for this, which you can only expressly use at this time. An error message will be issued if you call this method at another time.

As the first step in implementing the example, switch to the `on_ovs( )` event handler. The complete implementation structure has already been created; therefore, you can focus on the pending requirements and use the pregenerated parts. Phase 0 involves aspects of configuration that were implemented for the example in Listing 6.3.

```
METHOD on_ovs .
* Declaration of data structure for search fields and
* hit list columns
TYPES:
  BEGIN OF lty_stru_input,
* Fields for search
```

```
    name_class TYPE
      wd_this->element_class_sel_crit-name_class,
    category_class type SEOCATEGRY,
  END OF lty_stru_input,
* Fields for result list
  BEGIN OF lty_stru_list,
    name_class TYPE
      wd_this->element_class_sel_crit-name_class,
    descr_class TYPE
      wd_this->element_class_sel_crit-descr_class,
  END OF lty_stru_list.
* Definitions
DATA: ls_search_input TYPE lty_stru_input,
      lt_select_list   TYPE STANDARD TABLE OF lty_stru_list,
      ls_text          TYPE wdr_name_value,
      lt_label_texts   TYPE wdr_name_value_list,
      lt_column_texts  TYPE wdr_name_value_list,
      lv_window_title  TYPE string,
      lv_group_header  TYPE string,
      lv_table_header  TYPE string.
* References
FIELD-SYMBOLS: <ls_query_params> TYPE lty_stru_input,
               <ls_selection>    TYPE lty_stru_list.
* Analysis
* Which OVS phase?
CASE ovs_callback_object->phase_indicator.
* Configuration phase, optional
  WHEN if_wd_ovs=>co_phase_0.
* Texts for input fields in selection screen
* Name of class
    ls_text-name = `NAME_CLASS`. "Name=searchfieldname
    ls_text-value = `Name of class`. "the text
    INSERT ls_text INTO TABLE lt_label_texts.
* Category of class
    ls_text-name = `CATEGORY_CLASS`. "Name=searchfieldname
    ls_text-value = `Categorie of class`. "the text
      INSERT ls_text INTO TABLE lt_label_texts.
* Texts for columns in selection screen
* Name of class
    ls_text-name = `NAME_CLASS`. "Name=liststructure    ls_
text-value = `Class`. "the text
    INSERT ls_text INTO TABLE lt_column_texts.
* Another column for the description
```

```
    ls_text-name = `DESCR_CLASS`. "Name=liststructure
    ls_text-value = `Description`. "the text
      INSERT ls_text INTO TABLE lt_column_texts.
* Texts for title, GroupHeader, and TableHeader
    lv_window_title = 'Class search'.
    lv_group_header = 'Class group.
    lv_table_header = 'Name and description'.
* Set the configuration using CallBack object
    ovs_callback_object->set_configuration(
      label_texts  = lt_label_texts
      column_texts = lt_column_texts
      group_header = lv_group_header
      window_title = lv_window_title
      table_header = lv_table_header
      col_count    = 2
      row_count    = 5 ).
```

Listing 6.3 Handling OVS Phase 0 in the Event Handler

Configuring a search template and result table

The generated handler method begins with the declaration section. This is where the LTY_STRU_INPUT structure type for defining the fields you want to appear in the search template is prepared. The two fields name_class and category_class were extended and enable the user to enter a name and the class category for the selection. The name can be entered with wildcard symbols such as an asterisk (*), for example. The category stands for the class type such as GENERAL OBJECT TYPE or EXCEPTION CLASS.

The LTY_STRU_LIST structure type is used to define the result table. The fields you enter in this type will become the output table columns. The two fields name_class and descr_class were extended and, for this reason, the result table has two columns. Other declarations follow, which are used for transferring data to methods for the CallBack object.

Determining phases

The implementation part begins with the CASE ovs_callback_object->phase_indicator statement to find out which OVS phase contains the OVS component. The public phase_indicator instance attribute has the value for the current phase. The question about whether the OVS component is in phase 0 is WHEN if_wd_ovs=>co_phase_0.

The structures and tables are filled for phase 0 (configuration phase) to initialize the `OVS` component:

- `lt_label_texts`
  Is filled to define texts for selection fields.
- `lt_column_texts`
  Is filled to define headers for the result table.
- `lv_window_title`
  Is filled to define the title of the search and result window.
- `lv_group_header`,
  Is filled to define additional text for the title.
- `lv_table_header`
  Is filled to give the result table a title.

Finally, the `ovs_callback_object->set_configuration( )` method is called to return the values to the OVS component.

Object Value Selector: Phase 1 Event

Configuring a selection view

If you want to use the optional selection view of the `OVS` component, in phase 1, you must define the structure of the selection fields to be displayed and transfer it to the `OVS` component. You can also transfer initial values for the selection fields at the same time. You can use the `set_input_structure( )` method to do this.

The following also applies for this method: an error message will be issued if it is called at another time. If the method is not called, displaying the selection view will not apply and the result view will be displayed directly. Figure 6.24 shows the effects of handling `OVS` phases on the selection screen.

If the `OVS` phase 0 handling is implemented in the handler method, the selection screen can be explicitly arranged, as already explained for phase 0. If phase 0 is omitted, standard texts from the ABAP Dictionary (if available) will be used.

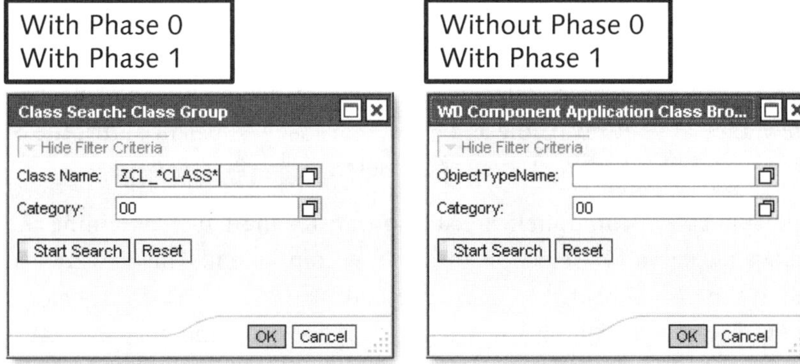

Figure 6.24 Effects of Handling OVS Phases on the Selection Screen

Although handling phase 1 is optional, the user should be offered the option of restricting the search result to an ABAP class name. To do this, you must take into account the search structure and user values already entered. Listing 6.4 shows the implementation for `OVS` phase 1.

```
* Search structure and default values phase, optional
* If they are omitted, no search view appears
WHEN if_wd_ovs=>co_phase_1.
* Determine values already entered by user from
* the InputField search field
ovs_callback_object->context_element->get_static_attributes(
  IMPORTING static_attributes = ls_search_input ).
* Transfer the values using the CallBack object
ovs_callback_object->set_input_structure(
  input = ls_search_input ).
```

Listing 6.4 Handling OVS Phase 1 in the Event Handler

Setting a selection screen

You can use the public `context_element` instance attribute of the `ovs_callback_object` `CallBack` object to determine the entry already made by the user. As always in context programming, the `get_static_attributes( )` method is available for this. Finally, you can transfer the structure with the data to the `set_input_structure( )` method of the `CallBack` object. This will complete the process of defining the selection screen.

Object Value Selector: Phase 2 Event

Determining a set of results

In phase 2, you must determine the set of search results from the using component. If values for selection parameters were entered in a selection view, they are now available as a `query_parameters` instance attribute of the `ovs_callback_object` event parameter.

The application component must also transfer the table containing the values available for selection to the `OVS` component. This is achieved using the `set_output_table( )` method of the `ovs_callback_object` event parameter. Calling `set_output_table( )` is mandatory and must be done in this phase.

Listing 6.5 shows the implementation details.

```
* Determine values for the hit list phase
WHEN if_wd_ovs=>co_phase_2.
* If phase 1 was implemented, use entry
* If not, use own values
  IF ovs_callback_object->query_parameters IS BOUND.
* Exception handling
    ASSIGN ovs_callback_object->query_parameters->*
      TO <ls_query_params>.
    IF NOT <ls_query_params> IS ASSIGNED.
* Initialize parameters
      ls_search_input-name_class = 'ZCL*'.
      ls_search_input-category_class = '00'.
    ELSE. "<ls_query_params> not ASSIGNED
* Transfer values from query_parameters
      ls_search_input-name_class =
        <ls_query_params>-name_class.
      ls_search_input-category_class =
        <ls_query_params>-category_class.
    ENDIF.
  ELSE. "Query_parameters not bound
* Initialize parameters
    ls_search_input-name_class = 'ZCL*'.
    ls_search_input-category_class = '00'.
  ENDIF.
* Determine values for the hit list
wd_comp_controller->getmodel_class_list(
  EXPORTING
    clstype = '0'"Search for classes
```

```
    clsname_pattern = ls_search_input-name_class
    category = ls_search_input-category_class
    langu = sy-langu
  IMPORTING
    clsnames_w_description = lt_select_list ).
* Set the hit list
ovs_callback_object->set_output_table(
  output = lt_select_list ).
```

Listing 6.5 Handling OVS Phase 2 in the Event Handler

query_parameter

A check is performed to see whether the public `query_parameters` instance attribute for the `ovs_callback_object CallBack` object is bound. This is done using the `IF ovs_callback_object->query_parameters IS BOUND` statement. This is the case if a selection screen was defined in phase 0 or 1.

However, it may be that `OVS` phases 0 and 1 were not processed in the handler method. You must react to this. In this example, you assign the `ZCL*` value to the `ls_search_input-name_class` auxiliary variable and `00` to the `ls_search_input-category_class` variable. This will ensure that general ABAP classes whose names begin with `ZCL*` are determined.

Business logic

The next part of the implementation involves determining the hit list; in other words, the business logic. In this example, the `getmodel_class_list( )` service method, based on the `SEO_CLASS_LIB_INTROSPECTION` function module that determines ABAP classes, was created using the service call wizard.

set_output_table( )

The values returned as an internal table by the service method are transferred to the `set_output_table( )` method of the `ovs_callback_object CallBack` object. In this case, the typing for the internal table delivered by the service method is identical to the hit list structure. This means that the data in the internal table does not need to be converted to the hit list typing. The `OVS` component then ensures that the hit list, as shown in Figure 6.25, is displayed. The appearance of the search is controlled by using phases 0 and 1.

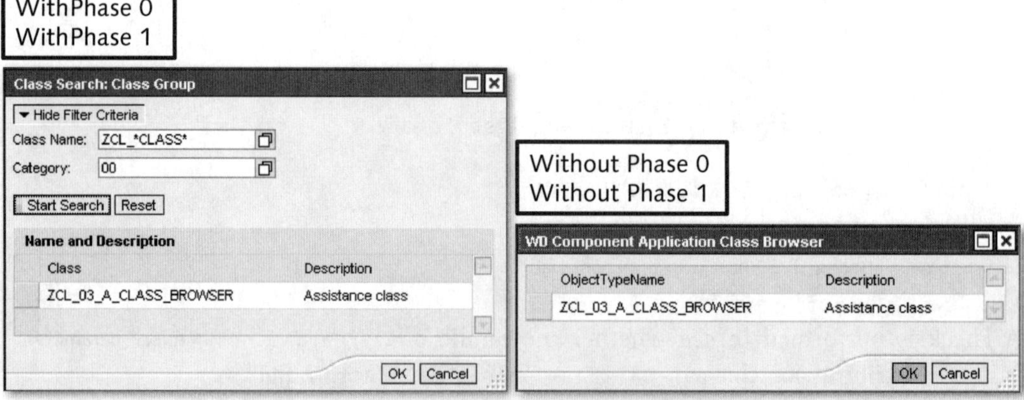

Figure 6.25 Different Displays for Selection View and Result View

Object Value Selector: Phase 3 Event

Transferring the user selection

The search result was displayed in the result view of the OVS component. The user now has the opportunity to select one or more table rows. However, the latter is only possible if a multiple selection for the result table was configured in the first phase of the process using the `set_configuration( )` method.

Only one result table row can be selected in the standard configuration for the OVS component. The content of the selected row is then available for reading in the `selection` instance attribute of the `ovs_callback_object` event parameter. The details for this are shown in Listing 6.6.

```
WHEN if_wd_ovs=>co_phase_3.
* Read data
IF ovs_callback_object->selection IS BOUND.
* De-reference data to read it
ASSIGN ovs_callback_object->selection->* TO <ls_selection>.
IF <ls_selection> IS ASSIGNED.
* Put data back in selection conditions
ovs_callback_object->context_element->set_static_attributes(
  static_attributes = <ls_selection> ).
ENDIF.
ENDIF.
ENDCASE.
ENDMETHOD.
```

Listing 6.6 Handling OVS Phase 3 in the Event Handler

The user selection is de-referenced by the following statement:

Setting selected values in view fields

```
ASSIGN ovs_callback_object->selection->* TO <ls_selection>.
```

The values selected by the user are available in the `<ls_selection>` field symbol and can be placed into view fields. The `set_static_attributes( )` method for `context_element` from the `ovs_callback_object` `CallBack` object was used for this.

The OVS phase 3 handling also completes the handler method implementation for the OVS event.

6.2.5 Input Help Mode: Freely Programmed

IWD_VALUE_HELP

Another input help mode available is FREELY PROGRAMMED. This mode enables you to program your own input help as you wish: the Web Dynpro framework allows you to create and use your own input help components. A Web Dynpro component to be used as input help must implement the `IWD_VALUE_HELP` Web Dynpro component interface. After the freely programmed input help has been bound to a context attribute, the input help is automatically available for every `InputField` bound to this attribute.

6.3 SELECT-OPTIONS

Before, you had to struggle with manually compiling a selection view. You had to define view fields and program the handling of inconsistencies and incorrect entries. Although we mentioned that you can take search context into account when you integrate search help, you might have already noticed that something is missing.

SELECT-OPTIONS

When we look again at defining standard selection screens in ABAP programming, it is apparent that the `SELECT-OPTIONS` ABAP statement exists specifically for this purpose. This statement creates an interval entry option in a very user-friendly way for the developer and user. Figure 6.26 displays a selection screen that was defined using the following statement sequence:

```
DATA: ls_seoclass TYPE seoclassdf.
SELECT-OPTIONS: clsname FOR ls_seoclass-clsname.
```

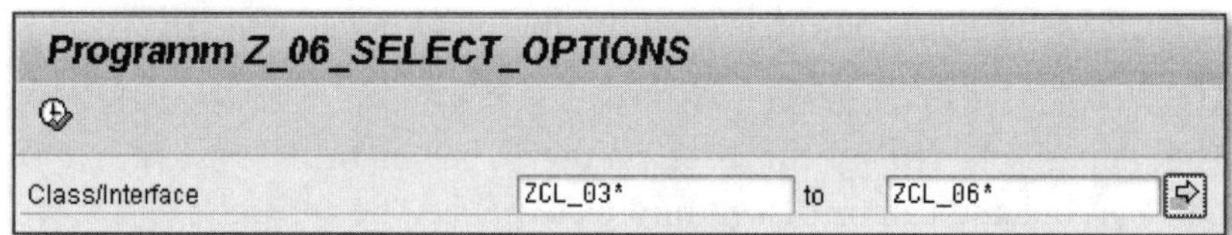

Figure 6.26 SELECT-OPTIONS in an Executable Program

Ranges table

This means individual entries and interval entries can be allowed that can be defined as inclusive criteria or as exclusive criteria. Within the program, an internal table with a header line is created from the SELECT-OPTIONS ABAP statement. The columns contained in this internal table are listed in Table 6.1.

Components	Type	Description
sign	C(1)	Specifies whether the result is included in or excluded from the overall set of results. Values are I for inclusion and E for exclusion.
option	C(2)	This is the selection option for the row specification in the form of logical operators, for example, EQ for equals.
low	SEOCLSNAME	This is the comparison value in single comparisons or the lower interval limit for interval limits.
high	SEOCLSNAME	This is the higher interval limit for interval limits.

Table 6.1 Columns in SELECT-OPTIONS Table

The type for the low and high columns is derived from the reference type for the SELECT-OPTIONS statement. This internal table is filled row by row with user entries and can be used for later operations.

WDR_SELECT_OPTIONS

You can also use SELECT-OPTIONS in Web Dynpro. The WDR_SELECT_OPTIONS Web Dynpro component is made available for this purpose. The interface controller for the WDR_SELECT_OPTIONS Web Dynpro component provides the init_selection_screen( ) method, which can be used to determine a reference to SELECT-OPTIONS with the IF_WD_SELECT_OPTIONS type. This reference provides the methods to arrange the corresponding options visually.

WND_SELECTION_SCREEN

The SELECT-OPTIONS visualization (see Figure 6.27, ❶), which is implemented in the WND_SELECTION_SCREEN interface view of the WDR_SELECT_OPTIONS Web Dynpro component, displays the standard functions (❹) CANCEL, CHECK, RESET, and COPY in the first row. You can deactivate these functions if you do not need them (set_global_options( ) method and m_display_btn_* constant from the IF_WD_SELECT_OPTIONS interface).

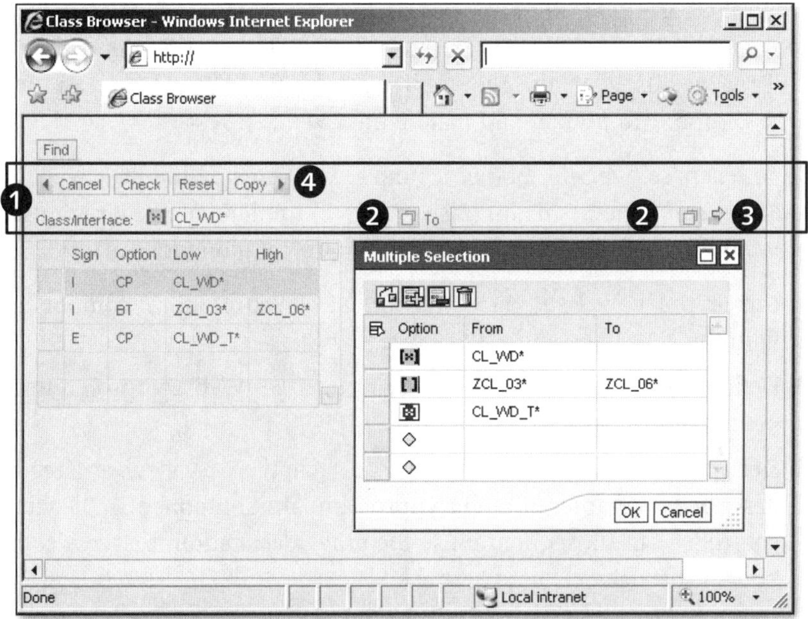

Figure 6.27 Web Dynpro Application with SELECT-OPTIONS

Selection and parameter fields

The area with selection fields and parameters follows under the functions; the user can configure this area as required (❷). In this example, a selection field was defined for entering an ABAP class name (create_range_table( ) and add_selection_field( ) methods of the IF_WD_SELECT_OPTIONS interface). As a result, the lower and upper limits of the selection field are displayed as input fields. If defined, input help is available for the fields and parameters. The user can use the MULTIPLE SELECTION button (❸) to open the MULTIPLE SELECTION dialog box for selection fields, where additional search criteria can be entered. Inclusive conditions are displayed in green, exclusive ones in red. The entries made by the user are placed in the created range table, visualized in this example in the `Table` UI element.

Functions and events

Another word about standard functions: events such as `ON_CHECK` are defined for standard functions in the interface controller of the `WDR_SELECT_OPTIONS` Web Dynpro component. These events are triggered when the corresponding button is clicked; for instance, the CHECK button. In the using component, an EVENT HANDLER must be defined that will register itself on the required event for the `WDR_SELECT_OPTIONS` Web Dynpro component and handle this event.

[✎]

As an exercise, we will look at a simple way of using the `WDR_SELECT_OPTIONS` component. In this case, you will implement the previously mentioned selection screen in a Web Dynpro component.

1. Create the new `ZWDC_06_CLASS_BROWSER` Web Dynpro component with the `V_SO` view and `W_MAIN` window.

Component usage

2. Define the usage for the `WDR_SELECT_OPTIONS` Web Dynpro component. Call this usage `USAGE_SO`.
3. Declare the COMPONENT USE for `USAGE_SO` in the `V_SO` view, as already described in Chapter 5, Web Dynpro Standard Components. The view controller can subsequently use the usage declaration to access component interface elements for the `WDR_SELECT_OPTIONS` Web Dynpro component.

View attributes

4. Define the two new object references in the view attributes:
   - `GO_SO`
     The `GO_SO` attribute provides the methods for configuring the selection screen (NAME: `GO_SO`, REFERENCE TYPE: `IF_WD_SELECT_OPTIONS`).
   - `GO_IC_SO`
     The `GO_IC_SO` attribute is used as a reference to the interface controller for the `SELECT-OPTIONS` component (NAME: `GO_IC_SO`, REFERENCE TYPE: `IWCI_WDR_SELECT_OPTIONS`).

5. Create the new `init_select_options( )` method in the view controller and implement it as shown in Listing 6.7:

   init_select_options( )

   - In the first step, check whether the component usage already has an active instance. You do this using the `has_active_component( )` method. If not, create an active instance for it using the `create_component( )` method.
   - Then, determine the reference to the interface controller (`wd_this->go_ic_so`). You will use this interface controller in the next step to determine the reference to the selection screen (`wd_this->go_so`). This reference is then used to create and configure the selection screen.
   - Create a range table for the `SEOCLSNAME` data element using the `create_range_table( )` method.
   - Finally, add the `add_selection_field( )` method to the new `CLSNAME` selection field. This method provides a range of parameters that control how the field is created. The option to define the explicit `SFBECLNAME` search help for the field has been used in this example.

```
METHOD init_select_options .
* The range table for the selection field
DATA: lt_range_table TYPE REF TO data,
* Reference to the select options usage controller
  lo_ref_cmp_usage TYPE REF TO if_wd_component_usage.
* Instantiate the usage component, if necessary
lo_ref_cmp_usage = wd_this->wd_cpuse_usage_so( ).
IF lo_ref_cmp_usage->has_active_component( ) IS INITIAL.
  lo_ref_cmp_usage->create_component( ).
ENDIF.
* Determine reference to the interface controller
wd_this->go_ic_so = wd_this->wd_cpifc_usage_so( ).
* Initialize selection screen
wd_this->go_so =
  wd_this->go_ic_so->init_selection_screen( ).
* Generate range table for data element
lt_range_table = wd_this->go_so->create_range_table(
  i_typename = 'SEOCLSNAME' ).
* Generate field in selection screen
wd_this->go_so->add_selection_field(
```

```
    i_id = 'CLSNAME'
    it_result = lt_range_table
    i_value_help_type =
      if_wd_value_help_handler=>co_prefix_searchhelp
    i_value_help_id = 'SFBECLNAME' ).
ENDMETHOD.
```

Listing 6.7 Initializing the Selection Screen

wddoinit( )

6. The next thing you must do is call the method in the `wddoinit( )` method of the view controller to ensure that the selection screen is initialized.
7. Define the `NAME_CLASS` node in the context. The context attributes correspond to the columns in the internal table for `SELECT-OPTIONS`; that is, `SIGN` (`CHAR1` type), `OPTION` (`CHAR2` type), `LOW` (`SEOCLSNAME` type), and `HIGH` (`SEOCLSNAME` type).

Creating a table and a button

8. In the view, create a table for the `NAME_CLASS` context node.
9. Create the `BTN_GO` button in the view and assign the `GO` action to the `onAction` button event. Switch to the implementation for the action handler method and implement this, as shown in Listing 6.8:
   - Use the `get_range_table_of_sel_field( )` method to read the range table of the `CLSNAME` field. What is interesting here is that the method returns a data reference (`TYPE REF TO DATA`).
   - You must de-reference the data reference to be able to continue working with it. You do this using a field symbol. After the de-referencing, you can use the field symbol as you would a normal variable.
   - The business logic in this example is minimal. Place the ranges table back into the context to display it.

```
METHOD onactiongo .
* Context node reference
DATA: lo_nd_name_class TYPE REF TO if_wd_context_node,
* User entries as the data reference
      rt_name_class TYPE REF TO data.
* To de-reference the range table
FIELD-SYMBOLS: <fs_name_class> TYPE table.
* Retrieve user entry
rt_name_class =
```

```
    wd_this->go_so->get_range_table_of_sel_field(
      i_id = 'CLSNAME' ).
* De-reference the data reference with field symbol
ASSIGN rt_name_class->* TO <fs_name_class>.
* Here comes the business logic
* Place the range table in the context
lo_nd_name_class = wd_context->get_child_node(
    name = `NAME_CLASS` ).
lo_nd_name_class->bind_table( <fs_name_class> ).
ENDMETHOD.
```

Listing 6.8 Action Handler for the GO Action

10. Create a ViewContainerUIElement in the view to embed the WND_SELECTION_SCREEN window of the SELECT-OPTIONS component.

ViewContainer UIElement

11. Switch to the window and embed the WND_SELECTION_SCREEN interface view in the VC_SO view container of the V_SO view.
12. Create a Web Dynpro application for the Web Dynpro component and test the application.

Testing

You have now used SELECT-OPTIONS in your Web Dynpro application – and thus opened up many possibilities for your future developments. With this new knowledge, you can now standardize the visual appearance of selection options and offer the user the familiar visual appearance and known input options of selection screens for classic ABAP reports.

6.4 Semantic Help

The general goal so far has been to provide users with input help to support them in specifically entering values into input fields; however, you may also need to explain *what* they are actually entering. This requires having to provide the user with explanations in the form of *semantic information* or *semantic help*.

The following options are available for this in Web Dynpro:

- Field-related help texts with tooltips
- Field-related explanation texts
- Field-related ABAP Dictionary help (F1 help)

- Non-field related explanations
- Application-related or window-related KW documents

Naturally, the principle of reuse once again forms the basis for the different approaches. Let us look at the different options in detail.

6.4.1 Help Texts with Tooltips

As already described, a number of properties exist for view elements. Among them is the TOOLTIP property, which is available for all UI elements because it is defined in the CL_WD_UIELEMENT ABAP class. This property enables the display of short texts up to a maximum length of 255 characters.

To display the help text in a yellow box known as a tooltip, you move the mouse cursor over the view element (see Figure 6.28). When you move the mouse cursor away from the field, the display disappears.

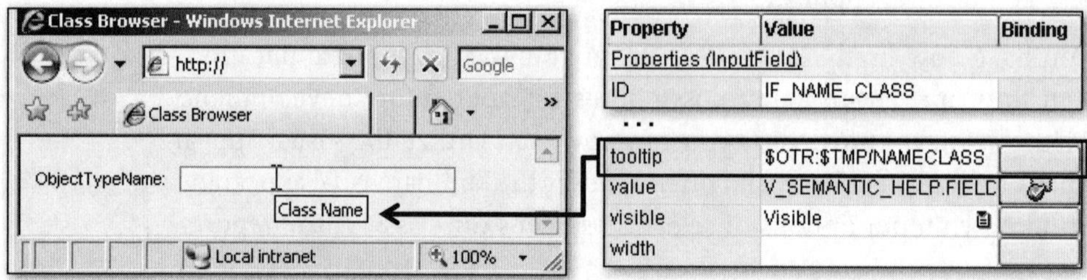

Figure 6.28 Tooltip with OTR Alias Short Text

tooltip property

The TOOLTIP property value can come from different sources: the property is entered directly, an OTR alias short text is used, or texts for the data element being used are used. In the example in Figure 6.28, the OTR alias short text $OTR:$TMP/NAMECLASS was used as the text source.

6.4.2 Explanation Texts

The next option is also implemented using view element properties, specifically, the EXPLANATION property. This property is only available for a subset of view elements (for example, Button, DropDown*, or InputField), not all of them.

The help text is displayed when you click a view element or move the mouse cursor on the view element label. This is displayed as underlined in green.

Explanation property

You can enter the EXPLANATION property value directly or by using OTR alias short texts. If the primary property of a UI element is bound to a context attribute, parts of the data element documentation can be presented to the user. To do this, you must use `DropDown` in the input field for the property or the CREATE BINDING... button to the right of the input field to open a maintenance dialog box for the explanation text and implement the required settings (see Figure 6.29).

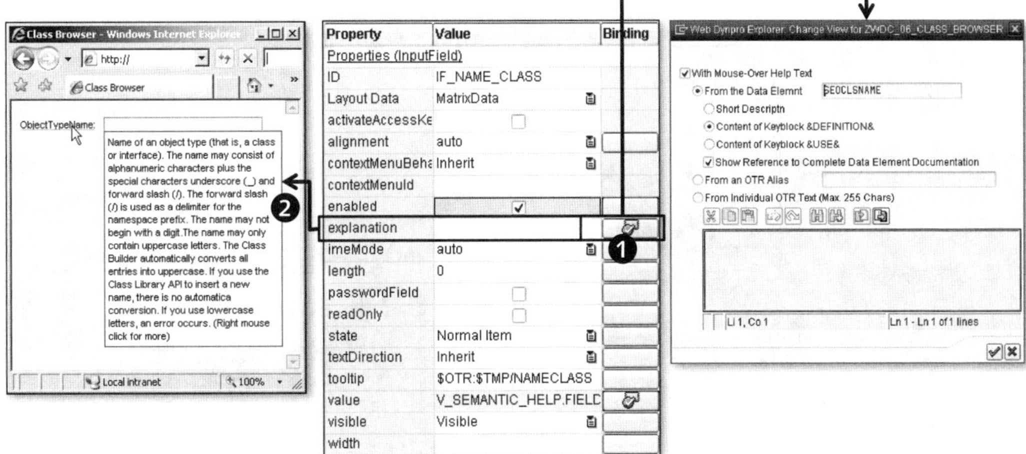

Figure 6.29 Maintaining and Displaying Explanation Values

SHORT DESCRIPTN, CONTENT OF KEYBLOCK &DEFINITION&, and CONTENT OF KEYBLOCK &USE& are available for displaying (❶). You can deactivate the display of explanation texts (❷) by selecting the HIDE QUICK HELP menu option in the context menu (anywhere in the view) or activate the display by selecting the DISPLAY QUICK HELP menu option. If you deactivate the display, you must refresh the Web Dynpro application for the setting to take effect.

6.4.3 ABAP Dictionary Help

You will most likely be familiar with F1 help for input fields from classic dynpro programming. This help is derived from data element documentation from the ABAP Dictionary.

For F1 help, the view element has to be bound to a context attribute that was typed with a data element. To now display the help, the user can activate it using the Ctrl + F1 key combination or the MORE FIELD HELP context menu option (see Figure 6.30).

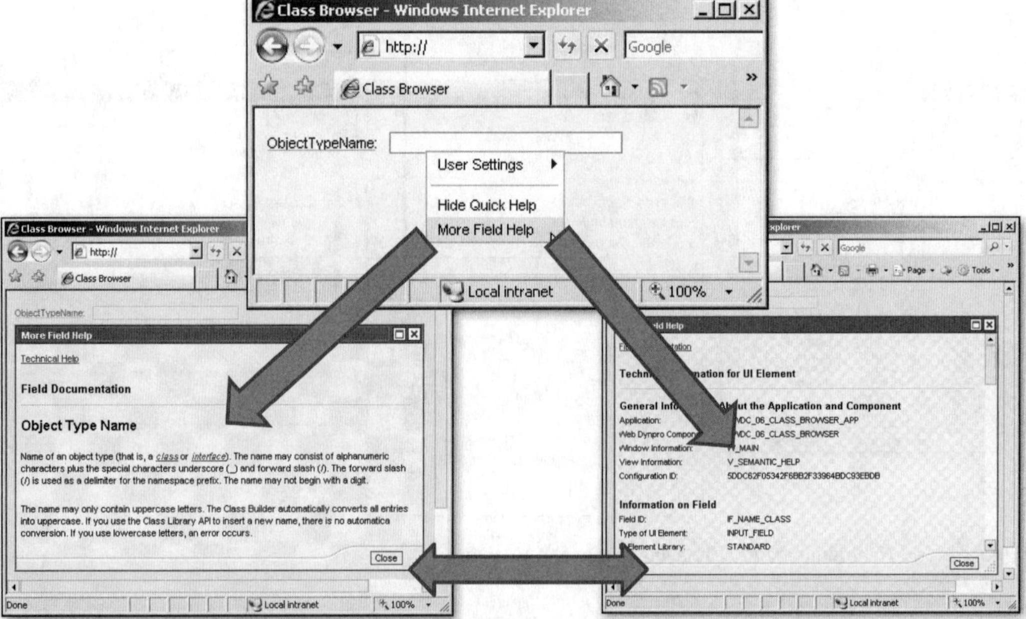

Figure 6.30 F1 Help with Field Documentation and Technical Help

Display

If data element documentation is available, field documentation is displayed for the user in the MORE FIELD HELP modal dialog box. The user can navigate via the TECHNICAL HELP link to the technical details for the field. These details consist of the following elements:

- **General Information About the Application and Component**
  Application, Web Dynpro Component, Window Information, View Information, and Configuration ID
- **Information on Field**
  Field ID, Type of UI Element, UI Element Library (Category)
- **UI Element Attributes**
  Attribute Name, Value, Context Path and Type of UI Element Attribute

If no data element documentation exists, the technical help is immediately displayed. It is also immediately displayed if the WDHIDEMOREFIELDHELPASDEFAULT application parameter is set to ABAP_TRUE. This means that no more data element documentation will be created, unless the EXPLANATION property was created for a field using the ABAP Dictionary.

6.4.4 Explanations

So far, all of the help had a reference to a view field. We will now look at non-field related help. You use the Explanation UI element to display help texts for a view element of a Web Dynpro application on one or more rows. An example is shown in Figure 6.31.

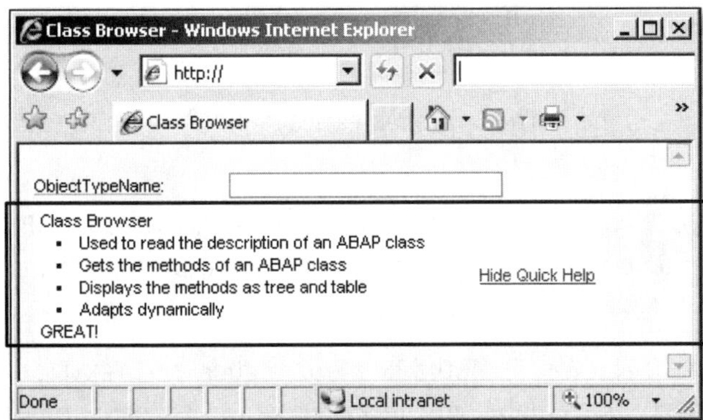

Figure 6.31 Explanation UI Element

The relevant documentation developer usually edits help text in the *Web Dynpro authoring environment* at design time.

Web Dynpro authoring environment

Web Dynpro Authoring Environment

One of the many text types stored in the Online Text Repository (OTR) are translatable texts. The ABAP Workbench provides a separate authoring environment called the *Web Dynpro Text Browser* for editing texts retrospectively without having to enter the development environment. You can activate the Web Dynpro Text Browser in Transaction SE80 by selecting the UTILITIES • SETTINGS... • WORKBENCH (GENERAL) path in the BROWSER SELECTION group and then choosing the WEB DYNPRO TEXT BROWSER menu option. After you confirm your selection by clicking the green checkmark, the Web Dynpro Text Browser now appears in your browser selection above the object list in the left-hand margin of the Workbench window.

When you click the WEB DYNPRO TEXT BROWSER button, only the Web Dynpro component views containing texts from the OTR that are ready for changing are displayed. These views are subject to the following restrictions:

- Only texts from the OTR and not from the ABAP Dictionary can be changed.
- All OTR texts for a Web Dynpro application can be edited only in the original logon language.
- Only text elements from active views can be changed; inactive views are not displayed in the Web Dynpro Text Browser.

Text property

The `Explanation` UI element has the TEXT property, to which you can assign a static text or a text from the OTR. You cannot bind a text to this field using data binding. This results in a maximum length of 255 characters.

Can longer texts be assigned? The approach varies depending on the SPS version.

SPS lower than 11

If you are using SAP NetWeaver Application Server 7.0 with an SPS lower than 11, the text must be dynamically assigned to the TEXT property in the `wddomodifyview( )` method.

SPS 11 or higher

If you are using SAP NetWeaver 7.0 SPS 11 or higher, the TEXTDOCUMENTNAME property is available in the `Explanation` UI element to directly specify the name of the documentation module to be displayed. Listing 6.9 shows an example of how you can assign a text or documentation module to the TEXT property of the `Explanation` UI element.

Assigning Explanation Text

The DOCU_GET function module makes the content of a documentation module available in an internal table. The format of the documentation corresponds to the SAPscript format. You can use the static cl_wd_formatted_text=>create_from_sapscript( ) method to convert the text into text to be displayed.

The DOCU_CREATE function module is used to create documentation modules. Select the General text entry for the Documentation Class, specify a name, and then switch to the SAPscript editor to maintain the text.

```
METHOD wddomodifyview .
* Reference to the explanation element
DATA: lo_explanation TYPE REF TO cl_wd_explanation,
* Document module text in internal table (for option 1)
      lt_tline TYPE text_line_tab,
* Formatted text for explanation (for option 1)
      lo_formatted_text TYPE REF TO cl_wd_formatted_text.
* Determine reference to view element
lo_explanation ?= view->get_element(
  id = 'EX_NAME_CLASS' ).
*** Option 1 (SPS lower than 11)**
** Read document module
*  CALL FUNCTION 'DOCU_GET'
*    EXPORTING
*      id     = 'TX' "General text
*      langu  = 'E'
*      object = 'ZTXT_06_CLASS_BROWSER'
*    TABLES
*      line   = lt_tline
*    EXCEPTIONS
*      OTHERS = 5.
*  IF sy-subrc <> 0.
*    EXIT.
*  ENDIF.
** Convert from SAPscript to Web Application Documentation
*  lo_formatted_text =
*    cl_wd_formatted_text=>create_from_sapscript(
*      sapscript_lines = lt_tline
*      type            = cl_wd_formatted_text=>e_type-wad ).
** Set text
*  lo_explanation->set_text(
```

```
*    value = lo_formatted_text->m_xml_text    ).
** Option 2 (SPS 11 or higher)**
* Set name of document module
lo_explanation->set_text_document_name(
  value = 'ZTXT_06_CLASS_BROWSER' ).
ENDMETHOD.
```

Listing 6.9 Dynamically Setting the Text Property of the Explanation UI Element

Option 1 (SPS lower than 11)

- In option 1, you see the dynamic option for an SPS lower than 11. The documentation module is read first using the DOCU_GET function module. This documentation module must have been created beforehand by the DOCU_CREATE function module. The function module returns an internal table with SAPscript formatting. The static cl_wd_formatted_text=>create_from_sapscript method converts this into Web Application Documentation (WAD) format and stores it in a CL_WD_FORMATTED_TEXT object in the public m_xml_text instance attribute. This attribute is then transferred to the set_text( ) method of the Explanation UI element.

Option 2 (SPS 11 or higher)

- Option 2, for SPS 11 or higher, is quite simple: you transfer the name of the documentation module to the set_text_document_name( ) method of the Explanation UI element.

You can use the DESIGN property (if you assign the emphasized value to it) to control whether the user is provided with a link for hiding the Explanation. Otherwise, the context menu is still available to hide the Explanation.

6.4.5 Knowledge Warehouse Documents

In the SAP Knowledge Warehouse (SAP KW), you can use created *information objects* (help texts) as help for a Web Dynpro application or a Window.

1. To be able to use SAP KW contents in your Web Dynpro application, switch to the PROPERTIES tab of the Web Dynpro application or to a window in your Web Dynpro component (see Figure 6.32).

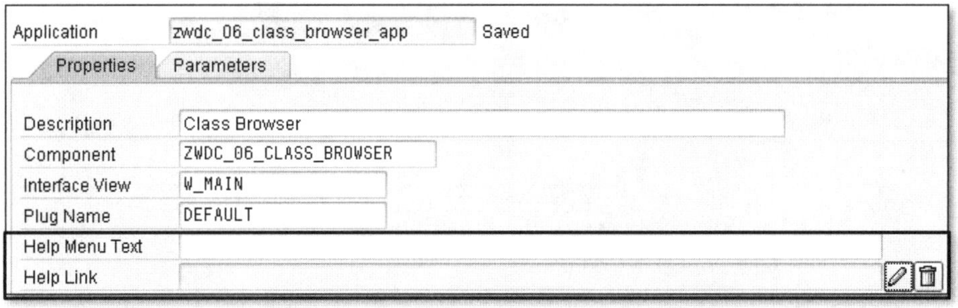

Figure 6.32 Integrating Information Objects from SAP Knowledge Warehouse

SAP Knowledge Warehouse

SAP KW is the SAP solution for all materials used in the areas of training, documentation, and manuals. It is an integrated environment for creating, translating, presenting, sharing, and managing information objects you can use for purposes such as the following:

- Documentation (help for applications)
- Training materials (for attendance-based training)
- Manuals (especially for quality management)

All contents managed in SAP KW are stored there as information objects. You can use structures, a particular type of information object, and hyperlinks to *link* information objects to multimedia hyperdocuments (for example, for training courses). Information objects with a common topic area are compiled and managed in *folders*. Information objects and folders are each assigned to an *area* (primary use).

Information objects are available in SAP KW in different *versions* that can be accessed using different *contexts*.

RFC connection

2. In the Help Menu Text field, enter the text for the help window title. You cannot maintain the Help Link field directly; instead, you must use the Create/Change Link to the right of the field. For your SAP KW system, you will need an `AIO_FOR_HELP_LINKS` RFC connection maintained using Transaction SM59.

Context

3. A dialog box appears that allows you to restrict the *search context* when searching for information objects in SAP KW. You can filter your search according to language, release, enhancement, and country (see Figure 6.33).

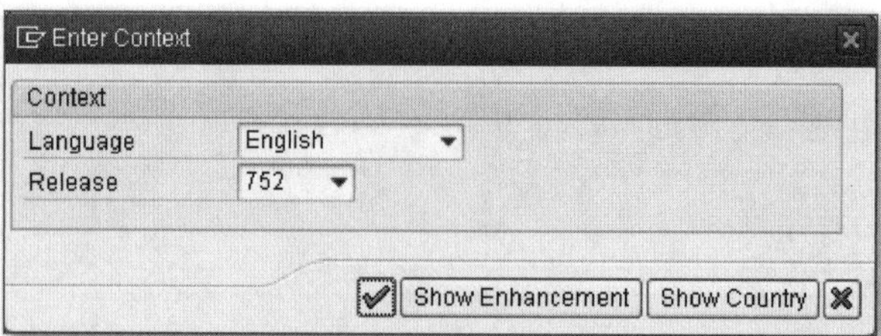

Figure 6.33 Defining the Context

4. After you have made your entries and confirmed them by clicking on the button with the green checkmark, a dialog box appears for selecting a topic area in SAP KW. Here, you can search for the information object (see Figure 6.34).

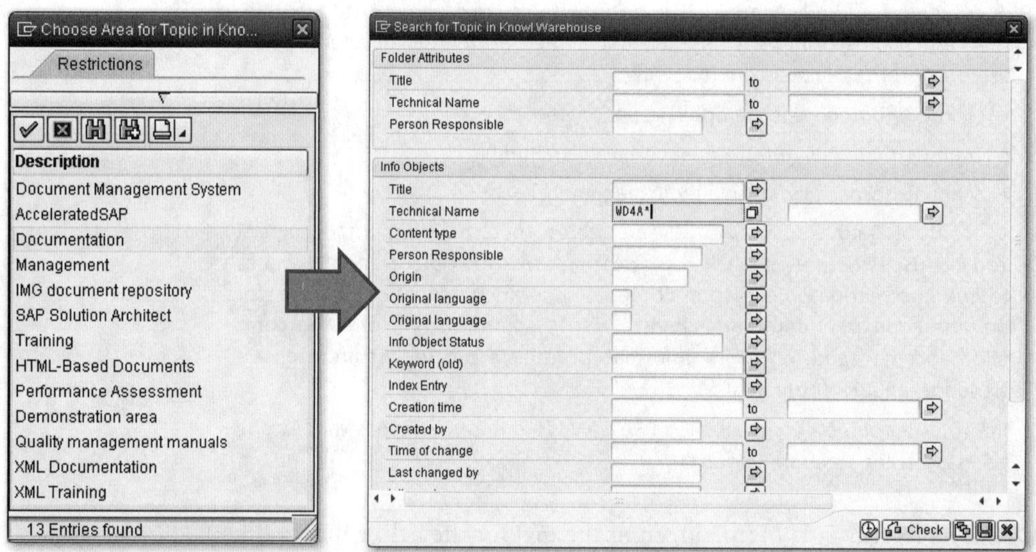

Figure 6.34 Selecting the Area and Topic

5. After you have made your selection – for example, DOCUMENTATION – and confirmed it by clicking on the button with the green checkmark, you go to the next dialog box. You can search for the information object using the numerous input fields provided.

For example, if you are interested in the documentation for Web Dynpro ABAP, select the TECHNICAL NAME input field to search for information objects with the technical name WD4A*.

Selecting an information object (content)

6. Confirm your entry by clicking on the button with the green checkmark. In the next screen, the search result for the information objects is displayed as a list, and you can select an entry (see Figure 6.35).

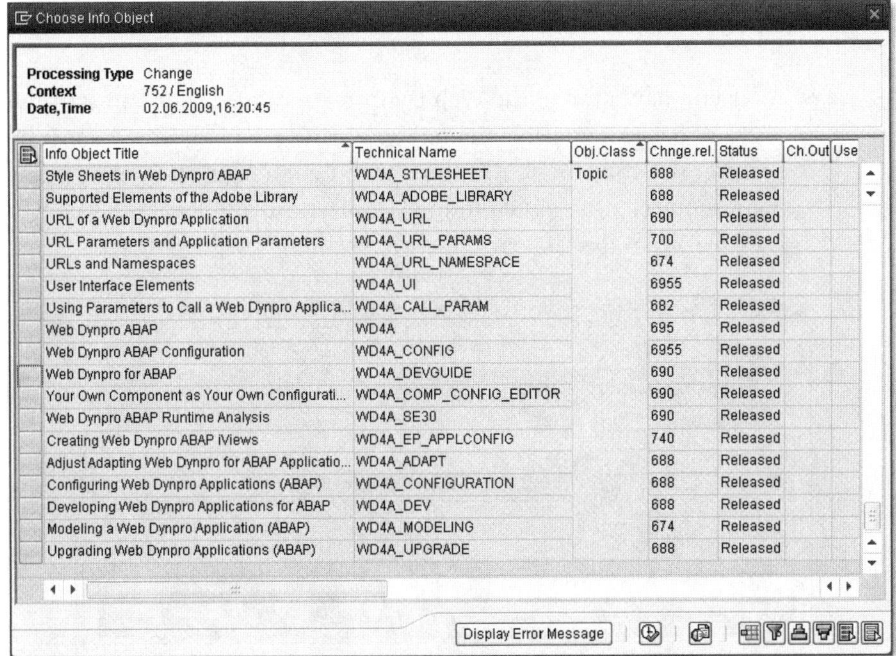

Info Object Title	Technical Name	Obj.Class	Chnge.rel.	Status	Ch.Out	Use
Style Sheets in Web Dynpro ABAP	WD4A_STYLESHEET	Topic	688	Released		
Supported Elements of the Adobe Library	WD4A_ADOBE_LIBRARY		688	Released		
URL of a Web Dynpro Application	WD4A_URL		690	Released		
URL Parameters and Application Parameters	WD4A_URL_PARAMS		700	Released		
URLs and Namespaces	WD4A_URL_NAMESPACE		674	Released		
User Interface Elements	WD4A_UI		6955	Released		
Using Parameters to Call a Web Dynpro Applica...	WD4A_CALL_PARAM		682	Released		
Web Dynpro ABAP	WD4A		695	Released		
Web Dynpro ABAP Configuration	WD4A_CONFIG		6955	Released		
Web Dynpro for ABAP	WD4A_DEVGUIDE		690	Released		
Your Own Component as Your Own Configurati...	WD4A_COMP_CONFIG_EDITOR		690	Released		
Web Dynpro ABAP Runtime Analysis	WD4A_SE30		690	Released		
Creating Web Dynpro ABAP iViews	WD4A_EP_APPLCONFIG		740	Released		
Adjust Adapting Web Dynpro for ABAP Applicatio...	WD4A_ADAPT		688	Released		
Configuring Web Dynpro Applications (ABAP)	WD4A_CONFIGURATION		688	Released		
Developing Web Dynpro Applications for ABAP	WD4A_DEV		688	Released		
Modeling a Web Dynpro Application (ABAP)	WD4A_MODELING		674	Released		
Upgrading Web Dynpro Applications (ABAP)	WD4A_UPGRADE		688	Released		

Figure 6.35 Found Information Objects with Single Selection

Structure area

7. After you select a row and confirm this selection by clicking on the button with the green checkmark, a dialog box for defining the structure area appears. This closely resembles searching for a topic area and can also be skipped.
8. In the next step, the link is created in the HELP LINK field (see Figure 6.36).

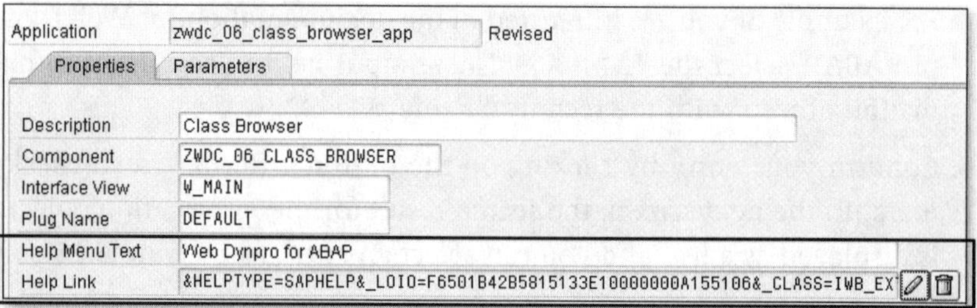

Figure 6.36 Result of Search – a Link

9. After you have started the Web Dynpro application, you can start the SAP KW-based help (Help Center) by pressing the F1 key. A separate browser window opens, like the one shown in Figure 6.37. The information object you defined in the Web Dynpro application properties is displayed in the WORTH KNOWING section.

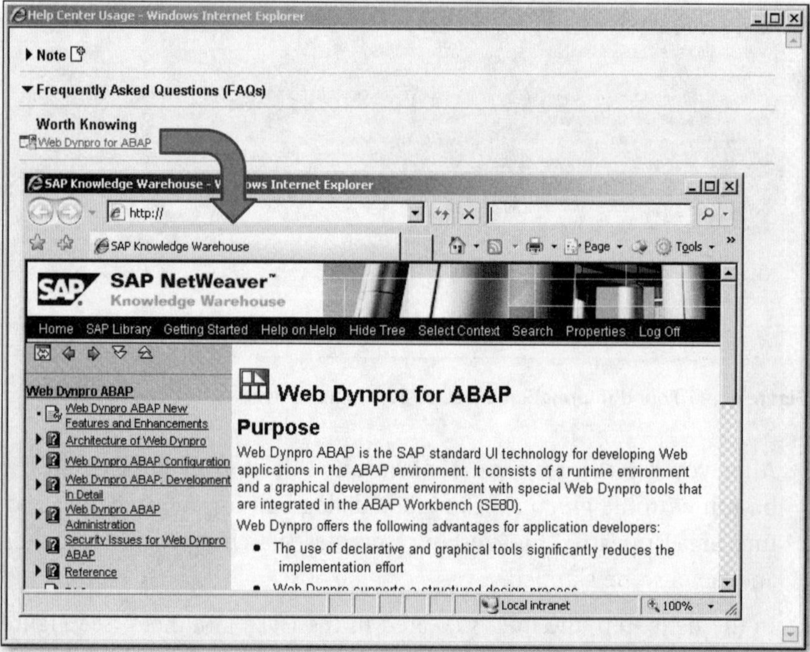

Figure 6.37 Help from SAP KW

10. By using an action handler, you can also trigger the display of the Help Center (see Listing 6.10). You can even change the stored link during runtime.

Triggering the display

```
* Reference to component controller API
DATA: lo_api_comp_controller TYPE REF TO if_wd_component,
* Reference to application
      lo_application TYPE REF TO if_wd_application.
* Determine API reference
lo_api_comp_controller = wd_comp_controller->wd_get_api( ).
* Determine reference to application
lo_application = lo_api_comp_controller->get_application( ).
* Open SAP KW help
lo_application->open_help_center( ).
```

Listing 6.10 Triggering the Display of Help in SAP KW

6.5 Summary

In this chapter, you learned about the options for providing users with input support. We explained the two major groups of selection options and input help in depth, and presented detailed examples for each group. The UI elements to which you were introduced in this chapter include DropDown, RadioButton, CheckBox, ItemListBox, and TriStateCheckBox.

The requirement to provide users with input options they can select (using optional input help) led us to the topic of input help. In this context, we comprehensively discussed the options for integrating input help, and presented practical examples. The WDR_SELECT_OPTIONS Web Dynpro component we used for illustration showed you one way that you can smartly implement selection screens through component usage. We ended this chapter with the topic of semantic help.

In Chapter 7 (Configuration, Customizing, and Personalization), you will learn about the different options available to adjust Web Dynpro applications. We will explain the concepts of personalization, customizing, and configuration, and use examples to deepen your understanding of the topics.

Web Dynpro components and applications can be customized at different levels without the need to change the implementation. This chapter describes these levels in detail and explains them using examples.

7 Configuration, Customizing, and Personalization

In practice, it is sometimes necessary to customize existing Web Dynpro applications according to individual requirements – be they standard SAP applications or applications you developed yourself. These requirements can range from enterprise-wide functional customizations, to industry-specific requirements, to user-specific changes to the interface or the navigation.

Applications that are created on the basis of Web Dynpro can be customized in different ways and for different target groups:

- **Configuration**
  Developers can create *configuration data sets*, which contain values for view element properties, context attributes, or both. These data sets enable the developer to override the values of view element properties using data binding, and thus to change the appearance of the user interface (UI) without having to modify the implementation.
- **Customizing**
  Settings for a specific user group in a particular client are made using the *Customizing* function. This function is controlled and regulated by authorizations. The Customizing options are wider in scope than the personalization options, which affect the settings for individual users only.
- **Personalization**
  Individual users can make individual UI settings using *personalization*.

These options are very restricted because the relevant settings depend on and affect only a single user.

Implicit and explicit customizations

Web Dynpro distinguishes between *implicit* and *explicit* customizations:

- Implicit customizations are provided by the Web Dynpro framework. Implicit changes do not require any programming or definition.

  As of SAP NetWeaver 7.0 EhP 2, implicit changes are referred to as *Web Dynpro built-in.*

- If the implicit change options are insufficient, the developer has additional options on the basis of context attributes. This kind of change is called *explicit customization*.

  As of SAP NetWeaver 7.0 EhP 2, explicit changes are referred to as *Web Dynpro component-defined.*

How are the options for configuration, Customizing, and personalization interrelated? Figure 7.1 shows the hierarchy of customization options.

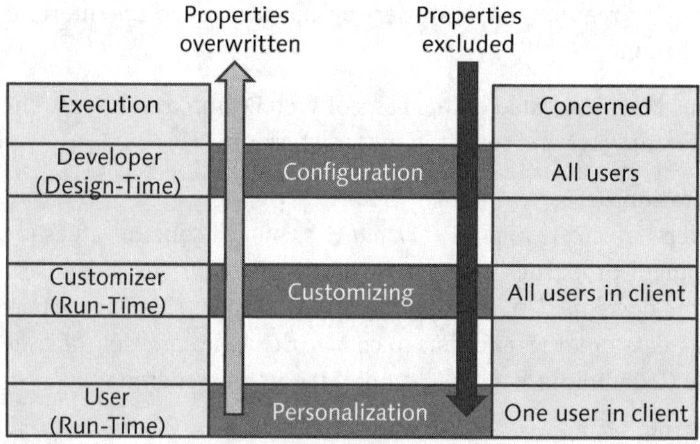

Figure 7.1 Hierarchy of Customization Options in Web Dynpro Applications

Customization hierarchy

The customization hierarchy defines who can set and overwrite property values, and where this can be done. It also shows how properties can be marked to ensure that no further changes are made to them. Customizations can then be made only if the user in question has the correct authorizations (this topic is dealt with in this chapter).

Topics Discussed

This chapter discusses the following topics:

- Configuration, which allows you to configure settings for Web Dynpro components and applications that are used by all system users.
- Customizing, which allows you to configure settings that apply to all users in a particular client.
- Personalization, which allows you to adapt a Web Dynpro application to your personal requirements.

7.1 Configuration

Let us begin by looking at the customization options at the highest level in terms of effect: configuration. As mentioned before, configuration affects the Web Dynpro components and applications that are used by all users in a system.

Configuration steps

Web Dynpro applications are configured using a *configurator* (*configuration editor*). The configurator is started automatically when configurations are created or changed, in two steps:

1. The developer creates configuration data sets for individual Web Dynpro components. These data sets are used to control the behavior or the UI of the individual views. Several data sets can be created for a single Web Dynpro component.
2. The application developer of a Web Dynpro application uses the configuration data sets for the Web Dynpro components to create an application configuration. The application configuration specifies which of the Web Dynpro components is used with which configuration.

Configuration data set

The data in the configuration data set that is created in the configuration editor is divided into three categories:

- **General administration data**
  This data includes, for example, the name of the configuration, the descriptive text and the name of the associated Web Dynpro component.

- **Explicit configuration data**
  The existence of a *configuration controller* is a prerequisite for this data. Each Web Dynpro component can have only one configuration controller. The configuration controller is a special instance of the custom controller.
- **Implicit configuration data**
  This data represents the values of the properties for the view elements. In a special usage of the Web Dynpro component in which certain properties are changed, the application developer creates a configuration that overrides the property values.

After this brief overview of configuration, we will provide you with a more detailed description of implicit and explicit configuration.

7.1.1 Implicit Configuration

Procedure

To customize a Web Dynpro application using implicit configuration, you need to create configuration data sets. A configuration data set provides the properties of the view elements for maintenance purposes. Maintaining these properties causes the appearance of the Web Dynpro application to be changed for all users when the set is used in an application configuration later on. Proceed as follows to create a configuration data set:

[✎]

1. In the Object Navigator (Transaction SE80), open the Web Dynpro component for which you want to create the configuration data set.

CONFIGURE_COMPONENT configurator

2. Open the context menu of the Web Dynpro component and select CREATE/CHANGE CONFIGURATION. This starts the standard configurator in the form of the Web Dynpro application `CONFIGURE_COMPONENT`.
3. Enter the name of the configuration data set in the CONFIGURATION ID input field, which in this case is `ZWDC_07_CLASS_BROWSER_C1` (see Figure 7.2, ❶). When entering the name, note that you must create your configuration data sets in the customer namespace and that these names have to be globally unique.

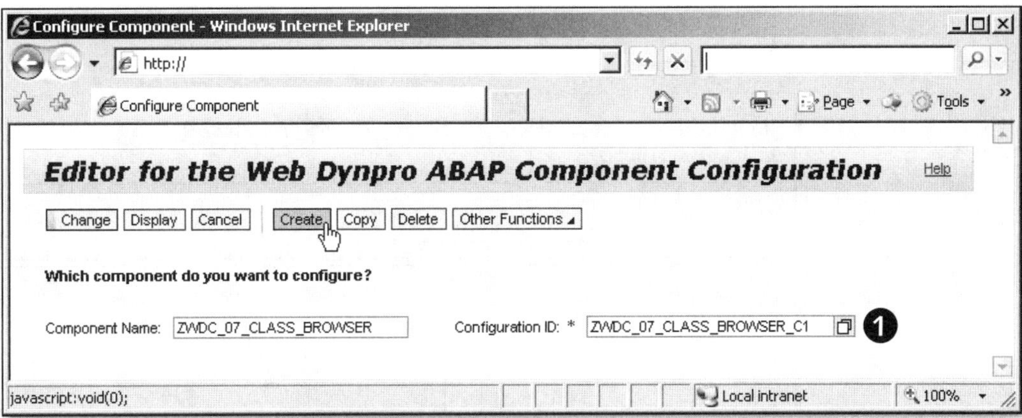

Figure 7.2 Creating a Configuration Data Set

Maintaining administration data

4. Select the CREATE function. A dialog box opens that contains the input options for the configuration administration data (see Figure 7.3). Enter the DESCRIPTION (❶) and the PACKAGE (❷) for the configuration data set and confirm your entries by clicking on OK.

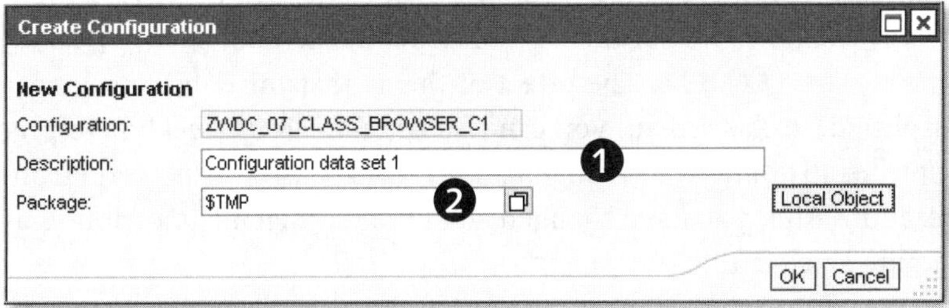

Figure 7.3 Maintaining the Configuration Data for the Configuration Data Set

Selecting a view

5. The configuration data set with the available functions and the selection option for the views of the configuration data set is displayed, as shown in Figure 7.4. The toolbar contains three views: ATTRIBUTES, COMPONENT-DEFINED (explicit configuration), and WEB DYNPRO BUILT-IN (implicit configuration) (❶).
6. Open WEB DYNPRO BUILT-IN. On the left, in a table, you will see a dropdown list with the views of the Web Dynpro components (❷), and, on the right, you will see the attributes that can be set (❸).

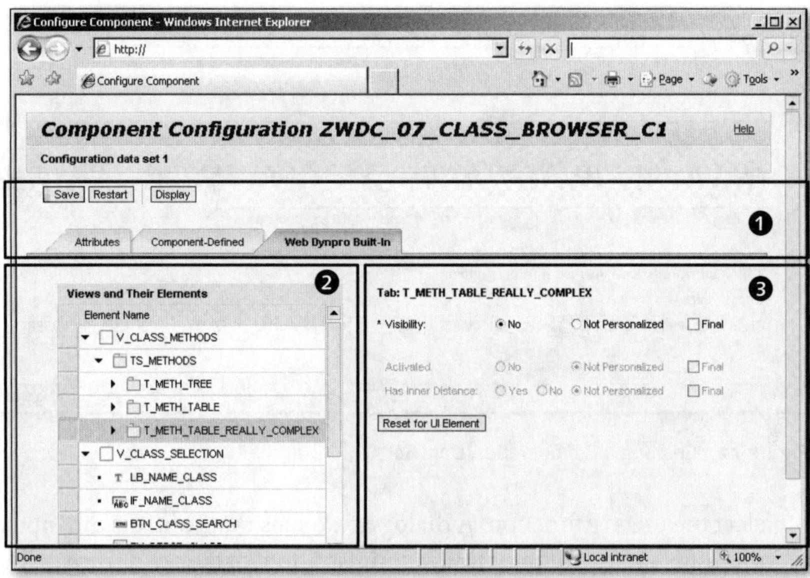

Figure 7.4 Maintenance Screen for a Configuration Data Set

Setting UI attributes

7. In this screen, you can now set the view element attributes as required. In this example, we set the VISIBILITY of `Tab` element `T_METH_TABLE_REALLY_COMPLEX` to `No`. The effect of this is that this tab is no longer displayed. In this screen, you can also use the FINAL checkbox to prevent the attribute from being changed using Customizing or personalization. After you have changed all of the view element attributes as required, select the SAVE FUNCTION.

Configuration data set in the Web Dynpro component object list

8. Close the browser window of the configuration application and update the object list of your Web Dynpro component in the Object Navigator. After you have updated the object list, the configuration data set is shown as a sub-element of the Web Dynpro component (see Figure 7.5, ❶).

Creating the application configuration

You can create the application configuration if the appropriate configuration data sets are available for all of the relevant Web Dynpro components that are used in your Web Dynpro application. Proceed as follows:

1. In the Object Navigator (Transaction SE80), open the Web Dynpro component and, from there, the Web Dynpro application for which you want to create the application configuration.

Start the configuration editor

2. Open the context menu of the Web Dynpro component and select CREATE/CHANGE CONFIGURATION (see Figure 7.6). This starts the configurator in the form of a Web Dynpro application (CONFIGURE_APPLICATION).

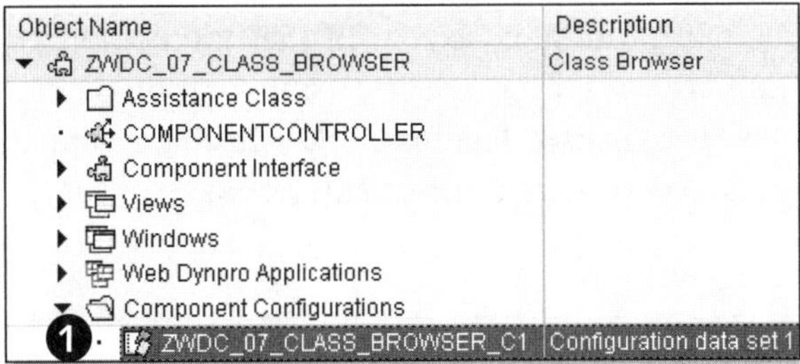

Figure 7.5 Configuration Data Set in the Object List of the Web Dynpro Component

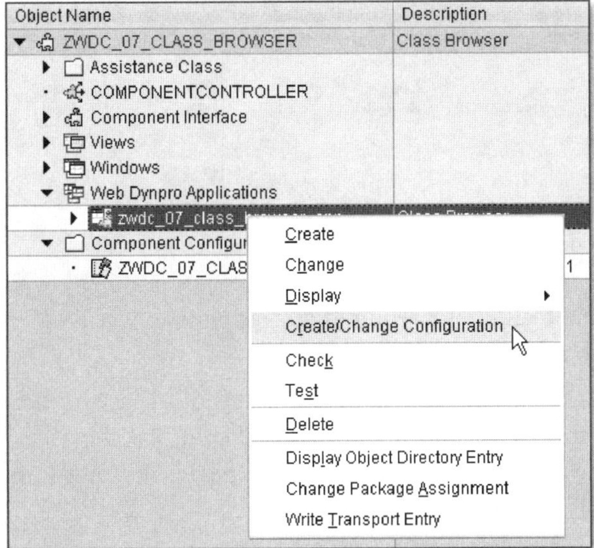

Figure 7.6 Creating the Application Configuration

3. Enter the name of the application configuration in the CONFIGURATION ID input field. When entering the name, note that you must create your application configuration in the customer namespace and that this name has to be globally unique.

4. Select the CREATE function. A dialog box opens that contains the input options for the configuration administration data. Enter the DESCRIPTION and the PACKAGE for the application configuration; for example, "Application configuration for the class browser" and "$TMP." Confirm your entries by clicking on OK.

Selecting a configuration data set for each Web Dynpro component

5. Select the STRUCTURE tab in the next screen. In the ASSIGNMENT OF COMPONENT CONFIGURATIONS group, select a configuration set for each Web Dynpro component (see Figure 7.7, ❶). In this example, the configuration set is COMPONENT CONFIGURATION `ZWDC_07_CLASS_BROWSER_C1` (❷).

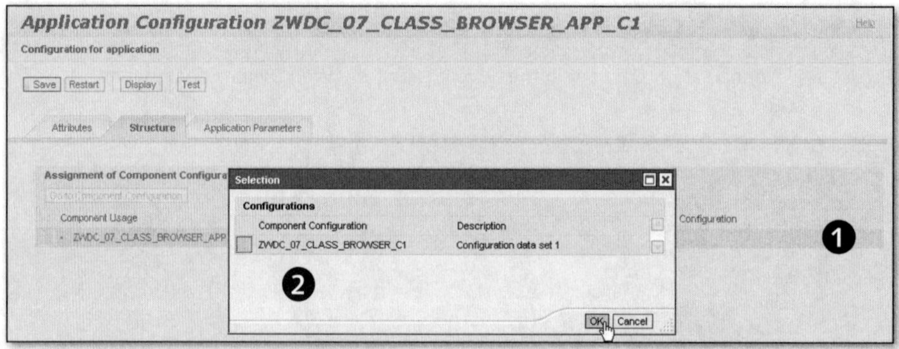

Figure 7.7 Selecting a Configuration Data Set for a Web Dynpro Component

Save

6. After you have made all of the required assignments, select SAVE to save the application configuration.
7. You can use the TEST function to check the effects of the application configuration on the Web Dynpro application. Figure 7.8 shows the test results for the settings that have just been made: the METHODS TABLE COMPLEX tab is now hidden.
8. Close the browser window of the configuration application and update the object list of your Web Dynpro component in the Object Navigator. After the update, the application configuration is displayed as a sub-element of the Web Dynpro application.

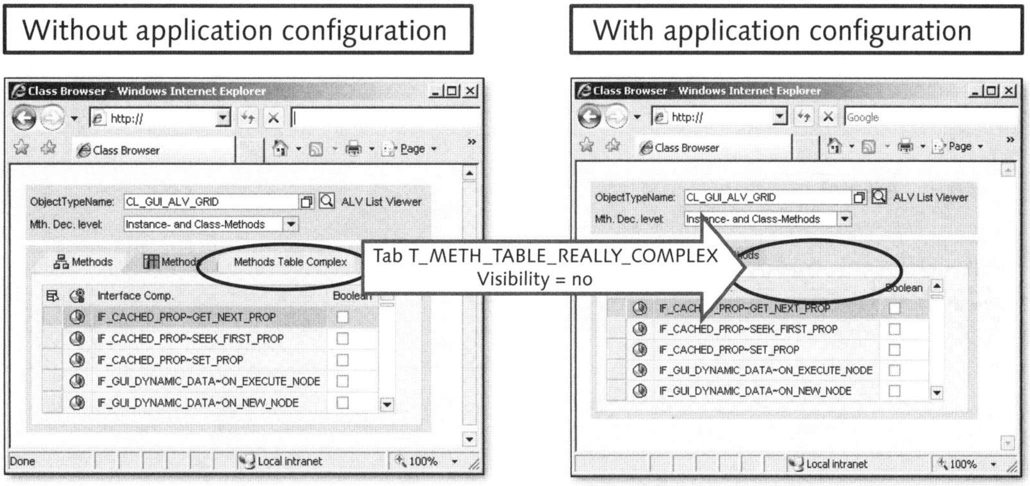

Without application configuration

With application configuration

Tab T_METH_TABLE_REALLY_COMPLEX
Visibility = no

Figure 7.8 Effects of the Application Configuration

Assigning the application configuration to the Web Dynpro application

To ensure that the application configuration has a real effect on the Web Dynpro application, you have to assign it to the Web Dynpro application. There are two ways of doing this (see Figure 7.9):

- Application parameters
  To make assignments using application parameters (❶), go to the PARAMETERS tab in the Web Dynpro application and create the parameter `WDCONFIGURATIONID` with the ID of the application configuration as a VALUE.
- URL parameters
  To make assignments using URL parameters (❷), append `[?|&]<parameter name>=<parameter value>` to the URL of the relevant Web Dynpro application. For testing purposes, you can enter this into the address bar of the browser after you have launched the application. Provide a hyperlink for users that points to the Web Dynpro application, including the URL parameter.

For more information on making assignments for the application configuration, see Section 7.3, URL Parameters and Application Parameters.

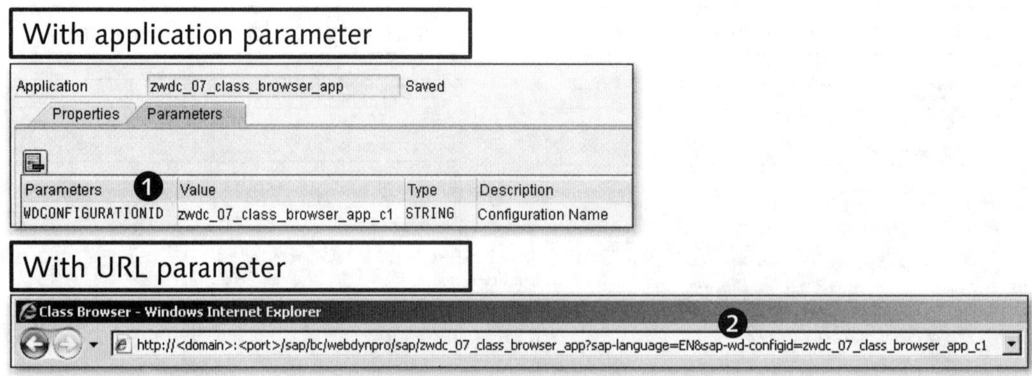

Figure 7.9 Assigning the Application Configuration to the Web Dynpro Application

7.1.2 Explicit Configuration

If implicit is not enough...

If the options provided by implicit configuration are not enough – because you want to influence the program flow using configuration, for example – you have to be prepared for some definition and programming work to enable explicit configuration. To do this, proceed as follows:

[✎]

1. In the Object Navigator (Transaction SE80), open the Web Dynpro component for which you want to enable explicit configuration.
2. Open the context menu of the Web Dynpro component and select CREATE • CUSTOM CONTROLLER.
3. The CREATE CONTROLLER dialog box opens. Here, enter the name of the custom controller in the CONTROLLER (❶) input field and the description in the DESCRIPTION (❷) field (see Figure 7.10). Confirm your entries using the button with the green checkmark.

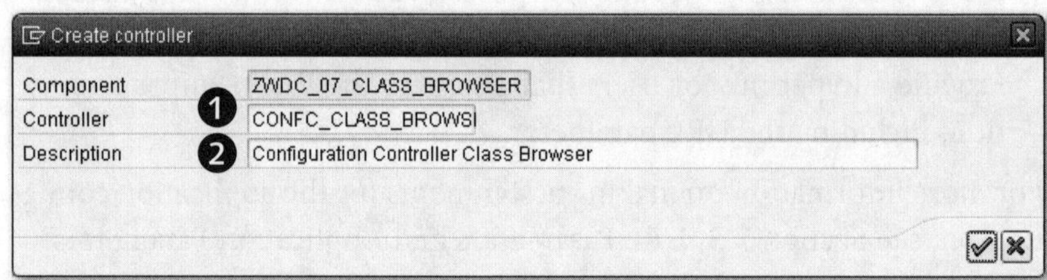

Figure 7.10 Maintaining the Attributes of the Custom Controller

4. The next screen that opens is the view for defining the elements of a custom controller (see Figure 7.11).

   Defining the custom controller context

   The CONTEXT tab allows you to define the context nodes (ICONS in this example) and context attributes (METHOD_KIND_ICON_NAME in this example) that the user can set later on in the explicit configuration.

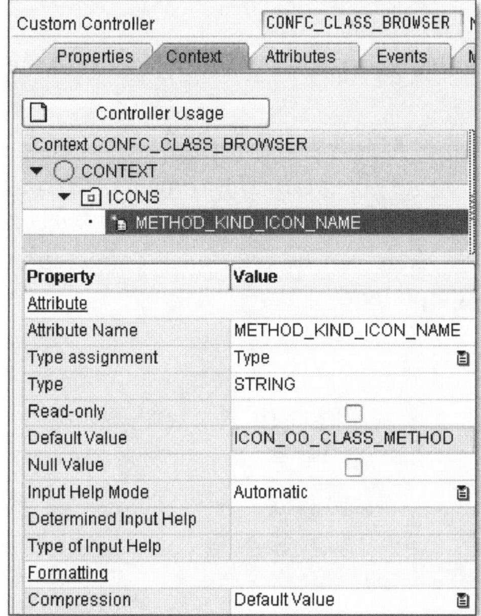

Figure 7.11 Defining the Context Node and Context Attributes for the Custom Controller

In addition to being used for the properties of view elements, the application developer can also take these context attribute values into account in the implementation.

When doing so, the developer has to be aware of the following rules, as set down in the Web Dynpro framework:

- When a node is created in the configuration controller context, recursion nodes are not allowed. If you go ahead and create a recursion node, you will not be able to maintain values for this node.
- Singleton nodes are also prohibited and cannot be created.

- The attributes have to have a simple type; in other words, no reference types or structured types.
- In the case of a *multiple node* (maximum cardinality n), one of the node attributes has to be marked in the properties as the PRIMARY ATTRIBUTE to ensure the uniqueness of the elements in relation to the primary attribute. This property is visible only in the configuration controller and not in the custom controller.

5. After SAVE, the custom controller is displayed in the object list of the Web Dynpro component.

From custom controller to configuration controller

6. Next, select (RE)SET AS CONFIG. CONTROLLER FROM THE CONTEXT MENU OF THE CUSTOM CONTROLLER YOU JUST CREATED. This converts the component controller to the configuration controller of the Web Dynpro component (see Figure 7.12). There can be only one configuration controller per Web Dynpro component.

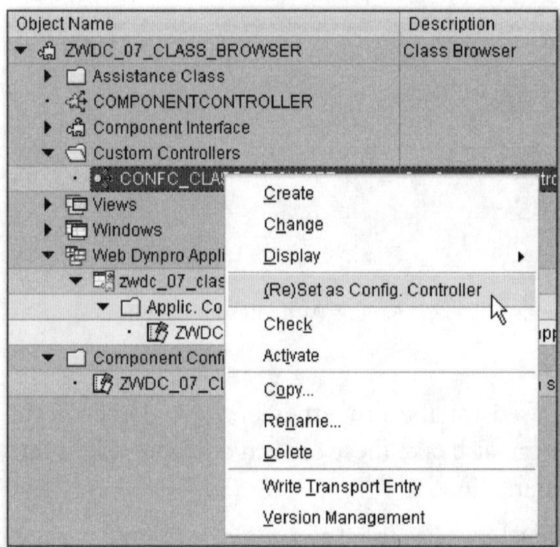

Figure 7.12 Converting a Custom Controller to a Configuration Controller

Context mapping and data binding

7. To be able to access the configuration controller data from any controller in the Web Dynpro component, you have to define the configuration controller as a used controller and then execute context mapping on the context nodes of the configuration controller. You

can then use the mapped context attributes in the implementation or in the data binding.

Figure 7.13 shows the definition of the configuration controller as a used controller (❶) and the context mapping of the configuration controller's context nodes to the context of a view (❷). Part (❸) of Figure 7.13 shows the effect of the context attribute data binding in the configuration controller on the ICONSOURCE property of the view element `Caption`; that is, the icon, which is stored in the DEFAULT VALUE of the context attribute of the configuration controller, is displayed.

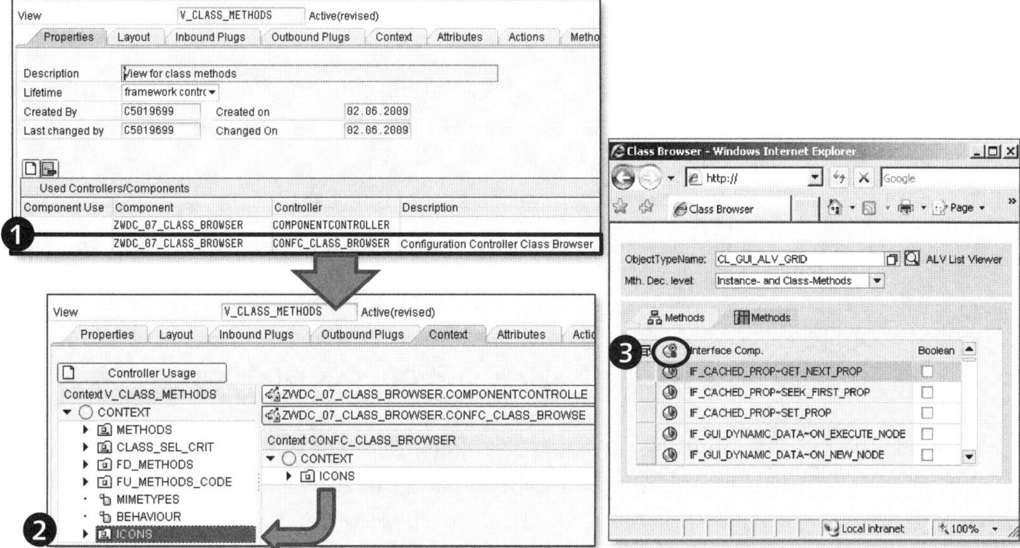

Figure 7.13 Using the Configuration Controller in a View

After you have finished creating the configuration controller, it is accessible in the definition of configuration data sets.

Explicit configuration

1. In order to use explicit configuration go to the configuration editor.
2. The context attributes that were created in the configuration controller are now located on the COMPONENT-DEFINED tab in the configurator, where you can set the values you require (see Figure 7.14).

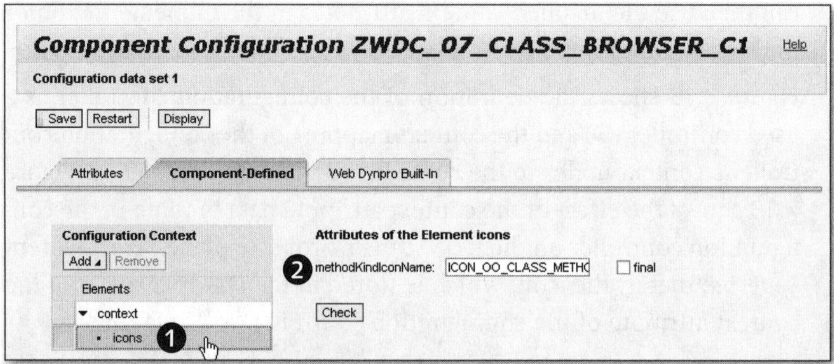

Figure 7.14 Explicit Configuration

Maintaining context attribute values

3. The defined context nodes from the configuration controller are listed in a table on the COMPONENT-DEFINED tab (❶). To the right of the table, the context attributes are displayed with their input options. The required values can be entered here (❷).
4. After making your entries, make the data persistent using the SAVE function.

7.2 Personalization and Customizing

Individualization

Aside from the configuration that affects the entire user group of a Web Dynpro application, individual users can also change some of the settings of the Web Dynpro application. These settings cover personal requirements and preferences. However, this is very restricted in comparison to the configuration because the performance of a Web Dynpro application must not be jeopardized by incorrect settings.

Customizing

The purpose of the Customizing function is to control settings that affect large user groups. An administrator with the appropriate authorizations can configure advanced settings by opening the Web Dynpro application in *Customizing mode*.

Another difference between configuration, Customizing, and personalization is the time at which changes are made. Whereas configuration changes are made at design time, Customizing and personalization changes are made at runtime. Furthermore, with Customizing, the Web Dynpro application CUSTOMIZE_COMPONENT can be used at design time.

Proceed as follows to carry out implicit Customizing:

[✎]

1. Start the Web Dynpro application in configuration mode. To do this, add the parameter name or parameter value pair sap-config-mode=X to the end of the URL of the Web Dynpro application.

Configuration mode

2. In the relevant view element, select SETTINGS FOR CURRENT CONFIGURATION from the context menu (see Figure 7.15). This opens the Customizing dialog box (provided that the user in question has the relevant authorizations).

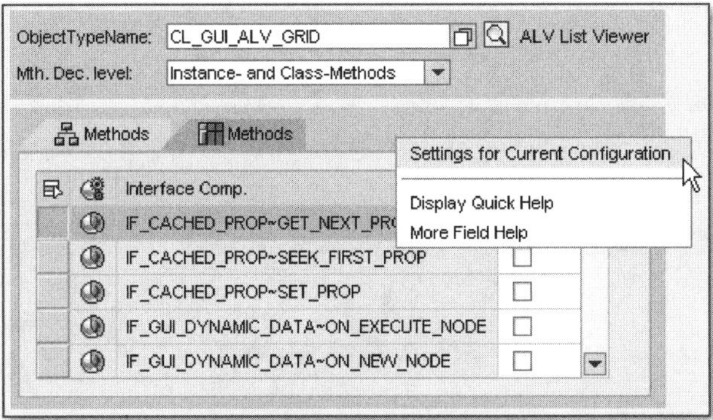

Figure 7.15 Implicit Customizing

3. In the next step, you should set the view element properties you require. In the example in Figure 7.16, the VISIBILITY (❷) property of the Tab (❶) view element is set to NOT PERSONALIZED, and the checkbox is checked to set the FINAL (❸) property to ABAP_TRUE. Properties that are marked as final in the configuration cannot be changed using personalization.

Setting values

With implicit personalization, proceed the same way as you did with implicit Customizing. You can change a restricted set of properties in the context menu of each view element such as the visibility of a view element (see Figure 7.17).

Personalization

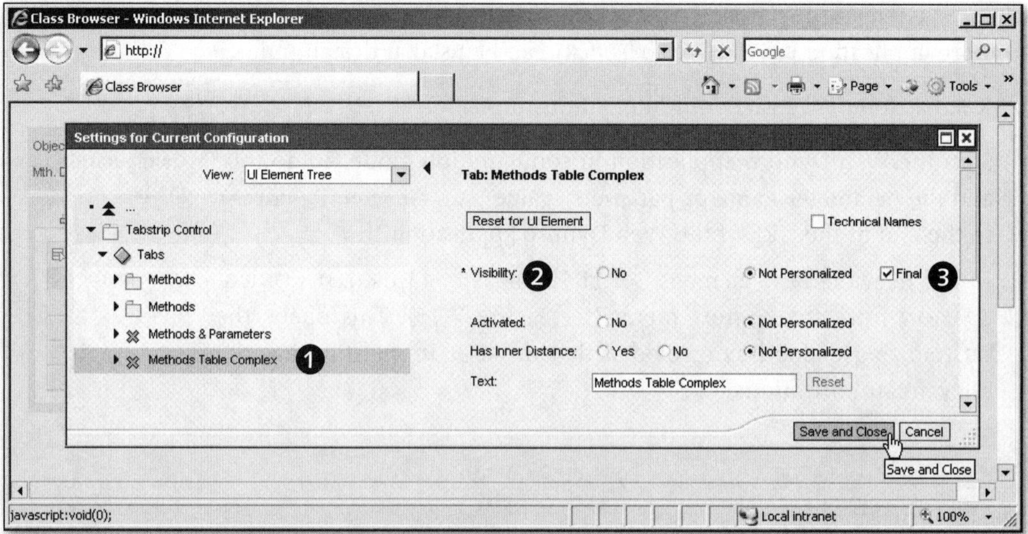

Figure 7.16 Setting Property Values in Customizing

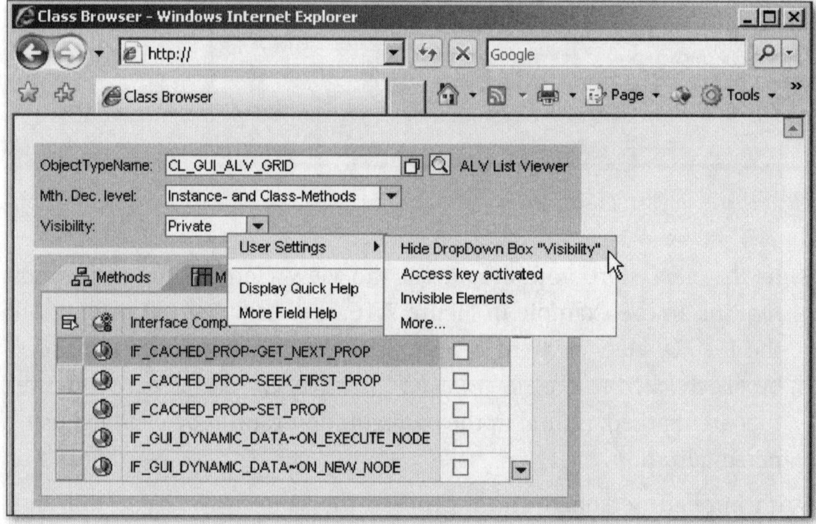

Figure 7.17 Personalizing the Web Dynpro Application

This also means that the user can reset view elements to visible that were previously set to invisible. Properties of view elements that were set to

FINAL in the configuration or in Customizing are not accessible using personalization.

7.3 URL Parameters and Application Parameters

As you have already seen, URL query string parameters can be included in a request URL to affect the properties of the Web Dynpro application or to switch to configuration or Customizing mode. The following section contains additional useful parameters and also describes several usable application parameters.

7.3.1 URL Parameters

The URL parameters for Web Dynpro applications are added to the standard URL of a Web Dynpro application. They all start with `sap-wd-` or `sap-`. These are prefixes that are reserved for SAP. Table 7.1 explains selected URL parameters.

Parameter	Value	Description
sap-wd-configId	ID of the application configuration	The application configuration ID is transferred with this parameter. The name of the relevant application parameter is WDCONFIGURATIONID.
sap-config-mode	X, config	Switches the user to configuration mode (config) or Customizing mode (X), provided that he has authorization S_DEVELOP or S_WDR_P13N.
sap-wd-ssrconsole	true	Displays the Web Dynpro console, which provides information on memory usage and runtime, among other things.

Table 7.1 Selected URL Parameters

7.3.2 Application Parameters

It is also possible to include application parameters in a Web Dynpro application in the Web Dynpro Explorer. You can do this on the PARAMETERS tab of the relevant Web Dynpro application. You can either define your own parameters or select one of the predefined parameters. Table 7.2 describes selected predefined parameters.

Parameter	Value	Description
WDCONFIGURATIONID	ID of the application configuration	The name of the associated URL parameter is `sap-wd-configId`.
WDDISABLEUSERPERSONALIZATION	`Boolean`	Disables personalization options (no URL parameter).

Table 7.2 Selected Application Parameters

Note

Note that the parameters specified in the URL are processed first, followed by the standard parameters that are defined for the Web Dynpro application.

7.4 Summary

Customizations to Web Dynpro components and Web Dynpro applications provide an elegant solution for modifying the appearance and behavior of Web Dynpro applications to suit the requirements of users and user groups without the need to undertake additional implementation efforts. The Web Dynpro framework contains the following levels of customization:

- Personalization, which enables the individual user to make changes to the UI
- Customizing, which enables users with the relevant authorizations to configure settings for a group of users

- Configuration, which enables application developers to configure settings in the form of configuration data sets for all users

The customization options that are provided by the Web Dynpro framework without the need for definition and implementation work are known as implicit customizations. If these options are not sufficient for a particular purpose, the application developer can define configuration controllers to create additional customization options. This kind of customization is known as explicit configuration.

Chapter 8, Practical Tips and Hints, describes more extension options provided by the Enhancement Framework, a comprehensive tool for making extensions to Web Dynpro components that is quite different in its approach to the methods discussed so far.

Even with many years of programming experience, you can still discover new Web Dynpro tools and features. This chapter describes these new tools and features.

8 Practical Tips and Hints

The Web Dynpro technology has been enhanced considerably in recent years. For example, the Web Dynpro Debugger is a tool you could only have imagined in the early days of Web Dynpro. Along with the technological progress, the know-how of the Web Dynpro developer community grew steadily. If you were to ask an experienced Web Dynpro today if he would design his first Web Dynpro component in the same way he did in the early days, he would most likely respond in the negative.

This chapter provides you with a discussion of technological innovations, enhanced by our many years of experience. Of course, you cannot substitute practical experience by reading a chapter. However, what we can do is share with you some of our experience. This chapter discusses the following topics:

- **Performance and memory optimization**
  Inadequate server configuration and lack of knowledge concerning the most important rules for developing highly-performing components frequently result in slow and inertly responding Web Dynpro UIs. Optimizing the server configuration and observing simple rules helps you develop Web Dnypro applications with good performance from the very beginning.
- **Debugging Web Dynpro applications**
  The Web Dynpro Debugger allows you to easily navigate through the active components and their sub-objects. For this, the debugger tool displays all active windows, views, controllers, and component usages in a hierarchical structure. The Web Dynpro Debugger facilitates your daily work and is an excellent tool for analyzing components.

- **Popup windows**
  Popup windows have become an essential part of modern UIs. Creating popup windows in Web Dynpro is very easy. Using a few method calls, you can display any window in a popup window.
- **Context change log**
  The context change log enables you to log user input. Using the change log, in turn, allows you to analyze and further process this user input.
- **Hotkeys**
  Hotkeys allow for defining shortcut key combinations to trigger actions such as a click on a button.
- **Context menus**
  By right-clicking on any part of a Web Dynpro application, you can open its context menu. The context menu can be enhanced by your own custom items with very little effort.

Topics Discussed

This chapter discusses the following topics:

- Optimizing the Web Dynpro system configuration
- Checklist for highly-performing Web Dynpro applications
- Analysis tools such as the performance monitor, trace tool, nesting analysis, and DOM analysis
- On-demand instancing of views and components
- Delta rendering
- Debugging Web Dynpro applications
- Creating simple popup windows
- Dialog boxes
- Using the context change log
- Defining hotkeys
- Creating context menus

8.1 Performance and Memory Optimization

If the degree of complexity of Web Dynpro applications increases, their memory consumption and response times to user actions likewise grows.

This can quickly lead to problems caused by high memory consumption or slowly responding UIs. Whereas most of the time high memory consumption does not occur until a later stage in a project – for example, during mass testing projects – slow response times of the UI to user actions can occur as early as the development phase.

Typical errors

However, poor system performance can often be avoided. In practice, it often appears that a lack of knowledge about the fundamental aspects of high-performance Web Dynpro development is the main reason for bad system performance. For example, few Web Dynpro developers know the concept of delta rendering optimization. Similarly, the global instancing of non-needed components is a typical error that frequently occurs.

Areas of analysis

In contrast to the performance and memory optimization of classical dynpros or ABAP applications, when optimizing Web Dynpro UIs, you must not only pay special attention to the application server but also to the client and its interaction with the backend. The following list contains the three most important aspects for optimizing Web Dynpro UIs. Each of them is discussed in this section.

- **Backend runtime**
  From the point of view of Web Dynpro, the backend runtime consists of the runtime of the application logic and the runtime of the Web Dynpro framework. It can be influenced by a large number of factors. For example, you can minimize the backend runtime by optimizing your own application logic. However, you have only limited options to influence the runtime of the Web Dynpro framework. With this, the most important thing is to observe the basic rules for developing highly-performing Web Dynpro applications.
- **Data volume transferred**
  Almost every user action entails an interaction between the frontend and backend. In this context, you should always try to reduce the volume of data that is transferred to a minimum. Because you cannot directly influence the flow of data between the frontend and backend, the transferred data volume can often be used only as an indicator for analyses.

- **Frontend rendering runtime**
  The frontend rendering runtime frequently represents a new aspect to ABAP developers. The data that has been transferred from the backend must be rendered by the browser, and with complex applications, slow client machines, and poor system configuration, the rendering process can take more than one second.

Analysis tools

You can use a number of tools to optimize the performance of Web Dynpro applications. For example, the backend provides the runtime analysis (Transaction SE30), which allows you to search for weak points in the coding as well as the Memory Inspector (Transaction S_MEMORY_INSPECTOR) for analyzing memory consumption. Furthermore, you can use the Debugger including its tools. To analyze the data flow, several tools are available on the Internet such as the Internet Explorer plug-in, HTTPWatch. In addition to the tools mentioned here, you can also use the Web Dynpro Trace tool, which is particularly useful for analyzing the delta rendering process.

The following sections provide an overview of the most important settings parameters, tools, and techniques for developing Web Dynpro applications with good performance.

8.1.1 Optimal System Configuration

By optimizing the system configuration, you can often achieve a significant performance improvement in the Web Dynpro area. An inadequate configuration can, for example, affect both the backend performance and the performance of the browser in the client. The following aspects are particularly important with regard to the performance of Web Dynpro applications:

- The `WD_GLOBAL_SETTING` component.
- The compression of the data flow between the browser and application server.

These two aspects are discussed in greater detail in the following two sections.

Global Web Dynpro Settings

The `WD_GLOBAL_SETTING` component is a standard component provided by SAP, which allows for the global configuration of Web-Dynpro-specific parameters. The parameters can be queried and modified via the `wd_global_setting` application that belongs to the component. Figure 8.1 shows a list of available settings parameters.

Globale Web Dynpro Settings	
Enable Accessibility Mode:	[*]
Delta Rendering:	ON
Do Not Allow Personalization by the User:	[*]
Display Splash Screen:	[*]
Force Use of External Stylesheet:	☑
Extended Help Off by Default (Exception per Field):	[*]
Inline CSS:	☐
Lightspeed Rendering:	☑
Save Application:	[*]
Runtime Repository as Shared Object:	[*]
Scroll Behavior of Tables:	SCROLLBAR
Stylesheet URI:	
Show Animation:	☑

Figure 8.1 Parameters of WD_GLOBAL_SETTING

Performance-relevant settings parameters

Three of the global settings parameters have a direct effect on the performance of Web Dynpro applications. These parameters are INLINE CSS, DELTA RENDERING, and SHOW ANIMATION:

- **Inline-CSS**

  Cascading stylesheets (CSS) are used to design the layout of Web Dynpro applications. They can either be transferred on demand into the output flow to the browser (Inline CSS), or read by the browser from an external CSS file on the server.

  Depending on the usage scenario, the use of Inline CSS can have a positive or negative effect on the performance of Web Dynpro applications. Experience has shown that you can significantly increase the speed of frontline rendering for complex UIs containing many different UI elements if you deactivate Inline CSS. Therefore, it is advisable to check out the optimal configuration of the Inline CSS parameter yourself.

- **Delta rendering**
  Normally, with each roundtrip, all views that are active in a window are transferred to the browser. However, in many cases this is unnecessary. After you have activated the delta rendering function, only the views that have actually changed will be transferred to the browser. This way, you can streamline your system in many respects – in the backend, with regard to the data throughput, and in the frontend. Consequently, you should only disable the delta rendering function if display problems occur.

  Section 8.1.3, Performance Tools, provides a detailed description of delta rendering.

> **Note**
>
> If you cannot find any delta rendering settings parameters, it is probably because delta rendering has only been available as of SAP_BASIS 7.00 Support Package 12.

- **Animations**
  The animation of some events, such as hiding the background during the opening of a popup window, is meant to make your daily work with Web Dynpro more intuitive. However, each animation slows down the workflow. Measurements have shown that a single animation can cost you up to 600 ms of time. You can save this precious time by disabling the animations function.

Compressing the HTTP Data Flow

Both on the Internet and in Web Dynpro, all data is transferred via TCP/IP. To minimize the network load, you can compress the data during the transfer using the GZIP algorithm. With Web Dynpro, this type of compression enables you to reduce the network load generated between the application server and the browser by approximately 85% to 95%. Thus, the compression is particularly useful with long and slow network connections.

You can activate the compression of the HTTP data flow in the HTTP Service Tree Maintenance (Transaction SICF).

Activating the HTTP compression

1. You can find the application by selecting Tools • Administration • Administration • Network from the SAP menu.

2. Skip the initial screen by pressing the [F8] key.
3. In the lower part of the next screen, you can see the HTTP service tree. Select DEFAULT_HOST • SAP • BC and double-click on the WEBDYNPRO node element.
4. Go to the settings item on the SERVICE DATA tab and select YES under COMPRESSION (see Figure 8.2).

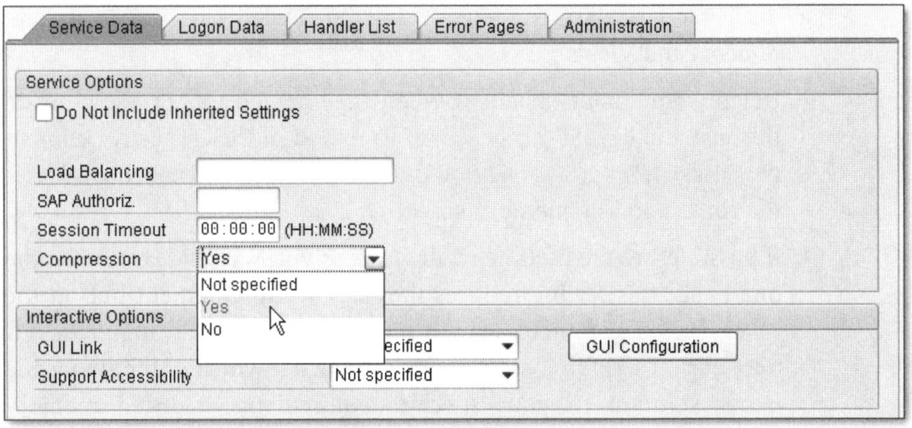

Figure 8.2 Activating HTTP Compression

8.1.2 Checklists for Developing High-Performing Web Dynpro Applications

Prior to looking at more complex topics such as delta rendering, in the following sections, we will take a look at a few basic rules that should be observed to develop Web Dynpro UIs with good performance.

Checklist: Components

At the level of components in particular, errors can occur from the point of view of the application performance, which is very difficult to undo later. The following checklist provides an overview of the most important basic rules of component performance:

- Use components only for programming UIs. Separate your application logic from the Web Dynpro controllers in such a way that you use classes for the application logic and controllers for managing components and views.

- Each component instancing affects the runtime and memory space. Do not develop one-view components but do not exaggerate either by creating large "monster components." Combine all views that are logically related in one component. In most cases, a sound mixture of five to ten views per component is ideal.
- Avoid the global instancing of external components in the `wddoinit( )` method. Do not instance an external component until you want to display it in the UI (see Section 8.1.4, On-Demand Instancing of Components and Views).
- Delete component instances when they are no longer used. To do this, use the `delete_component( )` method of the respective component usage (`IF_WD_COMPONENT_USAGE` type). Deleting an instance releases the corresponding memory space.
- If possible, set the lifetime of all views to WHEN VISIBLE. Note: On the one hand, this setting reduces the memory requirement but on the other hand, it can increase the runtime if a new instancing process is necessary. Therefore, you should ask yourself which of the two is the better solution to your specific requirements: reduced memory requirements or the probability of having to re-instance the views.

Checklist: Context

The context is responsible for the data exchange between the user interface and the Web Dynpro component; it is one of the most important elements of components. Therefore, it is also essential to observe certain rules concerning efficient context programming:

- Do not store all of the data in the context. Use the context only for data that is bound to UI elements.
- Do not create deeply nested contexts.
- Create local contexts as required; for example, in views.
- Avoid long context mapping chains.
- Update the context only if you really need to update the data.
- Use singleton nodes combined with a supply function if master-detail nestings are required.

- Pay attention to the following aspects for all nodes whose attributes are based on DDIC structures:
  - Transfer only required fields as attributes into the node.
  - If possible, use lean structures. Even if you include only a small portion of the fields of a structure in the attribute list of a node, the system internally requires the entire structure.
- Use the `set_static_attributes( )` method instead of `set_attribute( )` to update multiple context attributes of an element. Use the `bind_table( )` method to update entire nodes.

Checklist: UI Elements

Every generated UI element requires memory and computing time on the server, at the network level, and in the browser. For this reason, you should economize on the number of UI elements you use. The following checklist will provide assistance:

- Avoid any kind of scrolling. Do not use container scrolling or the scrolling function of the browser. In particular, with UIs that are ready for input, using scrolling containers reduces performance significantly.
- Avoid deep nestings of containers, groups, and tabstrips. Wherever possible, you should use the REPLACE ROOT ELEMENT function (see Chapter 2, Web Dynpro Architecture).
- If possible, do not use the UI element `Tree`.
- Use either `RowRepeater` or `MultiPane` for repeated UIs. Do not nest these two UI elements.
- Modify your UI elements only if they have really changed.
- If possible, avoid making changes to UI elements via view method `wddomodifyview( )`. Instead, use the importing parameter `first_time` for this.

8.1.3 Performance Tools

With the Web Dynpro framework, SAP provides a number of useful analysis tools. These tools specifically developed for Web Dynpro let you check your applications in a variety of ways, and include:

Web Dynpro analysis tools

- Performance monitor
- Nesting analysis
- Document Object Model (DOM) analysis
- Trace tool (contains the following sub-tools: delta rendering change tracking, detailed memory allocation information, and navigation information)

Traditional performance analysis tools

In addition to these tools, you can also use the traditional ABAP tools for performance measurement such as the runtime analysis, which we will briefly describe in this section.

> **Note**
>
> The tools and features described in this section require the availability of lightspeed rendering. Lightspeed rendering has been available as of SAP_BASIS 7.01.

Performance Monitor

[✎] The performance monitor allows you to easily display the most important performance-relevant key figures such as current memory consumption, end-to-end response time, as well as server-side and client-side rendering times.

Starting the performance monitor

1. To start the performance monitor, you can either append the `sap-wd-perfMonitor=X` parameter to the URL of your application, or simultaneously press the [Ctrl] + [Shift] + [Alt] + [P] keys in your browser. A small box with the performance monitor should appear in the upper right-hand corner (see Figure 8.3).

> **Tip**
>
> When you press the [Ctrl] + [Shift] + [Alt] + [H] keys simultaneously in the browser, a small popup window opens displaying an overview of all [Ctrl] + [Shift] + [Alt] shortcuts available.

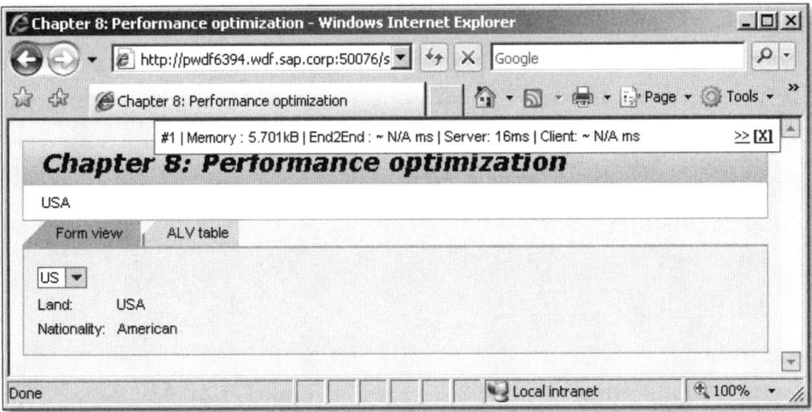

Figure 8.3 Performance Monitor

> **Caution**
>
> The data displayed in the Web Dynpro performance monitor is a set of values that lets you get a rough idea of performance; these values are by no means exact and cannot be used for comparative analyses.

Displaying details

2. To enhance the performance monitor and view additional details in different categories, click on the >> link.

3. Figure 8.4 shows the MEMORY category as an example. This category lets you view current memory consumption and the number of active components, active controllers, context nodes, and context elements. In addition, you can write a memory dump that can be analyzed using Transaction S_MEMORY_INSPECTOR.

Web Dynpro for ABAP SSR Console #3 << [X]

Overview | **Performance** | **Memory** | **Rendering** | **System Infos**

Write Memory Snapshot

Timestamp of measurement 25.05.2009 21:27:06

Memory	5.712kB
Max memory in step	8.183
Number of active WD-Components	2
Number of Controllers	6
Number of Context Nodes	10
Number of Context Elements	244

Figure 8.4 MemoryPerformance Monitor Category

Nesting Analysis

To trace deeply nested (and often unnecessary) containers, you can use the nesting analysis tool. This tool uses colors to highlight the different HTML tags used, as follows:

- `<TABLE>`
  Red highlighting
- `<DIV>`
  Blue highlighting
- `<SPAN>`
  Green highlighting

Starting the nesting analysis

You can start the nesting analysis in the browser window by pressing the [Ctrl] + [Shift] + [Alt] + [O] keys simultaneously. Figure 8.5 shows the nesting of an ALV table.

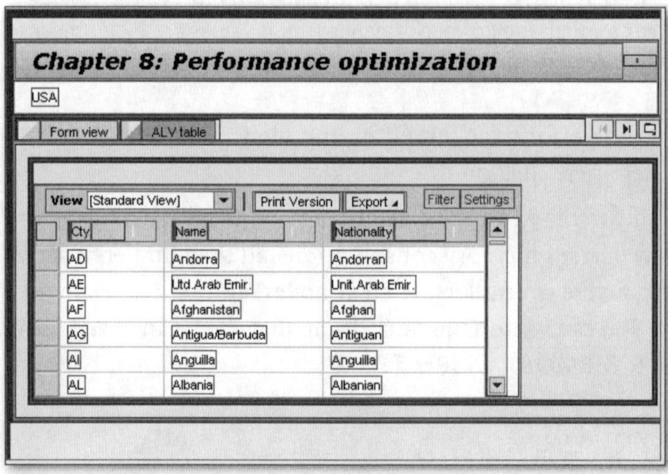

Figure 8.5 Nesting Analysis of an ALV Table

Goal of the nesting analysis

The nesting analysis lets you quickly identify and remove weak points. The higher the number of nestings that appear in a UI during analysis, the higher the number of UI elements that are generated in the backend, transferred to the client, and rendered by the browser in the frontend.

For performance reasons, you should reduce the rendering of HTML tables to an absolute minimum. HTML tables are used primarily with

MatrixLayout; in many cases, you can use the FlowLayout or GridLayout as an alternative.

Document Object Model Analysis

The Document Object Model (DOM) is a specification for accessing HTML or XML documents defined by the World Wide Web Consortium. DOM specifies the display of documents in a pedigree, which are interconnected using relationships.

Document Object Model analysis

The DOM analysis is particularly useful for checking the complexity of Web Dynpro applications. It simply counts the number of elements contained in a document and outputs this number in a popup window (see Figure 8.6). You can start the DOM analysis in the browser window by pressing the `Ctrl` + `Shift` + `Alt` + `D` keys simultaneously.

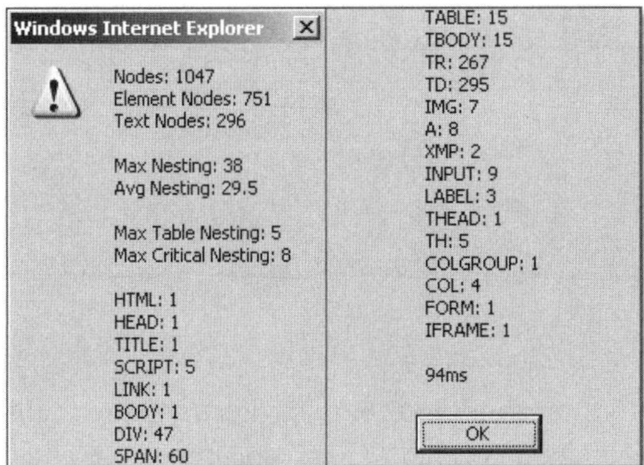

Figure 8.6 DOM Analysis for a Web Dynpro Application

Trace Tool

The trace tool is the most powerful tool among the Web Dynpro analysis tools. After it has been started, it logs entries about navigation events, memory consumption, events, components, and view changes during each roundtrip between the application server and the browser. You can either view these entries directly in the browser or download them in a ZIP file.

Using the trace tool

You can activate the trace tool in two different ways. The easiest way to do this is to simultaneously press the `Ctrl` + `Shift` + `Alt` + `C` keys in the browser window of the application to be analyzed. After you have activated the trace tool, a second browser window containing the trace tool opens below the window of the active application. Figure 8.7 shows this window.

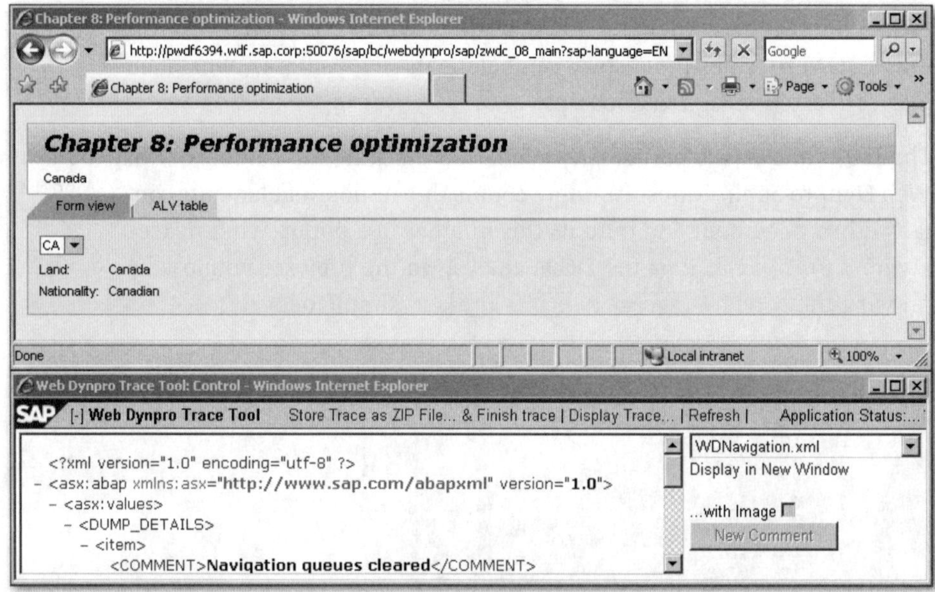

Figure 8.7 Web Dynpro Trace Tool

The dropdown list on the right enables you to toggle between the available traces. Most of the traces are displayed as XML documents. In addition to the display function, you can also store a comment for each trace roundtrip. When the measurements are finished, you can download the entire trace, including the comments in a ZIP file, by clicking on SAVE TRACE AS ZIP FILE... & END TRACE.

Transaction WD_TRACE_TOOL

Alternatively, you can activate the trace tool using Transaction WD_TRACE_TOOL (see Figure 8.8). Click on the ACTIVATE FOR THIS USER button within this transaction and confirm the two popup windows that appear by clicking on OK. Then, restart the Web Dynpro application. Aside from enabling you to activate the trace tool, the transaction also allows you to retroactively download completed traces in a ZIP file.

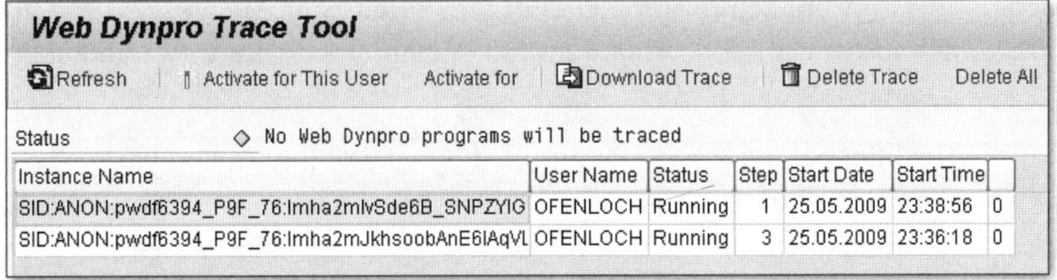

Figure 8.8 Transaction WD_TRACE_TOOL

More Tools

In addition to the tools that are specific to Web Dynpro, SAP provides the traditional tools for performance measurement such as the runtime analysis. Thus, you can also use the following tools for measuring and analyzing Web Dynpro applications:

- **Memory Inspector (Transaction S_MEMORY_INSPECTOR)**
  The Memory Inspector lets you carry out a detailed analysis of the memory dumps stored in the performance monitor.
- **Runtime analysis (Transaction SE30)**
  The runtime analysis is particularly useful for analyzing your own application coding. This type of analysis allows you to quickly identify weak points in your coding.
- **Workload Monitor (Transaction STAD)**
  The Workload Monitor can be used to exactly measure the response time of the application server during a roundtrip. In contrast to the runtime analysis, the measurement process does not distort the results.

8.1.4 On-Demand Instancing of Views and Components

An error that occurs very often, and that is particularly serious from the point of view of performance, is the global and premature instancing of non-visible views and components. These should not be instanced until you really need them; that is, when you want to display them in the browser. After using them for the last time, you should delete these views and components (`when visible/delete_component`). If you apply these rules, you can minimize the memory requirement of an application and ensure that instancings are equally distributed across the entire lifetime of the application.

Instancing views and components

To avoid premature instancing of views and components, you should first answer the following question: When exactly are views and components instanced?

The lifetime of a view is determined by its visibility. When you make a view visible, the system instances this view and keeps it in memory until the component is released. If its VIEW LIFETIME setting was set to `when visible`, it will be removed when the status changes to invisible.

However, you must not confuse the term "visible" with the normal meaning of the word as used in everyday speech: For example, a view can have the status "visible" in the system even though you cannot see it in the browser. Whether a view is visible or invisible to the system depends entirely on the window of the respective component. A view is instanced if it is embedded in a visible window and flagged as a default view or if it is addressed through its inbound plug. If the view is an interface view of an external component, this component is automatically instanced with its interface view. In addition, you can also instance external components using the `create_component( )` method of their component usage.

Behavior with Cross-Component Mapping

If you define a cross-component mapping between two or more components, these will be instanced irrespective of the visibility of their views.

Example

Let us now try to clarify what has been said in the previous paragraph using a small example. Figure 8.9 shows a simple application with two tabs and the associated window structure. The FORM VIEW tab is displayed in the browser. The user cannot see the other tab, ALV TABLE; that is, it is invisible to him. You might therefore assume that the `TABLE` interface view that is integrated in the second tab has not yet been instanced; this assumption is wrong though. It is the `W_MAIN` window that is solely responsible for the visibility of the `TABLE` interface view, not the browser window. However, because the `TABLE` view was flagged as a default view in the window, it is visible to the system. Consequently, it is instanced and transferred to the browser immediately upon startup of the application.

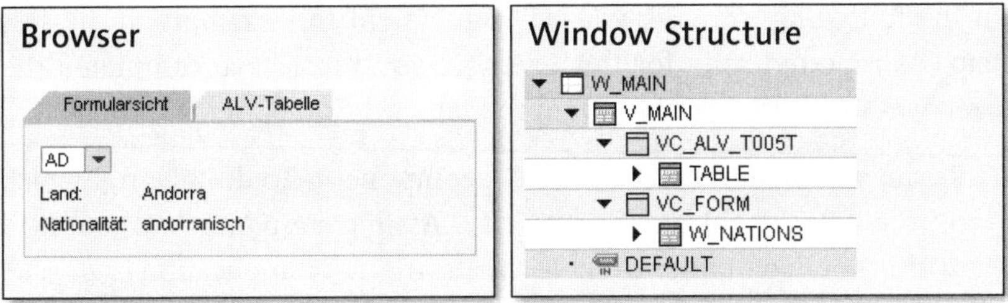

Figure 8.9 Visibility of Views

Restructuring the window

Now that you know that the window always instances all visible views, the next question is: How can you make the views that do not display in the browser invisible?

To accelerate the startup process of the sample application, you must prevent the automatic instancing of the visible TABLE interface view. The window must recognize the status of the TABLE interface view as invisible.

1. For this, you must first integrate an EMPTYVIEW in view container VC_ALV_T005T and flag this view as a default view.
2. Then, create a new outbound plug in V_MAIN to enable the navigation to the TABLE interface view. Link this outbound plug in the window with the default inbound plug of the TABLE interface view.
3. Finally, create an event that allows for navigating to the ALV TABLE tab. In this event, you trigger the outbound plug to the ALV table.

Figure 8.10 shows the restructured window structure.

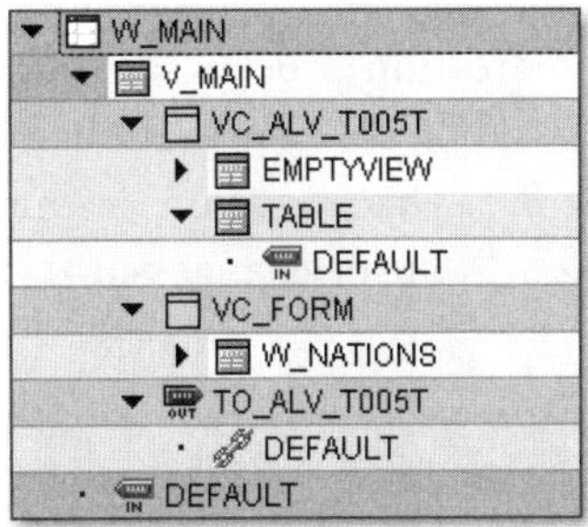

Figure 8.10 Invisible Interface View TABLE after Restructuring of W_MAIN

In the following exercise, you will implement this example in the system. As a prerequisite for this exercise, you must have completed the exercises in Chapter 5, Web Dynpro Standard Components.

1. Create a copy of the ZWDC_05_MAIN component. To do this, right-click on the component and select COPY. Assign the name ZWDC_08_MAIN to the new component. Then, create the new application zwdc_08_main. Next, adapt the label of the page header in V_MAIN to your requirements.

Measurement

2. Activate the component and test the application. Start the performance monitor and activate its detailed view. Go to the MEMORY tab and take note of the memory consumption and the number of active components.
3. Then, select the PERFORMANCE tab. Select a different element from the country ID dropdown list and then note the amount of data transferred during the roundtrip.
4. Delete the external context mapping. This will prevent the on-demand instancing of the ALV table. To do this, open the path COMPONENT USAGES • ALV_T005T • INTERFACECONTROLLER_USAGE in the object list of the component. Then, right-click on the DATA and select DELETE EXTERNAL MAPPING.
5. Go to the component controller and open the wddoinit( ) method. Delete the coding for the manual instancing of the ALV component from the method, up to the call of init_alv_t005t( ).
6. Navigate to V_MAIN. Create the outbound plug to_alv_t005t. Next, define a component usage for the interface controller of the ALV component. Select the LAYOUT tab and create the TAB_SELECTED action for the TabStrip event, ONSELECT. During the creation process, activate the flag for TRANSFER UI EVENT PARAMETERS and fill the new event handler method with the coding from Listing 8.1. This way, you ensure that the ALV component is instanced when the user changes to the ALV tab.

```
DATA: lo_cmp_usage             TYPE REF TO if_wd_
component_                                  usage,
      lo_interfacecontroller TYPE REF TO iwci_salv_wd_table,
      lo_node_t005t          TYPE REF TO if_wd_context_node.
CASE tab.
```

```
  WHEN 'TAB_1'.
    " Navigate to ALV table
    wd_this->fire_to_alv_t005t_plg( ).
    " Instance ALV component
    lo_cmp_usage = wd_this->wd_cpuse_alv_t005t( ).
    IF lo_cmp_usage->has_active_component( ) IS INITIAL.
      lo_cmp_usage->create_component( ).
      " Display node T005T in ALV table
      lo_interfacecontroller = wd_this->wd_cpifc_
alv_      t005t( ).
      lo_node_t005t =
        wd_context->get_child_node( wd_this->wdctx_t005t ).
      lo_interfacecontroller->set_data(
        r_node_data = lo_node_t005t ).
      ENDIF.
  ENDCASE.
```

Listing 8.1 Event Handler Method ONACTIONTAB_SELECTED

7. Go to the `W_MAIN` window. Integrate an `EMPTYVIEW` in view container `VC_ALV_T005T`, and flag this view as a default view. Then, bind outbound plug `to_alv_t005t` to the `default` inbound plug of the `TABLE` interface view.
8. Activate the component and test the application. Carry out the same performance measurement as you did at the beginning of this exercise.

Testing the application/ measuring

Comments on the exercise

The number of active components should have gone down from three to two. Similarly, the memory consumption of the application should have decreased considerably. Because the ALV table is now invisible to the window for the first time, it is no longer transferred automatically to the frontend. Only when the user selects the ALV table will the system read the data needed for displaying the table.

Without question, this exercise is far from perfect. For example, it would be conceivable to have the `delete_component( )` method remove the component usage that becomes invisible every time the user changes the tab. However, this gain in extra memory space would also result in a longer runtime during the next tab change. Thus, it is advisable to decide for each individual case whether you prefer better performance or lower memory consumption values. For components you only need once, it makes a lot of sense to delete such components right after their use.

8.1.5 Delta Rendering

Lightspeed rendering

The introduction of lightspeed rendering technology heralded a new Web Dynpro era; lightspeed replaces the traditional Web Dynpro rendering technology. Lightspeed rendering is based on the AJAX technology (Asynchronous JavaScript and XML). AJAX enables asynchronous communication between the browser and web server and is thus one of the key technologies for modern and powerful Web UIs. In addition, lightspeed offers a significantly larger set of UI elements and features.

Delta rendering

Along with lightspeed rendering came delta rendering. Delta rendering allows you to update only the portion of a page that has been modified by the application. Therefore, delta rendering leads to a significant improvement in performance under many circumstances because only a portion of the UI – instead of the entire UI – must be generated in the backend, then transferred, and then rendered in the browser. More complex UIs, in particular, benefit considerably from delta rendering with respect to performance.

Example

Figure 8.11 shows a simple example to demonstrate what delta rendering does. The example consists of views: an outer view containing a customer table and a second view embedded in the outer one, containing detailed information about customers that can be selected in the outer view. If a user changes the detailed information stored for a specific customer and presses the [Enter] key, a roundtrip occurs between the server and browser in the background. Depending on whether delta rendering has been activated, the server either transfers only the modified view (inner view), or all visible views to the browser where they will be rendered. The fact that only a portion of the UI is transferred has a positive effect on the server runtime, the network load, and also on the rendering time of the browser.

However, there is more you need to know about delta rendering. Although as an application developer you do not need to worry about handling the deltas (Web Dynpro does that for you), you should know how the delta rendering process works. This way, you will know to what you have to pay attention when developing your applications to ensure that delta rendering can be carried out without problems.

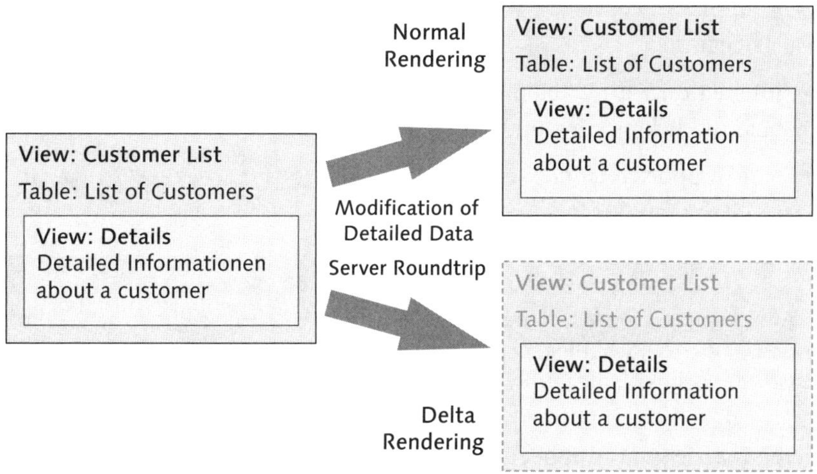

Figure 8.11 Example of the Delta Rendering Effect

Delta Rendering Functionality

Basic principles of delta rendering

Delta rendering is based on views. Each view has a what is called a *dirty flag*. If during a roundtrip, a visual change is made to a view, the system flags the entire view as *dirty*. At the end of each roundtrip, the rendering engine of the server analyzes the dirty flags of all visible views and generates a delta file for the browser from the smallest common superset of dirty views.

Dirty views

For delta rendering to be fully efficient, you must reduce the number of changes to the visual area of the views to an absolute minimum. Consequently, the question that arises is when or how a view can be declared dirty. The following list provides examples of actions that flag views as dirty:

- Changes to the context
  - Any changes to nodes or elements (attributes, properties, etc.)
  - Irrespective of whether the context change affects the currently visible view area

- Changes to UI elements
  - Typically in `wddomodifyview( )`
  - `set_visible( )`, `set_enabled( )` and others
- Navigation
- Interaction with UI elements (by pressing the [Enter] key in an input field or clicking on a button, etc.)
- Non-supported UI elements: `TimedTrigger`, `Gantt`, `Network`, `InteractiveForm`, and `OfficeControl`

Attention!

Any change to the visual areas of a view flags this view as dirty. The system does not check whether such changes also entail a value change. Note that views are already updated when just calling a changing method.

Granularity of changes

Even if a view has not been flagged as dirty, it can happen that the view must be rendered again. It is one of the specific features of delta rendering that only one area is updated at a time. Accordingly, the innermost of all common views that have been changed is the one rendered again. In the most adverse case, this is the outermost view of the application. To clarify this, Figure 8.12 contains three examples:

- **View A**
  View `A` has been changed. Although the `A_1` and `A_2` views are clean, they are children of `A` and must therefore be updated as well.
- **View B**
  The changes to view `B_1` only have a local effect. Views `B` and `B_2` do not need to be updated.
- **View C**
  Changes are made to views `C_1` and `C_2`. However, because only one area is updated at a time, view `C` will also be included in the update process.

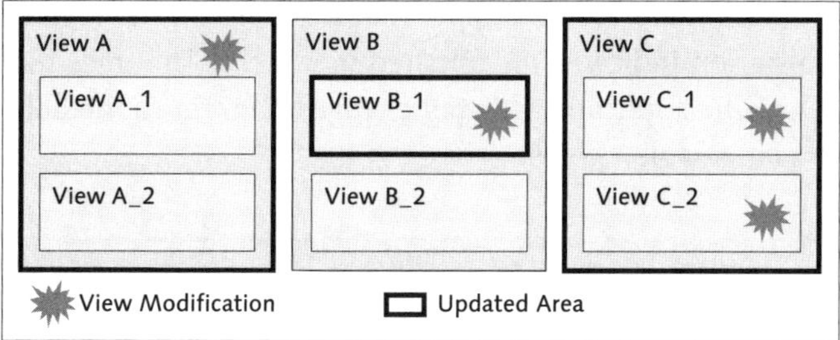

Figure 8.12 Rendering Clean Views

Consequences for Application Developers

Based on the information as to how the status of views changes to dirty, and in which cases they must be rendered anew, developers can draw a number of conclusions regarding the development of Web Dynpro UIs:

- Avoid making unnecessary changes to the context and UI elements.
- Compare the actual value with the planned value in advance.

```
IF lo_inputfield->get_visible( ) EQ abap_true.
  lo_input_field->set_visible( abap_false ).
ENDIF.
```

- Make a detailed plan of the structure and nesting of your views in advance. For example, answer the following questions:
  - Which of the views of a window change most often?
  - How can I keep a delta as small as possible?
  - How can I avoid using UI elements for data input, such as input fields, in outer views?
  - Would it even make sense to integrate additional views to keep the delta small?

Analyses using the Trace Tool

The trace tool enables you to very easily analyze the delta rendering in Web Dynpro applications. For example, after each user action, the tool displays an updated area within a green frame. In addition, the trace tool provides a list of the reasons for updates in a table.

Let us take a look at Figure 8.13. A frame that is displayed in green in the running application indicates the updated view area. The trace tool that displays below the application lists all changes relevant to the delta rendering process in a table.

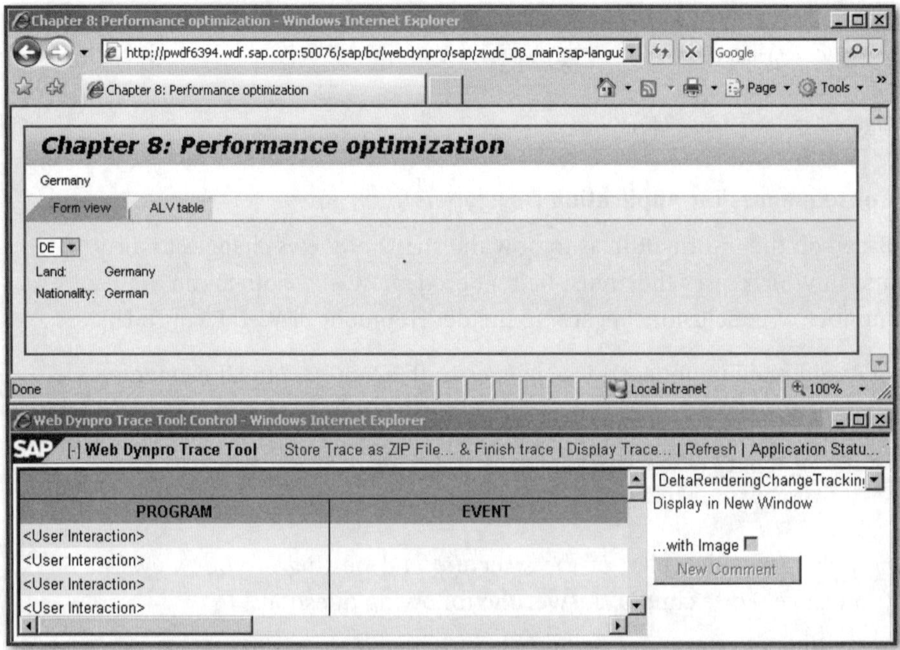

Figure 8.13 Tracing the Delta Rendering

In the following exercise, you will learn about the details of carrying out a delta rendering analysis using the Web Dynpro trace tool. For this purpose, you will analyze and discuss the `ZWDC_08_MAIN` component you created in the previous exercise. If you have not completed this exercise, you can also use the `ZWDC_05_MAIN` component from Chapter 5, Web Dynpro Standard Components.

1. Open the `ZWDC_08_MAIN` component and start its application.

Starting the trace tool

2. Start the trace tool. To do so, use Transaction `WD_TRACE_TOOL`, or go to the browser window and press the [Ctrl] + [Shift] + [Alt] + [C] keys simultaneously; if this key combination does not work, the focus is probably not on that page. The trace tool should now appear in a new window below your application.

3. Go to the delta rendering tool of the trace tool. To do this, select DELTARENDERINGCHANGETRACKING.XML from the trace tool's dropdown list (see Figure 8.14).

Figure 8.14 Trace Tool – Changing the Tool

4. Select a different country in the country ID dropdown list. A green frame (see Figure 8.15) around all visible elements indicates that the entire UI was rendered again and transferred to the browser. In this example, there are two reasons for this:

Changes to the dropdown list

 - If you change the lead selection, visible areas both in the page header and in the FORM VIEW tab must be updated.
 - The T005T node is mapped across the two views, V_NATIONS and V_MAIN.

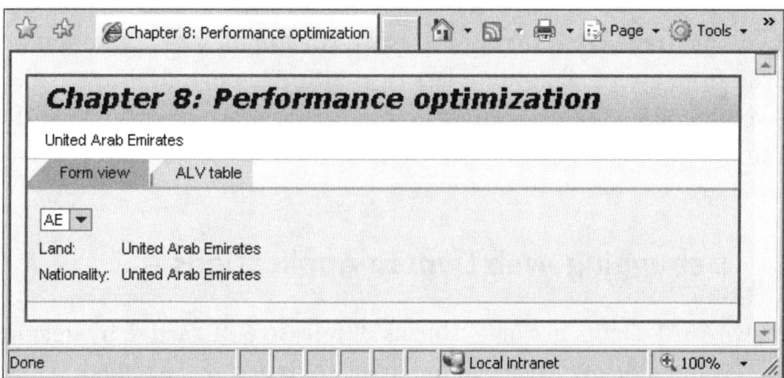

Figure 8.15 Changing the Dropdown List

5. Then, take a look at the trace tool (see Figure 8.16). The table of the delta rendering tool indicates that a <USER INTERACTION> has occurred in the ZWDC_05_NATIONS component of the V_NATIONS controller. This is because you changed the lead selection. Due to this change,

V_NATIONS has been flagged as dirty. What this table does not contain is the V_MAIN view of the main component, although it is also affected via the mapping of the T005T node.

CHANGES									
PROGRAM	EVENT	LINE	COMPONENT_NAME	CONTROLLER_NAME	OBJECT_TYPE	OBJECT_NAME	SUB_OBJECT_NAME	SUB_OBJECT_TYPE	REASON
<User Interaction>		0	ZWDC_05_NATIONS	V_NATIONS					ClientEvent
<User Interaction>		0	ZWDC_05_NATIONS	V_NATIONS					ClientEvent
<User Interaction>		0	ZWDC_08_MAIN	COMPONENTCONTROLLER	NodeName	T005T			ContextLeadSelectionChange
<User Interaction>		0	ZWDC_08_MAIN	V_MAIN	NodeName	T005T			ContextLeadSelectionChange
<User Interaction>		0	ZWDC_05_NATIONS	COMPONENTCONTROLLER	NodeName	T005T			ContextLeadSelectionChange
<User Interaction>		0	ZWDC_05_NATIONS	V_NATIONS	NodeName	T005T			ContextLeadSelectionChange

Figure 8.16 Trace Tool – Changing the Lead Selection

Scrolling through the ALV Table

6. Go to the ALV TABLE tab and scroll through the table a bit. At this stage, only the ALV table should have a green frame. Then, check the delta rendering log of the trace tool. As you can see, changes have been made to the VIEW_TABLE of the ALV component. However, these changes were limited to views in the ALV component, which means that the update could also be limited to the ALV table.

A look ahead

In this section, you learned about several aspects of the delta rendering process and the functionality of Web Dynpro. Delta rendering and on-demand instancing provide the greatest potential for improving Web Dynpro performance. Experience has shown, for example, that the data volume transferred for simple entries in complex UIs can often be reduced from an initial 20Kb to less than 3Kb. This significantly smaller data volume has a dramatic effect on the performance of both the back-end and the frontend.

8.2 Debugging Web Dynpro Applications

The new ABAP Debugger (available as of release 6.40; active by default since release 7.0) provides a number of tools for the detailed analysis of applications at runtime, including a Web Dynpro debugging tool. You can use the Web Dynpro Debugger to quickly and easily navigate through the tree of active components and analyze their objects:

- Controllers (window, view, component, and custom controllers)
  - Attributes
  - Nodes and elements of the context

- Views
  - UI elements and their properties
- Window structures

[✎] This section describes how the Web Dynpro Debugger works in a live system. For this purpose, you will debug the `ZWDC_08_MAIN` component. Of course, you can also analyze any other component of your choice in the Debugger.

Setting a breakpoint

1. Open the `ZWDC_08_MAIN` component.
2. Go to the component controller and set a breakpoint in the first line of the `wddoinit( )` method. To do this, move the cursor to the first line and click on the breakpoint icon (see Figure 8.17).

Figure 8.17 Setting a Breakpoint

3. Then, go to the `V_MAIN` view and set another breakpoint in the `wddomodifyview( )` method.

Starting the application and the debugger

4. Start the component via the application. The new Debugger should open in a SAP GUI window.

   If the classical debugger opens instead, you can activate the new Debugger via the menu of the component. To do this, select UTILITIES • SETTINGS • ABAP EDITOR • DEBUGGING and click on the NEW DEBUGGER radio button.

Problem: The Breakpoint Does Not Work

If your applications do not stop despite the fact that they contain an activated breakpoint, one of the following tips usually provides help:

- Check how many SAP GUI windows you have opened. The majority of systems are configured in such a way that you can open six windows at the same time in one system.
- Check on which application server the breakpoint was created. The Debugger will stop only if the browser uses the same server.

Replacing a tool

5. Open the Web Dynpro Debugger. To do this, click on the Replace Tool icon, as shown in Figure 8.18. In the popup window, select the Web Dynpro tool from the Special Tools menu.

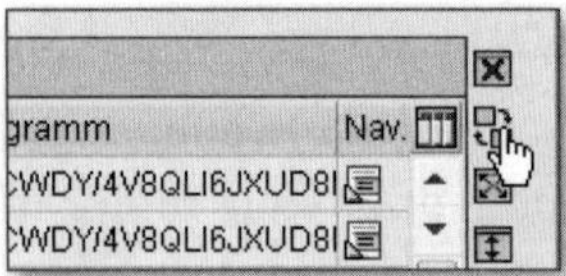

Figure 8.18 Selecting the Debugger Tool

> **Tip**
>
> To avoid having to reconfigure all tools for every new debugging session, you can save the layout in the Debugger. To do this, select Debugger • Debugger Session • Save Layout from the menu.

Exploring the debugger

6. The system now displays the Web Dynpro Debugger (see Figure 8.19). Take a look at the component usages for the `ZWDC_08_MAIN` component. As you can see, there is only one component at this point.

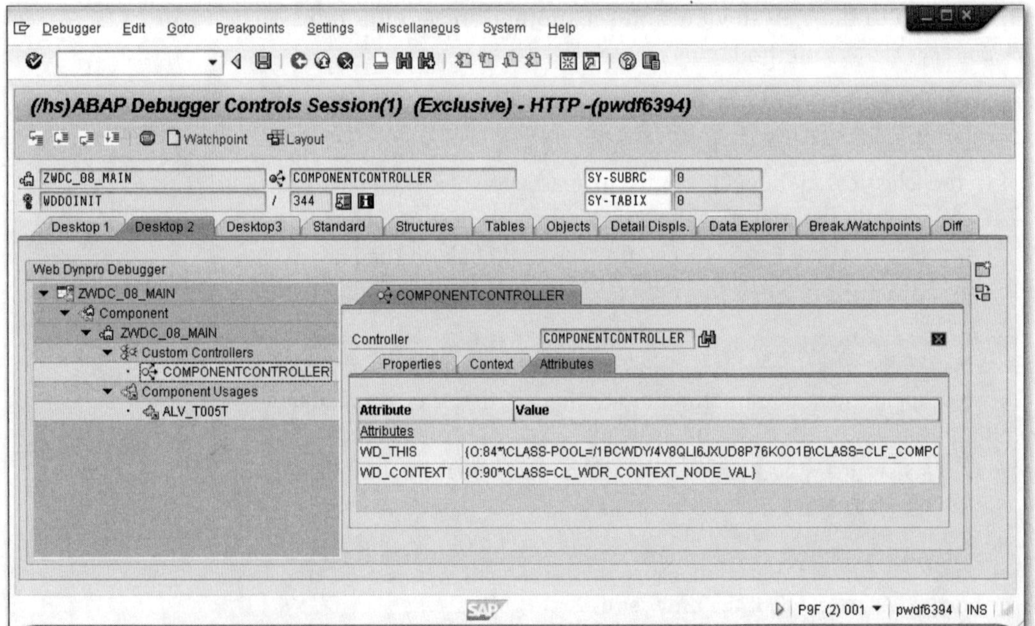

Figure 8.19 Web Dynpro Debugger After Startup

Instancing the component

7. Next, go to the view that contains the SOURCE CODE Debugger tool. Use the Debugger to jump over the `create_component( )` method. Calling this method simultaneously generates an instance of the nations component.
8. Return to the Web Dynpro view and compare the component usages with each other. You will see that there is now an instance of the nations component. Exit the Debugger by pressing the [F8] key twice.
9. At this point, your application has been fully instanced. Start the Debugger again by selecting a different country in the dropdown list. This action should cause the breakpoint in `wddomodifyview( )` to open the Debugger.

Context analysis

In addition to the component controller and component usage, the Web Dynpro tool now also displays views and windows. Open the `V_MAIN` view and go to the CONTEXT tab. This tab allows you to view the details of all existing nodes and elements of the context such as the values stored in the elements (see Figure 8.20).

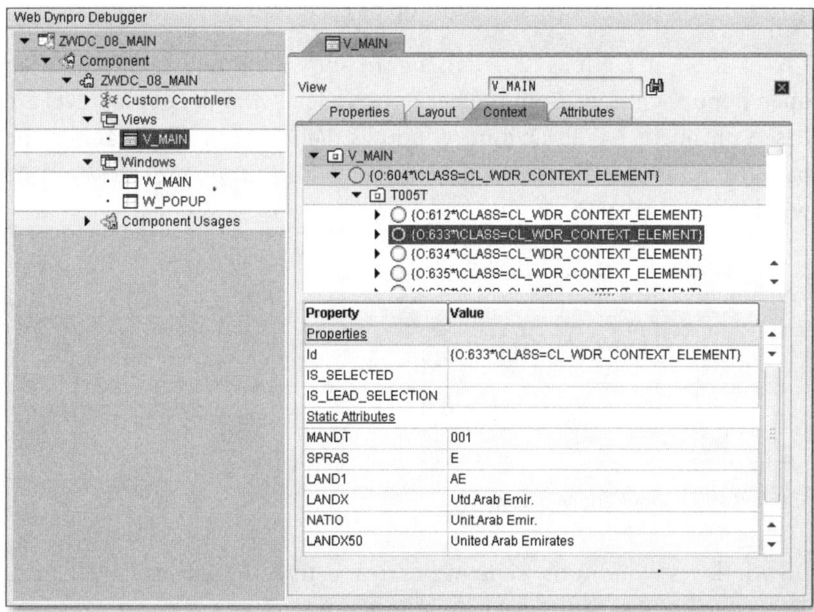

Figure 8.20 View Context in Detail

The Web Dynpro Debugger is especially useful for taking a quick look at the context. It allows for fast navigation through your components to obtain an overview of all active contexts. This Web Dynpro tool is also very useful for performance analyses. For example, a few clicks of the mouse enable you to see which components are currently active and which views are currently being used in the window.

8.3 Popup Windows

Using popup windows makes sense in many application scenarios. From simple popup messages to OK/CANCEL queries to complex UIs with any number of UI elements – countless scenarios are conceivable for the use of popup windows.

Modularity of popups Web Dynpro currently supports only modal popup windows. As long as a modal popup is opened, the level below the popup displays in a darker color and does not allow for data entries. It is also possible to open another popup window from within the existing one. This way, you can generate any number of levels on top of each other.

Levels in detail Take a look at Figure 8.21. This figure shows an application with an open popup window. Both the background level and the popup level are based on normal Web Dynpro windows. Whereas in this example the background is based on the W_MAIN window, the popup uses the W_POPUP window to display the popup level.

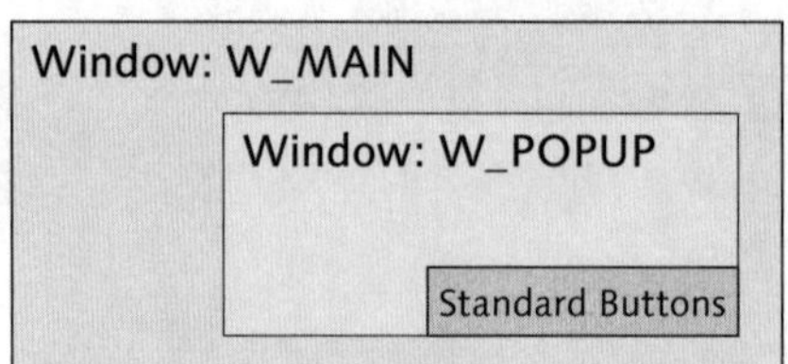

Figure 8.21 Popups and Windows

All windows work in the same way, irrespective of their displayed level. Thus, you can integrate views in a popup window in the usual manner and create a network of the views using plugs. Each popup has what is called a *window manager* that enables you to manage the basic properties of the popup window. You can use the window manager to define the popup title, and its dimensions or to define the default buttons such as CLOSE, OK, or CANCEL. The following sections describe how you can develop popup windows.

8.3.1 Creating Popup Windows

The window manager IF_WD_WINDOW_MANAGER allows you to create popup windows. The window manager provides three different methods for this, as shown in Table 8.1.

Method	Description
create_window( )	Creates a modal popup.
create_window_for_cmp_usage( )	Creates a modal popup for a component usage.
create_popup_to_confirm( )	Creates a simple dialog box.

Table 8.1 Overview of Window Manager Methods

Obtaining the window manager

Before you can initialize a popup window, you must obtain an object instance of the window manager from the component. You can get this object instance using the get_window_manager( ) method of component API IF_WD_COMPONENT. You can get the component API of the IF_WD_COMPONENT type via the wd_get_api( ) component controller method. Listing 8.2 shows how you can use the component controller to obtain the window manager.

```
DATA: lo_component_api   TYPE REF TO if_wd_component,
      lo_window_manager TYPE REF TO if_wd_window_manager.
lo_component_api  = wd_this->wd_get_api( ).
lo_window_manager = lo_component_api->get_window_manager( ).
```

Listing 8.2 Reading a Window Manager Instance

Creating a simple popup window

The create_window( ) method enables you to create popup windows. Calling this method does not pose any problem. You only need to transfer the mandatory window_name parameter during the call. The framework then initializes the window (IF_WD_WINDOW type) and returns its instance. In addition to the window name, you can also provide several other parameters such as the popup title (title) or the default buttons (button_kind).

Don't worry! The following exercise describes how to use the most important parameters of create_window in the system. Listing 8.3 contains an example of the creation of a simple popup window.

```
DATA: lo_window TYPE REF TO if_wd_window.
* Create simple window
CALL METHOD lo_window_manager->create_window
  EXPORTING
    window_name = 'W_POPUP'
    title       = 'Popup Window'
    button_kind = if_wd_window=>co_buttons_close
  RECEIVING
    window      = lo_window.
```

Listing 8.3 Creating a Simple Popup Window

Popups from external components If you want to integrate an interface view of an external component directly in a popup, you can use the window manager method create_window_for_cmp_usage( ) instead of create_window( ). If you do so, you must transfer an interface view, interface_view_name, and the component usage component_usage_name instead of a window.

Dialog boxes In many cases it is advisable to use a Web Dynpro dialog box instead of custom popup windows. You can create dialog boxes using the window manager method create_popup_to_confirm( ); the button_kind parameter allows you to define the buttons to be displayed in the dialog box.

The message_type parameter enables you to define the type of the dialog box. For this, Web Dynpro provides the following types: INFORMATION, WARNING, ERROR, CANCEL, and QUESTION. Figure 8.22 shows a simple dialog box of the WARNING type, which was generated via Listing 8.4.

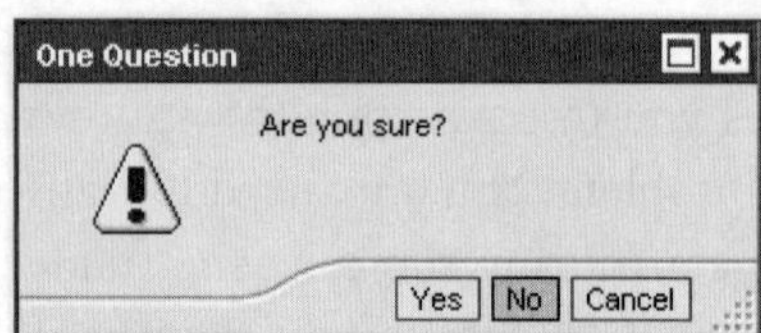

Figure 8.22 Dialog Box Created via create_popup_to_confirm( )

```
DATA: lo_window TYPE REF TO if_wd_window,
      lt_text   TYPE string_table.
APPEND 'Are you sure?' TO lt_text.
* Create dialog box
CALL METHOD lo_window_manager->create_popup_to_confirm
  EXPORTING
    text           = lt_text
    button_kind    = if_wd_window=>co_buttons_yesnocancel
    message_type   = if_wd_window=>co_msg_type_warning
    close_button   = abap_true
    window_title   = 'One Question'
    default_button = if_wd_window=>co_button_no
  RECEIVING
    result         = lo_window.
```

Listing 8.4 Creating a Dialog Box

Opening and closing popups

If you have already tried to reproduce the previous examples in the system, you were probably disappointed by the fact that no popup window opened. This is because one small building block was still missing for the display of a popup window. After creating the popup window, you must open it by using its `open( )` method. You can close the popup by calling `close( )`.

Opening External Browser Windows

You can also use the window manager to open Web Dynpro windows or any kind of address in external browser windows. For this, the window manager provides the `create_external_window( )` method.

[✎]

In the following exercise, you will create a new component with two windows: `W_MAIN` and `W_POPUP`. After you have started the application, you want a new popup window with window `W_POPUP` to open automatically.

Preparatory work

1. Create a component called `ZWDC_08_POPUP` with window `W_MAIN` and view `V_MAIN`. Create a new Web Dynpro application for this component.

2. Create a new V_POPUP view. This view is supposed to be displayed in a popup window. Integrate a TextView element containing the text "Hello Popup!" in the view. Save the view and create a W_POPUP window. Integrate V_POPUP into W_POPUP.

Opening the popup

3. Go to the wddoinit( ) method in the V_MAIN view. Implement the coding required to open the popup window. The popup should provide the buttons YES/NO/CANCEL. Listing 8.5 contains the solution.

```
DATA: lo_component_api  TYPE REF TO if_wd_component,
      lo_window_manager TYPE REF TO if_wd_window_manager,
      lo_window TYPE REF TO if_wd_window.
lo_component_api = wd_comp_controller->wd_get_api( ).
lo_window_manager = lo_component_api->get_window_manager( ).
* Create window
CALL METHOD lo_window_manager->create_window
  EXPORTING
    window_name = 'W_POPUP'
    title       = 'Popup Window'
    button_kind = if_wd_window=>co_buttons_yesnocancel
  RECEIVING
    window      = lo_window.
* Open window
lo_window->open( ).
```

Listing 8.5 Opening the W_POPUP Window in the Popup

Changing the Window Size

By default, Web Dynpro defines the size of a popup window automatically. However, you can change the size manually by calling the set_window_size( ) method in the window object.

Testing the application

4. Activate the component and start the application. The popup window should open with W_POPUP and V_POPUP immediately after the startup process. To close the popup, you must click on one of the buttons. Figure 8.23 shows the result of this exercise.

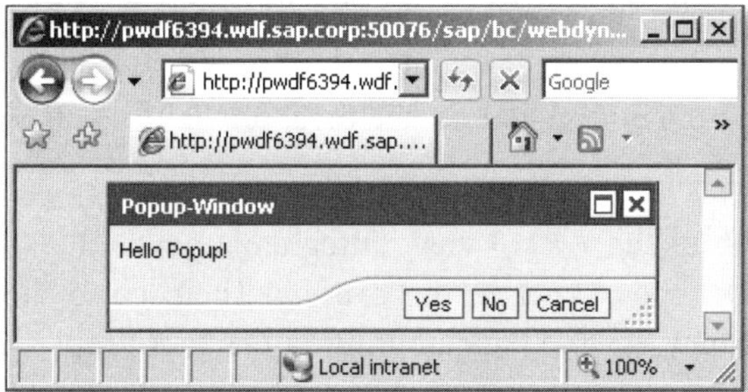

Figure 8.23 W_MAIN Displayed in the Popup

8.3.2 Standard Button Actions

In Section 8.3.1, Creating Popup Windows, you created a component with two windows. After you have started the application with the first window, the second one opens automatically in a popup window. This popup window contains three standard buttons: YES, NO, and CANCEL. The popup closes automatically when you click on one of the buttons.

Registering for button events

To determine on which button the user clicked, you must register an action for the event of each button. Because the popup window does not provide any direct access to the standard buttons and their events, you must carry out the registration process dynamically using the `subscribe_to_button_event( )` window method.

Example

Listing 8.6 shows the registration of the `BUTTON_CLICKED` action for the YES button as an example. As you can see there, you need the API of the view to register the button. You can obtain the API using view controller method `wd_get_api( )`. This should remind you of the component controller. For the YES button, the `IF_WD_WINDOW` interface provides the `co_button_yes` constant. Similar constants, all based on the same structure, are provided for all buttons.

```
DATA: lo_view_api TYPE REF TO if_wd_view_controller.
lo_view_api = wd_this->wd_get_api( ).
CALL METHOD lo_window->subscribe_to_button_event
  EXPORTING
    button      = if_wd_window=>co_button_yes
    action_name = 'BUTTON_CLICKED'
    action_view = lo_view_api.
```

Listing 8.6 Registering a Popup Button Action for an Event

[✎] In the following exercise, you will register the three buttons from the previous exercise for the BUTTON_CLICKED action of the V_MAIN view. After this, you will output the button you clicked on as text in the V_MAIN view.

1. Select the CONTEXT tab of the V_MAIN view. Integrate a new BUTTON_CLICKED attribute with type STRING in the context. Then, go to the LAYOUT tab and add a new TextView element. Bind the TEXT property to the BUTTON attribute.

Creating an action

2. Create the action, BUTTON_CLICKED. Double-click on the action to open its event handler method and insert the coding from Listing 8.7 into the event handler. This coding makes sure that the button selected by the user is output in V_MAIN.

```
wd_context->set_attribute(
  EXPORTING
    name = 'BUTTON_CLICKED'
    value = wdevent->name ).
```

Listing 8.7 Outputting the Selected Button

Registering buttons

3. Enhance the wddoinit( ) method. First, you must obtain the view API. Next, you must register the YES, NO, and CANCEL buttons for the BUTTON_CLICKED action by inserting the coding from Listing 8.8 into the method.

```
DATA: lo_view_api TYPE REF TO if_wd_view_controller.
lo_view_api = wd_this->wd_get_api( ).
CALL METHOD lo_window->subscribe_to_button_event
  EXPORTING
    button      = if_wd_window=>co_button_yes
    action_name = 'BUTTON_CLICKED'
    action_view = lo_view_api.
CALL METHOD lo_window->subscribe_to_button_event
  EXPORTING
    button      = if_wd_window=>co_button_no
    action_name = 'BUTTON_CLICKED'
    action_view = lo_view_api.
```

```
CALL METHOD lo_window->subscribe_to_button_event
  EXPORTING
    button      = if_wd_window=>co_button_cancel
    action_name = 'BUTTON_CLICKED'
    action_view = lo_view_api.
```

Listing 8.8 Registering the Standard Buttons in the wddoinit( ) Method

Testing the application

4. Activate the component and start the application. Click on one of the three popup buttons. This will close the popup window and display the technical name of the button that has been clicked on in `V_MAIN`. Figure 8.24 shows the result after clicking on the CANCEL button in the popup.

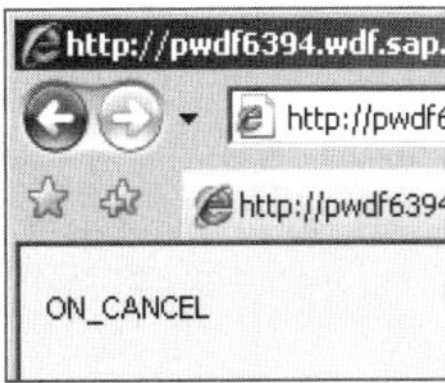

Figure 8.24 Output of the Button Clicked in the Popup

This section has described the most important aspects of developing popup windows. You now know how to create and open popup windows and how to register standard popup button events. In addition to these important functions, several other interesting methods are available for controlling popups; you can find these methods in the interface of the window. For example, you can define the display position of the popup window according to your requirements.

8.4 Context Change Log

Imagine the following situation: A user modifies a few data records in a table that contains several hundreds of rows. To save these changes in a database, you can apply different strategies:

- You read the node of the table in its entirety and update all data records in the database.

- You read the node of the table in its entirety and identify the changes using a before/after comparison of the data records. You then update the modified data records in the database.
- You use the context change log. This log records all changes implemented by the user in a table; after this, you can read the changes.

Thus, using the context change log represents the most elegant and efficient way to analyze the changes that have been made to the node. The context change log lists all user changes to the context in a single table.

Activating the change log

The change log is deactivated in the default settings of a controller. Therefore, you must activate it in the context of the respective component, if necessary. To do this, you can use the `IF_WD_CONTEXT` interface. You can obtain the reference to the context via the `wd_context->get_context( )` method. You can then activate the change log by calling the `enable_context_change_log( )` method (see Listing 8.9).

```
DATA: lo_context TYPE REF TO if_wd_context.
lo_context = wd_context->get_context( ).
lo_context->enable_context_change_log( ).
```

Listing 8.9 Activating the Context Change Log

> **Note**
>
> The change log records only the changes made by users. Changes to context elements that have been entered by the program are not listed.

Reading the change log

You can read the change log by calling the `get_context_change_log( )` in the `IF_WD_CONTEXT` interface. This will return a table of type `WDR_CONTEXT_CHANGE_LIST`. The optional importing parameter `and_reset` allows you to delete the change log after reading it. Note that with mapped nodes, you can read the change log only in the original node. Table 8.2 provides a brief overview of the change log methods of `IF_WD_CONTEXT`.

The analysis of the `WDR_CONTEXT_CHANGE_LIST` change log table is self-explanatory and is not described further in this book. Nevertheless, the change log should be part of your Web Dynpro toolbox. In particular, you should use it for complex Web Dynpro architectures.

Method	Description
`enable_context_change_log( )`	Activates the logging of user entries for this controller.
`disable_context_change_log( )`	Deactivates the logging function.
`get_context_change_log( )`	Provides the current content of the change log table and resets the table automatically (the reset property is activated by default but can be deactivated at any time).
`reset_context_change_log( )`	Resets the change log table.
`add_context_attribute_change( )`	Enables you to manually enter context attribute changes into the change log table.

Table 8.2 Change Log Methods in IF_WD_CONTEXT

8.5 Hotkeys

Hotkeys, also referred to as *shortcuts* or *shortcut keys*, were introduced in Web Dynpro along with the lightspeed rendering technology. Hotkeys enable you to trigger the events of buttons and other UI elements via your keyboard instead of using the mouse. Therefore, they represent a significant contribution to an increase in productivity and acceptance of Web Dynpro applications among power users. For example, like other applications, Web Dynpro also allows you to implement the classical shortcut [Ctrl] + [S] for saving documents.

UI elements with hotkey support

You can define hotkeys in the properties of supported UI elements. The following UI elements support the use of hotkeys: `Button`, `ToolBarButton`, `LinkToAction`, `MenuActionItem`, `ToolBarLinkToAction`, `ToolBarLinkToURL`, and `LinkToURL`.

After you have selected a hotkey, the corresponding action stored in the UI element is triggered for the `onAction` event. Note that for the `ToolBarLinkToURL` and `LinkToURL` elements, the corresponding URL is opened in a new browser window instead of the event. Figure 8.25 shows the example of a SAVE button with hotkey [Ctrl] + [S].

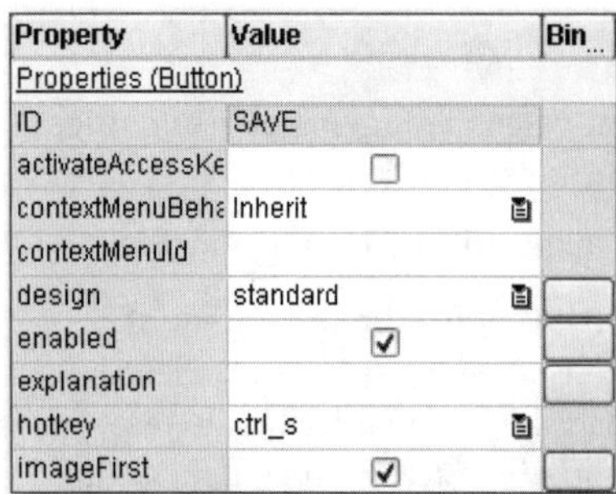

Figure 8.25 Save Button with Hotkey

Supported shortcuts

When defining hotkeys, you can choose from a limited number of key combinations:

- `Ctrl` + [0 – 9]
- `Ctrl` + [F2 – F12]
- `Ctrl` + [A – Z]
- `Ctrl` + `Shift` + [F1 – F12]

> **Note**
>
> Note that browser add-ins such as HTTPWatch in Internet Explorer also use shortcuts and therefore may be able to block shortcuts you define in Web Dynpro. This goes beyond the control of the Web Dynpro ABAP framework.

Global and local hotkeys

Web Dynpro distinguishes between local and global hotkeys. Whereas global hotkeys are valid for the entire visible area, local hotkeys are only valid within their local area. You can define local areas via the HANDLEHOTKEYS property of the UI element. This property is available for the UI elements `TransparentContainer`, `Table`, `Group`, and `Tray`.

Example

Figure 8.26 shows an example for global and local hotkeys. View A contains two containers and a total of three buttons. Button2 has a unique hotkey, `Ctrl` + `2`, and Button1 and Button3 share hotkey `Ctrl` + `1`. However, Button3 is located within a container whose HANDLEHOTKEYS property is activated. The question now is at which cursor position you can trigger which hotkey.

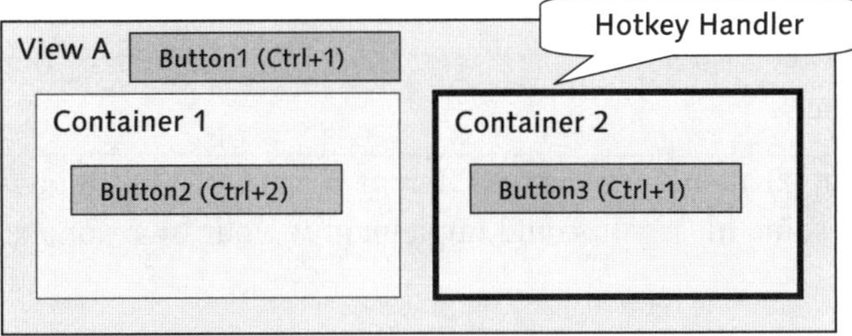

Figure 8.26 Global and Local Hotkeys

- **Button1**
  The Ctrl + 1 hotkey for Button1 is valid in all views and containers except for Container 2.
- **Button2**
  The Ctrl + 2 hotkey is valid in all views and containers.
- **Button3**
  Button3 is only valid within Container 2. Because this container is a hotkey handler, all buttons defined in it are only valid within this area.

Displaying Hotkeys

The respective key combination for a hotkey is automatically added to the tooltip of the associated UI element. If a text for the tooltip exists already, the text is appended to the end of the tooltip.

If you use hotkeys intelligently, they can significantly contribute to increased productivity of users working in Web Dynpro applications. It is therefore advisable to define hotkeys for your most important UI elements, provided they support the use of hotkeys. Because it is very easy to implement hotkeys, there is no need for a practical exercise in this section.

8.6 Context Menus

Context menus can be opened at any time in Web Dynpro applications using a right-click. Depending on the area you click on, Web Dynpro provides a collection of different system menu items. For example, you can hide unused input fields or define entered values as default values. As of SAP NetWeaver 7.0 Support Package 13, you can also create your own context menus.

Usage scenarios

You can use context menus in many different scenarios. The following list contains some ideas you could implement in your own context menus:

- **Standard date**
  Right-clicking on a date field allows you to select a default value from the context menu. This can either be the current date or a future date. The value you select is stored in a configuration controller. When you load the view, the context attribute of the date field is assigned the calculated date value.
- **Customization of views**
  Another example involves showing or hiding entire areas of a view via the context menu. This way you can customize your views according to your requirements.
- **Calling actions**
  Right-clicking on a view area enables you to call your own actions. An example of this scenario is the RESET menu item, which allows you to reset the attributes of a context element.

8.6.1 Standard Context Menu

Web Dynpro provides a set of default context menu items. This set of menu items is referred to as the *system menu*. Depending on the view area you click on, the system menu provides different items for you to select. For example, Figure 8.27 shows the system menu of an input field from Chapter 2, Web Dynpro Architecture.

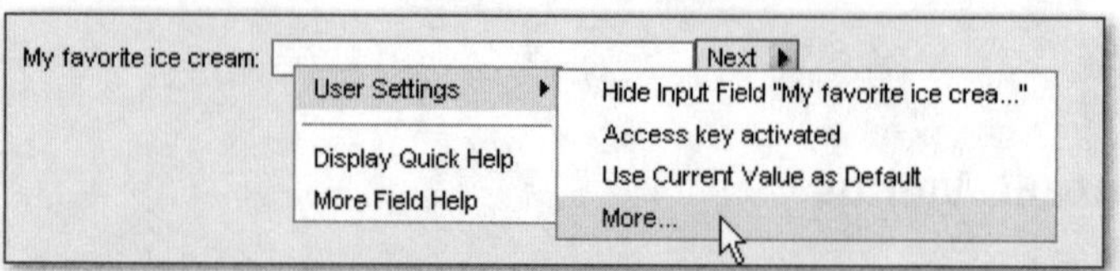

Figure 8.27 System Menu of an Input Field

Take a look at the individual system menu items in detail:

- **User Settings**
  This menu item enables you to enter user-specific settings for the UI.
  - **Hide Input Field "My favorite ice cream flavors"**
    Visibility
    Clicking on this menu item allows you to hide the MY FAVORITE ICE CREAM FLAVORS input field, including its label. The context menu will then contain an item called INVISIBLE ELEMENTS, which enables you to show the hidden elements again.
  - **Access key activated**
    Access keys
    Access keys enable you to quickly access UI elements using the keyboard. After an access key has been activated, you can use the key combination `Alt` + [first letter of field label] to set the focus directly to the respective field. If the labels of multiple fields begin with the same letter, you can toggle between these fields by repeatedly pressing the same key combination. Press the `Alt` key to view a list of currently active access keys. For this purpose, Web Dynpro underlines the first character of a field that has an active access key.

Note

By default, access keys are deactivated in the layout editor. You can activate the access key function for a specific UI element using the ACTIVATEACCESSKEY UI element property in the view designer. In addition, any user can store settings via the context menu of the respective UI element.

But be careful! Due to browser restrictions, not every letter can be used as an access key.

- **Use Current Value as Default**
  Default values
  When this item is selected, the Web Dynpro framework saves the value entered by the user as the default value. On initialization of the view, the stored value is automatically entered into the field.

  However, note that this setting works only for UI elements that have a unique ID. Consequently, you cannot use the default value function in conjunction with the `RowRepeater` and `MultiPane` elements.

- **More**

  By selecting the MORE item, you can view all available settings for the respective field and for all hidden UI elements in a popup window.

- **Display Quick Help**

  Help texts

  The DISPLAY QUICK HELP item lets you show and hide the quick help for a UI element. For this function to work, you must first configure the EXPLANATION property of the corresponding UI element.

- **More Field Help**

  Technical details

  Finally, the MORE FIELD HELP item allows you to call the field help (also referred to as [F1] help). If no field help is configured for a selected element, the system displays the technical details of the UI element instead. Therefore, this menu item is particularly helpful for analyzing unknown UIs. When you click on the menu item, a popup window opens displaying technical details for the respective UI element that has been clicked on. An example is provided in Figure 8.28.

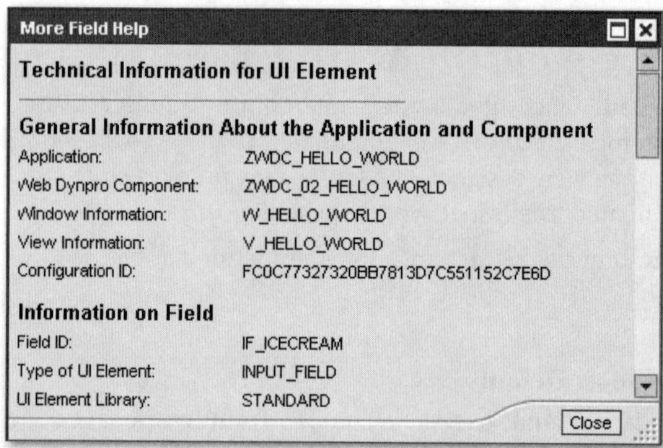

Figure 8.28 More Field Help Context Menu Item

8.6.2 Developing Custom Context Menus

Developing your own context menus is very easy. Similar to normal UI elements, you use the view designer to create them in the element hierarchy under the CONTEXT_MENUS root node. After this, you define the new menu statically as a context menu for the respective UI element via the CONTEXTMENUID property. In addition, you can also assign a context menu to a UI element dynamically using hook method `wddooncontextmenu( )`. This is all you need to do to implement a context menu.

Creating context menus

Return to the context menu creation function in the view designer. Here you have a choice between the following menu elements:

- `Menu`
  The `Menu` element represents the root of every context menu and is the only element that can be added directly under the `CONTEXT_MENUS` root node. In this position, it serves as a container for any number of child context menu elements. This way, the `Menu` element enables you to implement a hierarchical menu structure.
- `MenuActionItem`
  This UI element represents a concrete menu item. If you click on a `MenuActionItem` element, an action is executed in the view.
- `MenuCheckBox`
  This UI element provides a checkbox. For this, you must bind its CHECKED property to an attribute.
- `MenuRadioButton`
  This UI element provides a radio button. For this, you must bind the SELECTEDKEY property to an attribute.
- `MenuSeparator`
  This UI element provides a separator to separate individual context menu items from each other.

Unfortunately, you cannot drag the menu items of the context menu from a toolbar into the view, which is possible with UI elements. Therefore, you must compile the new menu by clicking through the context menu in the element hierarchy of the view designer.

Assigning a context menu to a UI element

Let us now take a look at the process of assigning context menus to UI elements. As mentioned earlier, this assignment can be carried out either statically in the view designer or dynamically via the `wddooncontextmenu ( )` method. In contrast to a static assignment, the dynamic variant is much more flexible.

- **Static assignment**
  The static assignment can be carried out via the UI element property CONTEXTMENUID in the view designer. The CONTEXTMENUBEHAVIOR property allows you to set the inheritance properties of the UI element. If you select provide, the system uses the value contained in CONTEXTMENUID. If the element in question is a container, the menu is available upon clicks within the entire container area. For example, a menu contained in ROOTUIELEMENTCONTAINER is available within the entire view.
- **Dynamic assignment**
  The dynamic assignment of a context menu occurs in the wddooncontextmenu( ) method. For this purpose, you can read the ID of the UI element that has been clicked on via context_menu_event->originator->id. You can then read the context menu using the context_menu_manager->get_context_menu( ) method and directly append the menu return parameter (see Listing 8.10).

```
CASE context_menu_event->originator->id.
  WHEN 'DATE_INPUT_FIELD'.
    menu = context_menu_manager->get_context_
menu( 'DATEMENU' ).
  ...
ENDCASE.
```

Listing 8.10 Example – wddooncontextmenu( ) Method

[✎] Here comes another exercise in which you will control the ready for input status of a date input field through a context menu. In addition, you will create an action that lets you enter the current date into the date field using the context menu.

Preparation

1. Create a component called ZWDC_08_CONTEXT_MENU. Next, create an application to enter into the component.
2. Go to the new view. Create the following two attributes in the context: ENABLE_DATE with type WDY_BOOLEAN and DATE with type DATS.
3. Go to the LAYOUT tab and add a new input field. Bind the VALUE property to the DATE attribute, and then bind the ENABLED property to the ENABLE_DATE attribute.

4. Next, create a context menu. This menu allows you to control the ready for input status of the input field and to fill it with the current date.

Creating the context menu

5. Right-click on the CONTEXT_MENUS root in the element hierarchy. Select CREATE CONTEXT MENU and enter the MENU_DATE ID in the popup that opens. Confirm your entries with the [Enter] key.

Menu for the date

6. Click on the new element and select INSERT MENU ITEM. Enter the SET_TODAY ID and select the MENUACTIONITEM type. Fill the TEXT property with the value "Today." Then create the SET_TODAY action from within the UI element. Insert the coding from Listing 8.11 into the associated event handler method. This coding fills the DATE attribute with the current system date.

```
wd_context->set_attribute(
  EXPORTING
    name  = 'DATE'
    value = sy-datum ).
```

Listing 8.11 Event Handler ONACTIONSET_DATE

7. Return to the LAYOUT tab. Add a new menu and enter the ID MENU_ENABLED into the popup window. Then, add a new item called SET_ENABLED with type MENUCHECKBOX into the menu. Bind its CHECKED property to the ENABLE_DATE attribute and enter "Date ready for input" as TEXT.

Menu for input status

This completes the creation of your context menus. Figure 8.29 shows the complete structure of the view.

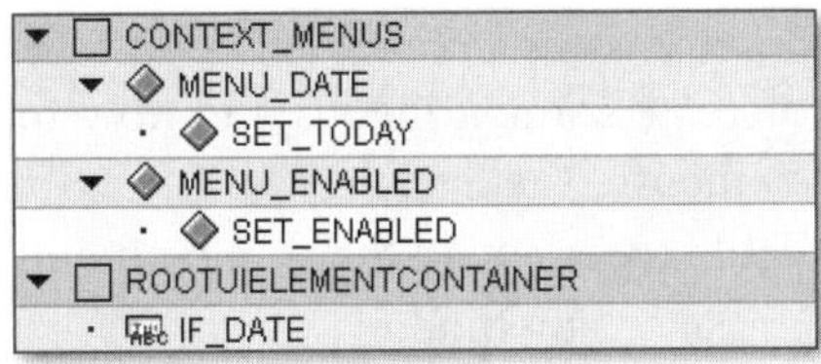

Figure 8.29 Element Hierarchy of the View with Context Menus

8. If you were to activate the entire component at this point, the framework would not yet display the context menus. This is because you must first assign the menus to their respective UI elements. To do this,

Assigning the context menus

click on the ROOTUIELEMENTCONTAINER and enter the MENU_ENABLED menu below the CONTEXTMENUID property. Set the CONTEXTMENUBEHAVIOR property to provide. Then, select the date field and fill the same property with the MENU_DATE menu. Select provide for the CONTEXTMENUBEHAVIOR property.

Testing the application

9. Activate the component and start the application. Right-click on a free area of the view. Then, click on DATE READY FOR INPUT; the input field should now open. After you click on the TODAY context menu item in the date field, the current date should appear in the field. Figure 8.30 shows the context menu of the date field.

> **Note**
>
> Shortly before this book went into print, the Web Dynpro development department implemented a correction for static context menus. Therefore, it may happen in some systems that the context menu does not function as described in this exercise. If this happens, you should implement SAP Note 1310110 to solve the problem.

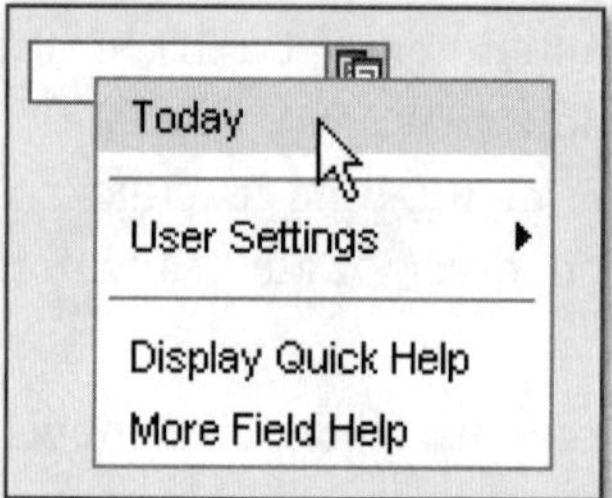

Figure 8.30 Entering the Current Date via the Context Menu

In this exercise, you learned how to create context menus and how to assign these menus statically to UI elements. The exercise can certainly still be improved. For example, you could try to assign the context menu dynamically using the `wddooncontextmenu( )` method.

8.7 Summary

In this chapter, you learned about important performance optimization aspects regarding Web Dynpro applications. The chapter provided three checklists that should help you optimize Web Dynpro components. The two most important ways of optimizing your components are on-demand instancing and delta rendering. The section on performance was then rounded off by a description of the two major Web Dynpro analysis tools. In addition to this, you were introduced to the Web Dynpro Debugger. This tool allows you to analyze the structure of components and contexts quickly and easily. Next, you learned how to create popup windows. Web Dynpro currently supports only modal popup windows. The context change log allows you to respond effectively to context changes made by users. The final sections of the chapter provided you with a description of how to create context menus, which allow you to generate local menus by right-clicking the mouse.

Chapter 9, Web Dynpro in the Enhancement Framework, describes how you can use the Enhancement Framework to customize external components according to your requirements without modifying them.

Very few development projects start with a "clean slate." However, although you can customize your own components according to new requirements at any time, this is not usually possible with third-party components. For this reason, SAP provides enhancements, a concept that enables you to create modification-free extensions.

9 Web Dynpro in the Enhancement Framework

In large customer projects, the standard SAP software often has to be customized according to the individual customer's requirements. In such cases, the customer ideally decides to implement a Business Add-In (BAdI). If there is no suitable BadI, the only remaining option is to modify the standard coding using the modification wizard. However, every new modification is a further deviation from the standard, and the customer then has to deal with any resulting long-term problems. Modifications pose a particular challenge when it comes to upgrades.

Enhancement Framework

With the goal of simplifying and unifying the process of making individual changes to development objects in mind, SAP introduced the *Enhancement Framework* in SAP NetWeaver 7.0. This new kind of extension concept is a technology for modifying, extending, and reusing development objects. In the Enhancement Framework, changes are made using the *Enhancement Builder*, which is integrated into the ABAP Workbench.

Implicit and explicit changes

Enhancements can be made at any point in the coding of the development object you want to change. Thus, enhancements are implicit enhancements; this is in contrast to explicit changes, which can be made at points defined in advance by the application developer only. The best-known example of explicit enhancements is the BAdI.

Development objects that are modified in the Enhancement Builder can be managed in the Switch Framework. This framework enables you to group together your changes to individual development objects in switches and in what are known as *business function sets*. The switches and the enhancements they contain can then be activated and deactivated in any way you like in the Switch Framework.

Topics Discussed

This chapter discusses the following topics:

- Enhancement Framework
- Implicit and explicit enhancements
- Creating Web Dynpro enhancements
- Enhancing controller methods
- Pre-exits, overwrite exits, and post-exits
- Context enhancements
- Customizing view layouts

9.1 Enhancements in Web Dynpro

First, let us look at an example of how to use enhancements. Imagine that you have purchased a standard software package for booking airline flights. The software is based on Web Dynpro. However, the software does not have an airline-specific search function, and you are also dissatisfied with the search results display. Therefore, you decide to add an airline search field to the Web Dynpro components of the software and to adapt the results display to suit your requirements. At the end of this chapter, we will use an enhancement to implement this example.

We will start at the beginning and look at how to create Web Dynpro enhancements. Because the Enhancement Builder is fully integrated into the ABAP Workbench, the processes of extending components and processing components are not very different.

Creating enhancements

1. To create a new enhancement, click on the menu of the relevant component object and select ENHANCE. For example, to enhance a view, click on VIEW • ENHANCE or press the key combination Ctrl + F4 (see Figure 9.1).

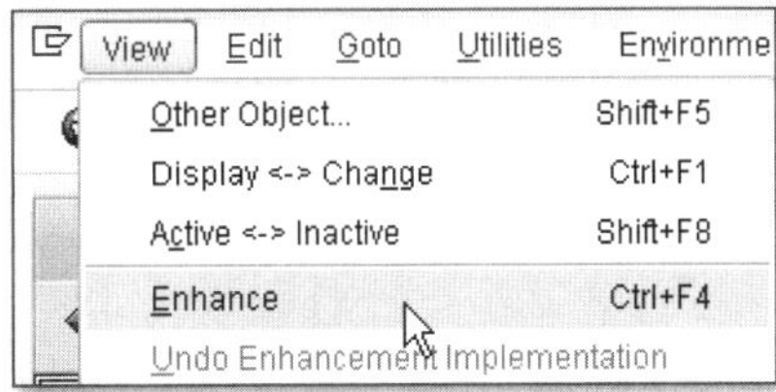

Figure 9.1 Enhancing a View

2. After you select ENHANCE, the CREATE ENHANCEMENT IMPLEMENTATION popup opens, as shown in Figure 9.2. Here, enter the name of the enhancement you want to create and a description.

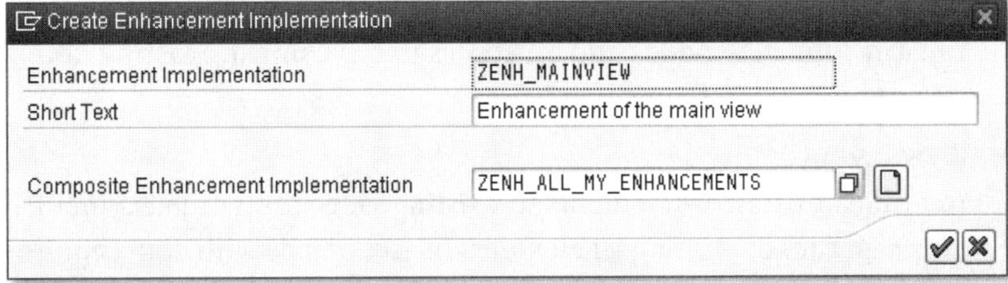

Figure 9.2 Creating an Enhancement Implementation

You can also specify a superordinate COMPOSITE ENHANCEMENT IMPLEMENTATION for the new enhancement. Composite enhancement implementations are used to bundle simple enhancements in accordance with semantics; in other words, they can be used to combine simple enhancements to form useful units.

3. Click on the button with the green checkmark to close the popup. The system then creates the enhancement. In the following section, we will look at the various enhancement options.

Selecting Enhancements

After you have created your first enhancement, the Create dialog box is no longer displayed automatically. Instead, Web Dynpro opens a dialog box where you can select from existing enhancements. Of course, you can also create a new enhancement in this dialog box.

9.1.1 Web Dynpro Enhancements in Detail

Examples of enhancements

Let us now take a detailed look at the enhancement options in Web Dynpro UIs. As a general rule, every part of a component can be enhanced:

- **Components**
  You can create additional component usages. However, component interfaces may not be implemented.
- **Controller**
  You can create pre-exits, post-exits, and overwrite exits for methods and event handlers. You can also define new actions and events, create new methods, and copy new attributes to the controller.
- **Context**
  You can copy new nodes and attributes to the context. Existing nodes cannot be modified, however.
- **View layout**
  You can copy new UI elements to existing views. You can also modify the properties of existing UI elements in accordance with your requirements. It is even possible to delete UI elements.
- **Plugs and navigation links**
  You can create new plugs and connect them with each other in the window editor using navigation links.

We will now take a closer look at some of the options in the Enhancement Framework.

Enhancing Controller Methods

Enhancing methods is one of the most important functions of the Enhancement Framework. Unlike modifications, with enhancements, the original methods are not changed directly; instead, the Enhancement Framework provides pre-exit, post-exit, and overwrite exit methods.

Properties of exits

Exits can be implemented for any method in a controller. You can also create new methods in an enhancement in the controller:

- The Framework executes pre-exits and post-exits either before or after the controller method itself is called.

- Overwrite exits, as the name suggests, replace the method. After an overwrite exit is created, the original method cannot be called again.

All three exit types have access to the same import, change, and export parameters as the original methods.

Example

Figure 9.3 shows the METHODS tab of an enhanced view. Simply click on one of the CREATE buttons next to the methods to create a new exit method. After the enhancement is implemented, the Create icon on the button changes to a Source Code icon. Click on this button to go to the source code of the enhancement in question. You can use the DELETE button on the toolbar to delete method enhancements.

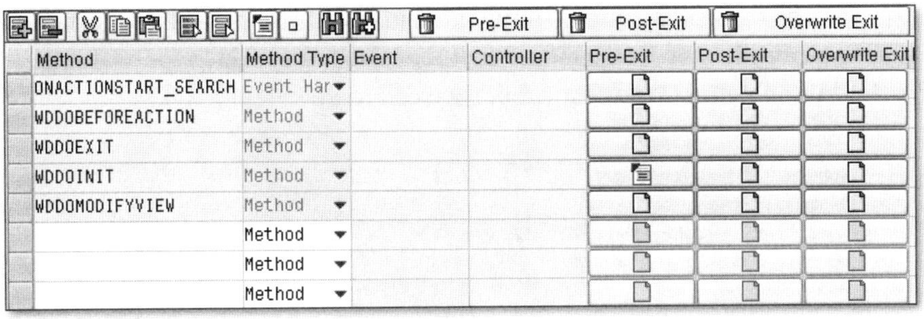

Pre-Exit | Post-Exit | Overwrite Exit

Method	Method Type	Event	Controller	Pre-Exit	Post-Exit	Overwrite Exit
ONACTIONSTART_SEARCH	Event Har					
WDDOBEFOREACTION	Method					
WDDOEXIT	Method					
WDDOINIT	Method					
WDDOMODIFYVIEW	Method					
	Method					
	Method					
	Method					

Figure 9.3 Enhancing Controller Methods

Enhancing the Context

In addition to the methods discussed in Section 9.1.1, Enhancing Controller Methods, you can also use the Enhancement Framework to enhance the context. Context enhancements are somewhat more restricted than method enhancements. For example, with context enhancements, no changes may be made to the original node. You are permitted to create new nodes and add new attributes only; however, the latter can also be created under existing nodes. It is also a simple matter to map attributes between controllers.

Enhancing View Layouts

Usually, the most important consideration in enhancements to Web Dynpro components is to adapt the existing view layouts to specific requirements. You can make the following changes to the view layout in enhancement mode:

- Create new UI elements
- Change the properties of existing UI elements
- Hide existing UI elements

In the view, you can also add enhancements to methods, actions, plugs, attributes, and the context.

Creating UI elements

From the technical point of view, the process of creating new UI elements in enhancement mode is no different than creating the same elements in normal editing mode. All of the UI elements that are added as part of the enhancement implementation can be processed normally. You can identify UI elements that were added at a later point by their additional ENHANCEMENT property (see Figure 9.4).

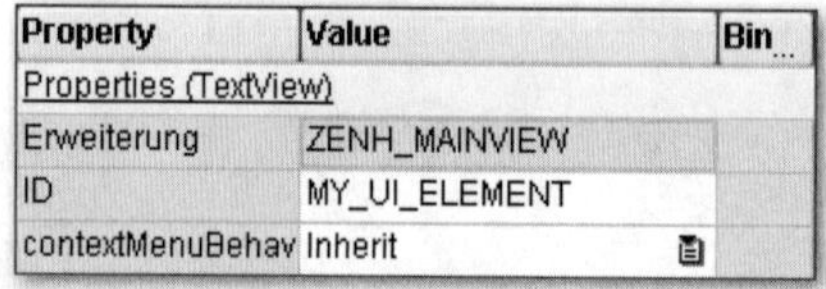

Property	Value	Bin...
Properties (TextView)		
Erweiterung	ZENH_MAINVIEW	
ID	MY_UI_ELEMENT	
contextMenuBehav	Inherit	

Figure 9.4 Enhanced TextView Element MY_UI_ELEMENT

The properties of existing UI elements can be changed in any way you like in enhancement mode. For example, you can change the existing binding of an input field or customize its design.

Deleting UI elements

It is also possible to delete existing UI elements in enhancement mode. To do so, right-click on the element in question and select DELETE ELEMENT. However, the original element is not deleted directly in the view; instead, it is marked with a red X in the BINDING column (see Figure 9.5). You then have the option to restore the original UI element by selecting UNDO DELETE.

Property	Value	Bin...
Properties (Group)		
Erweiterung	ZENH_MAINVIEW	✖
ID	INPUTGROUP_CP	

Figure 9.5 Example of a UI Element Deleted From an Enhancement

> **Generating Deleted UI Elements**
>
> When you delete a UI element, this element is no longer generated. You need to keep this in mind especially for dynamically-programmed components for the following reason: If an attempt is made during the runtime of the original component source code to access a deleted element, this immediately causes program errors, and possibly program termination.

9.1.2 Exercise: Additional Search Field

At the beginning of Section 9.1, Enhancements in Web Dynpro, we gave you an example of a Web Dynpro component extension in the form of a flight booking component that needs an extra "airline" search field. Let us now return to this example.

Enhancement of component WDT_FLIGHTLIST

In the following exercise, you will get a chance to practice what you have learned using the Enhancement Framework and the SAP standard test component `WDT_FLIGHTLIST`. The goal is to add an "airline" search field to the search screen in the `MAINVIEW` view of this component. We will then hide some table columns we do not require from the event table of the same view. Figure 9.6 shows the component before the enhancement is added.

Airline	Airline	Flight Number	Date	Dep. airport	Depart.city	Dest. airport	Arrival city	Departure	Arrival Time	Arrival date	Airfare	Airline Currency	ISO code
AC	Air Canada	0820	20.12.2002	FRA	FRANKFURT/MAIN	YUL	MONTREAL-DORVAL	10:00:00	12:00:00	20.12.2002	1.222,0000	CAD	CAD
AF	Air France	0820	23.12.2002	FRA	FRANKFURT/MAIN	FDF	FORT DE FRANCE	10:00:00	15:00:00	23.12.2002	2.222,0000	EUR	EUR
LH	Lufthansa	0400	28.02.1995	FRA	FRANKFURT	JFK	NEW YORK	10:10:00	11:34:00	28.02.1995	899,0000	DEM	DEM
LH	Lufthansa	0454	17.11.1995	FRA	FRANKFURT	SFO	SAN FRANCISCO	10:10:00	12:30:00	17.11.1995	1.499,0000	DEM	DEM
LH	Lufthansa	0455	06.06.1995	SFO	SAN FRANCISCO	FRA	FRANKFURT	15:00:00	10:30:00	06.06.1995	1.090,0000	USD	USD

Figure 9.6 Component WDT_FLIGHTLIST Before Enhancement

Opening the component

1. Open the SAP test component `WDT_FLIGHTLIST`. Start the `wdt_flightlist` application and familiarize yourself with both this application and the component.
2. Go to the `MAINVIEW` view and select the LAYOUT tab. We will now add the required search field to the search screen for the airport of departure and the airport of destination. The current status is shown in Figure 9.7.

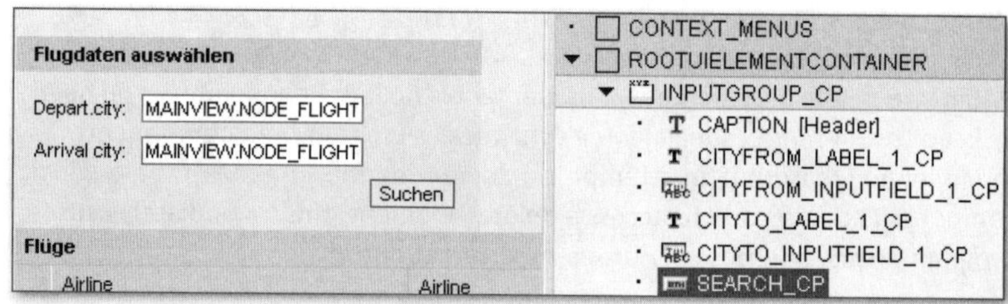

Figure 9.7 Search Screen Before Enhancement

Creating the enhancement

3. Start by enhancing the view. To do this, select VIEW • ENHANCE FROM THE MENU. A popup opens that allows you to create the new enhancement. In this popup, enter the value `ZENH_MAINVIEW` into the ENHANCEMENT IMPLEMENTATION field. Enter a short text and create the enhancement by clicking on the button with the green checkmark, as shown in Figure 9.8.

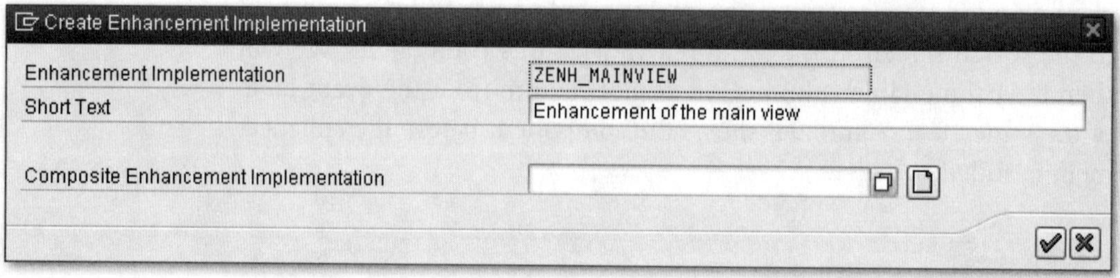

Figure 9.8 Creating an Enhancement

Creating a search field

4. You can now enhance the view. First, you need to enter a new "airline" attribute in the context. To do this, select the CONTEXT tab and create a new attribute called `ENH_CARRID` of the type `S_CARR_ID` under `CONTEXT`. Then, go back to the LAYOUT tab and enter a label and an input field for the airline under the group element `INPUTGROUP_CP`. Bind the VALUE property of the input field to the `ENH_CARRID` attribute.

Creating an overwrite exit

5. Next, you have to enhance the event handler of the `START_SEARCH` action. To do this, go to the METHODS tab and open `onactionstart_search( )`. Select the entire source code and copy it to the clipboard. Then, go back to the method list and, in the event handler row, click the CREATE icon in the OVERWRITE EXIT column (see Figure 9.9). The overwrite exit of the event handler is now open.

Method	Method Type	Pre-Exit	Post-Exit	Overwrite Exit	Enh.Impl.
ONACTIONSTART_SEARCH	Event Har				
WDDOBEFOREACTION	Method				

Figure 9.9 Creating an Overwrite Exit for the Search

6. Paste the source code from the clipboard into the overwrite exit. Next, modify the pasted source code so that it is suitable for the airline search function (see Listing 9.1). To do this, read the ENH_CARRID attribute from the context and transfer its value to the function module

```
* Insert this coding
DATA lv_carrid TYPE s_carr_id.
wd_context->get_attribute( EXPORTING name = 'ENH_CARRID'
                           IMPORTING value = lv_carrid ).
* Adapt the function call BAPI_FLIGHT_GETLIST
CALL FUNCTION 'BAPI_FLIGHT_GETLIST'
  EXPORTING
    airline          = lv_carrid
    destination_from = ls_from
    destination_to   = ls_to
  TABLES
    flight_list      = lt_flights.
```

Listing 9.1 Adapting the Event Handler onactionstart_search( )

Deleting a column

7. You have now completed the search enhancement. In the last step, you will reduce the number of visible table columns. To do this, go back to the LAYOUT tab and open the node of the FLIGHTTAB UI element. Right-click on the last element, FLIGHTTAB_CURR_ISO_1, and select REMOVE GROUP COLUMN, as shown in Figure 9.10. The element is still displayed in the element hierarchy, but is now marked as deleted.

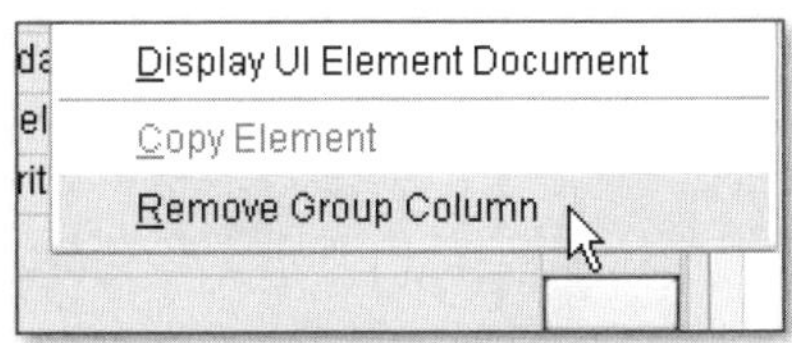

Figure 9.10 Deleting the ISO Code Column

This completes the exercise. Activate the component and test the application by entering the airline code "LH" in the search field and clicking on the SEARCH button. The table that no longer contains the ISO CODE column displays all Lufthansa flights, as shown in Figure 9.11.

Airline	Airline	Flight Number	Date	Dep. airport	Depart.city	Dest. airport	Arrival city	Departure	Arrival Time	Arrival date	Airfare	Airline Currency	ISO code
LH	Lufthansa	0400	28.02.1995	FRA	FRANKFURT	JFK	NEW YORK	10:10:00	11:34:00	28.02.1995	899,0000	DEM	DEM
LH	Lufthansa	9981	21.12.2002	FRA	FRANKFURT	DRS	DRESDEN	16:40:00	17:35:00	21.12.2002	222,0000	EUR	EUR
LH	Lufthansa	3577	28.04.1995	FCO	ROM	FRA	FRANKFURT	07:05:00	09:05:00	28.04.1995	6.000,0000	LIT	
LH	Lufthansa	2402	30.08.1997	FRA	FRANKFURT	SXF	BERLIN	10:30:00	11:35:00	30.08.1997	485,0000	DEM	DEM
LH	Lufthansa	2402	25.08.1997	FRA	FRANKFURT	SXF	BERLIN	10:30:00	11:35:00	25.08.1997	490,0000	DEM	DEM

Figure 9.11 Testing the Enhanced Component

Reconciling Enhancements After Upgrades

When a system is upgraded, conflicts can exist between enhancements you have added and the new development objects. Use Transaction SPAU_ENH to analyze and reconcile such conflicts.

9.2 Summary

In this chapter, you learned about the Enhancement Framework from the perspective of Web Dynpro. You gained practical experience of enhancing third-party components and their controllers in accordance with your own specific requirements. From now on, you will also find it easy to enhance context nodes and adapt view layouts.

A Appendix

The first section of this appendix suggests relevant additional reading for you, including sources and important references. The second section, on naming conventions, describes all of the conventions used in this book for variables, methods, view elements, and so on.

A.1 Recommended Reading

This is a list of the literature and sources used in the creation of this book.

- *http://sdn.sap.com*

  The SAP Developer Network is a treasure trove of high-quality discussions on the subject of Web Dynpro ABAP.

- *http://help.sap.com*

  The SAP Help Portal contains a useful collection of topics about Web Dynpro ABAP.

- Stefan Ehret, *NET310 ABAP Web Dynpro*. Participant Handbook for the SAP standard training course, version 2006/Q3, material number 50085725.

  This is the Participant Handbook for the SAP standard training course for basic Web Dynpro programming.

- Stefan Ehret, *NET311 Advanced ABAP Web Dynpro*. Participant Handbook for the SAP standard training course, version 2006/Q3, material number 50084905.

  This is the Participant Handbook for the SAP standard training course for more in-depth information on Web Dynpro.

- Stefan Ehret, *NET312 UI Development with Web Dynpro for ABAP*. Participant Handbook for the SAP standard training course, version 2006/Q2, material number 50089128.

  This is the Participant Handbook for the SAP standard training course for in-depth information on how to use view and UI elements.

A.2 Naming Conventions

Table A.1 contains the naming conventions for development objects.

Convention	Usage
Web Dynpro component	
ZWDC_<name>	Web Dynpro component
ZWDC_<name>_[ANW|APP]	Web Dynpro application
Controller	
CC_<name>	Custom controller
CONFC_<name>	Configuration controller
Window/View	
W_<name>	Window
V_<name>	View
Plugs	
TO_<target>	Outbound plug
FROM_<SOURCE>	Inbound plug
View elements	
BTN_	Button
CAPTION_	Caption
CB_	CheckBox
CBG_	CheckBoxGroup
DDBI_	DropDownByIndex
DDBK_	DropDownByKey
FD_	FileDownload
FU_	FileUpload
GR_	Group
IF_	InputField
ILB_	ItemListBox
IMG_	Image

Table A.1 Naming Convention

Convention	Usage
LB_	Label
PH_	PageHeader
RB_	RadioButton
RBGI_	RadioButtonIndex
RBGK_	RadioButtonKey
T_	Tab
TBL_	Table
TBLH_	TableHeader
TBLC_	TableColumn
TBLCE_	TableCellEditor
TBLCH_	TableColumnHeader
TIT_	TreeItemType
TNT_	TreeNodeType
TR_	Tree
TS_	TabStrip
TSCB_	TriStateCheckBox
TV_	TextView
VC_	ViewContainerUIElement
Usages	
USAGE_<name>	Usage
ABAP Classes	
ZCL_A_<name>	Assistence class
Controller methods	
IS_<condition>	Is condition fulfilled?
GETCTX_<NAME>	Read data from context
SETCTX_<name>	Put data in context
GETMODEL_<name>	Read data from model

Table A.1 Naming Conventions (Cont.)

Convention	Usage
SUPPLY_<name>	Supply function
ON_<event>	Event handler
Method parameters	
ID_	Import data (simple type)
IS_	Import structure
IT_	Import table
IO_ or IR_	Import object reference
ED_	Export data (simple type)
ES_	Export structure
ET_	Export table
EO_ or ER_	Export object reference
RD_	Return data (simple type)
RS_	Return structure
RT_	Return table
RO_ or RR_	Return object reference
Global variables	
GD_ or GV_	Global data (scalar)
GS_	Global structure
GT_	Global table
GO_ or GR_	Global object reference
Local variables	
LD_ or LV_	Local data (scalar)
LS_	Local structure
LT_	Local table
LO_ or LR_	Local object reference
ABAP Dictionary	
ZST_<name>	Structure

Table A.1 Naming Conventions (Cont.)

B The Authors

Dominik Ofenloch studied Business Information Systems at the University of Cooperative Education in Mannheim, Germany. Even before graduating, he was involved in programming various UI technologies at SAP AG in Walldorf, Germany. After completing his degree in 2006, he started his development career in the SCM department at SAP. He worked in this department until August 2009, where he developed software for user interfaces and Web Dynpro in the Transportation Management (SAP TM) area. In September 2009, he joined ENERGY4U GmbH of Siemens in Karlsruhe, Germany, where he works in the SAP Utilities area as a consultant and developer.

If you have comments or feedback on this book, Dominik would like to hear from you: *mail@dominikofenloch.de*.

Dr. Roland Schwaiger studied Computer Science at Bowling Green State University, Ohio, USA, and Applied Computer Science and Mathematics at the University of Salzburg, Austria, where he completed his doctorate in Mathematics.

After several years of working as an assistant professor at the University of Salzburg, he joined SAP AG in 1996. There, he worked as a Human Resources software developer for three years, which gave him the opportunity to develop his skills in an exciting and inspirational working environment. In 1999, Roland became a freelance trainer, editor, consultant, and developer. In this capacity, he applies his academic qualifications and the software development know-how he gained at SAP to real-world development projects and SAP training courses. In turn, he is able to transfer the knowledge he gains as a freelancer back to his academic work, thus creating a positive feedback loop between theory and practice.

Roland invites comments and feedback on this book; he can be contacted at *roland.schwaiger@facet.at*.

Index

D

J

K

L

M

N

O

Q

R

S

V

W

Z

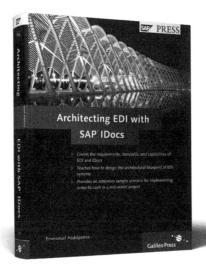

Tools for performance analysis: Code Inspector, runtime analysis, performance trace, and more

Performance aspects in development: SQL queries, internal tables, buffer, data transfer

Application design: general performance and parallelization

Hermann Gahm

ABAP Performance Tuning

This book for ABAP developers details best practices for ABAP performance tuning. Covering the most critical performance-relevant programming issues and performance monitoring tools, this book will show you how to best analyze, tune, and implement your ABAP programs.
Starting with a description of the client/server architecture, the book moves on to discussing the different tools for analyzing performance. Programming techniques are then analyzed in detail, based on numerous real-life examples. This book will help you ensure that your ABAP programs are tuned for best performance.

348 pp., 2009, 69,95 Euro / US$ 69.95
ISBN 978-1-59229-289-9